HOW THE UNITED STATES
RACIALIZES LATINOS

HOW THE UNITED STATES RACIALIZES LATINOS

WHITE HEGEMONY AND ITS CONSEQUENCES

Edited by

José A. Cobas, Jorge Duany, and Joe R. Feagin

Paradigm Publishers

Boulder • London

The editors agree with the goals of colleagues who want to affirm the dignity of women by modifying standard Spanish language terms. However, we do not follow in this book all of their specific language practices.

We observe standard Spanish grammar in respect to grammatical gender. We also adhere to standard Spanish grammar's rules on diacritics. Two exceptions are the names of individuals who do not use diacritics and the titles of existing publications.

Published in the United States by Paradigm Publishers, 3360 Mitchell Lane Suite E, Boulder, CO 80301 USA.

Paradigm Publishers is the trade name of Birkenkamp & Company, LLC,
Dean Birkenkamp, President and Publisher.

Library of Congress Cataloging-in-Publication Data

How the United States racializes Latinos : white hegemony and its consequences / edited by José A. Cobas, Jorge Duany, and Joe R. Feagin.
    p. cm.
  Includes bibliographical references and index.
  ISBN 978-1-59451-598-9 (hardcover : alk. paper)
  ISBN 978-1-59451-599-6 (paperback : alk. paper)
  1. Hispanic Americans—Government policy—United States. 2. Hispanic Americans—Social conditions. 3. United States—Race relations. 4. Racism—United States. I. Cobas, José A. II. Duany, Jorge. III. Feagin, Joe R.
  E184.S75H74 2009
  305.868'073—dc22

                                                                              2008042253

Designed and Typeset by Straight Creek Bookmakers.

13 12 11 10 09   1 2 3 4 5

To the late Bernard Farber and Joe Feagin
Eminent scholars, generous friends

José A. Cobas

Contents

Figures and Tables

FIGURES

TABLES

INTRODUCTION

Racializing Latinos

Historical Background and Current Forms

José A. Cobas, Jorge Duany, and Joe R. Feagin

Despite its scientific disrepute, the concept of "race" remains a powerful social determinant in the United States. The racialization of Latinos refers to their definition as a "racial" group and the denigration of their alleged physical and cultural characteristics, such as phenotype, language, or number of children. Their racialization also entails their incorporation into a white-created and white-imposed racial hierarchy and continuum, now centuries old, with white Americans at the very top and black Americans at the very bottom. Thus, one can speak about the intense racialization of daily life, including health, housing, education, work, friendship, and marriage patterns. In this introductory chapter, we trace the modern concept of race in Europe from its origin in the fifteenth century and the racialization of Latinos and Latin Americans in the United States since the nineteenth century. We also provide a brief overview of the main contributions of the individual chapters of this volume.

THE ORIGIN OF THE CONCEPT OF RACE IN EUROPE

In the fifteenth century, the Portuguese became the first Europeans to travel to Africa and establish trading posts on its western coast. They initially exchanged such goods as metal pots and wine for Africans' gold and spices. As the demand for enslaved Africans increased and made their transport more profitable than trade in nonhuman goods, enslaved Africans became the cargo of many Portuguese ships.

The Spanish nation-state was the first to colonize on a large scale indigenous societies in the Americas for their resources, but its growing wealth and military apparatus were soon countered by the imperial expansion of competing English, Dutch, and French nation-states. Early on, Spanish and English conquerors and enslavers in the Americas rationalized the oppression of indigenous and African peoples in both Christian religious terms (uncivilized, un-Christian) and physical-biological terms (ugly, apelike). The massive enslavement of Africans awakened the interest of European and North American scholars. Some of the latter had even invested in the slave trade, and many others began to accent European superiority and African inferiority. By the last few decades of the 1600s, British and other European thinkers were laying the groundwork for a hierarchy of biologically distinctive "races," which developed more fully over the eighteenth century. England's Sir William Petty, a leading anatomist, portrayed enslaved "blacks" as physically and culturally inferior to "whites." Drawing on European travelers' accounts of the Americas and Africa, Petty advocated a ladder-like ranking of unchangeable human "species" or "races" characterized by physical and social differences. He insisted that natives of the southern tip of Africa were the "most beastlike of all the souls of men with whom our travelers are well acquainted" (quoted in Shore, 2000:87; see also Feagin, forthcoming).

In Germany, the West's leading philosopher, Immanuel Kant, taught philosophy and what would later become social science. His treatise, "On the Distinctiveness of the Races in General" ([1775] 1950), laid out one of the first hierarchical models of human "races." Kant's work, which he claimed was based on science, conceived "races" as "differences in the human genus" shaped by different environments. Races varied in physical traits such as skin color, physiognomy, and body type, as well as in psychological temperament. Kant paid special attention to "Negro" traits. A physiological process ending with the evaporation of the acids of phosphorous, Kant asserted, "makes Negroes stink." Although in his racist view blacks were well prepared for physical labor, they were also "lazy, soft and dawdling" ([1775] 1950:22). This early white racial framing of people of African descent influenced most subsequent models of the racial hierarchy in Western societies.

Shaped by English thinkers such as Petty in the late 1600s and early 1700s, the first conceptualizations of "race" in North America developed over the next century on the basis of a belief in the supremacy of the "Anglo-Saxon" race, supposedly linked to superior Germanic groups (Horsman, 1981). Variations on this Anglo-Saxon myth were widely popular in North America. Thomas Jefferson, the most famous of the U.S. founders and a patrician slaveholder himself, was the first American intellectual to write extensively on racial matters. Jefferson led in creating self-satisfying rationalizations for the enslavement of African Americans. In a passage reminiscent of David Hume's stereotyping of Africans (Morton, 2002) and of Kant's overtly racist thinking ([1764] 1965), Jefferson argued that enslaved African Americans did not have any achievements that would demonstrate their human equality: "But never yet could I find a black had uttered a thought above the level of plain narration; never saw even an elementary trait of painting or sculpture" (quoted in Gossett, 1997:43). A man with great influence over the next century, Jefferson read and was influenced by the earlier work of scientists such as Petty, including their negative views of black Americans. In Jefferson's only intellectual book, the influential *Notes on the State of Virginia,* he articulated what Joe Feagin (2006:25, 28) has called the "white racial frame": "An organized set of racialized ideas, stereotypes, emotions, and inclinations to discriminate.... Critical to the white racial frame is an interrelated set of cognitive notions, understandings, and metaphors that whites have used to rationalize and legitimate systemic racism."

By the eighteenth century, an increasingly elaborate racialized discourse targeting African Americans, and to a lesser but significant degree Native Americans, was found in all major U.S. institutions—the economy, law, politics, education, and religion. By the latter part of the nineteenth century, the concept of race and the racial hierarchy in the United States were aggressively linked to the ascendant school of "Social Darwinism." The English philosopher Herbert Spencer, creator of that term and most important thinker in its tradition, saw human evolution as the outcome of individual competition for survival (Spencer [1873], 1972). The "fittest" American groups would supposedly prevail over "inferior" ones, and in this manner humanity would cleanse itself of unfit "races." Spencer argued that human competition occurred in varying environments and that human beings developed specific skills needed for survival. For him, this competition explained the purportedly higher development of the intellect among "white" Europeans, who had to rely on their wits to survive vis-à-vis groups such as African "Bushmen," who were alleged to depend on their brawn, not on their intelligence. Spencer put it as follows: "That superiority of sight which enables a Bushman to see further with the naked eye than a European with a telescope, is fully paralleled by the European's more perfect intellectual vision" ([1873] 1972:7). Spencer's writings won wide use and acclaim among white leaders and intellectuals in the United States, and some of his books became bestsellers. His thought drew on and reciprocally fostered the dominant racist ideology that had already emerged in the United States.

By the late nineteenth century, the dominant racist frame had coalesced in the momentous U.S. Supreme Court decision in *Plessy v. Ferguson* (1896), which provided the basis for the "separate but equal" doctrine of Jim Crow segregation. Homer Plessy contended in his lawsuit that being forced by a Louisiana law to ride in a separate train car violated his constitutional rights. In an astonishing display of racial arrogance and highly specious thinking, the all-white Supreme Court justices justified their decision to uphold Louisiana's law, claiming that the plaintiff's complaint was based only on his erroneous perception and not on reality: "We consider the underlying fallacy of the [black] plaintiff's argument to consist in the assumption that the enforced separation of the two races stamps the colored race with a badge of inferiority. If this be so, it is not by reason of anything found in the act, but solely because the colored race chooses to put that construction on it" (*Plessy v. Ferguson,* 1896:551).

THE RACIALIZATION OF LATIN AMERICANS AND LATINOS

The first major cases of North American racialization involved Indians and, as previously noted, enslaved Africans. The latter's vilification seemed to increase as slave labor became ever more important in U.S. agriculture, especially with advances in cotton farming in the South by the late 1700s. Beyond African Americans and Native Americans, whites created systems of oppression for other "Americans of color," including people of Latin American origin. White American leaders and the rank-and-file have belittled the physical appearance, Spanish language, Catholic traditions, and family values of Latin Americans at least since the 1830s.

The Spanish colonies in North America suffered from sequential imperialistic domination and racialization by Spain and then by the emerging United States. Spain's whites had mixed with the Indian and African-descended populations of Mexico and other Spanish American colonies, which resulted in a racially heterogeneous (mestizo) population. In the aftermath of the 1840s Mexican-American War, moreover, the ever-expanding United States seized much of northern Mexico, thereby incorporating about 110,000 Mexicans into U.S. territory.

The U.S. racialization process has had a cross-border dimension within the Americas. By the mid-1800s, the U.S. racial hierarchy and its rationalizing frame had become extended as white entrepreneurs and political leaders brought in more non-European labor and territories. The white Americans' racial frame soon classified all Mexicans as a racially inferior people who could not govern themselves. In Texas and California, among other areas, whites often spoke of Mexicans as "niggers" or "dirty mongrels"; the notorious adventurer Stephen Austin, in particular, referred to them as a "mongrel Spanish-Indian and Negro race" (quoted in DeConde, 1992:29). Over the coming decades, Mexicans were further described by whites as a mixed-race people who needed to be taught the Eurocentric way to advance their inferior civilization (Horsman, 1981).

The vituperation against Mexicans could also be heard in the nation's capital. In 1848, Senator John C. Calhoun, a vociferous opponent of the proposed annexation of Mexico, injected the language of the white racist frame into his jeremiad against Mexicans:

> We have never dreamt of incorporating into our Union any but the Caucasian race—the free white race.... I protest against such a union [the U.S. annexation of Mexico] ... Ours, sir, is the Government of a white race. The greatest misfortunes of Spanish America are to be traced to the fatal error of placing these colored races on an equality with the white race.... And yet it is professed and talked about to erect these Mexicans into a Territorial Government, and place them on an equality with the people of the United States.... Are we to associate with ourselves as equals, companions, and fellow-citizens, the Indians and mixed race of Mexico? Sir, I should consider such a thing as fatal to our institutions. (2007 [1848])

Clearly, the influential Senator Calhoun, a former U.S. vice president and secretary of state, put Mexicans "in their place" by insisting that they were not white but down the racial hierarchy among the "colored races."

As the oldest and largest group of Latin American origin in the United States, Mexicans have undergone the longest and most sustained history of racial oppression among Latinos. White American stereotypes of Mexicans emerged out of their earliest contacts in the U.S. Southwest during the first half of the nineteenth century. As Joan Moore and Harry Pachon (1985:4) have noted, "these first encounters with Mexicans tended to fix some basic outlines and to become the prototypes of later Anglo-Saxon images of all Hispanics." For instance, many white settlers, interlopers in the northern provinces of Mexico, scorned their native inhabitants as backward, lazy, cowardly, fatalistic, superstitious, violent, dangerous, and cruel. In this stereotyped imagery, whites drew on the racist framing used for centuries against African Americans and Native Americans. Such negative characteristics were supposed to have been passed on, as a result of the racial mixture between Spanish and Indian. Derogatory terms such as "spic" and "greaser" were coined to describe Mexicans in Texas, California, and elsewhere. The myth of racial inferiority helped to justify the U.S. conquest of a large part of Mexico's territory, as well as the low status of Mexican Americans in the racial hierarchy of the emerging Southwest. Although Mexican Americans gained U.S. citizenship after the Treaty of Guadalupe Hidalgo in 1848, they were denied full access to their legal rights.

European Americans who annexed huge areas of northern Mexico by force already shared a strong racist framing of other peoples, mainly African Americans and Native Americans, as we saw in the previous discussion of founders like Jefferson, who died a few years before the Mexican-American War. That long-standing white frame, which by the 1840s focused on white supremacy and black (and Indian) inferiority, has long been adaptive, and its central racist doctrines have regularly been imposed on other "people of color." The "Anglo-Saxon race" and its "Manifest Destiny" (a term created during this era) to rule the Americas were hailed enthusiastically as the Mexican "race" and the country of Mexico were increasingly berated.

The white-generated racial frame was applied not only to Mexico but to other Latin American countries as well. In the 1850s, President James Polk, who feared that the British might acquire Cuba, attempted to buy it from Spain. Ultimately Spain refused Polk's offer, but in the interim several influential individuals expressed their concern. Noted journalist James Shepherd Pike wrote that the United States did not want a territory filled "with black, mixed, degraded, and ignorant, or inferior races" (quoted in Horsman, 1981:282). Various U.S. presidents—from Polk to Ulysses S. Grant in the 1870s—also considered acquiring all or parts of the Dominican Republic. But here, too, one of the main impediments to annexation was the Americans' common belief that most Dominicans were of African origin or mixed race. For instance, in 1873, the pro-annexation American journalist Samuel Hazard wrote that "the great majority [of Dominicans] ... are neither pure black nor pure white; they are mixed in every conceivable degree" (quoted in Candelario, 2007:55). In the end, the U.S. government annexed neither the Dominican Republic nor Cuba, but Puerto Rico, which was perceived at the time to have a whiter population.

White feelings of superiority over Mexicans and other Latin Americans (as well as Native Americans) were well developed by the 1830s, when the current region of the southwestern United States was portrayed as "empty land" to be taken by white "settlers." Disparaging images of Latin American peoples, which had consolidated during the Mexican-American War of 1846–1848, intensified during the Spanish-Cuban-American War, commonly referred to as the "War of 1898." Mexicans and Native Americans, as well as Cubans, Puerto Ricans, and Filipinos, were largely imagined by whites to be outside the "American" community. Highly negative, racialized portraits of all these conquered groups were popularized through paintings, caricatures, photographs, postcards, and films between the last third of the nineteenth century and the first third of the twentieth. After the War of 1898, the inhabitants of the newly acquired territories of Cuba, Puerto Rico, and the Philippines were often pictured as dark-skinned, childlike, effeminate, poor, and primitive peoples (see Duany, 2002; Thompson, 2007)—once again, standard themes from the old white racist frame. A recurrent theme of these portrayals was that of "Uncle Sam's burden": the white man's mission to "save" the black children—sometimes dubbed "picanninies"—of the former Spanish colonies in the Caribbean and the Pacific.

At least since the Spanish-Cuban-American War, the racial composition of Puerto Rico's population has puzzled American travelers and public officials. Initially, many U.S. government reports (including those issued by the War Department and, later, the Census Bureau) insisted that the Puerto Rican population was predominantly of European rather than African origin. In 1898, an American travel writer, Trumbull White, called Puerto Rico "the whitest of the Antilles." A year later, the census found that 61.8 percent of the island's population was white. Other American observers remarked on the "surprising preponderance of the white race" in Puerto Rico, as the *National Geographic* magazine noted in 1900. In a widely distributed book, the geologist Robert T. Hill (1903:165) reiterated that "Porto Rico [sic], at least, has not become Africanized, as have all the other West Indies excepting Cuba." Such reports helped to allay the common racist fear that the U.S. government had annexed a predominantly black population after the War of 1898. Such a view still surfaces in contemporary debates about the island's political status, albeit indirectly. To many Americans, Puerto Ricans are not "pure whites" but racially mixed people.

U.S. racial discourses on Cuba long acknowledged that much of the island's population was of European ancestry. Since the end of the nineteenth century, American travel writers and photographers have depicted a white Cuban elite that could eventually govern the country according to U.S. democratic standards. Nevertheless, high-ranking military officials such as General Samuel B. M. Young and Major George M. Barbour, who participated in the Spanish-Cuban-American War, described most Cubans as a degenerate, savage, irresponsible, ignorant, and stupid people. Governor General Leonard Wood, who oversaw the U.S. military occupation of Cuba from 1899 to 1902, wrote: "[W]e are dealing with a race that has steadily been going down for a hundred years and into which we have to infuse new life, new principles and new methods of doing things" (quoted in Pérez, 2006:139). In 1902, the U.S. government grudgingly recognized the formal independence of the Cuban Republic, but only after imposing the Platt Amendment on the Cuban Constitution, allowing the United States to intervene freely in the island's internal political affairs until 1934.

During the second half of the nineteenth century, large numbers of Latin Americans began to move to the United States, in addition to those who already lived in the territories annexed after the Mexican-American War. In the Southwest, Mexicans were quickly dispossessed from their lands through legal and illegal means. New Mexico was a site for numerous conflicts between whites and Hispanics whose ancestors had lived there for generations. After 1880, thousands of Mexicans moved to the railroad, mining, and agricultural centers of Texas, Arizona, and California. In the Southeast, black Cubans worked in the cigar industries of Tampa, Key West, and other Florida cities, where they were routinely segregated from whites under the Jim Crow laws. In the Northeast, especially in New York City, Cubans joined Puerto Ricans and Spaniards in what was to become one of the leading U.S. Hispanic communities. They settled primarily in working-class enclaves such as Spanish Harlem and the Lower East Side of Manhattan. Although few in number, these pioneers set the pace for the massive migration from Latin America to the United States during the twentieth century. As their totals grew, U.S. Latinos—often called "Spanish," "Hispanic," or "Spanish American"—became increasingly racialized as a separate minority group.

Throughout the twentieth century, Latinos were consistently portrayed in the white-controlled U.S. media as unwanted and disreputable aliens. As Otto Santa Ana (2002) has argued, the image of a "brown tide rising" has characterized much of the media's discourse on migration from Latin America, particularly from Mexico. Moreover, Leo Chavez (2001) has shown that Mexican immigrants are typically considered an external threat and an internal enemy of the United States. In general, popular representations of U.S. Latinos continue to emphasize their lower-class origins, dark skin color, and foreign language and culture. Even today, Hispanics—especially undocumented immigrants—are often portrayed in terms of a thinly disguised white racist framing based on nineteenth-century Social Darwinism. For instance, the common notion of "illegal aliens" (or "wetbacks") serves to justify their treatment as animals without any human rights. The racial connotations of current public policies designed to "stem the tide" of undocumented immigrants, primarily from Mexico, China, and other Latin American and Asian countries—but not from Canada or Ireland—may be covert but are nonetheless very powerful. Similarly, the post-9/11 security efforts to "close the borders" of the United States have targeted Middle Eastern–looking and other dark-skinned persons, including Latinos.

Immigrant and "foreign" status has again become central to the racialized identification of Latin Americans. From its beginnings in the 1600s, the white racial frame has insisted that "Americans of color" (initially Indians, then Africans) are not only inferior biologically and intellectually but also uncivilized, dangerous, and foreign to the "American way of life." This anti-foreign view has been extended to Latin American immigrants in more recent decades. "Illegal," an epithet meaning "foreign and dangerous," has become a regular part of the United States' vernacular, but only in reference to Latin American immigrants.

Unauthorized entrants from countries such as Russia or Israel, and there are many, are not designated as "illegal." Citizens of other Western countries who violate U.S. immigration laws and regulations are excluded from the "illegal" category and are not routinely abused and targeted by the U.S. government.

In Phoenix and other southwestern cities, Latinos and Latin American drivers who display what law enforcement authorities perceive as "illegal" clues, such as an old car with "Mexican trappings" or the playing of certain kinds of music, are routinely stopped under the pretext of a traffic violation, yet with the main purpose of checking their immigration status. Indeed, the salience of this "illegal" imagery in the anti-Latino version of the contemporary racial frame has resulted in many bodily injuries and even in the deaths of immigrants, especially those targeted by white supremacists and xenophobes. Today, racialized framing and violence are facts of life for Latinos coming into and living in the United States. During the nineteenth century, Latinos and Latin Americans were often considered inferior "mongrels" who had to be saved by the Anglo-Saxon race. Today, Latinos are frequently treated as "problems," such as welfare chiselers or irresponsible propagators of children. They are often considered a serious menace to U.S. culture.

As Clara Rodríguez (1997) and Arlene Dávila (2001) have thoroughly documented, U.S. Latinos are stereotyped as having a particular physical appearance characterized by olive or brown skin and dark, straight hair. Their body type is ambiguously located by whites as somewhere between the dominant images of whiteness and blackness (see Mendible, 2007). Similarly, the U.S. government, mass media, police, and other major institutions increasingly refer to "Hispanics" as distinct from both non-Hispanic whites and blacks. Although all Latinos have been racialized, each group has followed its own path toward racialization, depending on its historical background, socioeconomic characteristics, and mode of incorporation into the host society. The following chapters focus on several groups of Latin American immigrants in the United States—including Mexicans, Puerto Ricans, Cubans, Dominicans, Salvadorans, Guatemalans, Colombians, Peruvians, and Chileans. Overall, their experiences suggest that Latino (including the closely linked term "Hispanic") has become a color-coded category. This process has many nuanced consequences and dimensions, as the savvy contributors to this volume consistently show.

BRIEF OVERVIEW OF CHAPTERS

In this book, we analyze how Latinos, both in the United States and in their countries of origin, have been racialized in various ways. Here, noted Latin American, Latino, and U.S. social scientists address the extent and costs of U.S. racial hegemony at home and abroad. In particular, our collaborators examine the multiple histories, causes, forms, and consequences of the racialization of Latinos and Latin Americans. Immigration restrictions, instauration of U.S.-style racism, violence, suppression of the Spanish language, and intergroup conflict are some of the racially based developments discussed in this volume.

Historically, Mexicans were the first sizable group of Latin American origin to be incorporated into the United States as a racialized and subordinated group. Yet, as Laura Gómez points out, many U.S. scholars have insisted that Mexican Americans are not a "race" but, rather, just another "ethnic group." She asserts that the failure to recognize the racialized status of Mexican Americans has contributed to the misperception that the history of U.S. race relations chronicles white-on-black oppression only. This limited view has interfered, for example, with the recognition of the important role played by Mexican Americans in the "who is white" question.

Racialization often entails minimizing historical, cultural, and linguistic differences among peoples from the same region—including, for example, those in various Latin American countries. Such labels as "Hispanic" typically collapse diverse peoples into a single overarching group according to criteria devised by the dominant white majority. In two separate chapters, Rubén Rumbaut and Clara Rodríguez discuss the byzantine histories of the broad panethnic labels applied to groups referred to today as "Hispanics" or "Latinos." From their beginnings, these categories subsumed culturally and geographically heterogeneous groups with separate identities and histories. The great inadequacy of these labels has been demonstrated in censuses since 1980, as many members of the so-called Hispanic or Latino population refuse to identify themselves with any of the racial labels they are offered on census forms and instead place themselves in the "other" category. As Rumbaut argues, the creation of a catchall term for people of various Latin American and Spanish origins has contributed to their racialization in the United States. In her analysis, Rodríguez adds that Latinos often resist their classification according to U.S. racial categories that tend to pigeonhole them as "not white."

The dilemmas of racial, ethnic, and panethnic definitions are prominent among Salvadorans, Guatemalans, and other Central Americans, who often become an "invisible minority" in the United States. Nestor Rodriguez and Cecilia Menjívar discuss racialized groups from Central America (especially Indians and blacks) who have been victims of massive killings in their homelands, perpetrated by national armies under the pretext of "anti-Communist" campaigns, often with the support of the United States. Like many other Latin Americans, these oppressed people have migrated, with and without documents, in search of a better and more peaceful life. Upon entering the United States, many blend with a local Latino community and experience the "anti-illegal" xenophobia and indifference or hostility of local governments. Rodriguez and Menjívar speculate that Central American immigrants are faced with two options: either become part of the pool of Latino "cheap" labor or join other Latin Americans and Latinos in a common cause to bring about change.

The adoption of a Hispanic or Latino identity, beyond the immigrants' specific national and ethnic identities, is still an emergent and contested process. Many Latinos are increasingly embracing a panethnic label in an effort to resist widespread stereotypes and advance their plight as a racialized minority. Whether identification as Latino or Hispanic will eventually replace specific national markers such as Mexican, Puerto Rican, or Dominican remains unclear.

Zulema Valdez provides further evidence of the complicated nature of racialization in her study of business owners of Latin American origin in Houston. Her informants overwhelmingly identified themselves by national origin. At the same time, however, they used panethnic labels to express animosity against some Latino groups, and to disassociate their national origin from widespread U.S. stigmatization of Latinos.

Some sources of interethnic and interracial friction between groups classified as Latinos in the United States begin at home. Both Jorge Duany and Wendy Roth deal with racialization in Puerto Rico and the Dominican Republic, but their foci are different. Duany examines the racialization of Haitians in the Dominican Republic and of Dominicans in Puerto Rico. In both countries, the victims face major economic and social obstacles because they are defined as "black" by their oppressors. Identifying the basic similarities and differences between the two cases, Duany argues that the precarious status of Haitians in the Dominican Republic and of Dominicans in Puerto Rico is primarily due to their racialization. The denigration of these groups externalizes racial prejudice and discrimination against foreign "others," who are largely excluded from dominant discourses of national identity.

Roth argues that a white Americanized view of race has crept into Puerto Rico and the Dominican Republic, affecting even those who have never left their homelands. Traditionally, Dominicans and Puerto Ricans have thought of their racial mixture as part of their uniqueness, which distinguishes them from unmixed Americans. Nevertheless, U.S. attitudes exert a secondary but significant influence on the process of racialization in these countries. Not all Puerto Ricans and Dominicans blindly accept American racial categories; many actively resist their imposition from abroad. However, others accommodate the U.S. language of racial classification—even though it may conflict with the local framing that accents a continuous model of race with multiple intermediate categories between white and black.

Although a more fluid racial classification system characterizes much of the Caribbean and Brazil, racial differentiation has recently increased in Cuba and among Cuban Americans. In particular, Lisandro Pérez discusses the multiple disadvantages faced by black Cubans, both at home and abroad. In the early 1960s, many white middle-class Cubans left for the United States as a result of the revolution led by Fidel Castro. In the 1990s, in the midst of a profound economic crisis, the Cuban government encouraged exiles to send dollars to their relatives. Having few relatives abroad, most black Cubans could not take advantage of family remittances. When Cuba's tourism industry was reestablished, competition for desirable jobs intensified. Yet many foreign managers preferred to hire white Cubans, and black Cubans again found themselves excluded from employment opportunities. Black Cubans who came to the United States did not fare well, either. They were often segregated in black urban areas, apart from their white Cuban friends and acquaintances. Pérez's prediction that racialization will persist among Cubans on and off the island is particularly relevant given the striking social, economic, and political disparities between Cubans at home and those in the diaspora.

Although the U.S. Census Bureau officially recognizes that "Hispanics can be of any race," it tends to treat them as a separate race from white and black non-Hispanics. Similarly, the mass media reproduce the popular (especially white) view that Hispanics are racially distinct from other groups, such as African Americans. Xóchitl Bada and Gilberto Cárdenas address Latino–African American relations in Los Angeles and Chicago. They underline that African Americans and Latinos share major economic interests and goals on which they can work together. To build successful coalitions, Latinos and African Americans should focus on their common needs, such as opportunities to work for fair wages, and reduce their disagreement over issues such as bilingual education.

Relations between different groups of Latin American immigrants can also be tense. In their chapter, Elizabeth Aranda, Rosa Chang, and Elena Sabogal show that Latin American and Caribbean immigrants frequently characterize fellow immigrants as economic and cultural threats to U.S. national identity and security. Although Miami immigrants hail the city's Latino cultural and linguistic environment, they harbor conflicting attitudes toward increasing migration from Latin America. According to Aranda and her colleagues, the racialization of Latinos—such as Cubans, Puerto Ricans, Colombians, and Peruvians in Miami—depends on their class backgrounds, national origins, and legal statuses, which in turn reflect the social constructs of "deserving" and "undeserving" immigrants. Thus, for example, some immigrants hold other immigrants responsible for growing income inequality and contracting public services, rather than blaming institutionalized racism and other structural sources of these trends. One of the main public concerns about the growing "Latinization" of cities like Miami has been the common (again, especially white) fear of the displacement of the English language by the Spanish language. Jane Hill contends that pressure against the public—and even private—use of Spanish and campaigns to proclaim English the "official language" of the United States are too copious to attribute to bona fide efforts to protect the status of English. In fact, she asserts, they are attempts to deride and ultimately squelch Spanish in the United States. "Mock Spanish," despite its surface appearance as bonhomie, shares these goals. When whites use supposedly Spanish expressions, such as "No problemo," in a linguistically disorganized way, they are appropriating and ridiculing one of the most important components of Latin American cultures: their language.

Ofelia García traces the history of pervasively negative attitudes toward the Spanish language and bilingualism in the United States since the mid-nineteenth century. She argues that Spanish was initially stigmatized as the language of the conquered and colonized as a result of the Mexican-American War (1846–1848) and the Spanish-Cuban-American War (1898). In the mid-twentieth century, the large-scale influx of Mexicans and Puerto Ricans (and, later, Cubans) expanded the need for bilingual education programs in the United States. In 1968, Congress authorized the Bilingual Education Act to improve the educational opportunities of the children of immigrants. But bilingual education's checkered history has continued since then as well. Today, bilingualism is increasingly scorned in influential educational and political circles. García argues that the U.S. government has maintained a policy of eradicating Spanish, by encouraging the shift to English and linking its use to poor and uneducated immigrants.

Violence against people of Latin American origin in the United States has been physical as well as symbolic. William Carrigan and Clive Webb address the mob violence visited upon by at least 597 Mexicans between 1848 and 1928. They argue that the lynching of Mexicans was one of the mechanisms used by local and national whites to consolidate their hegemony. These crimes occurred with the connivance of public authorities. Most notorious were the Texas Rangers, who by some estimates killed or seriously injured thousands of Mexicans. On one occasion, in 1881, they crossed the Mexican border illegally to apprehend a suspect, Onofrio Baca. The Rangers handed the prisoner to a white mob that quickly hanged him. Carrigan and Webb clearly document the intertwined histories of Mexicans and African Americans, particularly regarding racial violence by whites seeking to maintain full control of the racial hierarchy.

According to Fernando Purcell, Chileans were among the first to arrive in northern California after the Gold Rush began in 1848. Most Chileans thought of themselves as "white" but were racialized as nonwhites upon arrival. White U.S. miners did not want "foreign" competition, and conflict ensued. Chileans resisted but were victimized by the miners with the complicity of local authorities. Purcell argues that the shared experience of discrimination, as well as growing ties between Mexicans and Chileans during the 1860s, nurtured an early sense of a Hispanic American "race" in the San Francisco Bay Area. In short, the racialization of Chileans and other Latin American immigrants in California by whites fostered a panethnic Hispanic identity.

CONCLUSION

Together, the contributors to this volume demonstrate clearly and thoroughly how U.S. racialization is based on the centuries-old white racial frame—a white-generated worldview in which Latinos and Latin Americans appear as an inferior "race." This racist worldview has been echoed in the halls of Congress, printed in newspapers, and proclaimed from pulpits since the first days of the United States. It has provided ideological support for the seizure of Mexican land, annexation of former Spanish colonies, military intervention in sovereign Latin American nations, and alliances with Latin American dictatorships.

At home, the white racial frame has been employed to cast a wide net under which Latinos and Latin Americans are dumped for better political control and economic exploitation by white officials and employers. It has given impetus to establishing English as the official language of the United States and to pointing an accusing finger at the Spanish language because its speakers are considered "foreign" and "un-American." It has placed racialized groups in the position of enforcing the white racial frame for still other or newer racialized groups. And it has provided a vocabulary that racialized Latinos and Latin American immigrants can use to vilify each other, or other "Americans of color."

Sometimes the ideologies in particular interpretive frames have unintended and beneficial consequences. But racialization is incapable of generating decency, compassion, or progress for any human group. It has been evil through and throughout its operations since the seventeenth century. Why does it persist? The white racial frame and its associated racial hierarchy serve the interests of U.S. white elites splendidly, and they have the resources to support and propagate this frame. As part of that racial frame, common sense makes injustice appear inevitable.

REFERENCES

Calhoun, John C. [1848] 2007. "Conquest of Mexico." Retrieved December 13, 2007. (http://teachingamericanhistory.org/library/index.asp?document=478)

Candelario, Ginetta E. B. 2007. *Black Behind the Ears: Dominican Racial Identity from Museums to Beauty Shops.* Durham, NC: Duke University Press.

Chavez, Leo R. 2001. *Covering Immigration: Popular Images and the Politics of the Nation.* Berkeley: University of California Press.

Dávila, Arlene. 2001. *Latinos Inc.: The Marketing and Making of a People.* Berkeley: University of California Press.

DeConde, Alexander. 1992. *Ethnicity, Race, and American Foreign Policy: A History.* Boston: Northeastern University Press.

Duany, Jorge. 2002. *The Puerto Rican Nation on the Move: Identities on the Island and in the United States.* Chapel Hill: University of North Carolina Press.

Feagin, Joe R. 2006. *Systemic Racism: A Theory of Oppression.* New York: Routledge.

———. Forthcoming. *The White Racial Frame.* New York: Routledge.

Gossett, Thomas F. 1997. *Race: The History of an Idea in America.* New York: Oxford University Press.

Hill, Robert T. 1903. *Cuba and Porto Rico, with the Other Islands of the West Indies,* 2nd ed. New York: Century.

Horsman, Reginald. 1981. *Race and Manifest Destiny: The Origins of American Racial Anglo-Saxonism.* Cambridge, MA: Harvard University Press.

Kant, Immanuel. [1764] 1965. *Observations on the Feeling of the Beautiful and Sublime.* Berkeley: University of California Press.

———. [1775] 1950. "On the Distinctiveness of the Races in General." Pp. 16–24 in Earl W. Count (ed.), *This Is Race: An Anthology Selected from the International Literature on the Races of Man.* New York: Henry Shuman.

Mendible, Myra (ed.). 2007. *From Bananas to Buttocks: The Latina Body in Popular Film and Culture.* Austin: University of Texas Press.

Moore, Joan, and Harry Pachon. 1985. *Hispanics in the United States.* Englewood Cliffs, NJ: Prentice-Hall.

Morton, Eric. 2002. "Race and Racism in the Works of David Hume." *Journal on African Philosophy* 1:1–27.

National Geographic. 1900. "The First American Census of Porto Rico." 11(8):328.

Pérez, Louis A., Jr. 2006. *Cuba: Between Reform and Revolution,* 3rd ed. New York: Oxford University Press.

Plessy v. Ferguson. 1896. 163 U.S. 537, 551.

Rodríguez, Clara E. (ed.). 1997. *Latin Looks: Images of Latinas and Latinos in the U.S. Media.* Boulder, CO: Westview Press.

Santa Ana, Otto. 2002. *Brown Tide Rising: Metaphors of Latinos in Contemporary American Discourse.* Austin: University of Texas Press.

Shore, Bradd. 2000. "Human Diversity and Human Nature." Pp. 81–104 in Neil Roughley (ed.), *Being Humans: Anthropological Universality and Particularity in Transdisciplinary Perspective.* Berlin: Walter de Gruyter.

Spencer, Herbert. [1873] 1972. *On Social Evolution: Selected Writings,* edited by J. D. Y. Peel. Chicago: University of Chicago Press.

Thompson, Lanny. 2007. *Nuestra isla y su gente: La construcción del "otro" puertorriqueño en* Our Islands and Their People. Río Piedras, PR: Centro de Investigaciones Sociales, Universidad de Puerto Rico.

White, Trumbull. 1898. *Our New Possessions.* Boston: Adams.

CHAPTER 1

Pigments of Our Imagination

On the Racialization and Racial Identities of "Hispanics" and "Latinos"

Rubén G. Rumbaut

Why should Pennsylvania, founded by the English, become a Colony of Aliens, who will shortly be so numerous as to Germanize us instead of our Anglifying them, and will never adopt our Language or Customs, any more than they can acquire our Complexion?

—*Benjamin Franklin (1751)*

"Race" is a trope of ultimate, irreducible difference.

—*Henry Louis Gates, Jr. (1986)*

I have been telling my students since the 1970s that "race is a pigment of our imagination." The play on words of the definition is meant as a *double entendre,* both to debunk baseless biological pretensions and to focus attention on the social, legal, and political construction of categories meant to put people "in their place" in hierarchies of power and privilege. "Race" is a social status, not a zoological one; a product of history, not of nature; a contextual variable, not a given. It is a historically contingent, relational, intersubjective phenomenon—yet it is typically misbegotten as a natural, fixed marker of phenotypic difference inherent in human bodies, independent of human will or intention. What is called "race" is largely the sociopolitical accretion of past intergroup contacts and struggles,

15

which establish the boundaries and thus the identities of victors and vanquished, of dominant and subordinate groups, of "us" and "them," with their attendant conceits of superiority and inferiority and invidious taxonomies of social worth or stigma. As such, "race" is an ideological construct linking supposedly innate traits of individuals to their rank and fate in the social order. Racial statuses and categories (and the putative differences they connote) are imposed and infused with stereotypical moral meaning, all the more when they become master statuses affecting all aspects of social life. The dominant "racial frame" (Feagin, 2006) that evolved in what became the United States, during the long colonial and national era of slavery and after it, was that of white supremacy. Benjamin Franklin's words in the epigraph above are illustrative; they were written in 1751, a quarter of a century before he signed the Declaration of Independence with no hint of irony, back when not even Germans were imagined to be "white," mixing nativism and racism in what would become a familiar, habitual American blend.

How do "Latinos" or "Hispanics" fit in the country's "white racial frame"? Are they a "race"—or, more precisely, a racialized category? If so, how and when were they racialized? Why has the U.S. Census Bureau insisted since the 1970s on putting an asterisk next to the label—uniquely among official categories— indicating that "Hispanics may be of any race"? Is it a post-1960s, post–Civil Rights Era term, not fraught with the racial freight of a past in which for more than a century—in Texas since 1836 and in the rest of the Southwest after 1848—"Mexican" was disparaged as a subordinate caste by most "Anglos"? (Almaguer, 1994; Foley, 2004; Montejano, 1987). The use of the label "Latino" or "Hispanic" is itself an act of homogenization, lumping diverse peoples together into a Procrustean aggregate. But are they even a "they"? Is there a "Latino" or "Hispanic" ethnic group, cohesive and self-conscious, sharing a sense of peoplehood in the same sense that there is an "African American" people in the United States? Or is it mainly an administrative shorthand devised for statistical purposes, a one-size-fits-all label that subsumes diverse peoples and identities? Is the focus on "Hispanics" or "Latinos" as a catchall category (let alone "the browning of America") misleading, since it conceals the enormous diversity of contemporary immigrants from Spanish-speaking Latin America, obliterating the substantial generational and class differences among the groups so labeled, along with their distinct histories and ancestries? How do the labeled label themselves? What racial meaning does the panethnic label have for the labeled, and how has this label been internalized, and with what consequences? This chapter considers these questions, focusing primarily on official or state definitions and on the way such categories are incorporated by those so classified.

Newcomers and Old-Timers

The classification of "Hispanic" or "Latino" itself is new, an instance of a panethnic category created by law decades ago. But the groups subsumed under that label—Mexicans, Puerto Ricans, Cubans, Dominicans, Salvadorans, Guatemalans, Colombians, Peruvians, Ecuadorians, and the other dozen nationalities from Latin America and even Spain itself—were not "Hispanics" or "Latinos" in their countries of origin; rather, they only became so in the United States. That catchall label has a particular meaning only in the U.S. context in which it was constructed and is applied, and where its meaning continues to evolve.

The peoples it subsumes are rapidly transforming the country's demographic and geographic composition. The "Hispanic" or "Latino" population of the United States, as it has come to be reified by both ascription and assertion, reached 45 million in 2007, comprising 15 percent of the U.S. population (U.S. Census Bureau, 2008). (That total excludes another 4 million on the island of Puerto Rico, although they are U.S. citizens by birthright.) The rapid growth of this population—which was estimated at only 4 million in 1950—has been stunning. The Census Bureau announced that in 2003, Hispanics surpassed African Americans to become the largest minority in the country—and for the first time in decades their growth is now due more to natural increase than to immigration (Tienda and Mitchell, 2006). Given current trends, Latinos will account for 60 percent of total U.S. population growth between 2005 and 2050 (they already accounted for half the growth of the U.S. population between 2000 and 2005). By 2050 they are projected to increase to an estimated 128 million people or 29 percent of the national total, significantly exceeding the proportions of all other minorities combined. By comparison, the non-Hispanic black population in 2050 is projected to comprise 13 percent of the national total, and the Asian population 9 percent (Passel and Cohn, 2008).

"Hispanics" or "Latinos" are an extraordinarily diverse lot—an *arroz con mango*—made up both of recently arrived newcomers and of old-timers with deeper roots in American soil than any other ethnic group except for the indigenous peoples of the continent. They comprise a population that can claim both a history and a territory in what is now the United States that precede the establishment of the nation. But it is also a population that has emerged seemingly suddenly, its growth driven both by accelerating immigration from the Spanish-speaking countries of Latin America—above all from Mexico, which shares a 2,000-mile border with the United States—and by high rates of natural increase. Forty-five percent of the total Hispanic population of the United States today is foreign-born, and another 31 percent consists of a rapidly growing second generation of U.S.-born children of immigrant parents (Rumbaut, 2006).

Although a single label implies otherwise, "Hispanics" or "Latinos" are not a homogeneous entity, and should not be presumed to be so. Even the newcomers among them differ notably in national and social-class origins, cultural backgrounds, phenotypes (many mixing indigenous pre-Columbian ancestries with European, African, and Asian roots), migration histories, legal statuses, and contexts of reception in the United States. Nonetheless, despite sometimes profound group and generational differences among the nationalities so subsumed, the tens of millions of persons so classified do share a common label that symbolizes a minority group status in the United States, a label developed and legitimized by the state, diffused in daily and institutional practice, and finally internalized—and racialized—as a prominent part of the American mosaic. That this outcome is, at least in part, a self-fulfilling prophecy does not make it any less real (see Alba, Rumbaut, and Marotz, 2005; Aleinikoff and Rumbaut, 1998).

HISTORICAL CONTEXTS OF INCORPORATION AND INEQUALITY

Despite the rapid emergence of "Hispanics" or "Latinos" as a new, prominent—and official—part of the American mosaic, with the sole exception of the indigenous inhabitants of the Americas, the country's Spanish roots are older than those of other groups. They antedate by a century the creation of an English colony in North America and have left an indelible if ignored imprint, especially across the southern rim of the United States, from the Atlantic to the Pacific (Weber, 1992). By the time of the American Revolution, Spain had cast a wide net of communities stretching from coast to coast; there are regions of the country in which every town and village bears a Spanish name, and in them can be found the first missions, ranches, schools, churches, presidios, theatres, public buildings, and cities in U.S. history. Indeed, between the two coasts, as David Weber (1992) has noted, Spain claimed at least half of the present U.S. mainland, and governed these areas for well over two centuries, a period longer than the United States has existed as an independent nation. In U.S. popular culture and in official narrative and ritual, the American past has been portrayed as the story of the expansion of English America, suppressing if not silencing the Spanish presence from the nation's collective memory (see Walton, 2001). But origins shape destinies, and no understanding of "Hispanics" or "Latinos" in the United States today, or of the category under which they are now grouped, can ignore the complex historical and geographic contexts of their incorporation—including, for many of these populations, what has been called their "double colonization" (Gómez, 2007).

In the United States, the collective memory of these silent antecedents remains clouded by remnants of prejudices and stereotypes, whose roots go to colonial rivalries in the sixteenth century between Spanish America and English America, and to anti-Spanish propaganda in Protestant Europe and America that built into the *Leyenda Negra* (black legend), now centuries old, whose original intent was to denigrate Catholic Spanish culture and to portray Spaniards as a uniquely cruel and depraved race (Maltby, 1968). That legend was kept alive whenever conflict arose between English- and Spanish-speaking societies in America in the 1800s, especially during the Texas Revolt (1836), the Mexican-American War (1846–1848), and the Spanish-Cuban-American War (1898). The Mexican War (remembered in Mexico as *la invasión norteamericana*) was the United States' first foreign war and transformed the nation into a continental power; the Treaty of Guadalupe Hidalgo that ended it, along with the annexation of Texas that preceded it, expanded the territory of the United States by an area about the size of Western Europe, while severing half that of Mexico (which had achieved its independence from Spain only as recently as 1821). Five decades later, the Spanish-Cuban-American War gave the United States possession of

Spain's last remaining colonies in Cuba, Puerto Rico, and the Philippines, and transformed it into a global power. The incorporation of these territories was legitimized as fulfilling the nation's divinely preordained "Manifest Destiny" to spread the benefits of U.S. democracy and civilization to the lesser peoples of the continent. The U.S.-dictated terms of settlement after each war shaped subsequent patterns of political and military inequality between the United States and Latin America and the Caribbean.

The peoples of the conquered territories were absorbed into the expanding boundaries of the United States as second-class citizens—*de facto* if not *de jure*—and often depicted as "half-civilized" mixed-race "mongrels" and "half-breeds." This was the case above all in the American (formerly the Mexican) Southwest: For a century after the 1840s, Mexican Americans were subjected to laws, norms, and practices akin to the Jim Crow apartheid system that discriminated against blacks after the Civil War—injustices, most deeply rooted in Texas (which entered the Union in 1845 as a slave state and was among the first to secede from it as part of the Confederacy), that caused Mexicanos (and Hispanos, Tejanos, and Californios) in the Southwest to see themselves as foreigners in their native land (Foley, 2004; Gómez, 2007; Montejano, 1987; Weber, 1973). In Puerto Rico, occupied and formally acquired by the United States in 1898, the status of the islanders was left ambiguous until the passage of the Jones Act in 1917, which gave Puerto Ricans U.S. citizenship; these provisions remained after 1952, when a new constitution defined Commonwealth status for Puerto Rico, a status that distinguishes Puerto Ricans from all other Latin Americans (see Duany, 2002). Cuba, the target of repeated efforts at annexation by the United States throughout the nineteenth century and a main focus of U.S. trade and capital investment, never became a recruiting ground for agricultural workers, as did Mexico and Puerto Rico. But Cuba remained subordinated to the United States after 1902 under the terms of the Platt Amendment, attached by the U.S. Congress to the Cuban Constitution, which formalized the right of the United States to intervene in Cuban internal affairs. U.S. economic penetration of the island increased sharply after the 1898–1902 military occupation, and by 1929 U.S. direct investment in Cuba totaled more than one-fourth of all U.S. investment in Latin America (Rumbaut and Rumbaut, 2007).

The countries of the Caribbean Basin—especially Mexico, Puerto Rico, and Cuba—have felt most strongly the load, and the lure, of the U.S. hegemonic presence. They include countries that, since the days of Benjamin Franklin (who already in 1761 had suggested Mexico and Cuba as goals of American expansion) and Thomas Jefferson, were viewed as belonging as if by some "laws of political gravitation" (the phrase is John Quincy Adams's in 1823, who also crafted the "Monroe Doctrine") to the "Manifest Destiny" of the United States, in a Caribbean long viewed as "the American Mediterranean" (the term is Alexander Hamilton's, writing in *The Federalist* in 1787). Under the "Roosevelt Corollary" to the Monroe Doctrine enunciated by Theodore Roosevelt in 1904, the United States intervened frequently in the region, including at least twenty Marine landings in the Caribbean from 1905 to 1965 (see Langley, 2003). The United States "took" Panama in 1903 (then a province of Colombia) and built the Canal between 1904 and 1914; the Panama Canal Zone operated thereafter as a U.S. territory until 1979. U.S. Marines occupied the Dominican Republic from 1915 to 1924, and again in 1965. The Marines were in Nicaragua almost continuously from 1912 to 1933; after the end of the Somoza dictatorship in 1979, the United States supported the opposition "Contras" from bases in Honduras in the 1980s. U.S.-backed coups in post–World War II Guatemala (1954) and Chile (1973), support for the governments of El Salvador and Guatemala during the wars of the 1980s, and other interventions—above all economic and cultural, not solely military—have ironically resulted in expanding migration flows to the United States. As an unintended consequence of this history, many "Hispanics" today come from countries whose ties with the United States are more recent, but who have emerged as major sources of Latin American immigration since the 1980s— notably the Dominican Republic, El Salvador, Guatemala, and Colombia, with other sizable flows from Honduras, Nicaragua, Peru, Ecuador, Venezuela, and elsewhere. Given the economic, political, military, and cultural influence established over the decades, it is precisely these countries whose people have most visibly emerged as a significant component of American society.

WHITE BY LAW: CITIZENSHIP ELIGIBILITY AND STATUS LIMINALITY

A paradox of this history of incorporation and inequality since 1848 and 1898 is that the peoples now construed as "Hispanics" or "Latinos" occupied a liminal, intermediate position in a white supremacist state, fraught with status ambiguity. Mexicans in the United States have been legally and officially classified as "white" (and Hispanic elites historically asserted white identities for themselves and their communities), yet socially treated as "nonwhite." As Neil Foley points out, "[i]t is difficult to generalize about the status of Mexicans in the U.S., both citizens and noncitizens, because their racial status differed from region to region, from state to state, and often from town to town" (2004:343). The original "white racial frame" did not recognize those who today are called "Hispanics." The first eight decennial censuses counted "free whites" and "free colored" ("black or mulatto"), along with separate slave schedules; "Indian" and "Chinese" were added as racial categories after the Civil War, along with "white" and "black." Writing in the early 1830s (before the Mexican War, before the coming of the Chinese, before mass immigration), Alexis de Tocqueville saw but "three races in America." A chapter of his classic *Democracy in America* addressed "the present state and probable future of the three races that inhabit the territory of the United States," and the different effects of the tyranny of the Europeans on the Negroes and the Indians: "Chance has brought them together on the same soil, but they have mixed without combining, and each follows a separate destiny" (1969 [1832]:316).

As Aristide Zolberg (2006) has argued in a masterful analysis, the United States has been "a nation by design," engineering immigration and naturalization laws and policies to meet the interests of dominant social and economic groups, and restricting by "race" and origin (until relatively recently in its history) those populations it would lure and those it would bar. The Chinese Exclusion Act of 1882 (extended until 1943), the ban on virtually all other Asian immigration in 1917, and the national origin quotas imposed in the early 1920s, which privileged northwest Europeans (not abolished until 1965), all aimed at the racial exclusion of immigrants from the Eastern Hemisphere—but Latin Americans were exempted from these legal exclusions. Largely at the urging of American growers and ranchers, no limits were set on Western Hemisphere countries: It was understood that cheap, unskilled Mexican labor could be recruited when needed, as happened during World War I and the 1920s, and again during the Bracero Program beginning in the 1940s; and that those laborers could be deported en masse when they were no longer needed, as happened during the 1930s and again during "Operation Wetback" in the mid-1950s.

From the outset, U.S. law decreed, on racial grounds, which aliens would be excluded from national citizenship. The Naturalization Law of 1790 passed by the first Congress limited citizenship to "white persons." This racial prerequisite for becoming a citizen lasted variously for 162 years (until 1952); it was a crucial legal restriction, since persons "ineligible for citizenship" were subsequently denied access to other basic rights (e.g., California's "Alien Land Law" of 1913 used that pretext to prevent Asian immigrant farmers from owning land in the state). In the decades after the Civil War and the Reconstruction era, mass immigration reached record highs and countless people argued their racial identity in order to naturalize, but who was "white" (the meaning of which was itself changing over time) turned out to be a complicated question that was adjudicated in state and federal courts. Ian Haney López (2006), in a nuanced study of the legal construction of "race," analyzed fifty-two racial "prerequisite cases" heard by the courts (including the U.S. Supreme Court) between 1878 and 1952. Only one of the fifty-two involved a Mexican (*In re: Rodríguez*, 1897). Of the others, Chinese, Japanese, Burmese, Koreans, Filipinos, Hawaiians, Native Americans, and Afghanis (including those with mixed European ancestry) were found to be "not white"; Asian Indians, Punjabis, Syrians, and Arabians were found to be "white" in some cases but "not white" in others; Armenians and Mexicans were deemed "white" by law and thus eligible for citizenship. (Puerto Ricans, as noted, have had statutory U.S. citizenship since 1917.)

The 1897 *Rodríguez* case, the first court case addressing the liminal racial status of Mexicans, is instructive. In 1848, the Treaty of Guadalupe Hidalgo had granted U.S. citizenship to those who chose to remain in the newly acquired territories, though relatively few were in fact accorded the privileges reserved for whites. Half a century later, Ricardo Rodríguez, a Mexican immigrant from Guanajuato who had settled in San Antonio, applied to become a naturalized citizen. Legal briefs were filed in opposition, seeking to deprive Mexicans as a class of their right to naturalize and thus to vote, by arguing that Rodríguez was not a "white person" under the provisions of U.S. naturalization law but "a pure-blooded Mexican [with] dark eyes, chocolate brown skin, and high cheek bones" who could not pass as "Spanish," and that "Indians, Mongolians, or Aztecs" were ineligible for citizenship (Foley, 2004: 343). But the judge ruled that while Rodríguez "would probably not be classed as white ... from the standpoint of the ethnologist," he was nonetheless legally eligible to naturalize under the treaty of 1848.

Ironically, being deemed white by law would later work perversely against the interests of Mexican Americans, who remained subordinated in daily life. In 1954 in *Hernández v. Texas* (the first case tried by Mexican American lawyers before the U.S. Supreme Court, as part of a legal strategy to attack three key pillars of American racial apartheid: school and residential segregation and jury exclusion), the Court ruled that the systematic exclusion of persons of Mexican ancestry from juries in a Texas county violated the Constitution, thereby extending to them the Equal Protection Clause of the Fourteenth Amendment (Olivas, 2006). To put Mexican Americans on juries was tantamount to elevating them to equal status with whites, deeply violating Texas's racial caste system. The state of Texas had argued that the Fourteenth Amendment covered only two racial groups, whites and blacks; that Mexican Americans were classified as white, not black; and therefore that Hernández's rights had not been violated inasmuch as the juries that indicted and tried him were "composed of members of his race." The fact that no person with a Spanish surname had served on any type of jury for at least twenty-five years, according to the state, was mere happenstance. His lawyers challenged those claims with evidence that discrimination and segregation were common practices, and that Mexican Americans were shunned as a class apart. Yet the Supreme Court did not decide *Hernández* as a "race" case, since every party agreed and argued that Mexican Americans were "white."

Similarly, in 1849 the California State Constitutional Convention deemed Mexicans to be "white" for legal purposes, a status denied to blacks, Asians, and American Indians (Almaguer, 1994); Mexican Americans in California were also exempted from miscegenation laws that applied to other minorities. But that did not prevent California from passing an anti-loitering law in 1855, known as the "Greaser Act," which applied to "all persons who are commonly known as 'Greasers' or the issue of Spanish and Indian blood ... who go armed and are not peaceable and quiet persons." That nineteenth-century statute bears more than a passing resemblance to the local ordinances and state laws being passed across the United States in the twenty-first century in attempts to remove or to make life so miserable for undocumented immigrants (most of whom hail from Mexico and Latin America) that they will "self-deport." A key issue today is once more the lack of citizenship and legal status, this time pursued under cover of a new "colorblind racism."

CREATING A "HISPANIC" AND "LATINO" CATEGORY IN OFFICIAL STATISTICS

Beginning in 1850, the U.S. Census relied on objective indicators, such as country of birth (or decades later, parent's birthplace, mother tongue, or "Spanish surname"), to identify persons of Mexican origin in its decennial counts. Mexicans were coded as "white" for census purposes from 1850 to 1920. They were then classified as a separate "race" in the 1930 census, amid the Great Depression. During that tumultuous decade, perhaps a million or more were forcibly "repatriated" to Mexico, including many U.S. citizens (see Johnson, 2005; Kanstroom, 2007; Ngai, 2004); but Mexican American civil rights groups, with the support of the Mexican government, demanded not to be so designated. That racial usage was subsequently eliminated and Mexicans were again classified as "white" in the 1940 census and thereafter.

It was only in the 1950s, a decade in which more Puerto Ricans came to the U.S. mainland than did immigrants from any other country, that the Census Bureau first published information on persons of Puerto Rican birth or parentage. Tabulations on people of Cuban birth or parentage were first published in 1970, following the large flows that came to the United States after the 1959 Cuban Revolution. Efforts to demarcate and enumerate the "Hispanic" population as a whole, using subjective indicators of Spanish origin or descent, date back to the late 1960s. At that time—in the context of surging civil rights activism, new federal legislation that required accurate statistical documentation of minority groups' disadvantages, and growing concerns over differential census undercounts—Mexican American organizations pressed for better data about their group (Choldin, 1986). The White House ordered the addition of a Spanish-origin self-identifier on the 1970 census (in the "long form" sent to a 5 percent sample); to test it, the same question was inserted in the November 1969 Current Population Survey (the first time that subjective item was used). Later analyses by the Census Bureau, comparing the results nationally of the (subjective) Hispanic self-identification in the CPS versus the (objective) use of Spanish surnames, found wide-ranging differences between the two measures, raising questions of validity and reliability. For example, in the Southwest, only 74 percent of those who identified themselves as Hispanic had Spanish surnames, while 81 percent of those with Spanish surnames identified themselves as Hispanic; in the rest of the United States, only 61 percent of those who identified as Hispanic had Spanish surnames, and a mere 46 percent of those with Spanish surnames identified as Hispanic (U.S. Census Bureau, 1975).

In 1976, the U.S. Congress passed a remarkable bill—Public Law 94-311—a joint resolution "[r]elating to the publication of economic and social statistics for Americans of Spanish origin or descent." Signed by President Gerald Ford in June 1976, it remains the only law in the country's history that mandates the collection, analysis, and publication of data for a specific ethnic group, and goes on to define the population to be enumerated. The law, building on information gathered from the 1970 census, asserted that "more than twelve million Americans identify themselves as being of Spanish-speaking background and trace their origin or descent from Mexico, Puerto Rico, Cuba, Central and South America, and other Spanish-speaking countries"; that a "large number" of them "suffer from racial, social, economic, and political discrimination and are denied the basic opportunities that they deserve as American citizens"; and that an "accurate determination of the urgent and special needs of Americans of Spanish origin and descent" was needed to improve their economic and social status. Accordingly, the law mandated a series of data-collection initiatives within the Federal

Departments of Commerce, Labor, Agriculture, and Health, Education, and Welfare, specifying among other things that the Spanish-origin population be given "full recognition" by the Census Bureau's data-collection activities via the use of Spanish-language questionnaires and bilingual enumerators, as needed; and that the Office of Management and Budget (OMB) "develop a Government-wide program for the collection, analysis, and publication of data with respect to Americans of Spanish origin or descent" (Rumbaut, 2006).

In 1977, as required by Congress, the OMB's Statistical Policy Division, the Office of Information and Regulatory Affairs, issued "Directive 15: Race and Ethnic Standards for Federal Statistics and Administrative Reporting" to standardize the collection and reporting of "racial" and "ethnic" statistics and to include data on persons of "Hispanic origin." Directive 15 specified a minimal classification of four "races" ("American Indian or Alaskan Native," "Asian or Pacific Islander," "Black," and "White") and two "ethnic" backgrounds ("of Hispanic origin" and "not of Hispanic origin"), and allowed the collection of more detailed information as long as it could be aggregated within those categories. Since that time, in keeping with the logic of this classification, census data on Hispanics have been officially reported with a footnote indicating that "Hispanics may be of any race." (For usage rules, see U.S. Census Bureau, 2003.)

Tellingly, however, the term "Hispanic" led to the development of two other categories, "non-Hispanic white" (a catchall for persons who identify as white but whose ancestry does not include a Spanish-speaking nation) and "non-Hispanic black" (synonymous with "African American"), which typically have been set against "Hispanics" and the other racial minority categories, conflating the distinction. In the news media, as well as in academic studies, government reports, and popular usage, the "ethnic" constructs "Hispanic" and "Latino" have come to be used routinely and equivalently alongside "racial" categories such as "Asian," "Black" and "non-Hispanic White," effecting a *de facto* racialization of the former. It is now commonplace to see media summaries of exit polls tallying the "Latino vote" alongside "white" and "black" rates, or similar tallies "by race" of school dropout, poverty, and crime rates; or to hear local TV news crime-beat reporters quoting police sources that "the suspect is a Hispanic male," as if that were a self-evident physical description; or to read newspaper articles that report matter-of-factly that the country's first "Hispanic" astronaut was Franklin Chang-Díaz, a Chinese Costa Rican; or that the first "Latina" chancellor of a University of California campus is France A. Córdova, a French-born physicist who majored in English at Stanford, whose mother is an Irish American native New Yorker and whose father came to the United States as an eight-year-old from Tampico.

Later criticism of these additional categories led to a formal review of Directive 15, beginning in 1993 with congressional hearings and culminating in revised standards, which were adopted in 1997 (U.S. Bureau of the Census, 1997; see also Fears, 2003; Snipp, 2003). The changes now stipulated five minimum categories for data on "race" ("American Indian or Alaska Native," "Native Hawaiian or Other Pacific Islander," "Asian," "Black or African American," and "White"); offered respondents the option of selecting one or more racial designations (an option used for the first time in the 2000 census); and reworded the two "ethnic" categories into "Hispanic or Latino" and "not Hispanic or Latino." "Hispanic or Latino" was defined as "a person of Cuban, Mexican, Puerto Rican, South or Central American, or other Spanish culture or origin, regardless of race. The term, 'Spanish origin,' can be used in addition to 'Hispanic or Latino.'" The notice in the *Federal Register* of these revisions to OMB Directive 15 (as adopted on October 30, 1997) pointedly added: "The categories in this classification are social-political constructs and should not be interpreted as being scientific or anthropological in nature.... The standards have been developed to provide a common language for uniformity and comparability in the collection and use of data on race and ethnicity by Federal agencies." Nonetheless, Directive 15's definitions of "racial" and "ethnic" populations are used not only by federal agencies but also by researchers, schools, hospitals, business and industry, state and local governments—and are conflated, abridged, and diffused through the mass media, entering thereby into the popular culture and shaping the national self-image.

ASSERTING IDENTITIES: NATION, "RACE," AND PLACE IN THE 2000 CENSUS

Much has been made in the media and even in academic discourse about "the browning of America," a misnomer based on stereotypes of phenotypes presumed to characterize peoples of Latin American origin. Do Hispanics differ significantly from non-Hispanics by "race," as they do by place, socioeconomic status, and national origins? The American system of racial classification, employed variously since the first census of 1790, has been the *sine qua non* of externally imposed, state-sanctioned measures of group difference, distinguishing principally the majority "white" population from "black" and American Indian minority groups and, later, from Asian-origin populations (Snipp, 2003). Yet, as noted above, "Hispanics" were incorporated in official statistics as an "ethnic" category and conceived as being "of any race." Moreover, prior to 1970, Mexicans were almost always coded as "white" for census purposes, and were deemed "white" by law (if not by custom) since the nineteenth century. In addition, neither "Hispanic" nor "Latino" is a term of preference used by Latin American newcomers in the United States to define themselves; rather, the research literature has consistently shown that they self-identify preponderantly by their national origin. How then are racial categories internalized by Hispanics? Are there intergroup and intragroup differences in their patterns of racial self-identification? The 2000 census asked separate questions for "Hispanic" or "Latino" origin and for "race," permitting a cross-tabulation of the two—and thus an examination of how "Hispanics" or "Latinos" self-report by "race" as well as by national origin.

Despite growing diversification and accelerating immigration from Latin American countries over the past few decades, persons of Mexican, Puerto Rican, and Cuban origin still comprised 77 percent of the 35.2 million Hispanics counted by the 2000 census. Those of Mexican origin alone numbered 22.3

million—63 percent of the U.S. total at the time. Puerto Ricans on the mainland accounted for another 10 percent and Cubans for 4 percent. (If Puerto Ricans living on the island [who are U.S. citizens by birthright] were added to the calculation, those three groups would comprise 80 percent of the total.) Much of the remainder was accounted for by six nationalities of relatively recent immigrant origin: Dominicans, Salvadorans, and Guatemalans make up 7 percent of the Hispanic total, while Colombians, Peruvians, and Ecuadorians combine for nearly 4 percent more. Hence, nine ethnic groups accounted for nine out of ten (88 percent) Hispanics in the U.S. mainland. Their size and evolution reflect both the varied history of their incorporation in the United States and the relative geographical proximity of their source countries to the United States: Mexico, El Salvador, and Guatemala from Mesoamerica; Puerto Rico, Cuba, and the Dominican Republic from the Caribbean; and Colombia, Peru, and Ecuador from South America. Persons who trace their ethnic identities to the ten other Spanish-speaking countries of Central and South America, plus Spain, comprised only 4 percent of the Hispanic total. And only 8 percent self-reported as "other Spanish, Hispanic, or Latino" in the 2000 census, without indicating a specific national origin.

Hispanics as a whole are much more likely than non-Hispanics to consist of relatively recent newcomers to the United States: 45 percent of Hispanics are foreign-born, compared to fewer than 8 percent of non-Hispanics. Only "other Spanish, Hispanic, or Latino" is overwhelmingly a native-born population (94 percent)—some with ancestries that can be traced back many generations. Aside from that special case, Mexicans and Puerto Ricans—the two populations of longest residence in the United States, and the largest by far—are the only ethnic groups that consist mainly of natives (58 percent of the Mexicans and 60 percent of the Puerto Ricans were born in the U.S. mainland). All others are primarily foreign-born populations—from two-thirds of the Cubans and Dominicans to more than three-fourths of all the other groups.

Intergroup Differences: Self-Reported Race Among Latinos in the 2000 Census

Table 1.1 compares Hispanics and non-Hispanics, as well as the largest Hispanic ethnic groups, by the main racial categories employed in the 2000 census. Of the 246.2 million non-Hispanics counted by that census, 97 percent reported their race as either white (79 percent), black (14 percent), or Asian (4 percent). In sharp contrast, among the 35.2 million Hispanics, only half reported their race as white (48 percent), black (1.8 percent), or Asian (0.3 percent). Most notably, there was a huge difference in the proportion of these two populations who chose "other race": While scarcely any non-Hispanics (a mere 0.2 percent) reported being of some "other race," among the Latin Americans that figure was 43 percent—a reflection of more than four centuries of "mestizaje" (racial mixture) in Latin America and the Caribbean, as well as differing histories and conceptions of "race." In addition, Hispanics in the 2000 census were more than three times as likely to report an admixture of "two or more races"—6.4 percent of Hispanics versus only 2 percent of non-Hispanics—although among Hispanics who listed "two or more races," the overwhelming majority (85 percent) specified "white" plus another race. Still, the main divide among Hispanics was between the 48 percent who racially self-identified as "white" and the 43 percent who rejected all the official categories and reported "some other race" instead. (The Census Bureau is considering eliminating the "some other race" option in the 2010 census in order to force respondents to choose from among the five standard racial options mandated by the OMB directive.)

Examining these results for each of the main Hispanic ethnic groups, we find that the proportions who identified racially as "white" ranged from a low of 22 percent among Dominicans to a high of 84 percent among Cubans. More than half of the Dominicans (59 percent) and Salvadorans and Guatemalans (55 percent) reported "another race," as did 46 percent of the Mexicans, 42 percent of the Peruvians and Ecuadorians, 38 percent of the Puerto Ricans, 28 percent of the Colombians, and fewer than 8 percent of the Cubans. The most likely to identify as "black" were Dominicans (8.2 percent), while the "other Spanish, Hispanic, or Latino" were the most likely to identify as multiracial (10.7 percent). The meaning of "race," however, is problematic for several reasons. Consider, for example, the importance of geographic context in the determination and variability of self-reported racial identities in the census.

Location, Location, Location:
Intragroup Differences by Race and Place

Self-reported "race" varies not only between Latin American–origin groups but also within them—and over time and place as well. Table 1.2 presents 2000 census data on self-reported "race" for the largest Hispanic groups, now broken down by the largest states: California and Texas in the Southwest (where Mexicans, Salvadorans, and Guatemalans are most concentrated) and New York, New Jersey, and Florida along the East Coast (where Caribbean groups are concentrated). The differences are striking: In California 40 percent of the Mexican-origin population reported as "white," but in Texas 60 percent were "white"; and 53 percent reported as "other race" in California, compared to only 36 percent in Texas. A 1998–2002 longitudinal survey in Los Angeles and San Antonio found that Mexican Americans in San Antonio were five times more likely to identify as "white" than those in Los Angeles (Telles and Ortiz, 2008:272, 312). Similar if less pronounced patterns were observed for Salvadorans and Guatemalans in those two states: They were significantly more likely to be "white" in Texas and "other" in California. Even more striking are the differentials in the geography of "race" among Caribbean groups: All were far more likely to be "white" in Florida than in New York and New Jersey. In Florida, 67 percent of the Puerto Ricans reported that they were "white," compared to only 45 percent in New York and New Jersey; the respective percentages for Cubans were 92 versus 73 percent; for Dominicans, 46 versus 20 percent; for Colombians, 78 versus 46 percent. The gap was wider still for the Peruvians and Ecuadorians: 74 versus 43 percent. In all cases, as Table 1.2 shows, the reverse obtained for self-reports of "other race."

Table 1.1 Hispanic/Latino Ethnic Identity by Self-Reported "Race," 2000 Census, Ranked by Proportion Identifying as "Other Race"

Ethnic Identity	Total N	Race (Self-Reported)					
		% "Other" Race	% White	% Two or More Races	% Black	% Asian	% Indigenous[a]
Total U.S. Population	281,421,906	5.5	75.1	2.6	12.2	3.6	1.0
Not Hispanic/Latino	246,217,426	0.2	79.0	2.0	13.7	4.1	1.0
Hispanic/Latino	35,204,480	42.6	47.8	6.4	1.8	0.3	1.1
Dominican	994,313	58.8	22.4	9.4	8.2	0.2	0.9
Salvadoran, Guatemalan	1,532,512	55.2	35.8	7.2	0.6	0.1	1.1
Mexican	22,293,812	45.8	46.8	5.2	0.7	0.2	1.2
Peruvian, Ecuadorian	697,798	41.7	47.9	8.5	0.6	0.4	0.8
Puerto Rican	3,537,351	38.1	46.9	8.1	5.8	0.4	0.7
Other Central American	903,574	37.7	44.7	9.5	7.1	0.2	0.9
Colombian	648,731	28.2	62.0	8.2	1.1	0.2	0.4
Other South American	494,186	20.6	70.0	8.0	0.8	0.3	0.4
Cuban	1,311,994	7.6	84.4	4.1	3.6	0.2	0.2
Other Spanish, Hispanic, Latino	2,790,209	34.7	49.2	10.7	2.5	1.0	1.9

[a]Includes American Indians, Alaskan and Hawaiian natives, and other indigenous Pacific Islanders.
Source: 2000 U.S. Census, 5% IPUMS.

Those systematic patterns across so many different nationalities are unlikely to be explained by selective migrations, but rather invite a contextual, counterintuitive explanation: The more rigid racial boundaries and "racial frame" developed in the former Confederate states of Texas and Florida, and the severe stigma historically attached to those marked as nonwhite there, may shape defensive assertions of whiteness when racial status is ambiguous; in states like California and New York, the social dynamics have been more open to ethnic options and a rejection of rigid U.S. racial categories. If "race" was an innate, permanent trait of individuals, no such variability would obtain. Instead, these data exemplify how "race" is constructed socially and historically—and spatially as well.

These striking contextual differences are supported by other relevant data. For example, the 2000 census conducted in Puerto Rico found that 81 percent of the population on the island self-reported as "white"—notably higher than the 67 percent of Puerto Ricans who self-reported as "white" in Florida, versus 45 percent in the New York region. A census conducted by the United States when it occupied the island in 1899 found that 62 percent of the inhabitants were "white," as were 65 percent of those counted in the 1910 island census; but that proportion grew to 73 percent in 1920, and 80 percent by 1950—an increase attributed by Mara Loveman and Jerónimo Muñiz (2007) to changes in the social definition of whiteness and the influence of the "whitening" ideology on the island, since they could not be accounted for by demographic processes, institutional biases, or other explanations. Similarly, a study of racial self-identification of Puerto Ricans surveyed in the United States and Puerto Rico (Landale and Oropesa, 2002) found that mainland Puerto Ricans more strongly reject the conventional U.S. notion of race than do their island counterparts. Contexts shape the meanings of identity assignments and assertions (Rumbaut, 2005).

ASSERTING IDENTITIES:
THE MALLEABLE MEANINGS OF "RACE"

Varieties of Racial Identification Among Dominicans

The meaning of "race" also varies depending on the history of the group, on the way questions are asked, and even on the response format provided in conventional surveys. In a survey of more than 400 Dominican immigrants in New York City and Providence, Rhode Island, the adult respondents were asked three questions about their racial self-identification (Itzigsohn, 2004). First they were asked, in an open-ended format, how they defined themselves racially. Next they were given a closed-ended question, asking if they were white, black, or other (and if other, to specify). Finally, they were asked how they thought that "mainstream Americans" classified them racially. The results are summarized in Table 1.3. In response to the first open-ended question, 28 percent gave "Hispanic" as their "race," another 4 percent said "Latino," and still others offered a variety of mixed "Hispanic" or "Latino" answers; 13 percent said "Indio"; and another 13 percent

**Table 1.2 Self-Reported "Race" by Largest Hispanic Groups
in Selected States, 2000 Census**

Ethnic Identity	Total N	Race (Self-Reported)		
		% "Other"	% White	% Two or More Races
Hispanic/Latino (U.S. total):	35,204,480			
In California	10,928,470	51.6	39.7	6.4
In Texas	6,653,338	36.7	58.0	4.1
In New York–New Jersey	3,972,595	43.3	42.1	7.6
In Florida	2,673,654	16.6	75.0	5.4
Mexican	22,293,812			
In California	9,025,952	52.7	39.7	5.6
In Texas	5,706,532	35.8	59.6	3.6
Salvadoran, Guatemalan	1,532,512			
In California	667,273	61.1	30.2	7.2
In Texas	146,781	54.1	40.0	5.2
Puerto Rican	3,537,351			
In New York–New Jersey	1,462,393	40.5	45.4	6.5
In Florida	496,122	22.9	66.9	6.2
Cuban	1,311,994			
In New York–New Jersey	151,744	13.3	72.6	5.5
In Florida	878,289	3.9	91.6	2.5
Dominican	994,313			
In New York–New Jersey	709,755	62.4	19.8	8.9
In Florida	92,785	33.9	45.5	9.2
Colombian	648,731			
In New York–New Jersey	224,391	34.0	56.4	8.1
In Florida	192,397	14.5	77.8	6.4
Peruvian, Ecuadorian	697,798			
In New York–New Jersey	336,769	47.2	43.4	7.8
In Florida	96,754	18.5	73.6	6.9

Source: 2000 U.S. Census, 5% IPUMS.

gave their Dominican nationality as their race. Only 6.6 percent chose "black," and 3.8 percent "white."

The rest of their responses showed the extraordinary range of racial categories and labels common in the Spanish-speaking Caribbean—as well as the very significant responses obtained depending on the question asked, even though all three were ostensibly reflecting the respondents' racial identity. When asked to choose from the closed-ended format of the second question, the largest response remained "Hispanic" (written in by 21 percent of the sample, in addition to 3 percent who chose "Latino"), though the categories "black" and "white" now more than doubled to 16.8 and 11.6 percent, respectively. And when asked how they thought that others classified them racially, the category "black" dramatically increased to 37 percent (reflecting the reverse way in which the "one-drop rule" functions in the United States versus the Dominican Republic) while "white"

**Table 1.3 Dominican Immigrants' Answers to Three Racial
Self-Identification Questions[a]**

Responses	How do you define yourself racially? (Open-ended Q) %	Are you: white, black, or other? (If other, specify) (Closed-ended Q) %	How do you think most Americans classify you racially? %
Black	6.6	16.8	36.9
White	3.8	11.6	6.4
Hispano or Hispana (Hispanic)	27.5	21.1	30.4
Latino or Latina	4.1	2.8	3.2
Indio or India	13.1	18.8	4.0
Dominicano or Dominicana	12.8	2.0	0.2
Mestizo or Mestiza	4.7	8.0	1.0
Trigueño or Trigueña	4.1	4.5	1.0
Moreno or Morena	1.9	2.0	2.2
Mulato or Mulata	0.3	1.5	0.0
Indio or India, Hispano or Hispana	4.1	1.0	0.2
Black Hispano or Hispana	0.6	1.0	2.0
White Hispano or Hispana	0.6	0.3	0.5
Mixed Hispano or Hispana	0.6	1.3	0.2
Latino-americano or Latino-americana	0.3	0.5	0.5
Latino or Latina, Hispano or Hispana	0.3	0.5	0.5
Jabao or Jabá, Indio or India, Claro or Clara	0.3	1.3	0.2
Amarillo or Amarilla (yellow)	0.3	1.0	0.2
Oscuro, Prieto, de Color	0.3	0.8	1.0
American	0.6	0.0	0.5
Puerto Rican	0.0	0.0	0.2
Human race, other	6.9	1.5	0.7
Do not know	5.0	1.3	6.9

[a]Based on a survey of Dominican immigrants in New York and Providence, Rhode Island
(N = 418).
Source: Adapted from Itzigsohn (2004).

decreased to 6.4 percent. "Hispanic" was still given by almost a third of the sample (30.4 percent) as the "racial" category that they perceived others used to classify them. "Hispanic" was the label most consistently given by the respondents to characterize their own *racial* identity, whether asserted by themselves or imposed upon them by others.

Intergenerational Differences: The "Race" of Immigrant Parents and Their Children

Another recent study found that, in addition to significant change in ethnic self-identities over time and generations in the United States (as measured by open-ended questions), the offspring of Latin American immigrants were by far the most likely to define their racial identities in sharp contrast to their own parents (Portes and Rumbaut, 2001; Rumbaut, 2005). During the 1990s, in South Florida and Southern California, the Children of Immigrants Longitudinal Study (CILS) surveyed a sample of more than 5,200 1.5- and second-generation youths, representing 77 different nationalities, including all of the main Spanish-speaking countries of Latin America. Their immigrant parents were also interviewed separately. In one survey (conducted when the youths were seventeen to eighteen years old), respondents were asked to answer a semi-structured question about their "race" and were given the option to check one of five categories: "white," "black," "Asian," "multiracial," or "other"; if the latter was checked, they had to specify what that "other race" was. The results are presented in Table 1.4.

Among Latin American–origin youths, fewer than a fourth of the total sample checked the conventional categories of white, black, or Asian; 12 percent reported being multiracial; and more than 65 percent checked "other." When those "other" self-reports were coded, two-fifths of the sample (41 percent) wrote down "Hispanic" or "Latino" as their "race," and another fifth (19.6 percent) gave their nationality as their "race." The explicit racialization of the "Hispanic-Latino" category as well as the substantial proportion of youths who conceived of their nationality of origin as a racial category is noteworthy both for its potential long-term implications in hardening minority-group boundaries and for its illustration of the arbitrariness of racial constructions—indeed, of the ease with which an "ethnic" category developed for administrative purposes becomes externalized, diffused, objectified, and finally internalized and imagined as a marker of essentialized social difference.

The latter point is made particularly salient if we directly compare the youths' notions of their "race" with that reported by their own parents. The closest match in racial self-perceptions between parents and children was observed among Haitians, Jamaicans, and other West Indians (most of whom self-reported as black), among Europeans and Canadians (most of whom labeled themselves white), and among most of the Asian-origin groups (except for Filipinos). The widest mismatches by far (and hence the most ambiguity in self-definitions of "race") occurred among all of the Latin American–origin groups without exception: About three-fifths of the Latino parents defined themselves as "white," compared to only one-fifth of their own children. More specifically, 93 percent

Table 1.4 Self-Reported "Race" of Children of Immigrants and Their Parents, by National-Origin Groups

National Origin	Respondent (Parent/Child)	Self-Reported Race						
		White %	Black %	Asian %	Multiracial %	Hispanic, Latino %	Nationality as Race %	Other %
Latin American	Parent	58.1	1.5	1.1	14.7	6.4	8.3	9.8
	Child	21.9	0.8	0.0	12.1	14.0	19.6	4.6
Mexico	Parent	5.7	0.0	2.1	21.6	15.9	26.1	28.5
	Child	1.5	0.3	0.0	12.0	25.5	56.2	4.5
Cuba	Parent	93.1	1.1	0.3	2.5	1.1	0.5	1.4
	Child	41.2	0.8	0.0	11.5	36.0	5.5	4.9
Dominican Republic	Parent	30.6	11.1	0.0	44.4	0.0	5.6	8.3
	Child	13.9	2.8	0.0	13.9	55.6	8.3	5.6
El Salvador, Guatemala	Parent	66.7	4.2	4.2	16.7	8.3	0.0	0.0
	Child	20.8	0.0	0.0	12.5	58.3	4.2	4.2
Nicaragua	Parent	67.7	0.5	1.6	22.0	5.4	0.5	2.2
	Child	19.4	0.0	0.0	9.7	61.8	2.7	6.5
Other Central America	Parent	48.0	24.0	4.0	20.0	0.0	4.0	0.0
	Child	8.0	8.0	0.0	40.0	44.0	0.0	0.0
Colombia	Parent	84.6	1.1	0.0	9.9	2.2	0.0	2.2
	Child	24.2	1.1	0.0	9.9	58.2	1.1	5.5
Peru, Ecuador	Parent	61.8	0.0	0.0	26.5	2.9	2.9	5.9
	Child	32.4	0.0	0.0	11.8	55.9	0.0	0.0
Other South America	Parent	87.8	0.0	0.0	6.1	2.0	2.0	2.0
	Child	28.6	2.0	0.0	14.3	40.8	14.3	0.0

Source: Children of Immigrants Longitudinal Study (CILS); Portes and Rumbaut (2001); Rumbaut (2005).

of Cuban parents identified as white, compared to only 41 percent of their children; 85 percent of Colombian parents defined themselves as white, but only 24 percent of their children did so—proportions that were similar for other South Americans; two-thirds of the Salvadoran, Guatemalan, and Nicaraguan parents saw themselves as white, but only one-fifth of their children agreed; and about a third of the Dominican parents reported as white, more than twice the proportion of their children who did so.

The children, instead, largely adopted "Hispanic" or "Latino" as a racial label (41 percent—the largest single response), whereas scarcely any of their parents did so (6 percent); or they gave their nationality as their race (20 percent of the children versus 6 percent of their parents). Well over half of the Dominican, Salvadoran, Guatemalan, Nicaraguan, Colombian, Peruvian, and Ecuadorian youth reported their race as "Hispanic" or "Latino." Among Mexicans, whose pattern differed from all of the others, the children preponderantly racialized the national label, whereas Mexican parents were more likely to use "other" and "multiracial" as descriptors. These results point to the force of the acculturation process and its impact on children's self-identities in the United States: They provide another striking instance of the malleability of racial constructions, even between parents and children in the same family, residing in the same place.

More fully exposed than their parents to American culture and its ingrained racial notions, and being incessantly categorized and treated as Hispanic or Latino, the children of immigrants learn to see themselves in these terms—as members of a racial minority—and even to racialize their national origins. If these intergenerational differences between Latin American immigrants and their U.S.-raised children can be projected to the third generation, the process of racialization could become more entrenched still. It is indeed ironic that in a nation born in white supremacy, where citizenship was restricted on racial grounds until 1952 and immigration until 1965, and where it took a civil rights revolution to overthrow the legal underpinnings of racial apartheid, the children of Latin American immigrants, historically "white by law," should learn to become "nonwhite" in the post–Civil Rights Era.

REFERENCES

Alba, Richard D., Rubén G. Rumbaut, and Karen Marotz. 2005. "A Distorted Nation: Perceptions of Racial/Ethnic Group Sizes and Attitudes Toward Immigrants and Other Minorities." *Social Forces* 84(2):899–917.

Aleinikoff, T. Alexander, and Rubén G. Rumbaut. 1998. "Terms of Belonging: Are Models of Membership Self-Fulfilling Prophecies?" *Georgetown Immigration Law Journal* 13(1):1–24.

Almaguer, Tomás. 1994. *Racial Fault Lines*. Berkeley: University of California Press.

Choldin, Harvey M. 1986. "Statistics and Politics: The 'Hispanic Issue' in the 1980 Census." *Demography* 23(3):403–418.

Duany, Jorge. 2002. *The Puerto Rican Nation on the Move: Identities on the Island and in the United States*. Chapel Hill: University of North Carolina Press.

Feagin, Joe R. 2006. *Systemic Racism: A Theory of Oppression*. New York: Routledge.

Fears, Darryl. 2003. "The Roots of 'Hispanic': 1975 Committee of Bureaucrats Produced Designation." *Washington Post,* October 15, p. A21.

Foley, Neil. 2004. "Straddling the Color Line: The Legal Construction of Hispanic Identity in Texas." Pp. 341–357 in Nancy Foner and George Frederickson (eds.), *Not Just Black and White: Historical and Contemporary Perspectives on Immigration, Race, and Ethnicity in the United States.* New York: Russell Sage Foundation.

Franklin, Benjamin. 1751. "Observations Concerning the Increase of Mankind, Peopling of Countries, &c." Retrieved July 27, 2008.

Gates, Jr., Henry Louis. 1986. *"Race," Writing, and Difference.* Chicago: University of Chicago Press.

Gómez, Laura E. 2007. *Manifest Destinies: The Making of the Mexican American Race.* New York: New York University Press.

Haney López, Ian. 2006. *White by Law: The Legal Construction of Race,* revised and updated edition. New York: New York University Press.

Haub, Carl. 2006. "Hispanics Account for Almost One-Half of U.S. Population Growth." *PRB Report* (February). Washington, DC: Population Reference Bureau.

Itzigsohn, José. 2004. "The Formation of Latino and Latina Panethnic Identities." Pp. 197–216 in Nancy Foner and George Frederickson (eds.), *Not Just Black and White: Historical and Contemporary Perspectives on Immigration, Race, and Ethnicity in the United States.* New York: Russell Sage Foundation.

Johnson, Kevin. 2005. "The Forgotten 'Repatriation' of Persons of Mexican Ancestry and Lessons for the 'War on Terror.'" *Pace Law Review* 26(1):1–26.

Kanstroom, Daniel. 2007. *Deportation Nation: Outsiders in American History.* Cambridge, MA: Harvard University Press.

Landale, Nancy S., and Ralph Salvatore Oropesa. 2002. "White, Black, or Puerto Rican? Racial Self-Identification Among Mainland and Island Puerto Ricans." *Social Forces* 81:231–254.

Langley, Lester D. 2003. *The Americas in the Modern Age.* New Haven: Yale University Press.

Loveman, Mara, and Jerónimo O. Muñiz. 2007. "How Puerto Rico Became White: Boundary Dynamics and Inter-Census Racial Reclassification." *American Sociological Review* 72(6):915–939.

Maltby, William S. 1968. *The Black Legend in England: The Development of Anti-Spanish Sentiment, 1558–1560.* Durham, NC: Duke University Press.

Montejano, David. 1987. *Anglos and Mexicans in the Making of Texas, 1836–1986.* Austin: University of Texas Press.

Ngai, Mae N. 2004. *Impossible Subjects: Illegal Aliens and the Making of Modern America.* Princeton: Princeton University Press.

Olivas, Michael A. (ed.). 2006. *"Colored Men" and "Hombres Aquí":* Hernández v. Texas *and the Rise of Mexican American Lawyering.* Houston: Arte Público Press.

Passel, Jeffrey S., and D'Vera Cohn. 2008. *U.S. Population Projections: 2005–2050.* Washington, DC: Pew Hispanic Center.

Portes, Alejandro, and Rubén G. Rumbaut. 2001. *Legacies: The Story of the Immigrant Second Generation.* Berkeley and New York: University of California Press/Russell Sage Foundation.

Rumbaut, Luis E., and Rubén G. Rumbaut. 2007. "'If That Is Heaven, We Would Rather Go to Hell': Contextualizing U.S.-Cuba Relations." *Societies Without Borders* 2(1):131–152.

Rumbaut, Rubén G. 2005. "Sites of Belonging: Acculturation, Discrimination, and Ethnic Identity Among Children of Immigrants." Pp. 111–163 in Thomas S. Weisner (ed.), *Discovering Successful Pathways in Children's Development: New Methods in the Study of Childhood and Family Life.* Chicago: University of Chicago Press.

————. 2006. "The Making of a People." Pp. 16–65 in Marta Tienda and Faith Mitchell (eds.), *Hispanics and the Future of America*. Washington, DC: National Academy Press.

Snipp, C. Matthew. 2003. "Racial Measurement in the American Census: Past Practices and Implications for the Future." *Annual Review of Sociology* 29:563–588.

Telles, Edward E., and Vilma Ortiz. 2008. *Generations of Exclusion: Mexican Americans, Assimilation, and Race*. New York: Russell Sage Foundation.

Tienda, Marta, and Faith Mitchell (eds.). 2006. *Multiple Origins, Uncertain Destinies: Hispanics and the American Future*. Washington, DC: National Academies Press.

Tocqueville, Alexis de. [1832] 1969. *Democracy in America*, translated by George Lawrence and edited by J. P. Mayer. Garden City, NY: Doubleday Anchor.

U.S. Census Bureau. 1975. *Comparison of Persons of Spanish Surname and Persons of Spanish Origin in the United States*. Technical Paper No. 38. Washington, DC: U.S. Government Printing Office.

————. 1997. *Revisions to the Standards for the Classification of Federal Data on Race and Ethnicity*. Retrieved July 26, 2008.

————. 2003. "Guidance on the Presentation and Comparison of Race and Hispanic Origin Data." Retrieved July 26, 2008.

————. 2008. "U.S. Hispanic Population Surpasses 45 Million, Now 15 Percent of Total." Retrieved July 26, 2008.

Walton, John. 2001. *Storied Land: Community and Memory in Monterey*. Berkeley: University of California Press.

Weber, David J. 1992. *The Spanish Frontier in North America*. New Haven: Yale University Press.

Weber, David J. (ed.). 1973. Albuquerque: University of New Mexico Press.

Zolberg, Aristide. 2006. *A Nation by Design: Immigration Policy in the Fashioning of America*. New York: Russell Sage Foundation/Cambridge, MA: Harvard University Press.

CHAPTER 2

Counting Latinos in the U.S. Census

Clara E. Rodríguez

The way particular groups of people are classified is not always congruent with how they view themselves.[1] This difference has been referred to in various ways—for example, as the difference between imposed identity and self-identity (Chou and Feagin, 2008; Feagin, 2006) or, in classical anthropological texts, as the difference between state and folk (or popular) identity. Chantal Caillavet (2006) alludes to the divergence between the point of view of the passive "subjects" (the dominated) and those in power (the dominant society in a given period). The history of how the U.S. Census Bureau has counted—and considered counting—Hispanics/Latinos and of how Latinos have responded to these attempts in many ways reflects such divergence. This history also reflects the present volume's theme, which is the racialization of Latinos in the United States. Part of this history is the same contestation over impositions of identity that—with the escalating migration of peoples around the world—is becoming increasingly recognized as a global issue.

There are many views on how Latinos should be counted, with some discourses becoming more prominent at various points in time. Are Latinos a group with many races? This is the U.S. Census Bureau's current policy. Are Latinos a third race? Are they a mixed race? Are some national-origin groups of Latinos proportionally more white, black, or indigenous than others? Are Mexican Americans, Cuban Americans, and Puerto Ricans all nonwhite—as 151 white college students indicated in a recent survey? (Feagin, 2006:191). Are they a group outside of the U.S. racial structure, many of whom resist being classified according to U.S. race categories? Or do Latinos simply resist and deny their classification as nonwhite? In order to better contextualize these discourses and the current situation of Latinos reporting in the United States, I have found it useful to briefly review the history of racial classification in the U.S. Census.[2]

The History

As I and others have shown in earlier works (see Anderson, 1988; Rodríguez, 2000: chs. 4 and 5), throughout most of its history the U.S. Census has counted groups in terms of where they were seen to fit within an overarching dual racial structure (of white and nonwhite). In simplest terms, within this overarching structure were four presumed major color groups: white and three "nonwhite" groups—black, Asian or Pacific Islanders (yellow), and Native Americans or American Indians (red). The origins of this dual racial structure can be dated to the very first census in 1790, when three categories were listed: free whites, slaves, and all other free peoples. The free whites eventually came to be called on the census just "whites"; the slaves became "black or Negro," and "all other free peoples" were placed into the subsequent "free people of color" category. This definitive color line of white and nonwhite was established between 1790 and 1840, a bipolar racial structure that continued to evolve throughout the nineteenth and twentieth centuries. It is important to note that free whites were the initial reference point and that the question of whether a person or group was "white" or not continued to be the way in which the races of others were determined (Rodríguez, 2000: chs. 4 and 5). When other groups immigrated to the United States, the question of which socioeconomic queue they would enter was often influenced by whether they were seen as white or not. If they were perceived as white, then their entrance to jobs, housing, education, and other institutions was supposedly limited only by their talents, economic resources, networks, and availability.

Until 2000, census categories were also largely discrete; that is, respondents could choose only one category. A mulatto category was on the 1850–1920 censuses but not on the 1900 census. But the mulatto category—and other categories that appeared on the 1890 census—were considered a subset of the black or Negro category; the white component was ignored. This way of classifying individuals is referred to as the "one-drop" or hypodescent rule. In essence, if you had one drop of "black blood," you were considered black in the United States. When the case of *Plessy v. Ferguson* was argued in 1894, this was one of the issues addressed. Homer Plessy argued that he was seven-eighths white, looked white, and therefore should be allowed to sit in the white part of the train. The Supreme Court did not accept his argument and this decision resulted in the legitimation of Jim Crow facilities and legislation until the 1954 *Brown v. Board of Education* decision, which found that separate was not equal.

Most ethnic groups in the United States have been accommodated this way. Although questions about the "caliber" of whiteness often accompanied earlier immigrants, such as the Irish, the Italians, and Southern and Eastern Europeans, these groups still entered as whites and "became whiter" with time, assimilation, and upward mobility (Brodkin Sacks, 1994; Ignatiev, 1995; Jacobson, 1998). Although some Americans at the turn of the twentieth century may have referred to these groups as "different" and as being of inferior stock to native whites, I could find no reference to them as nonwhite in the census. Similarly, those who entered as African or West Indian immigrants were generally counted on the census as black, unless census takers considered them to be white and they were treated as white by their neighbors and relations. On the individual level, some people negotiated their identities by "passing," or denying that they had black or nonwhite ancestry.

On the whole, from the perspective of the U.S. government this slotting of groups into white and nonwhite categories has worked fairly well. When a group had grown sufficiently large or visible, new nonwhite categories were developed, such as Chinese and then Japanese categories, which were added in 1870 and 1880, respectively (Rodríguez, 2000: ch. 4).

Spanish-speaking immigrants from Latin America and the Spanish-speaking residents of territories acquired by the United States have had a very different history with respect to the census. In part, this is due to the fact that both Americas have been settled by peoples from all continents and that these peoples, in turn, have merged with indigenous populations—all of which has resulted in populations with a very wide variety of physical types that have not been easily slotted into existing U.S. race categories. Moreover, Latinos have evolved different constructions of race and ethnicity, which they bring with them to the United States, along with their own racial biases and histories of exclusion, slavery, and genocide. These histories and constructions also vary somewhat from country to country.

Further complicating this situation is the history of U.S. relations with its neighbors to the south. For example, the 1848 Treaty of Guadalupe Hidalgo, which added California, Nevada, Utah, and parts of Colorado, Arizona, New Mexico, and Texas to the United States, stipulated citizenship for the Spanish-speaking residents in these areas. Since nonwhites could not become naturalized citizens because of a law passed in 1790 (and overturned only after World War II), one could assume that these Spanish-speaking residents were considered "white." The 1898 Spanish-American War resulted in the acquisition of Puerto Rico and other Pacific territories (the Philippines and Guam), and in 1917 Congress made Puerto Ricans U.S. citizens by decree. In both cases, these Spanish-speaking peoples (of Mexican and Puerto Rican origin) became citizens of the United States at a time when Asians, for example, could not become naturalized citizens. However, despite these formal pronouncements of citizenship and implied white status, the reality of real citizenship eluded many. For example, many of the 1848 treaty provisions were not honored and many Spanish-speaking residents lost their lands and were disenfranchised and segregated in housing and educational settings. (The case of *Brown v. Board of Education* drew attention to these conditions a hundred years later.) Also, when Puerto Ricans were drafted by the U.S. armed forces during World War I, white/light-skinned Puerto Ricans were preferred and many fought in segregated units. In addition, when Puerto Ricans migrated to New York City, many were denied basic rights of citizenship (Rodríguez, [1989] 1991a: chs. 1 and 4).

In sum, the history of Latinos and the census has been multifaceted, but a recurring question has been how to accommodate Latino groups—which have their own earlier histories with the United States and are made up of many different types, groups, and views—within a basically white/nonwhite race order. Despite changes in the rigidity of that order, symbolized by the ability to now choose more than one race category, the Census Bureau and Latinos still struggle over this issue.

CLASSIFICATION OF LATINOS IN THE CENSUS

1930–1980

The U.S. Census has used various indicators to count the members of the group now called Latinos. In 1930, the Census Bureau included a separate category in the race question for one particular Latino group, "Mexican." This category was deleted in subsequent censuses. From 1940 to 1980, Puerto Ricans, Mexicans, and all other Latinos were classified as "white" unless the census interviewer determined (or the respondent indicated to the interviewer) that they were of some other race category, such as black or Asian. Prior to 1980, the U.S. Census Bureau had, at various times, also counted samples of Latinos using cultural indicators, such as whether the person's mother tongue was Spanish (1940) and whether he or she had a Spanish surname (1950) or was of "Spanish origin" (1970). (In other words, the census used language, surname, and ancestry—but not country of birth.)

Several significant changes occurred with the 1980 census, when the Bureau mailed every household a mail-back questionnaire. For the first time, people would classify themselves, by race, without an interviewer present. The 1980 census also introduced the "Hispanic identifier." This was a specific question, separate from the race question, that asked all residents whether or not they were Hispanic. If the respondent said "yes," they were instructed to check off one of four boxes—labeled "Mexican," "Cuban," "Puerto Rican," and "other Hispanic (specify)"—to indicate what kind of Hispanic they were. According to Harvey Choldin (1986), this question was introduced in response to political pressure from Hispanic organizations, but it also reflected an awareness that the numbers of Hispanics were increasing. The Hispanic identifier was included in the "short form" that went out to all residents. So in 1980, Hispanics were counted on a national basis in the United States for the first time. Although the Hispanic identifier has changed slightly over time (e.g., the word "Latino" was added), it is still included on the short form of the census.

The race question on the 1980 and 1990 forms included the following major categories: "white," "black," "Asian or Pacific Islander," "American Indian," and "other race." Because the 1980 questionnaire was mailed, it was the first census that asked respondents (Hispanics and non-Hispanics) to fill in their own race. Few anticipated that major difficulties would occur in moving from having race determined or reported by census takers to having individuals determine their own race. For decades, race had been described in many sociological texts and elsewhere as an ascribed characteristic—that is, as something that people were born with, like sex, that was easily recognizable and that did not change during their lifetime. Since its inception in 1790, the U.S. Census had assumed an either/or approach to race—one was of a particular race or one was not. The actual names of the categories changed over time, and the color lines blurred in many cases (see Rodríguez, 2000: chs. 4 and 5). However, it was not possible to be both black and white, or both enslaved and free. It was not possible—or desirable—to imagine other ways of thinking about "race." However, both these changes, the Hispanic identifier and self-reporting, dramatically affected the collection of race and ethnic data in the United States, for now all groups were to be identified in terms of whether they were Hispanic or not. This led, among many other things, to the introduction into academic literature and the popular discourse terms such as "non-Hispanic white" and "non-Hispanic black."

1990–2000

As the United States lumbered on toward the end of the twentieth century, several trends seriously challenged racial thinking and led to a major reassessment in how race and ethnicity were conceived. In 2000, they culminated in a major shift in how the United States counted its people. First were the broad demographic changes that the United States experienced, such as large-scale immigration from non-European countries, and the concentration, and consequently greater visibility, of racial and ethnic minorities in populous states and metropolitan areas (Edmonston, Goldstein, and Tamayo Lott, 1996). Many of the newer immigrant groups—such as Middle Easterners, Latinos, and Asian Indians— also brought with them a wide range of physical types. Second, although intermarriage rates between African Americans and whites were still relatively low, they had increased, as had rates of racial and ethnic intermarriage among other groups—particularly those of high socioeconomic status (Edmonston, Lee, and Passel, 1994; Kalmijn, 1993; Rolark, Bennett, and Harrison, 1994; Spickard, 1989). There was also greater affirmation of mixed-race identity and political mobilization along these lines. Practices with regard to racial classification were also changing. For example, in 1990 half (50.6 percent) of all children who were the product of interracial unions were classified as "white" on the census form by their parent(s) (Bennett, McKenney, and Harrison, 1995: table 5). In the past, census takers would most likely have classified such children according to the race of the nonwhite parent (Rodríguez, 2000).

In addition, a burgeoning and well-placed academic and scientific literature on the meaning of race emphasized the social constructedness of race. Research on DNA sequencing and other new technologies highlighted how "race" was at variance with scientific principles, often conflated with the concept of "ethnicity," which was unfixed, imperfectly measured, and increasingly under scientific criticism. This reexamination and questioning were not limited to ivory tower intellectuals but reached into more popular venues.[3] Dovetailing with these trends were demands from the politically conservative right to eliminate racial classifications as divisive and as entitling certain groups over others. As Newt Gingrich (then Speaker of the U.S. House of Representatives) and others assumed greater control in Congress, they began to question affirmative action policies and minority set-asides. All of these trends were changing not just the "face" of the United States but also how "race" was viewed by many individuals and policymakers.

Finally, accompanying such domestic trends were many changes occurring on a global scale, such as increased international monetary and labor flows worldwide; changing political regimes in South Africa, Latin America, and the Soviet Union; and the growth of mass media markets in heretofore uncovered areas. Within this larger context, "race" and "racial awareness" were also undergoing change around the world, as television and other media outlets made clear. All of these trends made for greater heterogeneity, and for an ever more insistent questioning of the concept and nature of "race" in the census and elsewhere (Edmonston, Lee, and Passel, 1994; Root, 1992, 1996). Indeed, such changes contributed to what was for the U.S. Census a radical departure from business as usual.

In the year 2000, the Census Bureau issued a form that allowed U.S. residents to choose more than one racial category, thus acknowledging, for the first time in its 200-year history, that persons could belong to more than one racial group. This, in effect, altered the long-standing hypodescent or one-drop rule, which required a person—regardless of appearance and the exact components of his or her ancestry—to occupy socially and administratively one category in the census—that is, the nonwhite category.

Another trend that has contributed to the recent reassessment of race and ethnicity in the U.S. Census, while receiving little attention, is the way in which Latinos/Hispanics have responded to questions on race over the last three decennial censuses (Martinez, 2001). As noted above, in 1980 the census shifted the way it determined race, from having census takers classify others' race to having individuals reporting their own race. For example, prior to 1980, various smaller censuses indicated that about 90 percent of Hispanics/Latinos were white, whereas in subsequent self-report censuses this proportion was much lower—in fact, less than half in the last nationwide decennial census. Hispanics/Latinos have responded to questions of race in ways quite different from non-Hispanics/Latinos. These Latino responses to race have confounded the Census Bureau, but they have also moved us to thinking about race in very different ways.

LATINOS AND RACE REPORTING IN THE CENSUS

As noted above, the 1980 census marked a turning point. The introduction of the Hispanic identifier fundamentally altered the whole racial classification schema of the census. The white category became the non-Hispanic white category, the black category, the non-Hispanic black category, and so on. In 2000, this all became more complex as people were allowed to choose more than one race category. Sixty-three races, including six single races (namely, white, black, Asian, Pacific Islander, Native American or American Indian, and some other race) and fifteen possible combinations, were noted. When divided by whether these groups were Hispanic or not Hispanic, a total of 126 race/ethnic categories became possible (Porter, 2001:B1). Although few reports utilize all of these categories, they indicate the impact of these shifts.

In addition, there were unanticipated results. As Figure 2.1 indicates, in the 2000 census, 47.9 percent of Latinos indicated they were white, 2 percent reported they were black, 1.2 percent said they were American Indian, and less than 1 percent said they were Asian, Native Hawaiian, or other Pacific Islander. A surprising 42.2 percent chose the "some other race" category and many of these wrote in a Latino descriptor, such as Mexican, Chicano, Puerto Rican, or Boricua (Grieco and Cassidy, 2001:10). This is "surprising" because, as Figure 2.2 shows, the proportion of non-Hispanics in the "some other race" (SOR) category is only 0.2 percent (Grieco and Cassidy, 2001:10). Although different national origin groups varied in the extent to which they chose SOR, they all chose it to a higher degree than did non-Latinos. According to Sonya Tafoya (2004: table 2), in the 2000 census, Cubans were the group who chose this category least frequently, only 7 percent, while Dominicans chose it most often, 58.4 percent. The groups also differed with regard to the degree to which they reported they were white, black, or two or more races. Up until 1980, the "other race" category had been generally seen as a miscellaneous or "none of the above" category. It had evolved in the census as a place to put new, but small, groups that did not have a separate racial category, such as Asian Indians, who were placed in this category at the turn of the nineteenth century.

The tendency of a large portion of Latinos to choose the "other race" category and to write in Latino descriptors has been consistent for the last three decennial censuses. In both the 1980 and 1990 censuses, about 40 percent of Latinos in the United States chose this category (Denton and Massey, 1989; Martin, DeMaio, and Campanelli, 1990; Rodríguez, [1989] 1991a, 1990, 1991b, 1991c; Tienda and Ortiz, 1986). The "other race" response continued despite various attempts by the U.S. Census to dissuade it. For example, the Census Bureau inserted the word "race" into the race question numerous times; reversed the questions, so that the Hispanic-origin question would precede the race question; and, in the 2000 census, added the word "some" to the "other race" category in an attempt to make clear that the race question was calling for a race response and not a national-origin or Latino descriptor. Some even saw the decision to allow respondents to choose more than one race category as an attempt to encourage Latinos to avoid choosing the "other race" category and to instead choose more than one traditional race category (Padilla, 2001). Nevertheless, only 6.3 percent of all Latinos chose the more-than-one race category—a proportion higher than the 2.4 percent of the total population who chose more than one race category, but far lower than the proportion of Latinos who chose the "some other race" (SOR) category—which continued to draw over 40 percent of all Latinos. The

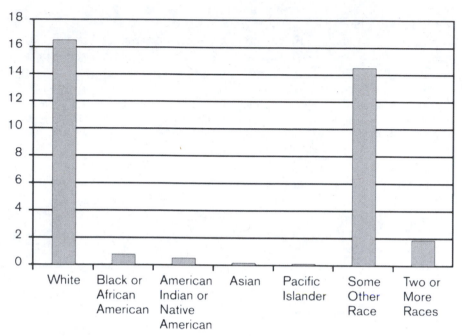

Figure 2.1 Hispanic/Latino Population in the United States, by Race, According to the Census, 2000 (in Millions)

Source: Grieco and Cassidy (2001).

number of Latinos choosing SOR has grown significantly (Guzmán and Diaz McConnell, 2002); in 2004 it was estimated at over 19 million people.

THE GOVERNMENT'S RESPONSE

Ignoring SOR

How did the government respond to Latinos' "other race" departure? In 1980, when the first census data appeared indicating that 40 percent of Hispanics reported they were of "other race," there was little government response. Many in the statistical, research, and government communities assumed either that this figure represented a mixed-race group or that many Hispanics did not understand the question. When the results were repeated in the 1990 census, the government began to take greater notice. But, even in the early 1990s, official reports tended to look obliquely at the tendency of Hispanics to choose "other race" and to collapse this issue into a more general "data quality" problem without mentioning Hispanic responses per se (U.S. General Accounting Office, 1993). Nevertheless, responses of "other race" represented a serious departure from the existing race structure—one that could not (and still cannot) be easily

**Figure 2.2 Total Non-Hispanic Population and Hispanic/Latino
Population in the United States, by Race,
According to the 2000 Census (Percentages)**

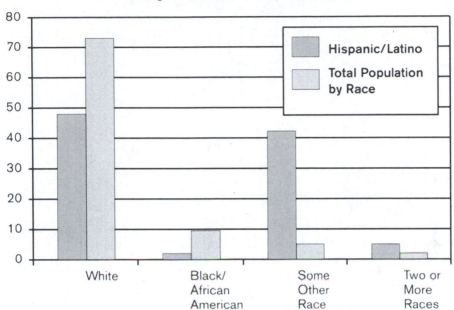

Note: The American Indian/Alaska Native, Asian, Native Hawaiian, and Other Pacific Islander categories were omitted from this figure because they constituted less than 1.2 percent of the Hispanic/Latino group.

Source: Grieco and Cassidy (2001).

accommodated. What was to be done with the millions of Latinos who chose the "other race" category—despite attempts to discourage this response? In the 1990 census, 10 million Latinos chose this category and in 2000 close to 15 million did so (U.S. Bureau of the Census, 2001:10). Although not all Latinos fell into this category, 95–98 percent of the "other race" category was "Hispanic" (U.S. General Accounting Office, 1993:26). The figure for 2000 was roughly 97 percent. Where were these "other race" folks to be put? How were they to be reported or tabulated? Bottom line: What race or color were they?

Post-1990: Studying SOR and Moving to Race

As the U.S. government made preparations for the 2000 census, all of the trends and issues noted above contributed to a radical reexamination of race and ethnic classifications (see Rodríguez, 2000: ch. 7). This reexamination involved numerous congressional hearings and scholarly conferences, as well as massive studies that included hundreds of thousands of households (Evinger, 1996). In addition to the studies discussed below, the U.S. Office of Management and Budget (1995:44690–44691) noted plans from the following agencies to examine racial classifications: the National Center for Health Statistics, the Centers for Disease Control and Prevention, the Department of Health and Human Services (DHHS), the National Center for Education Statistics, the Office for Civil Rights in the Department of Education, and the Office of the Assistant Secretary for Health.

The Proposal to Make Hispanics a Race

In preparation for the 2000 census, a proposal was advanced—it is not clear by whom—to include "Hispanic" as a category in the race question, so that there would be a white, black, Asian, Pacific Islander, Native American or American Indian, and Hispanic category, and respondents would have to choose one.[4] They could specify what type of Native American or American Indian, Asian or Pacific Islander, or some other race they were. But no Hispanic group enthusiastically endorsed this proposal, which came to be known as the "combined question format."

The Office of Management and Budget (OMB) tested the combined question format through a series of studies conducted by the Bureau of Labor Statistics, the Current Population Survey, the National Content Survey, and the 1996 Race and Ethnic Targeted Test (RAETT). These studies involved over 200,000 households. Their net finding was that use of the combined format resulted in the counting of fewer Hispanics and whites (Rodríguez, 2000; U.S. Department of Labor, Bureau of Labor Statistics, 1995: table 1). Accordingly, the proposal was abandoned and the 2000 census returned to the status quo; that is, Hispanics were an ethnic group that could be of any race.

Some researchers reexamined some of the data sets of the studies conducted by the government. Their results have led to somewhat different conclusions. For example, when Charles Hirschman, Richard Alba, and Reynolds Farley (2000) analyzed the RAETT data set, they found that in census tracts with a high concentration of Latinos, population counts were similar under both formats. They concluded their analysis by advocating the use of the combined format, maintaining that when one added "Hispanics who marked only the category Hispanic" to "those who marked the Hispanic plus another race," the response rates were comparable to using separate questions (Hirschman, Alba, and Farley, 2000:390). They also argued that the combined question format was preferable to the separate question format because it was "closer to popular understandings of 'origins'" and fewer respondents (in general) skipped the question. However, one limitation of the RAETT data set was that the response rate of Hispanics to the mail-back questionnaire was lower than that of other groups: only 44 percent compared to 71 percent of the white ethnic sample, for example.

Still other conclusions were reached by Mary Campbell and Christabel Rogalin (2006), who examined a different database commissioned by the Census Bureau, the May 1995 Race and Ethnicity Supplement to the Current Population Survey. They found that, under the combined question format, almost 20 percent of the sample chose a non-Latino category—an outcome that appeared to decrease the total number count of Latinos. Controlling for age, sex, national origin, education, language, region, percentage of Latinos in area of residence, nativity, non-Latino spouses, self or proxy responses for race classification, and inclusion of a multiracial category, they found that language use, local ethnic context, national origin, and age were all significantly related to the identification choices of Latinos. In essence, Mexican Americans/Chicanos, Puerto Ricans, and respondents who spoke Spanish at home were more likely to choose the Latino category in a combined format question, whereas Cubans and the oldest cohort in their sample were more likely to choose a non-Latino single-race identification (usually white). Although fewer than a third of the total chose more than one race category, the more-than-one choice was more common in cities with small Latino populations and in the Northeast. In contrast to Hirschman, Alba, and Farley (2000), Campbell and Rogalin (2006) proposed that the combined question format be retained but that a follow-up question be added, asking each respondent to choose the one label with which he or she "most identified," as the California Health Interview Survey did.

Post–2000 Census: Eliminating the SOR Category Completely and Using the Combined Question Format

Although little public attention was devoted to it at the time, the decision to allow people to choose more than one race category was also influenced by the tendency of Latinos to choose the "other race" category. Interviewing census officials after the 2000 census results were released, María Padilla (2001:A1) stated that "by allowing people to identify more than one race, the Census Bureau had hoped to minimize the number who would mark 'other.'" Claudette Bennett, head of the racial-statistics branch of the Census Bureau, noted that, in hindsight, "the 'Other Race' category should have been eliminated from the 2000 census" (Padilla, 2001:A1).

As part of its preparations for the 2010 census, the Census Bureau seriously considered eliminating the SOR category altogether. In 2004, it initiated a series of tests to see how a race question without the "some other race" category would be received. These questions were tested in what was designated as "the most diverse county in the U.S."—part of Queens, New York. This area was also, incidentally, 48 percent Hispanic. To my knowledge, the results of this test have not been made public.

However, even as studies were conducted and proposals advanced to eliminate the SOR category, those in the SOR group represented growing numbers of people. Already in 1990, those who had checked the "other race" category were the second-fastest-growing racial category in the country (after Asian and Pacific Islanders) (Rodríguez, 1991b:A14; U.S. General Accounting Office, 1993). The "other race" group also grew significantly between 1990 and 2000 (Guzmán and Diaz McConnell, 2002). By 2004, it had reached an estimated 18 million. Moreover, the general population of Latinos was and is growing at breakneck speed—much faster than the population of the nation as a whole. Between 1980 and 1990, Hispanics had increased by 50 percent, compared to the white (non-Hispanic) population, which had increased by only 6 percent

(U.S. Bureau of the Census, 1991: table 1; U.S. Bureau of the Census, 1993:2). By 1999, the number of Hispanics in the United States (30 million) was greater than the total population of Canada. In 2003, it officially became the largest minority ethnic group in the country (Alonso-Zaldivar, 2003) and, in 2007, was estimated at 45.5 million, or 14 percent of the nation's total population. However, this estimate did not include the 3.9 million residents of Puerto Rico, who were also U.S. citizens and would raise the total to 49.4 million.[5]

2010—A Political and Cultural Shift

As noted above, as part of its preparation for the 2010 decennial census the Census Bureau conducted extensive nationwide testing of the race question—without the SOR category. This ignited "a furious debate among Hispanic advocacy groups, statisticians, and officials over how the nation's largest minority group should be defined racially." It also highlighted "the difficulties the Census Bureau has encountered over the decades as it has struggled to find a racial home for Hispanics living in this country" (Swarns, 2004a:1). This testing was nearing its end when in mid-November 2004 Congressman José E. Serrano (D-NY) inserted language into Congress's "omnibus" conference report that disallowed the use of congressional funds "provided in this or any other Act for any fiscal year" for "the collection of Census data on race identification that does not include 'some other race' as a category" (Serrano, 2004).[6] In essence, funding for the testing of questions—without the SOR category—and for any other projects that would eliminate the SOR category was eliminated.

As the *New York Times* subsequently noted, "Census officials had hoped to eliminate the 'some other race' category from the 2010 questionnaire to encourage Hispanics to choose from among five standard racial categories"—that is, "white," "black," "Asian," "American Indian or Alaska native," and "Pacific Islander or Hawaiian native" (Swarns, 2004b). According to a press release from Congressman Serrano's office, his action would not "force all Americans to choose one of five racial identities." Hispanic organizations were "quick to praise the action." As Congressman Serrano, the ranking Democrat on the Appropriations Subcommittee that funds the Census Bureau, stated:

> Millions of American Latinos do not fit neatly into one of the Census Bureau's race categories.... I am happy that we were able to make sure that people have an additional option on the census form. This will ensure that Americans are not forced to racially self-identify in a way they are uncomfortable with, and will produce census results that better reflect the realities of race in America today. More accurate census results will help policy-makers make better decisions. (Serrano, 2004)

Also of interest, given current concerns over immigration and the growth of the Latino population, is the statement made by Serrano that eliminating SOR would ignore the evolving views of race across the country (Swarns, 2004b).

Whether one viewed this turn of events as the actions of a single member of Congress meddling in the operations of the census or as the outcome of a dialogue between the Bureau and a sizable number of Hispanic advocacy organizations, it appeared that, at this point in the process, the Bureau had failed in its attempt to impose a racial classification system over the objections of the group that would have been most affected. As of this writing, the 2010 census will retain essentially the same combined question format in the 2000 census, one for race, and another for Hispanic origin.

CONCLUSION

For the most part, people (whether or not they are Latinos) check off their "race" to the best of their understanding. Clearly, some may be expressing a political challenge, others a very conscious "identity," but most simply, humbly, or matter-of-factly check what seems to make the most sense to them. Although the "problem" of racial classification has been addressed through multitudinous studies, it has received minimal media attention outside of limited academic circles. Even the Spanish-language media have tended to sidestep it. In part, this is because discussions of race and the census are more complicated than measured media sound bites can generally accommodate and, in part, because "race" is a political issue, often highly personal and emotional, and so does not lend itself to easy answers.

The struggle over imposed identity and self-identity is evident in the fact that Latinos continue to choose "some other race," despite the many attempts made by the Census Bureau to dissuade this response. It is unmistakable in the dismay that Latinos and others expressed with regard to dropping "some other race" from the census, and in the political intervention that followed. On the other side, the struggle is apparent in various state attempts to alter the question on race so as to eliminate ambiguous responses. This was evident in the initial changes in question format, such as adding the term "race" numerous times and having the Hispanic item precede the race item. Then came many large-scale studies testing a race question that included Hispanics as a separate race. Finally, recent studies were conducted with the hope of eliminating the SOR category altogether.

Some might say that the consistent separation between race and Hispanic origin in the last three censuses represents a stasis in this struggle. Others would say it represents a victory against the further racialization of Latinos. Still others would argue that it represents the inability of Latinos to adapt to the United States' way of life. In any case, I suspect that the question of how best to count changing populations, both in the United States and elsewhere, will be one of the key public policy issues of the twenty-first century.

NOTES

1. The author would like to acknowledge the assistance of Jessie Richford and the contributions of Cordelia and David Reimers, John Nieto-Phillips, and Héctor Cordero-Guzmán to an earlier version of the present chapter. In addition, parts of this chapter borrow from the

author's book *Changing Race: Latinos, the Census, and the History of Ethnicity in the United States* (Rodríguez, 2000).

2. The following historical review is drawn from and builds upon Rodríguez (2000).

3. See, for example, the following cover stories and special issues: *Time* magazine, April 9, 1990; *Discover,* November 1994; *Newsweek,* February 13, 1995; *Mother Jones,* October 1997; and *The Sciences,* March/April 1997.

4. Prior to the 1990 census, similar proposals had been advanced, but because they were met with considerable opposition, they did not advance to the level of congressional consideration or become a point of departure for additional studies (McKenney and Cresce, 1994; Rodríguez, 2000:161ff).

5. For the most recent estimates of the Latino population, see U.S. Bureau of the Census (2007, 2008).

6. There is a long history of politicians effecting census changes. Recent examples include California Representative Robert Matsui, who is responsible for the long list of Asian races; Hawaii Senator Donna Ikeda, who separated Pacific Islanders from Asians; and Florida Representative Charles T. Canady, who added two questions about grandchildren to the 2000 census.

REFERENCES

Alonso-Zaldivar, Ricardo. 2003. "Latinos Now Top Minority." *Los Angeles Times,* June 19. Retrieved April 14, 2008. (http://azbilingualed.org/AABE%20Site/AABE%20NEWS%202003/latinos_now_top_minority_census.htm)

Anderson, Margo, J. 1988. *American Census: A Social History.* New Haven: Yale University Press.

Bennett, Claudette N., Nampeo McKenney, and Roderick Harrison. 1995. "Racial Classification Issues Concerning Children in Mixed Race Households." Paper presented at the annual meeting of the Population Association of America, San Francisco.

Brodkin Sacks, Karen. 1994. "How Did Jews Become White Folks?" Pp. 78–102 in Steven Gregory and Roger Sanjek (eds.), *Race.* New Brunswick, NJ: Rutgers University Press.

Caillavet, Chantal. 2006. "Commentary on Paper Entitled 'Comparative Perspectives: Latinos, the Census, and Race in the United States,' by Clara Rodríguez." Presented at the Conference "Des catégories et de leurs usages dans la construction sociale d'un groupe de référence: 'Race,' 'ethnie' et 'communauté' aux Amériques." Paris, France, December 13–15.

Campbell, Mary E., and Christabel L. Rogalin. 2006. "Categorical Imperatives: The Interaction of Latino and Racial Identification." *Social Science Quarterly* 87(5):1030–1052.

Choldin, Harvey. 1986. "Statistics and Politics: The 'Hispanic Issue' in the 1980 Census." *Demography* 23(3):403–417.

Chou, Rosalind, and Joe R. Feagin. 2008. *Model Minority Myths: Asian Americans Facing Racism.* Boulder, CO: Paradigm Books.

Denton, Nancy A., and Douglas S. Massey. 1989. "Racial Identity Among Caribbean Hispanics: The Effect of Double Minority Status on Residential Segregation." *American Sociological Review* 54:790–808.

Edmonston, Barry, Joshua Goldstein, and Juanita Tamayo Lott. 1996. *Spotlight on Heterogeneity: The Federal Standards for Racial and Ethnic Classification.* Committee on National Statistics, National Research Council. Washington, DC: National Academy Press.

Edmonston, Barry, Sharon M. Lee, and Jeffrey S. Passel. 1994. "U.S. Population Projections for National Origin Groups: Taking Race and Ethnic Ancestry into Account." *Proceedings of the American Statistical Association,* Social Statistics Section. Washington, DC: American Statistical Association.

Evinger, Suzanne. 1996. "How to Record Race." *American Demographics* 18(5):36–42.

Feagin, Joe R. 2006. *Systemic Racism: A Theory of Oppression.* New York: Routledge.

Gómez, Christina. 2000. "The Continual Significance of Skin Color: An Exploratory Study of Latinos in the Northeast." *Hispanic Journal of Behavioral Sciences* 22(1): 94–103.

Grieco, Elizabeth M., and Rachel C. Cassidy. 2001. *Overview of Race and Hispanic Origin: Census 2000 Brief.* Retrieved April 14, 2008. (www.census.gov/prod/2001pubs/c2kbr01-1.pdf)

Guzmán, Betsy, and Eileen Diaz McConnell. 2002. "The Hispanic Population: 1990–2000 Growth and Change." *Population Research and Policy Review* 21:109–128.

Hirschman, Charles, Richard Alba, and Reynolds Farley. 2000. "The Meaning and Measurement of Race in the U.S. Census: Glimpses into the Future." *Demography* 37(3):381–393.

Ignatiev, Noel. 1995. *How the Irish Became White.* New York: Routledge & Kegan Paul.

Jacobson, Mathew. 1998. *Becoming Caucasian: Whiteness and the Alchemy of the American Melting Pot.* Cambridge, MA: Harvard University Press.

Kalmijn, Matthijs. 1993. "Trends in Black/White Intermarriage." *Social Forces* 72(1):119–146.

Katzman, Martin T. 1968. "Discrimination, Subculture, and the Economic Performance of Negroes, Puerto Ricans, and Mexican-Americans." *American Journal of Economics and Society* 27(4):371–375.

Martin, Elizabeth, Theresa J. DeMaio, and Pamela C. Campanelli. 1990. "Context Effects for Census Measures of Race and Hispanic Origin." *Public Opinion Quarterly* 54(4):551–566.

Martinez, Anne. 2001. "New Choices on 2000 Census Fail to Offer Right Racial Fit for Latinos." *Mercury News,* May 24, p. 1.

Massey, Douglas S., and Nancy Denton. 1993. *American Apartheid: Segregation and the Making of the Underclass.* Cambridge, MA: Harvard University Press.

McKenney, Nampeo R., and Claudette E. Bennett. 1994. "Issues Regarding Data on Race and Ethnicity: The Census Bureau Experience." CDC-ATSDR Workshop, Public Health Reports, vol. 108(1):16–25.

McKenney, Nampeo R., Claudette Bennett, Roderick Harrison, and Jorge del Pinal. 1993. "Evaluating Racial and Ethnic Reporting in the 1990 Census." Reprinted from the Proceedings of the Section on Survey Research Methods of the American Statistical Association, pp. 66–74.

McKenney, Nampeo R., and Arthur R. Cresce. 1993. "Measurement of Ethnicity in the U.S.: Experiences of the U.S. Census Bureau." Pp. 173–221 in *Challenges of Measuring an Ethnic World: Science, Politics, and Reality.* Proceedings of the Joint Canada–United States Conference on the Measurement of Ethnicity, April 1–3, 1992. Washington, DC: U.S. Government Printing Office.

Padilla, María T. 2001. "America's Changing Face—It's Mixed: The 2000 Census Let People Identify Themselves as Multiracial for the First Time, and 6.8 Million Did." *Orlando Sentinel,* March 13, p. A1.

Porter, Eduardo. 2001. "Even 126 Sizes Don't Fit All." *Wall Street Journal,* March 2, p. B1.

Rodríguez, Clara E. [1989] 1991a. *Puerto Ricans: Born in the U.S.A.* Boulder, CO: Westview Press.

———. 1990. "Racial Identification Among Puerto Ricans in New York." *Hispanic Journal of Behavioral Sciences* 12(4):366–379.

———. 1991b. "The Effect of Race on Puerto Rican Wages." Pp. 77–98 in Edwin Meléndez,

Clara E. Rodríguez, and Janice Barry Figueroa (eds.), *Hispanics in the Labor Force: Issues and Policies.* New York: Plenum Press.

———. 1991c. "Why 'Other' Is Our Second Fastest Growing Racial Category." Letter to the Editor, *New York Times,* April 4, p. A14.

———. 1992. "Race, Culture, and Latino 'Otherness' in the 1980 Census." *Social Science Quarterly* 73(4):930–937.

———. 1994. "Challenging Racial Hegemony: Puerto Ricans in the United States." Pp. 131–145 in Roger Sanjek and Steven Gregory (eds.), *Race.* New Brunswick, NJ: Rutgers University Press.

———. 1996. "Racial Themes in the Literature: Puerto Ricans and Other Latinos." Pp. 104–125 in Gabriel Haslip-Viera and Sherrie L. Baver (eds.), *Latinos in New York: Communities in Transition.* Notre Dame, IN: University of Notre Dame Press.

———. 2000. *Changing Race: Latinos, the Census, and the History of Ethnicity in the United States.* New York: New York University Press.

Rolark, Stanley, Claudette Bennett, and Roderick Harrison. 1994. "Tables on Multiracial Responses and on Interracial and Interethnic Couples and Children." Presentation at the Workshop on "Race and Ethnicity Classification: An Assessment of the Federal Standard for Race and Ethnicity Classification." Washington, DC: National Academy of Sciences, Committee on National Statistics.

Root, Maria P. P. (ed.). 1996. *The Multiracial Experience: Racial Borders as the New Frontier.* Newbury Park, CA: Sage Publications.

———. 1992. *Racially Mixed People in America.* Newbury Park, CA: Sage Publications.

Serrano, José E. Congressman. 2004. "Serrano Succeeds in Retaining 'Other' Race Option on Census Form, Hispanic Organizations Applaud Action." November 22, 2004, Press Release. Retrieved April 14, 2008. (http://serrano.house.gov/PressRelease.aspx?NewsID=1122)

Spickard, Paul R. 1989. *Mixed Blood: Intermarriage and Ethnic Identity in Twentieth-Century America.* Madison: University of Wisconsin Press.

Suro, Roberto, and Sonya Tafoya. 2004. *Dispersal and Concentration: Patterns of Latino Residential Settlement.* Washington, DC: Pew Hispanic Center.

Swarns, Rachel. 2004a. "Hispanics Debate Racial Grouping by Census." *New York Times,* October 24, p. 1.

———. 2004b. "Washington: 'Other Race' Stays on the Books." *New York Times,* November 23. Retrieved April 14, 2008. (http://query.nytimes.com/gst/fullpage.html?res=9E01EEDE173EF930A15752C1A9629C8B63&fta=y)

Tafoya, Sonya. 2004. *Shades of Belonging: Latinos and Racial Identity.* Washington, DC: Pew Hispanic Center. Retrieved May 29, 2008. (http://pewhispanic.org/files/reports/35.pdf)

Tienda, Marta, and Vilma Ortiz. 1986. "'Hispanicity' and the 1980 Census." *Social Science Quarterly* 67(March):3–20.

U.S. Bureau of the Census. 1991. "Census Bureau Releases 1990 Census Counts on Hispanic Population Groups." Press Release, June 12, Washington, DC.

———. 1993. *We, the American ... Hispanics.* Ethnic and Hispanic Statistics Branch, Population Division, U.S. Government Printing Office, November.

———. 2001. *The Two or More Races Population: 2000.* Retrieved April 14, 2008. (www.census.gov/prod/2001pubs/c2kbr01-6.pdf)

———. 2007. "Population of Puerto Rico." Retrieved May 21, 2008. (http://factfinder.census.gov/servlet/SAFFPopulation?geo_id=04000US72&_state=04000US72&pctxt=cr)

———. 2008. "2008 Estimates of the Population by Race and Hispanic Origin for the United States and States: July 1, 2007, Table 4: (SC-EST2007–04), Release Date: May 1, 2008." Retrieved May 21, 2008. (http://www.census.gov/popest/states/asrh/tables/SC-EST2007-04.xls)

U.S. Department of Labor, Bureau of Labor Statistics. 1995. "A CPS Supplement for Testing Methods of Collecting Racial and Ethnic Information: May, 1995." Bureau of Labor Statistics Statistical Working Papers series, November.

U.S. General Accounting Office (GAO). 1993. "Census Reform: Early Outreach and Decisions Needed on Race and Ethnic Questions." GAO/GGD-93-36 (January).

U.S. Office of Management and Budget. 1995. "Standards for the Classification of Federal Data on Race and Ethnicity; Notice." *Federal Register,* Part VI, vol. 60, no. 166, pp. 44674–44693 (August 28).

CHAPTER 3

Becoming Dark

The Chilean Experience in California, 1848–1870

Fernando Purcell

Chileans were among the first to arrive in California in 1848 after the Gold Rush began, and they became the second-largest Hispanic American contributor to California's population after Mexicans during the second half of the nineteenth century. Although the number varies according to different sources, it is safe to estimate a Chilean immigration of at least four or five thousand people during the period 1848–1870. Most of them were recruited to work in the gold mines, even though many performed different kinds of jobs in California. The great majority of the people who traveled to California from Chile belonged to the lower classes and were peons from central Chile, as passport lists, labor contracts, and reports of Chilean authorities make clear. The Chilean consul in San Francisco, for example, pointed out on September 2, 1851, that the great majority of Chileans who went to California were of the "inferior classes of the Chilean population" (Records of the Ministry of Foreign Affairs, National Archives, Chile, vol. 73, September 2, 1851, no page). His comment had a class rather than racial connotation, based on the predominant system of social stratification in Chile. The point here is not that race was irrelevant in Chile but, rather, that it had a different meaning than in the United States. At the time, most Chileans, whether of European descent or mestizos (mixed race), considered themselves "white" and together they comprised the great majority of the Chilean population. Hence, Chileans who traveled to California confronted new social and cultural challenges, the most important being their racialization by the dominant Anglo-American population. It was as though the skin of Chileans in California was abruptly "darkened" upon their arrival in San Francisco, and soon tensions arose with Anglo-Americans in California. In the following pages, I will analyze several episodes that help to clarify how this racialization process occurred, with particular attention to Chileans' responses to the facilitation of their incorporation into California society.

ENCOUNTERING THE "HOUNDS"

San Francisco during the Gold Rush was a city on the move, a gathering place for various peoples who perhaps never imagined they were going to participate in the creation of one of the most cosmopolitan cities in the world. For Chilean traveler Benjamín Vicuña Mackenna, San Francisco's social scenario was in 1852 a "hodge-podge of cities, a tower of Babel of all nationalities" (quoted in Beilharz and López, 1976:195). Despite the presence of myriad people, California quickly became controlled by a majority of Anglo-Americans who imposed their sociocultural hegemony. This process included ethnic and racial struggles with foreigners, which became crucial for the re-creation of California society after 1848 (Moore, 2003:96).

Chileans suffered the consequences of racial discrimination early in the summer of 1849 at the hands of the so-called Hounds, "a desperate set of young fellows" who "took this name from their custom of going throughout the places every night at eleven o'clock and barking like hounds as a sort of impudent serenade to the quiet and respectable people of San Francisco" (quoted in Oehler, 1950:168). This was a dispossessed and anxious group of young men who took advantage of the lack of strong authorities to keep peace and order in San Francisco in 1849. They became the protagonists of one of the first major violent events in California after the discovery of gold, the so-called attack on "Little Chile," an area near Telegraph Hill where most Chileans had settled.

The attack on Little Chile occurred on July 15, 1849, causing an enormous commotion in San Francisco. It was the result of ethnic and racial tensions combined with the anxieties generated by a group that targeted vulnerable "nonwhite" foreigners in the city. Benjamín Vicuña Mackenna (1956:4–5) described Little Chile as a place where "the female portion of Valparaíso" or prostitutes lived, while Hubert Bancroft (1888:261–262) argued that in 1851 the neighborhood was "a hollow filled with little wooden huts planted promiscuously, with numberless recesses and fastnesses filled with Chileans—men, women, and children."

The origins of the attack on Little Chile lie in a series of previous quarrels and incidents such as the assassination, on June 21, 1849, of Benjamin B. Beatty, a thirty-year-old native of Albany, New York, by a Chilean. Charles Frederick Winslow, a witness, wrote a letter to his wife on July 19, 1849, telling her that Beatty was shot by a Chilean "for intrusions on his wife in his tent. They [the

Hounds] were insolent and licentious, and having a pique against these Chileans only because they are foreigners, they insulted them and laid improper hands on their females" (quoted in Oehler, 1950:168). On July 15, there was a series of incidents after Samuel Roberts, one of the leaders of the Hounds, had problems with his mistress, a Chilean prostitute named Felicia Alvarez. Taking into account that women were scarcer than gold in California, tensions arose and, as a result, the Hounds attacked Little Chile at night. The *Alta California* (August 2, 1849, p. 1) reported that "tents were torn down and destroyed, their contents stolen or damaged, and their occupants knocked down, shot at, and otherwise maltreated." Moses Pearson Cogswell from New Hampshire wrote that these men had also "ravished their women, and committed other shameful outrages" (quoted in Hunt, 1949:54).

A meeting was called to establish the procedures for the trial. On July 17, prominent members of San Francisco society appointed a grand jury of twenty-four citizens. The trial lasted more than a week. In the end, Roberts was found guilty of all the counts, and eight others were found guilty of one or more of the charges against them. Roberts was sentenced to ten years in prison but his penalty was never enforced. This situation rarely happened in California when the accused was nonwhite. The attack on Little Chile was the first major incident in Gold Rush California in which foreigners suffered the consequences of racial discrimination. For Chileans, this was their initial challenge to understand that despite their self-perceived "whiteness"—some of the outraged Chileans were wealthy businessmen of European descent established in Valparaíso—they would suffer racial discrimination in California. Chileans underwent a process of racialization, of which they quickly became aware, as the Chilean consul in San Francisco Samuel Price made clear on August 14, 1850, stating that in California, "there is a belief among them [Anglo-Americans] that all South Americans are Indians, Zambos or Blacks and that because of this they do not deserve a social position equal to theirs" (Records of the Ministry of Foreign Affairs, National Archives, Chile, vol. 63, August 14, 1850, no page). The numerous illegal actions of the Hounds throughout 1849 "were directed chiefly against foreigners—Chileans, Peruvians and Mexicans, as being supposed less able to defend themselves, and who were likewise imagined to possess fewer sympathies from the community in their behalf" (Soulé, Gihon, and Nisbet, 1855:555).

Moreover, the assault on Little Chile, as many testimonies from the trial show, was racially selective. On many occasions, the Hounds asked who the owners of certain tents were before they proceeded to attack. For instance, they left untouched Anglo-Americans and Englishmen who were in Little Chile at the time. According to the *Alta California* (August 9, 1849, p. 1), Englishman Michael McNeil declared during the trial, "I have a tent and blacksmith shop. I heard a party pass, and say they would let me alone because I was an Englishman." Duncan McCallam, who lived with McNeil, said that they asked him, "Whose tent is this? I said an English tent. They said, 'all right,' and I laid down again." The same occurred to Anglo-American A. Dimmoch from Sausalito, who on that day happened to be in a tent adjoining a Chilean one. Thus, the riot was not a melee but the rational plot of a cluster of people who, despite being drunk, had a clear idea of whom they wanted to attack and for what reasons. As Bancroft (1887:101) wrote, the assault was a "coolly planned conspiracy" against the Chileans. Even during the trial, the defense of Roberts and the accused Hounds argued that foreigners were prohibited from working in the mines, insinuating that they had no rights to be in California in the first place. In an attempt to justify the action of the Hounds, defense attorney Myron Norton referred to several incidents directed against Anglo-Americans in which foreigners had participated. According to the *Alta California* (August 9, 1849, p. 2), using a xenophobic argument, Norton asked the judges, "And what is the feeling of these men [the accused]? Would not revenge be sought by all Americans placed under similar circumstances?"

News of the riot spread quickly and soon all Chile knew of the terrible fortune of some of their compatriots. On August 29, 1849, after receiving information about the attack, the Chilean House of Representatives authorized the president to spend 40,000 Chilean pesos to repatriate Chileans from California (Barros Arana, 1913:350). More important, the assault on Little Chile led to the establishment of the first Chilean consulate in San Francisco only one month later. Consul Pedro Cueto soon started informing Chilean authorities about the situation besetting their citizens living in California. In particular, he referred to a new problem for this Chilean community: the presence of Chilean indigents. On January 30, 1850, he warned the Chilean minister of foreign affairs about the "considerable number of dispossessed Chileans who want to return to their country; many of them have approached me looking for help but I do not have enough money to support them. This is why I feel compelled to beg you for help and I hope that you will be able to find a way to alleviate their suffering" (Records of the Ministry of Foreign Affairs, National Archives, Chile, vol. 63, January 30, 1850, no page). This situation remained unchanged in the following months, as the next Chilean consul, Samuel Price, reported: "[M]any Chileans are sick and with no economic resources to return to their country" (Records of the Ministry of Foreign Affairs, National Archives, Chile, vol. 63, February 28, 1850, no page). He not only continued imploring for economic resources to address these problems but also proposed to the Chilean minister of foreign affairs that the future emigration of Chileans to California be stemmed, because of the racially derogatory terms in which Anglo-Americans looked down upon Chileans.

THE WAR OF THE CALAVERAS OR CHILEAN WAR

The Calaveras incident in the California foothills during December 1849 and early January 1850 serves as a window on the interaction between Anglo-Americans and Chileans but also, and more significantly, on a fundamental aspect of the dynamics of racial stratification and social control imposed by Anglo-Americans in early-U.S. California. Manifest Destiny was an overarching racial ideology that transcended and influenced all kinds of intergroup relations in California. However, it was an abstract doctrine that could not have made much difference unless applied through concrete forms of social behavior. Law and lynching practices were effective ways to convert Manifest Destiny into something tangible, especially in the gold mines.

The relevance of law and justice to the imposition of racial supremacy over nonwhites becomes clear when we examine the so-called War of the Calaveras or Chilean War. This incident originated after Anglo-American miners, described by John Hovey (1849–1851:87) in his diary as "real 'Americans' and true to their country," gathered to "make law" and elected district authorities to preserve their "rights as American citizens." In a meeting held in early December 1849, these Anglo-Americans chose L. A. Collier as district judge in the mining area of Mockelumne Hill, Calaveras, and established that "no foreigners shall be permitted to work in these mines after the tenth day of December 1849" (Hovey, 1849–1851:85). This decision was accompanied by negative comments about immigrants in the area. For Abraham Nash, "the foreigners and especially these D'd [Damned] copper hides every one of them should be driven from our diggings they've got no business here in the first place" (Hovey, 1849–1851:88). Chilean miners refused to obey the order from Anglo-American miners to abandon the area, and on December 15, Anglo-American miners sacked the tents completely while their newly elected judge fined them because of their defiance. The next morning, on December 16, the Chileans, led by two people named Concha and Maturano, departed to Stockton, where they complained to the authorities, including sub-prefect W. Dickenson, Justice of the Peace G. Belt, Sheriff Young, and Judge Reynolds (Beilharz and López, 1976:120–124). As Argentine Ramón Gil Navarro wrote in his diary, the Chileans "ended up lodging a complaint against the judge of Mockelumne—Collier—saying that they had not been treated fairly by him" (quoted in Ferreyra and Reher, 2000:72).

Remarkably, the Chileans were able to obtain a warrant from the Stockton authorities. This warrant was put in the hands of a group of Chileans to arrest the Anglo-Americans responsible for the expulsion, fining, and sacking of the Chilean camp. The Chileans returned to Calaveras and went directly to talk to Calaveras's Judge Scollen, who had been sympathetic to them before. This time, however, Scollen hesitated to provide open support for the arrest, knowing that doing so could cause serious problems in the community. Navarro mentions in his diary that "there was much argument with Scollen because he says the order is not written correctly, since American citizens can never be arrested by foreigners" (quoted in Ferreyra and Reher, 2000:74). Without Scollen's support, eighty armed Chileans went to the Anglo-American camp in the area, killing several people and injuring others.

Unlike in San Francisco a few months earlier, Chilean miners in the foothills had established a network of protection among themselves and with other people from Latin America. This, plus the fact that they were living in an environment with a spatial mobility they could not afford in cities like San Francisco, bolstered their confidence in their procedures for self-protection. The Chileans took sixteen prisoners from the Anglo-American camp and escorted them to Judge Scollen's cabin. Scollen refused to see the Chileans because he did not want to become involved in the incident. Accordingly, the Chileans marched toward

Stockton with the prisoners, but a couple of days later the prisoners were rescued by a group of Anglo-Americans, and the Chileans passed from being captors to captives (Ayers, 1922:52). On December 30, the Chileans were brought back to Calaveras, where Anglo-American miners formed a jury that found them all guilty of murder in the first degree (Hovey, 1849–1851:81–82).

Soon thereafter, hundreds of miners arrived in Calaveras to witness the theatrical execution of the Chileans. Several of the latter were punished, including one, Ignacio Yáñez, who was sentenced to have his ears cut off. Three of the leaders were shot. The sentences were carried out on January 3, 1850. As Gil Navarro later wrote, the cutting of Yáñez's ears "was followed by a cry of pain such as one might hear in the last agony of a martyr. The ear with a part of the cheek was in the hand of the executioner who, after a moment, threw it aside and went after the other ear with the coldest insensitivity." Navarro continued his dramatic description: "A sea of blood inundated the face and clothing of the poor fellow, giving him a look more horrible than you can imagine." Later, the three other Chileans were tied to oak trees and shot one after another (quoted in Beilharz and López, 1976:145–149).

Race was certainly a factor in this episode, not only before but after the incident. The astonished editor of the *Pacific News* in San Francisco could not believe what his correspondent had written on January 3, 1850, about the origins of the incident:

> If we understand our correspondent right, the warrant was issued by the American authorities, and placed in the hands of *Chilians* [sic], for the arrest of American citizens. If this was the case, such a course was undoubtedly wholly injudicious in itself, and likely to produce the calamity which has arisen. We trust, however, that there is some mistake in this, and that the matter will be satisfactorily explained hereafter.

The correspondent had provided an accurate report of the incident and the incredulous editor continued by blaming Stockton authorities and stating that there was "culpable carelessness somewhere in this matter. Why send a party of *foreigners* to arrest Americans—especially foreigners who could not speak the English language, and who even did not take with them an interpreter? ... Shameful, indeed, is it, that an American was not sent to make the arrest, if there was any need of it" (*Pacific News*, January 3, 1850, p. 2).

For James Ayers, who ended up as a prisoner of the Chilean extralegal authorities, there was a "general consensus of opinion amongst the miners upon this subject, and it would have been a 'most lame and impotent conclusion' to permit an alien to exercise a privilege which was denied to an American citizen" (Ayers, 1922:61).

Several factors help explain Anglo-American animosities against the Chileans in Calaveras, including ethnic and racial prejudices (S. Johnson, 2000:193–234). Another ingredient was the fact that Chileans in Calaveras assumed a shared exercise of justice and law, which was unacceptable for Anglo-American miners. The latter group had appealed to justice throughout the Gold Rush not only as a way to impose "order" but also as a consistent and conscious form of establishing Anglo-Saxon superiority in the recently conquered and foreign-crowded territory of California (McKanna, 2002). In this case, the Anglo-Saxon racial agenda, carried out through the exercise of the law as well as through lynching, was turned the opposite way, because of the Chileans' attempt to make justice by themselves, which explains the tragic results for many of them.

Many Anglo-Americans were also executed during the Gold Rush, although in strikingly lower numbers than "Hispanics" (D. Johnson, 1981:575). The judgment of Anglo-Americans had a different connotation than that of South Americans. Behind their punishment was the idea of establishing order and law, not necessarily racial stratification. This agenda becomes clear when we compare the trial of the Hounds and the trial of Chilean miners in Calaveras, because we see that Anglo-Americans and Chileans were treated in a radically different way. The Hounds did not even complete their sentences, whereas Chileans experienced terrible consequences for their actions. The trial of the Hounds was longer than that of the Chileans in Calaveras. This distinct treatment suggests that the punishment of undesirable foreigners was motivated by the attempt to impose racial supremacy.

THE FOREIGN MINERS' TAX

Legal inequalities in the California mines were exerted not only through robbery, expulsion from the mines, or lynching, but also by the establishment of discriminatory laws. The Foreign Miners' Tax is a good example of how Anglo-Americans enacted specific laws against undesirable immigrants, who, despite all their suffering and discrimination in the goldfields, chose to remain in the business of gold extraction after 1849. This tax, passed by the state legislature on April 13, 1850, imposed a monthly fee of $20 on every foreigner working in gold extraction. Thomas J. Green, the author of the legislation, argued before the California Senate that "this bill requires the foreigner, upon the plainest principles of justice, to pay a small bonus for the privilege of taking from our country the vast treasure to which they have no right" (Journal of the Senate of the State of California, San Jose, 1850, p. 494). What Green considered a "small bonus" was actually a large amount of money that essentially sought the expulsion, rather than the exploitation, of certain foreign miners, especially Spanish-speakers. This explains why an anonymous English immigrant, who was in Chili Gulch in 1850, pointed out in his diary that the tax collector arrived at his place "armed to the teeth" and remained at his camp for the night, "but they never asked if we were naturalized Americans or not and did not solicit fragment from us." The man, who wrote a diary titled *Early Days in California* (October 1852), makes clear that the tax was collected from Spanish-speakers only. This anecdote illustrates that the legal measure was primarily aimed at Chileans, Mexicans, and Spanish-speakers in general (Purcell, 2004).

That the law was racially charged can be further demonstrated by considering the attitude of other foreigners toward it. Some non-American citizens, including the Irish portion of the so-called Sydney Ducks from Australia, used the tax as an opportunity to be considered "white" and to enjoy the privileges denied to Chileans and Mexicans. On November 23, 1850, the editor of the *Stockton Times* (p. 2) complained about the high sums of money that the Foreign Miners' Tax imposed on foreigners, stating that a lower amount would have been "attended by the most beneficent results, since it would have been protective in its nature, against the impositions and insults of that portion of the American, pseudo-American, and Sidney-American people who would banish or exterminate every 'foreigner' in the country."

This editorial implies that people such as the Sydney Ducks and "pseudo-Americans"—presumably English, Irish, and Germans—joined Anglo-Americans in opposition to a limited number of foreigners against whom the tax was imposed. Hence, some foreigners sided with Anglo-Americans to define themselves against the "undesirable" foreigners. This strategy eased their entry into California society. In the end, as Sucheng Chan (2000:60) points out, "the English, Irish, and Germans lined up on the side of Americans against the other foreigners, in the process solidifying their own standing as honorary Americans." For their part, Chileans refused to pay the tax; one even killed the tax collector at Bolivia Camp in May 1850 (Ferreyra and Reher, 2000:119). According to the *Stockton Times* (June 1, 1850, p. 3), a group of foreigners in Tuolumne County "presented a strong resistance to the enforcement of the late tax law" and "the sheriff of the county, in attempting to compel the foreigners to yield, was killed by them, and one or two of his posse wounded." Such actions by Chilean individuals or small groups were complemented with a broader pattern of resistance against the law, which usually implied the creation of intergroup alliances that sought to revert its discriminatory applications. One of the efforts to contest the mistreatment by Anglo-Americans was the initiative of a group of Chileans, Mexicans, and "Sonoreños" from Jesús María, Calaveras, who protested in May 1850 against the tax imposed upon them, by writing a letter to Governor Peter Burnett.

> Sir: We your humble petitioners being Chilians, Sonoreños, and other Mexicans apprehending some difficulty on account of our working on the gold mines, having been debarred from the privilege of working at some places and now being threatened to be driven off from our present encampment, and not wishing to resist the Americans or do any act contrary to the laws of your nation humbly beg your protection. And should it be contrary to your laws that we work in the mines and peaceably retire? But if it is lawful for us to remain and work in the mines we earnestly request your speedy intercession. (Governor Peter Burnett Papers, California Historical Society, Letters Received, May 1, 1850, pp. 47–48)

This letter is a good example of how Chileans and Mexicans assumed shared responsibility in the maintenance of a good environment where people from both nations could work unmolested by Anglo-Americans. Unfortunately for them, their petition was simply ignored, which led great numbers of them to abandon the Southern Mines and return to their homelands.

On August 14, 1850, the *Evening Picayune* of San Francisco wrote that, as a result of the Foreign Miners' Tax, "from fifteen to twenty thousand Mexicans, and perhaps an equal number of Chilenos are now leaving, or preparing to leave California for their own country" (Bancroft, 1888:234). Although it is difficult to specify the number of people who left the mines because of the Foreign Miners' Tax, the figures provided by the *Evening Picayune* were an exaggeration because those people who actually left the mines numbered only several thousand. However, many Chileans stayed, leading to what Susan Lee Johnson (2000:209–210) calls "unexpected alliances." Johnson (2000:216) recognizes that the Foreign Miners' Tax and other forms of discrimination against foreigners "had a profound effect on the strategies of resistance and accommodation remaining Spanish and French speakers pursued." However, she does not explore these new forms of resistance and accommodation, but simply refers to the lessons foreigners learned. The Mexicans and Chileans who remained in California took concrete actions, including organizing public protests, sending letters of complaint to authorities regarding the Foreign Miners' Tax, and sometimes committing violent actions against tax collectors. These strategies deepened their ties of solidarity even further and contributed to the development in the following decades of a broader ethnic identity beyond their national origins.

AFTER THE GOLD RUSH

Mexicans and Chileans became increasingly dependent on Anglo-American capital to secure jobs in California after the Gold Rush. The end of easy mining and the dissolution of independent companies, where Mexicans and Chileans worked side by side with other Spanish-speaking people and their *patronos* (employers), provoked crucial transformations in labor and social relationships between "Spaniards" and Anglo-Americans. Throughout the 1850s, miners, regardless of their national origin, were increasingly forced to work as wage laborers for large corporations, which attracted many early miners as well as new immigrants (Cornford, 1999:93). This change had profound repercussions on the daily lives of Chilean peons. In many cases, they lost the connections to their *patronos* and had to quickly adapt to new capitalist modes of labor control, to which they were unaccustomed. To make matters even worse for the miners, wages declined steadily throughout the 1850s (Paul, [1947] 1965:120).

Anglo-Americans, who controlled most industries in California and particularly mining industries, found new tools in labor control to impose their racial supremacy over nonwhites. These forms of control replaced public executions and other violent actions as the main strategies for the imposition of Anglo-American superiority in California—a scenario that was more than clear in mining towns like New Almaden, where Mexicans and Chileans suffered the consequences of segregation and mistreatment during the 1850s and the following decades.

As Stephen J. Pitti (2003:51) argues, Mexicans, Chileans, and many Californios who worked at New Almaden became the first "Latino" industrial workers in the United States. This mine started its operations before the California Gold Rush and attracted Mexicans from Sonora even before 1847. New Almaden expanded considerably after the Gold Rush, and its owners found a good-sized labor force in the thousands of unemployed foreigners in Northern California. As Pitti (2003:54–55) points out, Hispanic American laborers were segregated from white employees and usually performed the most dangerous jobs, and "rarely worked alongside New Almaden's Cornish or Irish residents in the 1850s and 1860s." Mexicans and Chileans worked ten-hour shifts, carrying up to 300 pounds of ore on their backs more than thirty times a day. It was common for them in their underground work to fall from ladders or be struck by falling rocks. Fires inside the mines were not rare, either. Indeed, Mexican and Chilean miners in New Almaden had higher fatality rates than Irish or Cornish miners, because of the dangerous work they performed (Pitti, 2003:58). Mexicans and Chileans also suffered spatial segregation in this mining town. As noted, they infrequently worked alongside Irish and Cornish miners, who enjoyed a certain degree of "whiteness" that made them different and more privileged. They lived in an area called "Spanishtown," with many restrictions to their mobility outside the mining town and the obligation to acquire supplies at the company store at higher prices (Pitti, 2003:56).

The story of Chileans and Mexicans after the Gold Rush is one of progressive movement toward the margins of society. After they became wage-earners in the mines and laborers in the cities, they occupied a marginal position in California society, both socially and spatially. This pattern had become clear in San Francisco. On May 22, 1853, the *Alta California* stated that

> [t]he Spanish as a class are very slow to learn English and to adopt American customs. They have no thought of becoming citizens. They feel their inferiority, and seem to have no hope, further than to live the few years that may be appointed to them. They hate the Americans, hate them bitterly, complain of injustice done, but the gold of California repays all. They call the Americans diablos [devils], imputing to them the malice as well as the power of demons. (p. 2)

This quote suggests that lower-class Mexicans and Chileans felt inferior to Anglo-Americans, a claim difficult to prove. Such an assertion probably reflects more what the writer thought about Chileans and Mexicans than what they thought of themselves. Nevertheless, it is possible to unearth examples that demonstrate that they felt excluded and uncomfortable in the society where they lived. This exclusion certainly contributed to the solidarity between Chileans and Mexicans, most of whom experienced similar forms of discrimination in California.

To make matters even worse, both Mexicans and Chileans were profiled as criminals because some members of their communities chose the path of delinquency as a way of life. Thus, all members of the Hispanic American community became stigmatized by the actions of a few. Anglo-Americans usually blamed whole communities and not only individuals for their crimes. This process of criminalization becomes clear when we review several events in which many paid the consequences of a few delinquents. In 1855, Thomas Seward, who had spent some time in the mines located in the foothills, wrote his wife Lucy Seward telling her about the robberies of Chileans in the mines and the sad consequences of them:

We are having pretty risky times up in the mines killing off Chilenos but I suppose you don't know what that is. They are inhabitants of Chile, one of the South American States and are a mixture of Spaniards and Indians. There are a great many here and have been committing murders and robberies for some time past and now the miners are shooting and hanging every one they meet. (Thomas Seward Papers, California Historical Society, Letters Received, August 15, 1855)

This letter uses a simple and cold-blooded language to tell a tragic story of persecution that embodied the complex racial dynamics that arose after the Gold Rush. But this case was not exceptional. Two years earlier, something similar had happened to Mexican mine workers. After the assassination of six people, presumably committed by a band of Mexican robbers, the pursuers of these Mexicans, according to Elias S. Ketcham's *Diary* (1853:35–36), "destroyed all the Mexican tents or dwellings that came in their way; which believed to be cruel and unjust, the Mexicans must suffer for the guilty in that case.—But many persons who are prejudiced say they are all alike, a set of cut throats and should be exterminated or drove out of the country" (quoted in Waldrep, pp. 81–82).

Collective vengeances targeting Hispanic Americans as criminals remained frequent throughout the 1850s and 1860s and soon raised international concern. *La Voz de Sonora* from Ures, Mexico, launched a staunch criticism against such actions between September and October of 1855. In an article entitled "The Persecution," the editor of this Mexican newspaper pointed out that in California "numerous individuals from the Spanish race are victims of atrocious events. Unfortunately, we have not known of any measures taken by the authorities to put an end to such horrendous scenes" (September 28, 1855, p. 3). The article then noted that many Mexicans and Chileans paid the consequences of the actions of bands of a few criminals, sometimes led by Anglo-Americans: "Why do they [Anglo-Americans] take actions against all individuals from the Spanish race in such vengeful, cruel and unfair manner for crimes committed by 4 or 6 Mexican or Chilean bandits when their leaders are North Americans?"

Two weeks later, the same newspaper denounced the discrimination suffered by Mexicans and all the other members of the "Spanish race" living in California. This time, the editor of *La Voz de Sonora* complained bitterly about lynching practices in California. On October 12, 1855, he pointed out that "the celebrated Lynch Law has served as a death instrument to satisfy racial hatred" (p. 2). Similar complaints were made by the same newspaper a year later. The editor argued that the hostile actions against Mexicans and "our brothers from South America" had not changed (July 11, 1856, p. 2).

A HISPANIC AMERICAN "RACE"

The common experience of discrimination, as well as the peculiar interethnic connections that Mexicans and Chileans developed during the 1860s (Purcell, 2004), nurtured an early Hispanic American panethnic identity. Mexicans and

Chileans living in California became enmeshed in the social networks between immigrants from different Hispanic American countries. The discourses of solidarity, cooperation, and unification that the Spanish press in California retrieved from Hispanic American countries, on the occasion of the French occupation of Mexico in 1862, gave an important impulse to mutual aid among Hispanics in California. Mexicans and Chileans had developed strong ties since the Gold Rush when, united against discriminatory practices against them, they established informal alliances in search of protection. Their common Gold Rush experience and the continuing discrimination against them by Anglo-Americans throughout the 1850s contributed to the emergence of a broader identity. It was precisely during the 1860s that self-references such as *raza hispano-americana* (Hispanic American race), *raza española* (Spanish race), and, to a lesser extent, *raza latina* (Latin race) became common denominators for Hispanics in California.

Some newspapers, such as *La Bandera Mexicana*, established in 1863, referred explicitly to this panethnic unity. *La Bandera Mexicana* claimed to have promoted the defense of Hispanic American interests as its basic principle. In a pamphlet distributed in San Francisco (November 23, 1863), its editor underlined the "*Unión de la América*" and solidarity among Hispanic American nations. Charitable organizations emerged, such as the Sociedad Hispano-Americana de Beneficencia Mutua, established early in 1862, and the Sociedad Patriótica Chilena de Beneficencia Mutua, which was created in San Francisco in 1865 because of the "sufferings and destituteness of the Latin race in this country [United States]" (La Voz de Chile y el Nuevo Mundo, June 5, 1868, p. 2). The latter's bylaws, published in La Voz de Chile y el Nuevo Mundo on June 5, 1868, established that this was a society open "to Chileans and all Hispanic Americans, without any distinction of sex, age, and nationality, who are residents of the State of California." At the same time, the bylaws expressed an interest in "the societies' hope that they propagate among the entire Latin race the spirit of association and mutual protection that characterizes the union of the Chileans, which in a foreign land is necessary and beneficial." This trend continued later with the Sociedad Latina Hispano Americana, which operated in the early 1870s, and the Sociedad Española de Beneficencia Mutua, founded in 1876, which joined together Spanish and Hispanic American members.

In short, Mexicans, Chileans, and other Hispanics developed a sense of belonging to what they usually called the Hispanic American race. Although Chileans who migrated to California had already advanced toward the consolidation of a national identity, Mexicans along the northern border—where most migrants to California at the time originated—had not yet developed strong national loyalties (Reséndez, 2005). The weakness of national identities among Hispanics in California—at least before the French occupation of Mexico and the War of the Pacific in Chile (1879–1883)—contributed to a racial and ethnic identity beyond national affiliations. The conformation and consolidation of this identity were the result of the actions and interests of Chileans, Mexicans, and other Hispanic Americans, but Anglo-Americans played a crucial role as well. The racialization of Chileans and other Hispanics by Anglo-Americans in California certainly fostered the rise of a new collective identity.

CONCLUSION

Chileans faced many challenges after their arrival in California in 1848. Here they encountered different cultures, labor practices, and ways of understanding race, ethnicity, nationalism, and even the law, which shaped their integration into California society. One of the most important challenges was a powerful process of racialization and the ensuing discrimination by Anglo-Americans. In the years that followed their arrival in San Francisco, Chileans were "darkened" and marginalized in the cities and mining towns where they settled. However, Chileans were not passive but active actors in this process: They negotiated and resisted their racialization as "nonwhite" people. Moreover, they established alliances with other immigrant communities, especially from Latin America. Chileans and Mexicans, for example, gathered together during and after the Gold Rush years, thus establishing alliances of protection and ethnic solidarity because of the discrimination they constantly faced. This eventually led to the creation of an early Hispanic panethnic identity in California, which crystallized in the 1860s.

REFERENCES

Ayers, James J. 1922. *Gold and Sunshine: Reminiscences of Early California*. Boston: Gorham Press.

Bancroft, Hubert. 1887. *Popular Tribunals*. San Francisco: The History Company.

————. 1888. *California Inter Pocula*. San Francisco: The History Company.

Barros Arana, Diego. 1913. *Un decenio de la historia de Chile (1841–1851)*, Vol. 2. Santiago de Chile: Imprenta, Litografía y Encuadernación Barcelona.

Beilharz, Edwin, and Carlos López (eds.). 1976. *We Were 49ers! Chilean Accounts of the California Gold Rush*. Pasadena, CA: Ward Ritchie Press.

Chan, Sucheng. 2000. "A People of Exceptional Character: Ethnic Diversity, Nativism, and Racism in the California Gold Rush." Pp. 44–85 in Kevin Starr and Richard J. Orsi (eds.), *Rooted in Barbarous Soil: People, Culture, and Community in Gold Rush California*. Berkeley: University of California Press.

Cornford, Daniel. 1999. "'We All Live More Like Brutes Than Humans': Labor and Capital in the Gold Rush." Pp. 78–104 in James J. Rawls and Richard J. Orsi (eds.), *A Golden State: Mining and Economic Development in Gold Rush California*. Berkeley: University of California Press.

Ferreyra, María del Carmen, and David S. Reher (eds.). 2000. *The Gold Rush Diary of Ramón Gil Navarro*. Lincoln: University of Nebraska Press.

Hovey, John. 1849–1851. "Journal of a Voyage from Newburyport, Mass to San Francisco, California." Unpublished manuscript, Huntington Library, San Marino, CA.

Hunt, Elmer M. 1949. *The Gold Rush Diary of Moses Pearson Cogswell of New Hampshire*. Concord: New Hampshire Historical Society.

Johnson, David A. 1981. "Vigilance and the Law: The Moral Authority of Popular Justice in the Far West." *American Quarterly* 33:558–586.

Johnson, Susan L. 2000. *Roaring Camp: The Social World of the California Gold Rush*. New York and London: W. W. Norton.

McKanna, Clare V. 2002. *Race and Homicide in Nineteenth-Century California*. Reno and Las Vegas: University of Nevada Press.

Moore, Shirley. 2003. "'We Feel the Want of Protection': The Politics of Law and Race in California, 1848–1878." *California History* 81:91–108.

Oehler, Helen Irving. 1950. "From Letters in the Winslow Collection." *California Historical Society Quarterly* 25:167–172.

Paul, Rodman W. [1947] 1965. *California Gold: The Beginning of Mining in the Far West*. Lincoln and London: University of Nebraska Press.

Pitti, Stephen. 2003. *The Devil in Silicon Valley: Northern California, Race, and Mexican Americans*. Princeton and Oxford: Princeton University Press.

Purcell, Fernando. 2004. *"Too Many Foreigners for My Taste": Mexicans, Chileans, and Irish in Northern California, 1848–1880*. Ph.D. dissertation, University of California, Davis.

Reséndez, Andrés. 2005. *Changing National Identities at the Frontier: Texas and New Mexico, 1800–1850*. Cambridge, UK: Cambridge University Press.

Soulé, Stephen, John Gihon, and James Nisbet. 1855. *The Annals of San Francisco*. New York, San Francisco, and London: D. Appleton.

Vicuña Mackenna, Benjamín. 1856. *Pájinas de mi diario durante tres años de viajes 1853–1854–1855*. Santiago de Chile: Imprenta del Ferrocarril.

Waldrep, Christopher, ed. 2006. *Lynching in America: A History in Documents*. New York: New York University Press.

CHAPTER 4

Repression and Resistance

The Lynching of Persons of Mexican Origin in the United States, 1848–1928

William D. Carrigan and Clive Webb

On November 16, 1928, four masked men tore into a hospital in Farmington, New Mexico, and abducted one of the patients as he lay dying in bed.[1] The kidnappers drove to an abandoned farmhouse on the outskirts of the city where they tied a rope around the neck of their captive and hanged him from a locust tree (*La Prensa* [San Antonio], November 17, 1928, p. 1; *Farmington Times Hustler*, November 16, 1928, p. 1). (For a full account of the lynching, see Carrigan and Webb, 2005.)

The dead man, Rafael Benavides, had been admitted to the hospital with a serious gun wound less than twenty-four hours earlier. His wound was inflicted by a sheriff's posse pursuing him after he assaulted a farmer's wife. According to one newspaper, "the fiendishness and brutality of his acts were such that the postal laws will not permit us to print them" (*Farmington Times Hustler*, November 23, 1928, p. 1). The abduction and execution of Benavides therefore elicited the approval of many local citizens relieved at the removal from their community of this dangerous menace. In the frank opinion of one newspaper editorial, "the degenerate Mexican got exactly what was coming to him" (*Durango Herald Democrat* [Colorado], quoted in *Farmington Times Hustler*, November 28, 1928, p. 9). Others were nonetheless more circumspect in their assessment of the lynching. While they did not dispute the guilt of the dead man, they contended that his due punishment could be determined only by a court of law. The *Santa Fe New Mexican* responded to the precipitous action of the mob by stating that it would "take San Juan County a long time to live down the bad name received by this lawless act" (quoted in *Farmington Times Hustler,* November 28, 1928, p. 9). Such an opinion reflected a new racial sensibility among many Anglos in the Southwest. For decades, lynch mobs terrorized persons of Mexican origin or descent[2] without reprisal from the wider community. The more critical attitude taken by the Anglo establishment created a political climate less tolerant of extralegal violence. Although acts of lawlessness continued, Rafael Benavides became the last Mexican in the United States to be lynched in such blatant defiance of the judicial system.

Although widely recognized in the Mexican community on both sides of the border, and among some scholars, the story of mob violence against Mexicans remains relatively unknown to the wider public. Two recent popular works on lynching—*Without Sanctuary* by James Allen and his colleagues (2000) and *At the Hands of Persons Unknown* by Philip Dray (2002)—reveal the extent to which the historical narrative of racial violence in the United States excludes Mexicans. In January 2000, the photographs that would later be published in Allen's *Without Sanctuary* went on display at the Roth Horowitz Gallery in New York City. This widely acclaimed exhibit, which was later shown at the New York Historical Society and the Martin Luther King, Jr. National Historic Site, contained fifty-four separate images and several artifacts relating to lynching. Forty-five of the images depicted the corpses of African American lynching victims. Seven other photographs showed Anglo fatalities. Images and artifacts relating to the mob murder of Sicilian, Jewish, and Chinese immigrants were also included. Yet neither the exhibition nor the accompanying book contained any reference to Mexicans. Although photographic evidence of numerous Mexican lynching victims exists, its omission from these venues created a false impression that Mexicans had not been the targets of organized racial violence.

Similar criticisms can be made of Dray's work. In 2002, Dray published the first national overview of lynching in the United States in more than a half-century. His book, *At the Hands of Persons Unknown,* was a bestseller and winner of a major literary award, the 2002 Southern Book Award for Non-Fiction. Dray rightfully focuses upon the thousands of African Americans who perished at the hands of Anglo mobs in the southern United States. Although the book contains some discussion of other racial and ethnic groups, not once in more than 500 pages does it mention Mexicans.

This chapter seeks to expand upon the existing work in the fields of lynching studies and Mexican American history by providing the first systematic analysis of Mexican lynching victims. Our conclusions are based on extensive archival research that adds substantially to the number of previously documented cases of anti-Mexican mob violence. For instance, the files at Tuskegee Institute contain the most comprehensive count of lynching victims in the United States, but they refer only to the lynching of 50 Mexicans in Arizona, California, New Mexico, and Texas. Our own research has revealed a total of 216 victims during the same time period.

This massive undercount is not the only problem. It is difficult to find even the 50 cases included in Tuskegee's records. In every publication and data summary of the Tuskegee materials, the lynching victims are divided into only two categories, "black" and "white." This neat binary division belies historical reality since the list of "white" victims includes Native Americans, Chinese, and Italians as well as Mexicans. Only through perusal of the original archival records is it possible to determine that 50 of the victims recorded by Tuskegee as "white" were of Mexican descent. Despite the methodological problems with its data, Tuskegee's binary division of blacks and nonblacks has been widely adopted by other groups collating lynching statistics and by scholars who have written about mob violence. The central aim of the present chapter is to broaden the scholarly discourse on lynching by moving beyond the traditional limitations of the black/white paradigm. Placing the experience of Mexicans into the history of lynching expands our understanding of the causes of mob violence and the ways in which individuals and groups sought to resist lynching and vigilantism.

Between 1848 and 1928, mobs lynched at least 597 Mexicans. Historian Christopher Waldrep (2000) has asserted that the definition of "lynching" has altered so much over the course of time as to render impossible the accurate collection of data on mob violence. It is therefore essential to familiarize the reader from the outset with the interpretation of lynching used to compile the statistics in this chapter. The authors regard lynching as a retributive act of murder for which those responsible claim to be serving the interests of justice, tradition, or community good. Although our notion as to what constitutes a lynching is clear, it is still impossible to provide a precise count of the number of Mexican victims. We have excluded a significant number of reported lynchings for which the sources do not allow for verification of specific data such as the date, location, or identity of the victim. The statistics included in this chapter should therefore be considered a conservative estimate of the number of Mexicans lynched in the United States.

Statistics alone can never explain lynching in the United States. More than other Americans, blacks and Mexicans lived with the threat of mob violence throughout the second half of the nineteenth and the first half of the twentieth century. The story of Mexican lynching is not a footnote in history but, rather, a critical chapter in the history of Anglo western expansion and conquest. If the story of lynching is essential to understanding the African American experience, then lynching is equally important to the story of the Mexican American experience.

As Table 4.1 demonstrates, the lynchings occurred most commonly in the four southwestern states where Mexicans were concentrated in largest numbers. Lynching patterns varied significantly across the southwestern states. A comprehensive treatment of the subject would emphasize the distinctive patterns of mob violence that developed in each of the four states. Mob violence in Texas, for example, differed significantly from lynching in California. Lynching varied within state borders too, as is readily apparent when we compare levels of anti-Mexican violence in Northern and Southern California. Yet in spite of the significant differences between states and regions, certain patterns do emerge.

Table 4.1 Lynchings of Mexicans, by State

State	Number of Lynchings
Texas	282
California	188
Arizona	59
New Mexico	49
Colorado	6
Nevada	3
Nebraska	2
Oklahoma	2
Oregon	2
Kentucky	1
Louisiana	1
Montana	1
Wyoming	1

LIMITATIONS OF TRADITIONAL FRONTIER VIOLENCE THEORIES

Historians of the western United States have traditionally portrayed extralegal violence as an essential function of the frontier. According to this interpretation, the economic and demographic development of the frontier rapidly outpaced the growth of legal and governmental institutions. Faced with the absence or impotence of proper legal authorities, frontiersmen were forced to take the law into their own hands. Vigilantism therefore served a legitimate purpose in the settlement of the American West, preserving the fragile order and security of frontier communities, and paving the way for the establishment of a formal legal system (Abrahams, 1998). Historian Richard Maxwell Brown is the best-known exponent of this interpretative model. In his opinion, vigilantism "was a positive facet of the American experience. Many a new frontier community gained order and stability as the result of vigilantism that reconstructed the community pattern and values of the old settled areas, while dealing effectively with crime and disorder" (1975:126).

Frontier conditions undoubtedly fostered the growth of vigilantism in general. Nonetheless, the conventional interpretation of western violence cannot be applied to the lynching of Mexicans. The most serious criticism of the "socially constructive" model of vigilantism espoused by Brown is that it legitimates the actions of lawbreakers. There is an implicit presumption of the vigilantes' civic virtue and of the criminal guilt of their victims. In truth, the popular tribunals that put Mexicans to death can seldom be said to have acted in the spirit of the law. According to Joseph Caughey (1957:222), vigilante committees persisted in their activities "long after the arrival" of the law courts. However, Anglos refused to recognize the legitimacy of these courts when they were controlled or influenced by Mexicans. Determined to redress the balance of racial and political power, they constructed their own parallel mechanisms of justice. This is precisely what occurred in Socorro, New Mexico, during the 1880s, when Anglo vigilance committees arose in opposition to the predominantly Mexican legal authorities (Fergusson, 1991:21–32). These committees showed little respect for the legal rights of Mexicans, executing them in disproportionately large numbers. Their actions therefore amounted to institutionalized discrimination (Pitt, 1966:154–155).

Another crucial factor to consider is that only a small number of Mexican lynching victims—64 out of a total of 597—met their fate at the hands of vigilante committees acting in the absence of a formal judicial system. Most were summarily executed by mobs that denied the accused even the semblance of a trial. These mobs acted less out of a rational interest in law and order than out of an irrational prejudice toward racial minorities. Their members expressed contempt for the due process of law by snatching suspected Mexican criminals from courtrooms or prison cells and then executing them. In June 1874, Jesús Romo was arrested for robbery and attempted murder near Puente Creek in California. Romo was grabbed from the arresting officer by a gang of masked men who tied a rope around his neck and hanged him. Such was the presumption of his guilt in the minds of the mob that it precluded the need for him to stand trial. The *Los Angeles Star* (June 13, 1874, p. 1) commended the decision to dispense with legal formalities, declaring that Romo was "a hardened and blood-stained desperado, who deserved richly the fate which overtook him." In this and other instances, the mob was motivated by unsubstantiated assertion and an impulsive instinct for vengeance. Their actions therefore did not so much uphold the law as oppose its proper implementation. A similar incident occurred in April 1886, when Andrés Martínez and José María Cordena were arrested for horse theft in Collins County, Texas. The two men never saw the inside of a courtroom but were instead seized from the custody of the authorities by ten masked men and shot dead (*New York Times*, April 21, 1877, p. 1).

The spatial distribution of Mexican lynchings also confounds those who suggest that remote locations forced vigilantes to take extralegal action. Although many episodes of anti-Mexican mob violence involved lynch mobs that broke into jails to retrieve their victims, lynch mobs did sometimes operate in isolated mining camps, in out-of-the-way gulches, or on sparsely settled ranchlands. In such cases, the lynch mobs likely sought out these remote locations in order to avoid the negative attention that more public lynchings would have generated. On July 13, 1877, masked men in San Juan, California, seized Justín Arajo, a Mexican arrested for the murder of an Anglo, and took him to a remote roadside, where they hanged him from a willow tree (*New York Times*, July 22, 1877, p. 5).

The lynching of Mexicans not only occurred in areas where there was a fully operating legal system, but often involved the active collusion of law officers themselves. In February 1857, a justice of the peace assembled an unwilling audience of Mexicans outside the San Gabriel mission to watch as he decapitated Miguel Soto and then stabbed repeatedly at the corpse (Monroy, 1990:209–210). The most systematic abuse of legal authority was by the Texas Rangers. Their brutal repression of the Mexican population was tantamount to state-sanctioned terrorism. Although the exact number of those murdered by the Rangers is unknown, historians estimate that it ran into the thousands (Johnson, 2003). In March 1881, Rangers crossed the border into Mexico and illegally arrested

Onofrio Baca on a charge of murder. Baca was returned without extradition orders to the United States, where he soon found himself faced by an angry mob. Baca was "strung up to the cross beams of the gate in the court house yard until he was dead" (*El Paso Times,* April 8, 1881; de Zamacona, 1880–1881). The terrorization of Mexicans continued well into the twentieth century. On October 18, 1915, Mexican raiders derailed a train traveling toward Brownsville, killing several passengers. Some who survived the crash were robbed and murdered by the Mexicans. The Rangers exacted brutal revenge. Two Mexican passengers aboard the train were shot for their supposed assistance of the raid. The Rangers then executed eight suspected Mexican criminals along the banks of the Rio Grande (Pierce, 1917:96, 97, 102, 110, 112, 114; *New York Times,* October 19, 1915, p. 1; *The Independent,* November 1, 1915, p. 177).

The legal system not only failed to protect Mexicans, it served as an instrument of their oppression. Only under pressure from the federal government were local and state authorities willing to investigate acts of mob violence. Even when these investigations were carried out, they inevitably failed to identify those responsible. As a result, almost no white man was ever made to stand trial for the lynching of a Mexican. As the U.S. consul in Matamoros, Thomas Wilson, testified to Congress: "[W]hen an aggression is made upon a Mexican it is not much minded. For instance, when it is known that a Mexican has been hung or killed ... there is seldom any fuss made about it; while, on the contrary, if a white man happens to be despoiled in any way, there is a great fuss made about it by those not of Mexican origin" (U.S. Congress, 1878:285).

RACE AND CONQUEST

The traditional interpretation of western violence will clearly not suffice. It is instead our conviction that racial prejudice was the primary force in fomenting mob violence against Mexicans in the United States. The lynching of Mexicans underlines the centrality of class and race in the colonization of the American West. The bitter racial enmity of the U.S.-Mexican War had an enduring legacy long after the Treaty of Guadalupe Hidalgo established nominal peace in 1848. Well into the twentieth century, the majority white population continued to utilize extralegal violence against Mexicans as a means of asserting its sovereignty over the region. The lynching of Mexicans was one of the mechanisms by which Anglos consolidated their colonial control of the American West. Mob violence contributed to the displacement of the Mexican population from the land, denial of access to natural resources, political disfranchisement, and economic dependency upon an Anglo-controlled capitalist order.

The racial identity of Mexicans was to a considerable degree determined by their class status. The earliest Anglo settlers of the Southwest saw the native ruling elite as a racial group superior to the mass of Mexican laborers. Travelers such as Richard Henry Dana asserted that the ruling classes could trace a direct line of descent from the Spanish colonists of the seventeenth century. Their racial purity elevated them to a position of social superiority over the majority of the Mexican population. As Dana put it, "each person's caste is decided by the quality of the blood, which shows itself, too plainly to be concealed, at first sight" (1981 [1840]:126–127). While most Mexicans were restricted to a status of permanent racial subordination, a small minority were therefore able to secure the social advantages of whiteness. Their position as whites acted as a protective shield against mob violence. Although the elite often suffered assaults against their property, they seldom experienced injury in person. On occasion, Anglos even invited their involvement in vigilance committees (Pitt, 1966:154–155).

In contrast to the elite, lower-class Mexicans were classified by Anglos as a distinct and inferior racial other. Mexican lynching victims were overwhelmingly members of the impoverished laboring class. The majority of Mexicans occupied a liminal position within the racial hierarchy of the southwestern states. Under the auspices of the Treaty of Guadalupe Hidalgo, Mexicans who became naturalized U.S. citizens in theory enjoyed the same legal protections as Anglos. However, the racial antipathy of Anglos undermined the *de jure* status of Mexican Americans. The contemporary discourse on race relations perpetuated the notion that lower-class Mexicans were a hybrid of Anglo, Indian, Spanish, and African blood. Their impure status pushed them to the margins of whiteness, precluding their entitlement to many of its social privileges. A track foreman interviewed in Dimmit County, Texas, made this comment in the late 1920s: "They are an inferior race. I would not think of classing Mexicans as whites" (Taylor, 1980:446).

The racial attitudes of Anglos had disastrous consequences. Mexicans found themselves dispossessed of their land by a combination of force and fraud. The new urban economy of the late nineteenth century afforded them few opportunities, confining them for the most part to poorly paid manual labor. The combined forces of economic discrimination and racial prejudice in turn restricted Mexicans to their own ethnic neighborhoods, or barrios, which became breeding grounds for poverty, disease, and crime. This spatial separation from Anglos compounded what the sociologist Roberta Senechal de la Roche describes as the cultural and relational distance between Mexicans and Anglos. The two peoples spoke a different language and practiced different forms of religious worship (Senechal de la Roche, 1996:106–109; Senechal de la Roche, 1997:52–53, 58–59).

These physical and psychological boundaries between the two "races" resulted in mutual misunderstanding and suspicion. In particular, they helped to perpetuate the racial stereotyping of Mexicans as a cruel and treacherous people with a natural proclivity toward criminal behavior. As one Anglo author observed, "The Spanish Americans are held in sovereign contempt by citizens, and are stigmatized with being filthy, ignorant, lazy and vicious" (Shaw, 1854:17). Such stereotypes instilled the conviction that Mexicans constituted a violent threat to the established social order. This belief in turn provided Anglos with the pretext for acts of repressive violence. In the words of California gold prospector Elias S. Ketcham (1853), "many persons who are prejudiced, say they are all alike, a set of cut throats should be exterminated, or drove out of the country."

The primacy of racial prejudice is underlined by the acts of ritualized torture and sadism that accompanied the lynching of Mexicans. As Table 4.2 shows, 52 of the Mexican lynching victims recorded in our data suffered some act of

Table 4.2 Mob Crimes

Crime	Number of Lynching Victims
Hanging	267
Shooting	213
Physical Mutilation	52
Burning	5
Unknown	60

physical mutilation. The most common forms of maiming were the burning and shooting of bodies after they had been hanged, although there were more extreme examples. In February 1856, the body of a Mexican horse thief was discovered in a ravine near the Californian Mission San Gabriel. The dead man had been shot four times, his body hacked by a knife blade, and his tongue cut out (*Los Angeles Star,* July 19, 1856, p. 2). Vigilantes in Virginia City, Montana, similarly dismembered a suspected Mexican murderer. Joe Pizanthia was hanged and his corpse first shot and then burned (Gard, 1949:179–180). Although Anglos also suffered at the hands of lynch mobs, their executions occurred without elaborate ceremony. By contrast, in turning the lynching of Mexicans into a public spectacle, Anglos sent a powerful warning that they would not tolerate any challenge to their cultural and political hegemony.

Racial prejudice alone cannot account for the lynching of Mexicans. An assessment of the supposed crimes committed by Mexican mob victims indicates the additional importance of gender. As Table 4.3 shows, Anglos lynched only 9 Mexicans for alleged transgressions of sexual norms. Among these victims was Aureliano Castellón, murdered by a mob in Senior, Texas, following an attempted assault on a fifteen-year-old girl (*San Antonio Express,* January 31, 1896, p. 8). This was nonetheless an exceptional incident.

An explanation for this phenomenon is to be found in the gendered construction of Mexican racial identity. The dominant discourse of the nineteenth century drew distinctions between "masculine" and "feminine" races. Mexicans were classified according to the latter category (Okihiro, 2001:64–65). Anglo stereotypes of Mexican males therefore emphasized their supposed lack of traditional masculine virtue. Mexican men were denied the attributes of honor, honesty, and loyalty. Instead, they were defined as unprincipled, conniving, and treacherous. "The men are tall and robust," wrote Theodore T. Johnson (1849:240), "but appear effeminate in their fancy serapas [*sic*] under which they invariably conceal their ready and cowardly knife." The feminization of Mexicans encouraged Anglos to accuse them of such crimes as cheating at cards or cowardly acts of murder. At the same time, it diminished their sexual menace to whites. As the economist Paul Schuster Taylor (1934:274) observed, Mexicans were less commonly seen as carnal predators than were African Americans.

Racism was also intertwined with another determining factor in mob violence against Mexicans: economic competition. Anglos considered Mexicans an innately lazy and unenterprising people who had failed to exploit the rich natural

Table 4.3 Alleged Crimes of Victims

Alleged Crime	Number of Lynching Victims
Murder	301
Theft or Robbery	116
Murder and Robbery	38
Being of Mexican Descent	10
Attempted Murder	9
Cheating at Cards	7
Rape or Sexual Assault	5
Assault	5
Witchcraft	3
Kidnapping	3
Courting a White Woman	2
Taking Away Jobs	2
Rape and Murder	1
Attempted Murder and Robbery	1
Refusing to Join Mob	1
Threatening White Men	1
Being a "Bad Character"	1
Killing a Cow	1
Being a Successful Cartman	1
Miscegenation	1
Refusing to Play the Fiddle	1
Taking White Man to Court	1
Protesting Texas Rangers	1
Serving as Bill Collector	1
Giving Refuge to Bandits	1
Unknown	83

resources of the Southwest. Thus it was the "Manifest Destiny" of the superior Anglo to develop the economic potential of the region. Mexican rivalry for land and precious metals was therefore considered an unacceptable challenge to the proprietary rights of Anglo pioneers. Anglos used racial arguments to justify their illegal expropriation of Mexican assets.

The most striking illustration of this justification is the California Gold Rush. As many as 25,000 Mexicans migrated to the mining regions of California between 1848 and 1852. The Mexicans not only arrived in the mines earlier than many Anglo prospectors but brought with them superior expertise and skills. Their rapid prosperity aroused the bitter animosity of those Anglos who believed in their own natural sovereignty over the mines. As the *Alta California* (August 9, 1850, p. 2) observed, Anglos reacted to "the superior and uniform success" of their ethnic rivals "with the feeling which has for some time existed against the Mexican miners, one of envy and jealousy." The introduction of a Foreign Miners' Tax in April 1850 fuelled ethnic violence inasmuch as it sanctioned the expulsion of prospectors who could or would not pay (Chan, 2000:64–65). At least 163 Mexicans were lynched in California between 1848 and 1860. Count-less others were driven from the mines in fear of their safety. According to a meeting organized by miners at Rodgers' Bar in August 1850, "Many persons of Spanish origin, against whom there had not been a word of complaint, have been murdered by these ruffians. Others have been robbed of their horses, mules, arms, and even money, by these persons, while acting as they pretended under the authority of the law" (*Alta California,* August 19, 1850, p. 2).

Mob violence became a common method of Anglo settlers as they sought to secure their control over the incipient capitalist economy of the southwestern states. The Texas Cart War of 1857 is a potent example. During the 1850s, Tejano businessmen developed a freight-hauling service between Indianola and San Antonio. Anglos resentfully turned upon the Mexican rivals, whose lower prices had beaten them out of business. According to a report by the Mexican Embassy in Washington, posses of armed men "have been organized for the exclusive purpose of hunting down Mexicans on the highway, spoiling them of their property and putting them to death" (Garrison, 1973:274; Mexican Lega-tion in the United States, 1821–1906; Rippy, 1931:179–180).

One further factor accounts for the phenomenon of mob violence: diplo-matic hostilities between the United States and Mexico. Although the Treaty of Guadalupe Hidalgo secured formal peace between the two countries, tensions persisted as a result of the turbulence along their mutual border. As Table 4.4 shows, the most serious outbreaks of anti-Mexican mob violence occurred during the 1850s, the 1870s, and the 1910s, decades characterized by intense ethnic strife in the borderlands. Diplomatic relations between the two nations deteriorated as each blamed the other for the troubles. As diplomatic tensions increased, so the violence in the borderlands became even more intense. Thus was created a downward spiral of recrimination and violence.

MEXICAN RESISTANCE TO MOB VIOLENCE

Mexicans implemented numerous strategies of resistance that challenged the legitimacy of mob law in the southwestern states. The discussion of this resistance

Table 4.4 Lynchings of Mexicans, by Decade

Decade	Number of Lynchings
1848–1850	8
1851–1860	160
1861–1870	43
1871–1880	147
1881–1890	73
1891–1900	24
1901–1910	8
1911–1920	124
1921–1930	10

that follows is necessarily episodic, highlighting particular individuals and events. Resistance, especially armed self-defense by individuals and localized groups, was near constant throughout the period. Protest by regional civil rights organizations and by the Mexican government occurred less regularly, though with increasing frequency in the twentieth century. We do not pretend to be comprehensive here but, rather, seek to outline the most common forms of resistance employed by Mexicans in the United States and to suggest something of the efficacy of these acts of protest.

It was inevitable that, without recourse to local or state authorities, Mexicans themselves would assume responsibility for avenging the victims of mob violence. Frustration at the indifference and delay that dogged official investigations fuelled the thirst for vigilante justice. Most acts of armed resistance were localized and ephemeral. Once the perpetrators had accomplished their purpose to correct an abuse of justice, their forces dispersed and the social order was restored. Yet occasionally the cumulative impact of white violence stirred such bitter resentment as to incite a coordinated counteroffensive. The conflict between Mexican "outlaws" and Anglo authorities, in particular, assumed the characteristics of a race war. While his actual historical identity is still contested by scholars, the most infamous of these "outlaws" was undoubtedly Joaquín Murieta. According to legend, Murieta was one of the thousands of Mexicans driven from the gold mines of California. Although he attempted to establish an honest trade around the camps as a merchant, he was accused of horse theft and severely whipped. His half-brother was hanged for the same offense. Twice a victim of white brutality, Murieta turned to violence until his death several years later (Coblentz, 1936:27; see also Shippey, 1948:136–140). Other resistance leaders included Tiburcio Vásquez and Juan Cortina, who between 1859 and 1873 engaged in a series of bitter and bloody confrontations with the U.S. military.

Scholars commonly describe these Mexican "outlaws" as "social bandits" (an influential concept coined by Eric Hobsbawm [1969]). Their criminal behavior was specifically conditioned by the racially oppressive climate of the Southwest. Dispossessed of their economic resources and their political rights, the "outlaws" launched a direct retaliatory assault upon the Anglo populace. Anglos refused to distinguish between general lawlessness and legitimate acts of resistance, indiscriminately labeling any challenge to their legal and political power as "banditry." Although some "bandits" did engage in indiscriminate acts of lawlessness, others explicitly assumed the mantle of political revolutionaries. Juan Cortina proclaimed that he was an instrument of divine retribution, sent to avenge those Mexicans murdered and dispossessed by whites. As he once observed: "There are to be found criminals covered with frightful crimes, but they appear to have impunity until opportunity furnishes them a victim; to these monsters indulgence is shown, because they are not of our race, which is unworthy, as they say, to belong to the human species" (McLemore, 1983:219–221; Thompson, 1991:88, 92; Thompson, 1994:6; Webb, 1965:176).

Although Mexican "outlaws" were brutally repressed by Anglos, their actions served an important psychological purpose. As Manuel Gonzáles observes (1999:89), they provided the Mexican population with a potent symbol of resistance against their oppression. The mere existence of men such as Tiburcio Vásquez and Juan Cortina constituted a direct challenge to the legitimacy of white mob rule. In the words of one Anglo, Cortina "was received as the champion of his race—as the man who would right the wrongs the Mexicans had received" (Ward, 1996:180). Though perceived as ruthless and unrepentant criminals by Anglos, the "bandits" were therefore hailed by Mexicans as folk heroes. Their lives became immortalized through the *corridos* sung on the southwestern border. These tales of heroism enabled a disempowered Mexican population to strike back at least rhetorically against those who sought to crush ethnic dissent. The spirit of cultural resistance implicit in the *corridos* is reflected in a first-person narrative about the life and legend of Joaquín Murieta:

> Now I go out onto roads
> To kill Americans
> You were the cause
> Of my brother's death
> You took him defenseless
> You disgraceful American. (Rosales, 1996:7)[3]

Armed resistance was not the only means by which Mexicans sought to counter Anglo aggression. Spanish-language newspapers such as *El Clamor Público* and *El Fronterizo* published numerous anti-lynching editorials that articulated the anger and frustration of their readers. The mainstream English-language press continued to accept the actions of lynch mobs largely without question. Mexican American newspapers thus provided an important counternarrative to the conventional discourse on ethnic violence (Sheridan, 1986:107).

It was not until the early twentieth century, however, that Mexicans organized in formal defense of their civil rights. One incident in particular appears to have provided the catalyst. In 1911, Antonio Gómez, a fourteen-year-old boy, was arrested for murder in Thorndale, Texas. Gómez was seized by a mob of over 100 people who hanged him and then dragged his corpse through the streets of the town. Mexicans acknowledged the need for urgent collective action through the establishment of new civil rights organizations. In June 1911, Mexican activists established a new organization, La Agrupación, in an effort to provide legal protection against Anglo aggressors. Three months later, in September 1911, 400 representatives assembled at El Primer Congreso Mexicanista in Laredo, Texas. The delegates denounced the brutal oppression of their people that had continued unchecked since the signing of the Treaty of Guadalupe Hidalgo. Out of these discussions came an agreement to establish a new civil rights organization with the express purpose of protecting its members against white injustice. La Gran Liga Mexicanista de Beneficencia y Protección intended to attract the support of wealthy philanthropists and the liberal press in order "to strike back at the hatred of some bad sons of Uncle Sam who believe themselves better than the Mexicans because of the magic that surrounds the word *white*" (De León, 1993:88; Limón, 1974:86–88, 97–98; *New York Times*, June 26, 1911, p. 4; Rosenbaum, 1998:49–50; Weber, 1973:248–250; Zamora, 1995 [1993]:81, 97,

149). Another civil rights organization, La Liga Protectora Latina, was founded in Phoenix, Arizona, in February 1915 (Rosales, 2000:114–115).

How successful these incipient civil rights groups were in their struggle to end lynching is difficult to assess. Mexicans were able to coordinate their resistance against lynching through the creation of a permanent organizational opposition. Yet the defense agencies also operated in a politically repressive environment that seriously impeded the momentum of their anti-lynching campaigns. In 1929, Mexicans founded another defense agency, the League of United Latin American Citizens (LULAC). The observations of one LULAC organizer underline the difficulties of mobilizing Mexican Americans, especially in small towns and remote rural areas. Like many of his colleagues, the organizer was confronted with a paradoxical problem. The only way to prevent further lynchings was for Mexicans to rally in protest. Yet it was the very fear of mob violence that frightened them into silence. "The Mexican people were afraid of coming into town for a meeting," observed the organizer, "because they thought they were going to be shot at or lynched if we had our meeting at the courthouse. The courthouse to them was just a medium or a means of being punished. Most of the time, even when they were innocent of what they were being accused of, somebody would just find a goat for something, and the goat would be a Mexican" (Simmons, 1974:465; see also Márquez, 1993).

More than any other form of resistance, it was ultimately the diplomatic protests of the Mexican government that proved decisive in the decline of mob violence. The Mexican government made repeated protests as early as the 1850s against the "unjustly depressed and miserable condition" of its citizens (Ceballos-Ramírez and Martínez, 1997:136; U.S. Congress, 1865–1866:208–210; U.S. Department of State, 1863, II:114–141). Diplomatic appeals became louder and more persistent with the election of Porfirio Díaz to the Mexican presidency in 1877. By the time Díaz assumed office, relations between the United States and Mexico had been stretched almost to the breaking point as each nation blamed the other for the lawlessness along their mutual border. Díaz was determined to reduce the deepening diplomatic tensions between the two nations in order to facilitate trade links. To this end, he instructed the appropriate consuls to compile reports on the condition of Mexican nationals along the Texas border. The reports documented numerous acts of brutality and abuses of justice. Yet despite the hopes of the Díaz administration, this initiative did not instigate a new era of mutual cooperation with the United States. The authorities in Washington declined to involve themselves even indirectly in the internal affairs of Texas (García, 1995:1–3; Richmond, 1982:277–278).

During the next two decades, Mexican officials continued to draw the U.S. Department of State's attention to the suffering of their citizens. But their outrage was ignored. In 1881, the Mexican ambassador reported to Secretary of State James Blaine about the lynching of an alleged horse thief in Willcox, Arizona. While conceding that the man was hanged illegally, Blaine commented that he and his accomplice "were probably outlaws" and that he therefore deserved his fate. This conclusion was based entirely on the testimony of local sheriff R. H. Paul. According to Paul, "The southeastern portion of the Territory has been under the control of the worst and most desperate class of outlaws" and "an example was needed in order to put an end to so deplorable a state of affairs" (de Zamacona, 1880–1881:840–844; García, 1995:5–8). The uncritical acceptance of this testimony was typical of the investigations conducted by the U.S. Department of State. Rather than send its own representatives to the scene of a lynching, it relied entirely upon reports written by local officials who condoned the actions of the mob—if indeed they were not actual members of it.

It was not until the 1890s that the protests of Mexican officials finally started to receive a positive response from the U.S. Department of State. On August 26, 1895, a mob stormed the jailhouse at Yreka, California, and seized four men awaiting trial on separate murder charges. The prisoners were hauled into the courthouse square and hanged from an iron rail fastened into the forks of two trees. One of the victims, Luis Moreno, was a Mexican (*Los Angeles Times,* August 27, 1895, p. 1; *New York Times,* August 27, 1895, p. 1; *San Francisco Examiner,* August 27, 1895, p. 1; *San Francisco Examiner,* August 28, 1895, p. 3; *San Francisco Examiner,* November 29, 1895, p. 8). The Mexican government demanded that those responsible be punished and that a suitable indemnity be paid to the heirs of Moreno. Although a grand jury failed to return any indictments against members of the mob, President William McKinley did recommend to Congress the payment of a $2,000 indemnity (*New York Times,* January 19, 1898, p. 1; U.S. Congress, n.d.:1–3). The Moreno case established a precedent for the later lynchings of Mexican nationals in the United States (note, for example, the indemnity paid to the family of a Mexican lynched in Cotulla, Texas, in October 1895 [U.S. Congress, n.d.]).

After the repeated failure of the federal government to respond to Mexican protests, what provoked this change of policy? By the late nineteenth century the United States was receiving criticism from governments throughout the world for its inability to protect foreign nationals on its soil. Although it continued to insist that it had no authority to intervene in the affairs of individual states, the federal government did endeavor to resolve any incipient diplomatic crises by providing financial compensation to the families of lynching victims. This occurred after the massacre of Chinese miners at Rock Springs, Wyoming, in 1888 and again following three separate attacks on Sicilian immigrants in Louisiana during the 1890s. Accordingly, the indemnities paid to the families of Mexican lynching victims should be seen in the context of efforts by the federal government to safeguard the international reputation of the United States. (On the continued complaints made by Mexican officials during the twentieth century, see Rippy, 1928:29.)

The diplomatic protests of the Díaz administration must also be seen as a response to growing grassroots pressure from the Mexican people. By the early twentieth century, the regime faced rising criticism for allowing the massive investment of U.S. capital to undermine Mexican economic autonomy (Garner, 2001:141). The Díaz administration therefore protested American mob violence as a means of demonstrating its protection of Mexican national interests. A case in point is the lynching of Antonio Rodríguez in Rock Springs, Texas. On November 3, 1910, a mob broke into the local jail where Rodríguez was awaiting trial for murder, smothered his body with oil, and burned him at the stake. According to local residents, "the action of the mob was justified as the lives of the ranchers' wives had been unsafe because of the attempted ravages of Mexican settlers along the Rio Grande." Newspaper reports, however, revealed no evidence connecting Rodríguez with the crime (*The Independent,* November 17, 1910, pp. 1061–1062; *New York Times,* November 11, 1910, p. 2; Rice, 1990:26–30).

The lynching provoked a storm of protest throughout Mexico. Rioting erupted in Mexico City on November 8 as angry demonstrators stoned the windows of American businesses and tore and spat at the U.S. flag. Three days later, rioters in Guadalajara wreaked similar damage against American property. In Chihuahua, U.S. citizens were openly mobbed in the streets. Tensions along the Rio Grande were so strained that an estimated 2,000 Texans armed themselves in advance of a suspected Mexican invasion. Although the Díaz administration denounced the violence, it reacted to popular pressure by imposing an economic boycott of U.S. imports (*The Independent,* November 17, 1910, pp. 1061–1062; *The Independent,* November 24, 1910, pp. 1120–1121; *New York Times,* November 10, 1910, p. 1; *New York Times,* November 11, 1910, p. 1; *New York Times,* November 12, 1910, p. 5; *New York Times,* November 13, 1910, pt. 3, p. 4; *New York Times,* November 15, 1910, p. 10; Rice, 1990:31–39, 49–51, 79; U.S. Department of State, 1918:355–357).

Whether or not the Díaz administration had ulterior motives in protesting the lynching of Antonio Rodríguez, diplomatic pressure prevailed. It was now increasingly evident to the United States that Mexico would not tolerate the continued abuse of its citizens. As *The Independent* asserted, the people of Mexico had risen "in righteous wrath" against Anglo oppression. Diplomatic tensions would deteriorate still further unless the federal government took decisive action to protect the rights of Mexican nationals (*The Independent,* November 17, 1910, pp. 1111–1112; *New York Times,* September 2, 1919, p. 1; *New York Times,* January 10, 1920, p. 3; *New York Times,* August 4, 1921, p. 10).

The persistence of international protests undoubtedly played a key role in the eventual decline of Mexican lynchings. At the same time, several other forces conspired to facilitate change, not only in Washington but throughout the Southwest. The end of the Mexican Revolution induced a new period of stability in the turbulent southwestern borderlands. It should also be stressed that lynching in all its forms was in decline by the 1920s. The regional campaigns of the Commission on Interracial Cooperation and the Association of Southern Women for the Prevention of Lynching worked in conjunction with the national lobbying of the National Association for the Advancement of Colored People to mobilize liberal opposition to mob violence. Although the protests of these civil rights organizations had little immediate impact upon the Southwest, their efforts served to delegitimize lynching throughout the United States (Brundage, 1993:248–249, 251).

Acts of racial violence against Mexicans continued sporadically throughout the 1920s. Yet where earlier administrations had signally failed to secure justice for the families of Mexican lynch victims, the federal government now took tough interventionist action. Perhaps the most telling example of the impact of Mexican protest is the case of four Mexicans lynched in Raymondville, Texas, in September

1926. Initial reports of the lynchings were wildly contradictory. According to Sheriff Raymond Teller, the Mexicans had been arrested for the murder of two of his officers. Teller was taking the suspects from jail out into the countryside in search of their cache of arms when he was ambushed. The prisoners were killed in the resultant gunfight. Yet according to other testimony, Teller and his officers had themselves tortured and then shot the Mexicans. For decades the Department of State had, in its investigations of Mexican lynchings, invariably taken the reports of local law officers at face value. These reports repeatedly failed to identify those responsible for the lynchings, instead concluding vaguely that the victims had met their deaths at the hands of persons unknown. This case demonstrated a new determination to avoid diplomatic tensions with Mexico over the lynching of its citizens on American soil. Not only did the Department of State reject the conclusions of the sheriff's report, but Teller and his fellow officers were tried for murder (*Atlanta Constitution,* October 24, 1926; *Atlanta Constitution,* January 8, 1927, p. 1; *Montgomery Advisor,* September 19, 1926, p. 1).

CONCLUSION

In 1916, a Wisconsin newspaper observed: "That there are still lynchings in the far west, especially along the Mexican border, would hardly seem to be open to question, although they escape the average collector of statistics. The subject is one that invites searching inquiry" (*La Crosse Tribune,* January 12, 1916, p. 1). During the course of more than eight decades, the lynching of Mexicans continued to elude systematic analysis. While the literature on mob violence against African Americans continued to expand in scope and sophistication, there was relatively little scholarly interest in Mexican lynchings. As a result, the explanatory models for mob violence constructed by scholars were restricted in their narrow racial and regional emphases on African Americans in the South. Investigation of the lynching of Mexicans emphasizes the need to expand the analytical parameters of lynching studies.

Scholars need not only to compare mob violence against African Americans and Mexicans, as a means of learning more about each as a discrete phenomenon, but also to probe the connections between them. In particular, it is important to recognize that many Anglo settlers in the American West, especially Texas, migrated from the South (White, 1991). These settlers brought with them a culture of violent racism that they used to impose their sovereignty over the other peoples of the region. In short, there are important, if underappreciated, connections between the history of Mexicans and the history of African Americans, and these connections await further scholarly investigation.

NOTES

1. An earlier version of this chapter appeared under the title "The Lynching of Persons of Mexican Origin or Descent in the United States, 1848 to 1928" in *The Journal of Social*

84 *William D. Carrigan and Clive Webb*

History 37, 2 (2003):411–438. The authors would like to thank the copyright holders for permission to republish portions of that article.

2. Some of the lynching victims described in this chapter were naturalized American citizens, while others were Mexican nationals resident in the United States. Despite the best efforts of the authors, it has not always proved possible to determine the citizenship of each individual. The authors have used the word "Mexican" to refer to all lynching victims of Mexican origin or descent.

3. For further analysis of the *corrido* as an expression of cultural resistance, see Paredes (1958).

REFERENCES

Abrahams, Ray. 1998. *Vigilant Citizens: Vigilantism and the State.* Cambridge, UK: Polity Press.

Allen, James, Jon Lewis, Leon F. Litwack, and Hilton Als. 2000. *Without Sanctuary: Lynching Photography in America.* Santa Fe, NM: Twin Palms.

Brown, Richard Maxwell. 1975. *Strain of Violence: Historical Studies of American Violence and Vigilantism.* New York: Oxford University Press.

Brundage, William Fitzhugh. 1993. *Lynching in the New South: Georgia and Virginia, 1880–1930.* Urbana: University of Illinois Press.

Carrigan, William D., and Clive Webb. 2005. "'A Dangerous Experiment': The Lynching of Rafael Benavides." *New Mexico Historical Review* 80(3):265–292.

Caughey, John W. 1957. "Their Majesties the Mob: Vigilantes Past and Present." *Pacific Historical Review* 26:217–234.

Ceballos-Ramírez, Manuel, and Oscar J. Martínez. 1997. "Conflict and Accommodation on the U.S.-Mexican Border, 1848–1911." Pp. 135–158 in Jaime O. Rodríguez and Kathryn Vincent (eds.), *Myths, Misdeeds, and Misunderstandings: The Roots of Conflict in U.S.-Mexican Relations.* Wilmington, DE: Scholarly Resources.

Chan, Sucheng. 2000. "A People of Exceptional Character: Ethnic Diversity, Nativism, and Racism in the California Gold Rush." Pp. 44–85 in Kevin Starr and Richard J. Orsi (eds.), *Rooted in Barbarous Soil: People, Culture, and Community in Gold Rush California.* Berkeley, Los Angeles, and London: University of California Press.

Coblentz, Stanton A. 1936. *Villains and Vigilantes: The Story of James King of William and Pioneer Justice in California.* New York: Wilson-Erickson.

Dana, Richard Henry, Jr. [1840] 1981. *Two Years Before the Mast: A Personal Narrative of Life at Sea.* Harmondsworth, UK: Penguin.

De León, Arnoldo. 1993. *Mexican Americans in Texas: A Brief History.* Arlington Heights, IL: Harlan Davidson.

de Zamacona, Manuel. 1880–1881. "Notes to James G. Blaine." October 30, 1880–April 19, 1881. Rolls 18–19, Notes from the Mexican Legation in the United States to the Department of State, 1821–1906. Washington, DC: National Archives.

Dray, Philip. 2002. *At the Hands of Persons Unknown: The Lynching of Black America.* New York: Random House.

Fergusson, Erna. 1991. *Murder and Mystery in New Mexico.* Santa Fe, NM: Lightning Tree Press.

García, Mario T. 1995. "Porfirian Diplomacy and the Administration of Justice, 1877–1900." *Aztlán* 16(1–2):1–25.

Gard, Wayne. 1949. *Frontier Justice.* Norman: University of Oklahoma Press.

Garner, Paul. 2001. *Porfirio Díaz.* Harlow, UK: Longman.

Garrison, George P. 1973. *Texas: A Contest of Civilizations.* Boston: Houghton Mifflin.

Gonzáles, Manuel G. 1999. *Mexicanos: A History of Mexicans in the United States.* Bloomington and Indianapolis: Indiana University Press.

Hobsbawm, Eric J. 1969. *Bandits.* London: Weidenfeld and Nicolson.

Johnson, Benjamin Heber. 2003. *Revolution in Texas: How a Forgotten Rebellion and Its Bloody Suppression Turned Mexicans into Americans.* New Haven: Yale University Press.

Johnson, Theodore T. 1849. *Sights in the Gold Region and Scenes by the Way.* New York: Baker and Scribner.

Ketcham, Elias S. 1853. "Diary." January 24. Huntington Library, San Marino, CA.

Limón, José. 1974. "El Primer Congreso Mexicanista de 1911: A Precursor to Contemporary Chicanismo." *Aztlán* 5(1–2):85–117.

Márquez, Benjamin. 1993. *LULAC: The Evolution of a Mexican American Political Organization.* Austin: University of Texas Press.

McLemore, S. Dale. 1983. *Racial and Ethnic Relations in America,* 2nd ed. Newton, MA: Allyn and Bacon.

Mexican Legation in the United States. 1821–1906. "Notes from the Mexican Legation in the United States to the Department of State." Microfilm 54, Reel 4. Washington, DC: National Archives.

Monroy, Douglas. 1990. *Thrown Among Strangers: The Making of Mexican Culture in Frontier California.* Berkeley: University of California Press.

Okihiro, Gary. 2001. *Common Ground: Reimagining American History.* Princeton: Princeton University Press.

Paredes, Américo. 1958. *With His Pistol in His Hand: A Border Ballad and Its Hero.* Austin: University of Texas Press.

Pierce, Franklin C. 1917. *A Brief History of the Lower Rio Grande Valley.* Menasha, WI: George Banta Publishing Company.

Pitt, Leonard. 1966. *The Decline of the Californios: A Social History of the Spanish-Speaking Californians, 1846–1890.* Berkeley and Los Angeles: University of California Press.

Rice, Harvey F. 1990. "The Lynching of Antonio Rodríguez." M.A. thesis, University of Texas, Austin.

Richmond, Douglas W. 1982. "Mexican Immigration and Border Strategy During the Revolution, 1910–1920." *New Mexico Historical Review* 57:269–288.

Rippy, J. Fred. 1928. "The United States and Mexico, 1910–1927." Pp. 3–103 in *American Policies Abroad: Mexico.* Chicago: University of Chicago Press.

———. 1931. *The United States and Mexico.* New York: Knopf.

Rosales, F. Arturo. 1996. *Chicano! The History of the Mexican American Civil Rights Movement.* Houston: Arte Público Press.

Rosales, F. Arturo (ed.). 2000. *Testimonio: A Documentary History of the Mexican American Struggle for Civil Rights.* Houston: Arte Público Press.

Rosenbaum, Robert J. 1998. *Mexicano Resistance in the Southwest.* Dallas: Southern Methodist University Press.

Senechal de la Roche, Roberta. 1996. "Collective Violence as Social Control." *Sociological Forum* 11(1):97–128.

———. 1997. "The Sociogenesis of Lynching." Pp. 48–76 in W. Fitzhugh Brundage (ed.), *Under Sentence of Death: Lynching in the South.* Chapel Hill and London: University of North Carolina Press.

Shaw, Pringle. 1854. *Ramblings in California.* Toronto: James Bain.

Sheridan, Thomas E. 1986. *Los Tucsonenses: The Mexican Community in Tucson, 1854–1941.* Tucson: University of Arizona Press.

Simmons, Ozzie G. 1974. *Anglo-Americans and Mexican Americans in South Texas: A Study in Dominant-Subordinate Group Relations.* New York: Arno Press.

Shippey, Lee. 1948. *It's an Old California Custom.* New York: Vanguard Press.

Taylor, Paul S. 1934. *An American-Mexican Frontier: Nueces County, Texas.* Chapel Hill: University of North Carolina Press.

———. 1980. *Mexican Labor in the United States: Dimmit County, Winter Garden District, South Texas.* Berkeley: University of California Press.

Thompson, Jerry D. 1991. "The Many Faces of Juan Nepomuceno Cortina." *South Texas Studies* 3:85–95.

Thompson, Jerry D. (ed.). 1994. *Juan Cortina and the Texas-Mexico Frontier, 1859–1877.* El Paso, TX: Texas Western Press.

U.S. Congress. 1865–1866. "The Condition of Affairs in Mexico." *House Executive Documents* 73, 39th Congress, 1st Session (1262), II.

———. 1878. "The Texas Border Troubles." *House Reports,* Misc. Doc. No. 64, 45th Congress, 2nd Session (1820).

———. N.d. "Indemnity to Relatives of Luis Moreno." House of Representatives, Document 237, 55th Congress, 2nd Session (3679), Vol. 51.

———. N.d. *Senate Report* 1832, 56th Congress, 2nd Session (4064).

U.S. Department of State. 1863–1918. *Papers Relating to the Foreign Relations of the United States.* Washington, DC: U.S. Government Printing Office.

Waldrep, Christopher. 2000. "War of Words: The Controversy over the Definition of Lynching, 1899–1940." *Journal of Southern History* 64:75–100.

Ward, Geoffrey C. 1996. *The West: An Illustrated History.* Boston: Little, Brown.

Webb, Walter Prescott. 1965. *The Texas Rangers.* Austin: University of Texas Press.

Weber, David J. (ed.). 1973. *Foreigners in Their Native Land: Historical Roots of the Mexican Americans.* Albuquerque: University of New Mexico Press.

White, Richard. 1991. *"It's Your Misfortune and None of My Own": A New History of the American West.* Norman and London: University of Oklahoma Press.

Zamora, Emilio. [1993] 1995. *The World of the Mexican Worker in Texas.* College Station: Texas A&M University Press.

CHAPTER 5

Opposite One-Drop Rules

Mexican Americans, African Americans, and the Need to Reconceive Turn-of-the-Twentieth-Century Race Relations

Laura E. Gómez

Despite the recognition that the United States today is a multiracial society, scholars and laypeople alike continue to view U.S. history as pivoting around race conceived in binary terms, as almost exclusively about white-over-black subordination. This is the case even though Mexican Americans have been part of U.S. society since 1845, when Texas became a state, and in very significant numbers since 1848, when a peace treaty ending the U.S.-Mexico War gave U.S. citizenship to more than 100,000 Mexicans. The belief that race is historically a matter of white/black relations has been exacerbated by the persistent tendency to see Mexican Americans as an ethnic, rather than a racial, group.[1]

Both racial and ethnic boundaries are sociologically significant, but, by invoking race rather than ethnicity to describe the Mexican American experience, I echo sociologists who have identified race as "the most powerful and persistent group boundary in American history, distinguishing, to varying degrees, the experiences of those classified as *nonwhite* from those classified as *white*, with often devastating consequences" (Cornell and Hartmann, 1998:25; emphasis added). In American society, sociologists have associated race with the quality of assignment (racial group membership is assigned by others, particularly by members of the dominant, white race) and ethnicity with the quality of assertion (ethnic group membership is chosen by members of the ethnic group). As sociologists Edward Telles and Vilma Ortiz have recently noted, however, both the ethnic and racial models described here originated in a black/white model of U.S. society (Telles and Ortiz, 2008:38).

A note on terminology is in order. I use the term "Mexican American" to refer to those people who were mestizo (Indian-African-Spanish) descendants of the Spanish colonizers of indigenous people in present-day Mexico and the United States who lived in the territory ceded by Mexico in 1848. As the reader will see, a substantial number of these persons became American citizens at that time, so it is a term that refers both to a particular ethnoracial group and to citizenship status. I use the term "Euro-American" to refer to the non-Mexican white population of the United States, including the portion that was ceded from Mexico in 1848. Because I will be discussing Mexican Americans' position as at once nonwhite and, yet, white or "off-white" in certain limited contexts, I do not simply refer to Euro-Americans as whites. I use the terms "black" and "African American" interchangeably to refer to Americans of African descent who are not Mexican American or Latino.

MANIFEST DESTINY RECONSIDERED

In this chapter, I call for reconceiving Mexican Americans in racial terms and to do so based on Mexicans' nineteenth-century history in the United States. Scholars typically see the middle to late nineteenth century as a key period in U.S. race relations, and they tend to emphasize the Civil War, the end of slavery, the constitutional amendments aimed at granting equal rights to the former slaves, and Reconstruction as key factors in the evolution of racial dynamics in the twentieth century. That standard story about race in the nineteenth century is flawed because it overlooks events related to Mexican Americans: the American colonization of northern Mexico beginning in 1846, the ceding by Mexico of half its territory to the United States in 1848, and the collective naturalization to American citizenship of 115,000 Mexicans following the war. All of these events occurred within a generation of the Civil War and Reconstruction, and yet virtually all scholars write about these events as representing two unrelated eras. Moreover, in the popular imagination, Manifest Destiny conjures a moment of national triumph before the dark years of conflict over slavery that culminated in the Civil War, exacerbating the tendency to see them as completely separate periods.

How does it change our thinking about U.S. race relations and about race itself to reconceive these nineteenth-century events as central forces that produced the racial order in the early twentieth century and that today continues to exert a powerful effect? Certainly, it results in a more accurate and more complex understanding of race, racial dynamics in the United States, and historic processes of racialization (Gómez, 2007). This approach shifts our gaze from North/South dynamics to the West and Southwest and to considering the causal links between Manifest Destiny and colonization in the 1830s and 1840s, on the one hand, and the crisis over slavery and the Civil War of the 1860s, on the other. This intellectual move allows us to better understand the dynamics of whiteness, of groups becoming white, and of contingent (or limited) white status as illustrated by the experience of Mexican Americans as well as that of other groups over the course of the nineteenth and twentieth centuries. Finally, reconceiving nineteenth-century race relations in this way leads us to eschew the false dichotomy often presented between racial dynamics in the United States and those in Latin American countries.

For many decades, American sociologists and historians have been taken with the comparison between U.S. and Latin American racial models, often concluding that the more fluid racial categories of Latin America were less pernicious than the more impermeable black/white divide that characterized the United States during slavery, Reconstruction, and the Jim Crow era.[2] Instead, linking Manifest Destiny and the American colonization of northern Mexico with slavery and the Civil War invites us to take seriously what I have termed the "double colonization" of the American Southwest: This region was colonized twice, first by Spain and then by the United States (Gómez, 2007). Both the Spanish and the American colonial enterprises were grounded in racism—in a system of status inequality built on presumed racial difference. While a central aspect of both the Spanish and American conquests was a racial ideology of white supremacy, the particular variants of the ideology differed under the two regimes (and, as well, varied regionally within them). The American colonizers of the Southwest thus did not start with a clean slate. Instead, a new racial order evolved in the looming shadow of the Spanish-Mexican racial order.

THE FIRST MEXICAN AMERICANS

The United States invaded Mexico in the summer of 1846 in the far northern Mexican region of Nuevo México, establishing a fort in Santa Fé within a manner of months.[3] U.S. military forces then moved west to Alta California, while troops at the Texas/Mexico border moved south, eventually taking Mexico City in September 1847. U.S. naval forces simultaneously proceeded to Monterey (in northern Alta California) and to the eastern Mexico seacoast. By late 1847, Mexican and American diplomats were attempting to negotiate an end to the war and eventually did so, in February 1848, with the Treaty of Guadalupe Hidalgo. The peace treaty provided for U.S. indemnification to Mexico for damages from the war in the amount of $15 million and for Mexico's ceding of roughly half its northern territories to the United States (including the requirement that Mexico relinquish its claim on Texas, which had broken from Mexico in 1836 and was admitted to the Union as a slave state in 1845). The so-called Mexican Cession consisted of 1.3 million square miles, an area 50 percent larger than the Louisiana Purchase of 1804. In order to fathom the massive scale of the Mexican

Cession, consider that, today, 85 million Americans live in states that formerly were Mexican territory.

Yet the peace treaty gave the United States not only land but also people. The ceded lands were home to unknown numbers of Indians from tribes who had never submitted to the Spanish and later Mexican governments, which had attempted to assert political and military authority over the region. Indians in this category very likely numbered in the tens of thousands in 1848. The ceded lands also were home to tens of thousands of Pueblo Indians (in what is now the state of New Mexico) and so-called Mission Indians in California and Texas, both of whom, under Mexican law, had political and social rights as "civilized Indians" (Rosen, 2007:6–7).

Small numbers of Euro-Americans (U.S. citizens and citizens of Canada and European nations) lived in Alta California (especially concentrated in the Monterey trading center) and New Mexico (especially concentrated in the fur-trapping and trading region of the Taos Valley), but Texas was a different story. By the mid-1830s, Euro-Americans outnumbered Mexicans in Tejas, even though it was still under Mexican control (Gómez, 2007:6, 165, n. 23). As historian Richard White has noted, as many as 40 percent of the Euro-Americans in Texas in the ten years before Texas broke away from Mexico were "illegal aliens," having immigrated to Mexico in violation of laws that required them to become Mexican citizens and Catholics (1991:65). Euro-American immigrants to Mexican Texas took black slaves with them (again in violation of Mexican law), and the number of slaves in Texas increased threefold between 1850 and 1860 (Gómez, 2007:18).

My focus here will be on Mexicans living in the Mexican Cession—people who were ancestrally a mixture of the indigenous, African, and Spanish people who had settled Mexico in the seventeenth and eighteenth centuries (Gómez, 2007; Menchaca, 2001). Mexico's mid-seventeenth-century population contained roughly equal numbers of those claiming Spanish descent (only a small minority of whom had been born in Spain, even at that time) and those who identified themselves (or were so identified in official records) as black (racially mixed persons, African slaves, and their descendants), but ten times as many mestizos (mixed Indian-Spanish people) and Indians as either of those groups (Menchaca, 2001:61). In a society in which miscegenation was not prohibited and in some respects encouraged, Mexico rapidly became a mestizo society that was a blend of the three racial populations. New Mexico's eighteenth- and nineteenth-century settler population (which needed to be almost entirely replenished after the Pueblo Revolt of 1680) was recruited mostly from Mexico's interior and reflected this racially mixed population (Esquibel, 2006:65–69). Moreover, some evidence suggests that persons living in Mexico's northern territories (Nuevo México, Alta California, Tejas) were much more indigenous and African than Spanish in their origins—precisely because such mestizo settlers had more to gain from the comparatively looser racial order on Mexico's frontier (Esquibel, 2006:65–69).

An estimated 115,000 such Mexicans lived in the land ceded by Mexico, who, by virtue of the peace treaty in 1848, became the first Mexican Americans.

Consider that, via this one law, as many Mexicans were simultaneously granted American citizenship as people who lived in the fifth-largest U.S. city at the time (New Orleans).[4] Some 14,000 Mexicans lived in California in 1850, and 25,000 Mexicans lived in Texas, but nearly two-thirds of all Mexicans in the Mexican Cession lived in present-day New Mexico (75,000) (Gómez, 2007:6, 164, n.20; Martínez, 1975; Montejano, 1987:31). Thus, the total number of Mexican Americans who lived in the New Mexico Territory, which Congress created in 1850 when it made California a state, was about the size of the nation's eighth-largest city (St. Louis, population 78,000) and considerably larger than the ninth- and tenth-largest U.S. cities at the time (Spring Garden, Pennsylvania, at 59,000 and Albany, New York, at 51,000).

The first Mexican Americans were "Americans" by express provision of the peace treaty, which had collectively granted naturalization to these former Mexican citizens. (The treaty also offered Mexicans living in the ceded lands the right to maintain their Mexican citizenship and thereby reject American citizenship; while significant numbers of persons initially did so, many of them eventually adopted U.S. citizenship [Gómez, 2007:43].) As the result of congressional action in 1790, not long after the ratification of the U.S. Constitution, the ability to become an American citizen was restricted to "free white persons." The 1848 treaty giving citizenship to more than 100,000 Mexicans was the first of several instances in which Mexicans received the benefit of what I have elsewhere termed an "off-white" racial status in law that did not correspond to Mexicans' otherwise nonwhite racial status. The belief that Mexicans were "but little removed above the Negro" was widespread among both elite and average Americans, and this view was displayed repeatedly in congressional debates, in newspapers, and in efforts to rally some 70,000 volunteers to fight against Mexico in the war (Gómez, 2007:59; Horsman, 1981; Rodriguez, 2007:93–97). Yet the significance of Mexicans' privilege should be underscored: They were collectively granted federal citizenship at a time when immigrants from Asia (including the Middle East), Africa, and elsewhere could not, under any conditions, become U.S. citizens because they were not considered "free white persons."[5]

One of the reasons this arrangement was palatable to President James Polk and the Senate (which had to ratify the treaty to make it law) was that, at this time, federal citizenship was inferior to state citizenship. The nature of "citizenship" rights conveyed to Mexicans under the treaty was, at best, legally vague and, at worst, a deliberate attempt to mislead the Mexican negotiators. The Mexicans believed they had protected the rights of Mexican citizens living in the ceded territory to elect American citizenship. What they probably did not understand, however, was the fact noted above—that, in the United States at the time, federal citizenship was inferior to state citizenship.

At mid-nineteenth century, one's political and civil rights stemmed largely from one's status as a citizen of New Jersey or Virginia and had very little to do with one's status as a citizen of the federal republic (Gómez, 2007:43–44). This would begin to change only as a result of the Civil War and the Reconstruction Amendments to the Constitution (particularly the Fourteenth Amendment of 1868), which considerably expanded the notion of federal rights and the idea that the states were in important ways inferior to the federal government. Substantial numbers of Mexicans in Texas and California held both federal and state citizenship and therefore had access to full political rights. Significantly, however, the evidence shows that some Mexicans were not enfranchised as state citizens in California and Texas because they were deemed "too Indian" or "too African" (Menchaca, 2001).

Recall that two-thirds of the first Mexican Americans lived in New Mexico (where Pueblo Indians also were concentrated), and that in 1850 Congress organized New Mexico (then extending as far west as Las Vegas, Nevada) into a federal territory. The vast majority of the first Mexican Americans thus lived in a contiguous colony of the United States: the federal territory of New Mexico, which Congress did not admit to statehood until 1912. Accordingly, although they had certain rights as persons "white enough" for naturalization under the treaty, at least two-thirds of the first Mexican Americans were severely limited in their political rights and inclusion as full citizens within the United States (Gómez, 2007:44–45). This history of entering the nation as a colonized people (rather than as immigrants) and the history of the vast majority of the first Mexican Americans as second-class citizens living in a contiguous colony have shaped the racialization of Mexican Americans in ways that have yet to be fully understood by scholars.

OPPOSITE ONE-DROP RULES: THE EVOLUTION OF DISTINCT RACIAL LOGICS FOR BLACKS AND MEXICANS

Each time the United States acquired additional territory, the executive and legislative branches vigorously debated whether slavery would be allowed in the new region. For example, the Missouri Compromise of 1819–1820 was crafted to settle the slavery debate in the remainder of the Louisiana Purchase that was not initially carved into states. Under the law, slavery was allowed south of the thirty-sixth parallel but banned north of it. During debates over the annexation of Texas in 1837 and 1844, Congress refused to admit Texas precisely because it was to be a slave state; in 1845, southerners got the upper hand and Texas was finally admitted. Congressional opposition to the U.S. invasion of Mexico, to the formal declaration of war, and to the peace treaty all were focused on the question of slavery, as repeated debates over the Wilmot Proviso showed. That measure specified that slavery would be prohibited in any additional lands taken from Mexico, and it passed the House of Representatives in both 1846 and 1847 (Gómez, 2007:132).

The crisis became most acute with the addition of Mexican territory in 1848, the single largest acquisition of territory by the United States. Congressional debates about whether to allow slavery in the New Mexico and Utah territories (the portion of the Mexican Cession that remained after Congress carved out the states of Texas and California) revealed a federal legislature increasingly fractured on the slavery question. It became unlikely that Congress would act at all, making judicial intervention almost inevitable. The Supreme Court spoke to the question of slavery in the newly acquired territories less than a decade after the end of the war with Mexico. In 1856, in *Dred Scott v. Sandford,* the

Supreme Court ruled that the Missouri Compromise was an unconstitutional exercise of congressional power. This case is also notorious because it ruled that black Americans (whether they were free or enslaved) lacked the basic requisites of federal citizenship, such as being able to file a lawsuit in federal court. In this way, the colonization of Mexico and the Civil War are inextricably linked: The massive addition of Mexican territory interrupted the uneasy truce over slavery that had held sway for decades and that propelled the nation to civil war.

Yet the racial subordination of Mexican Americans (accomplished via colonization) and the subordination of African Americans (accomplished via slavery) are linked in other ways as well. For example, at the turn of the twentieth century, we can trace the evolution of two racial logics, one applying to African Americans and one applying to Mexican Americans. These two racial logics were mutually reinforcing—they worked dialectically to promote the subordination of the other group, as well as the subordination of the group at which each was directed. What I describe as a hard or rigid racial logic applied to blacks: Black status came to be defined by the hypodescent rule, and little movement out of the black category was the result. Under the soft or flexible racial logic, which applied to Mexicans, a kind of reverse one-drop rule emerged: One drop of Spanish blood led in some circumstances to the definition of Mexicans as white by law.

African Americans

We can trace the evolution of the hard racial logic that applied to blacks by examining the Supreme Court's ruling in *Plessy v. Ferguson* in 1896. *Plessy* is infamous as the opinion that invoked the logic of "separate but equal" as a feature of American constitutional law: Legally segregated facilities for blacks and whites ("separate" schools, trains, theaters, swimming pools, etc.) comported with the Constitution's equal protection clause (the Fourteenth Amendment), so long as blacks were provided comparable facilities (equal, in a general sense). Not until 1954, in the midst of the modern Civil Rights Movement, did the nation's highest court reverse itself and thereby require school desegregation in *Brown v. Board of Education.*

Here my focus is on the social context of the case, especially its role as ushering in the hypodescent rule as the dominant American rule of defining black status. Homer Plessy was arrested for riding in the whites-only car of a New Orleans train. Under Louisiana law, the train company was required to have two separate passenger cars, one each for "the white and colored races" (Elliott, 2006:249). It was a crime punishable by fine or imprisonment to ride in the wrong car (subject to significant exceptions for black servants riding with their white employers), and Plessy was arrested, convicted, and sentenced for doing so (Elliott, 2006:249).[6]

Plessy was seven-eighths white and looked white, yet he lived his life as a member of the black community in New Orleans, where he was active in African American civil rights organizations (Elliott, 2006; Harris, 2004). For the civil rights lawyers who filed the litigation as a test of this new breed of Jim Crow legislation (which specifically mandated "equal but separate" accommodations for the races), Plessy was the perfect client precisely because his racial status was ambiguous (Elliott, 2006:264). His situation underscored both the irrationality and the unworkability of legalized (*de jure*) segregation.

Such laws were irrational because racial definitions were inherently irrational: Was Plessy a black man who looked white, or was he a white man who was part black? In an 1893 letter, one of Plessy's lawyers, Albion Tourgée, argued presciently that scientists had failed to define race with any precision because race was socially constructed rather than biologically meaningful (Elliott, 2006:260). In oral arguments in 1896, Tourgée asked pointedly of the Supreme Court justices, "Who [is] white and who [is] colored? By what rule then shall any tribunal be guided in determining racial character?" (Elliott, 2006:286). Plessy's legal team also argued that such laws were ultimately unworkable because they depended on subjective enforcement by actors, from train conductors to police officers, who necessarily had to engage in on-the-spot judgments about racial status.

Because Plessy looked white, he and his lawyers had to arrange in advance to have him arrested; without such a plan, he would have been allowed to ride in the whites-only car (Elliott, 2006:265). In his biography of Tourgée, historian Mark Elliott notes that the Louisiana railroad companies "were overwhelmingly opposed to the Separate Car Act because of its extra cost and inconvenience," so they were perfectly willing to assist in the constitutional challenge to the law (2006:265). Plessy's lawyers faulted the law because it provided no guidance to those who had to enforce it; it contained no definition of its terms "white" and "colored." They emphasized that individuals could appear white but be black by reputation (especially in Louisiana), as was the case with Plessy. In an argument that fits very well in the contemporary American moment, Plessy's lawyer told the Supreme Court in 1896: "Race-intermixture has proceeded to such an extent [that it is often] impossible of ascertainment [after careful study, much less] ... the casual scrutiny of a busy conductor" (Elliott, 2006:287).

In essence, Plessy's lawyers were arguing that race was socially constructed rather than an inherent quality that mattered on its own terms. But the Supreme Court refused to engage their arguments about the meaning of race, about racial categories, and about the difficulty of assigning persons to racial categories. The Supreme Court's only nod to these issues (which were central in the briefs submitted by Plessy's lawyers) was to acknowledge, in the penultimate paragraph of the opinion, a range of definitions of black status (and, correspondingly, of white status, though the Court did not put it that way). For example, the Court noted a variety of competing definitions of black status and added that these definitions included the idea that "any visible admixture of black blood stamps the person as belonging to the colored race"—the definition that would come to be known as the hypodescent rule (Gómez, 2007:145).

Perhaps disingenuously, the Court said it would leave the question of definitions to the various state and local legislative bodies. Yet the impact of *Plessy* was to lead legislatures to adopt the hypodescent rule, which within a matter of decades evolved into the dominant definition of black status in the United States. This was so because the effect of the decision in *Plessy* was to give the green light to state and local governments to pass Jim Crow laws, the Supreme Court having ruled that the Fourteenth Amendment prevented no bar to such laws. The result was the proliferation of anti-black segregation statutes across the nation (north and south, east and west) and in virtually every aspect of social life. And with the rise of such statutes came the dire need for a workable definition of "black" and "white": a definition that was easy to understand and easy to apply.

Only an easy definition would work because the management of this apartheid system would work only if individuals could assist, informally, in the process of enforcement (in all senses of the word) of racial categorization. The hypodescent rule under which one drop of black ancestry defines black status was the result and eventually emerged as *the* American rule by about 1930 (Telles, 2004:80). Prior to *Plessy,* however, it was far from inevitable that the one-drop rule would become the dominant U.S. rule. There had been a rich variety of definitions of white and black status for centuries in the United States. The revolutionary generation often defined someone as black only if one or more of the person's grandparents had been black (one-quarter or *more* black), and census enumerators had between 1850 and 1890 counted blacks, mulattoes, quadroons, and octoroons at various times, attesting both to the prevalence of black/white mixing and to the existence of competing state and local definitions (Gómez, 2007:144).

The hypodescent rule rose to become the dominant U.S. rule for defining black status, but looking closely at how this occurred (and exploring the law's central role in that process) reminds us that the racial order is historically contingent and socially constructed. This was no less so for racial logics directed at African Americans than for racial logics directed at Mexican Americans.

Mexican Americans

A year after the Supreme Court decided *Plessy,* a federal judge in San Antonio, Texas, issued a decision in a case called *In re: Rodríguez.* As a matter of legal precedent, there are vast differences between an opinion issued by the U.S. Supreme Court (like *Plessy*), which controls the law of the entire nation, and an opinion issued by a federal district court (like *Rodríguez*), which controls only the law in the particular jurisdiction out of which it arises (in this case, the Western District of Texas). The trial judge's ruling in *Rodríguez* was not appealed, so there is no appellate ruling in the case; yet it stands as the only reported naturalization case involving the determination of the racial status of a Mexican applicant in the nineteenth century. I compare the two cases here in order to illustrate the interaction between judicial opinions and the social context, and because they occur within a year of each other and allow us to see the contrasting racial logics that applied to blacks and Mexicans at the turn of the twentieth century.

In this case, Ricardo Rodríguez, a Mexican national, sought to become a naturalized U.S. citizen. Typically, naturalization cases occur as run-of-the-mill, little-publicized events (Gómez, 2007:139). Moreover, the case arose at a time when the 2,000-plus-mile U.S.-Mexico border was more symbolic than real. At this time and well into the twentieth century, substantial numbers of Mexican nationals crossed the porous border without any difficulty whatsoever, as did Americans entering Mexico. Procedures to regulate Mexican immigration across the border did not become institutionalized until the 1940s (Sánchez, 1993:38–62). Prior to that time, Mexicans entered the United States freely and blended into Mexican American communities, in many cases without perceiving naturalization to American citizenship as necessary or desirable.

We know very little about Rodríguez himself or what motivated him to seek U.S. citizenship, but it is clear that this case entered the public spotlight when Euro-Americans organized to block Rodríguez's naturalization application because they believed too many Mexicans were becoming citizens and, specifically, voting in San Antonio elections. Similar sentiments appear to drive the contemporary anti-immigrant movement, except that, today, Mexicans' racial status is not openly touted as a reason for opposing Mexican immigration (it is a barely-below-the-surface subtext). But in 1897 those who opposed the citizenship application filed by Rodríguez could openly talk about race: Only "white" or black immigrants could become naturalized citizens under U.S. law. In the wake of the Civil War, Congress amended the law in 1870 to allow white persons as well as "persons of African nativity or African descent" to become American citizens. Under this law, Asian immigrants to the United States in the nineteenth and twentieth centuries were prevented from becoming citizens (though their American-born children were citizens via the Fourteenth Amendment's establishment of birthright citizenship in 1868).

Rodríguez claimed he was white and therefore eligible to become a U.S. citizen, but some Euro-American politicians intervened to argue that Mexicans were not white and therefore not eligible to naturalize, hoping to stem the rising tide of Mexican American voters in San Antonio. The judge considered whether Rodríguez was white via two commonly relied upon tests, the *common sense test* (sometimes called the ocular test in that it relied on the judge's or other persons' assessment of the applicant's appearance) and the *scientific approach* (under which the judge speculated about how "scientists" would classify the applicant) (Haney López, 1996). In this case, the judge took notice of Rodríguez's "copper-colored or red" complexion and "dark eyes, straight black hair and high cheek bones" to conclude that he was not white in appearance (Rodriguez, 2007:169). He also conceded that anthropologists would probably not conclude that Rodríguez was white: "If the strict scientific classification of the anthropologist should be adopted, he would probably not be classed as white," said the judge (as quoted in Gómez, 2007:141). Either one of these "tests" would have been a sufficient basis for concluding that Rodríguez was ineligible for citizenship, if the judge had wanted to reach that conclusion.

Instead, the judge reached back to nineteenth-century events to decide that Rodríguez was "white enough." His rhetorical strategy was to emphasize the laws that historically gave Mexicans political rights, suggesting that these laws had conferred white status on Mexicans, along with substantive rights. He specifically relied on three legal moments to make his case. First, in 1836, the constitution of the Republic of Texas conferred citizenship on all men except "Africans and their descendants" and "Indians," thereby including Mexicans by default (Gómez, 2007:141). When Congress voted in 1845 to annex Texas as a state, it similarly conferred state citizenship on the Mexicans who were in Texas in 1836. Yet the judge elided the vigorous debate in the 1830s, 1840s, and 1850s about the racial status of Mexicans. For example, in the context of implementing these two laws, some Mexicans were deemed not white enough (or too Indian or too black) to become Texas citizens (Menchaca, 2001:228). The third law relied upon by the judge was the 1848 grant of collective naturalization to the Mexicans living in the ceded territory as a condition for ending the war with Mexico. (While the treaty itself did not contain racial restrictions on Mexican naturalization, racial prerequisites were included in the constitutions of several states carved out from the Mexican Cession, as well as in the congressional legislation that established New Mexico as a federal territory [Gómez, 2007:141].)

Lurking behind the scenes—and unstated in the opinion—was a social context in which Euro-American elites were bitterly divided over whether Mexicans should be encouraged to immigrate and naturalize. In the last decade of the nineteenth century, an acute labor shortage resulted from federal legislation in 1882 to prohibit Chinese laborers from entering the United States—a shortage that would soon be exacerbated by the 1907–1908 curtailment of Japanese immigration. For the first time, American agricultural, railroad, and other employers were beginning to actively recruit Mexican laborers to come to the United States. Yet white workers who competed with Mexican workers and whites who feared Mexican Americans' political power in towns like San Antonio vigorously opposed both Mexican labor recruitment and Mexican naturalization. Other Euro-Americans wanted the United States to remain attractive for Mexican workers.

Less than two decades after this decision, Congress passed a major immigration bill that consolidated the anti-Chinese efforts into a virtual ban on immigration from any Asian country (creating the so-called Asiatic Barred Zone from which immigrants could not enter the United States) (Ngai, 2004:18). In the same bill, Congress created the first exception for temporary Mexican workers: sojourners who would be allowed into the United States as contract laborers for a limited period of time. Actively recruited by employers and U.S. government agents, tens of thousands of Mexicans entered the United States in the 1920s under the temporary-worker provision. For these workers, naturalization was not an option; the United States invited them only as temporary workers without the option of becoming permanent members of the nation. If the 1917 immigration law permitted some Mexicans the opportunity for short-term economic improvement, it also constituted a huge exception to the naturalization opportunities created by the *Rodríguez* case.

UNMASKING THE REVERSE ONE-DROP RULE AS RACIAL IDEOLOGY

The early twentieth century thus saw the consolidation of opposing ideologies of race that together helped constitute the twentieth-century racial hierarchy that we take for granted today. Without understanding how they worked—and how they worked in tandem—we cannot fully understand U.S. racial dynamics in the twentieth century and beyond. For African Americans, the hypodescent rule came to define black status in an expansive fashion and, in turn, to signal devastating legal disabilities. For Mexican Americans, the reverse one-drop rule operated to open up white status to Mexicans, and thereby the assumption of some political rights, but it also operated to impose a contingent whiteness. While Mexican Americans were relegated to second-class citizenship in virtually all areas of social and political life, they had access to whiteness in certain legal contexts. In the national order in the early twentieth century, Mexican Americans occupied a middle position as a wedge group, between whites above them and blacks below them. Like other wedge groups (at that time and since then), Mexican Americans were bought off with honorary white status and, to be honest, with the accompanying privileges, and in exchange they became complicit in policing the one-drop rule for African Americans.

The evolution of separate racial ideologies with respect to Mexican Americans and African Americans highlights the complexity and the internal contradictions within white supremacy. Whereas the racial ideology that we most commonly associate with this period of American history resulted in the hardening of the black racial category (under the one-drop rule), an ideology emerged for Mexicans that depended on racial boundaries being flexible and permeable. Sociologists and historians of U.S. race relations often have cited Latin American contexts as illuminating counterexamples to U.S. racial dynamics, but this approach overlooks the ways in which U.S. racial dynamics themselves substantially evolved from Spanish colonial models of race (dynamics that typically have been mislabeled as "ethnic" in the U.S. context). The myopic tendency to view American race relations as only about white-over-black relations and as centered on a North/South axis has obscured the ways in which Latin American–style race relations have existed both historically and as a powerful legacy today within the United States.

Moreover, the unmasking of these processes of racialization as they affected Mexican Americans makes visible the ideological work that labeling these dynamics as "ethnic" accomplished. The formal "white enough to naturalize" status initially afforded by the collective naturalization of Mexicans in 1848 and then consolidated in the *Rodríguez* opinion encouraged Mexican Americans, collectively and individually, to distance themselves from blacks and other nonwhite groups. Indeed, any group or person seeking equality appreciated the extent to which it paid to be perceived as white (or white enough) under the law. For Mexican Americans, that meant distinguishing themselves from blacks, but also from Indians, Chinese, and Japanese, depending on the region.[7]

The silence in American public discourse about the reverse one-drop rule as it has governed Mexican Americans speaks volumes. Talking openly about the way the one-drop rule operated for Mexicans would have exposed the tensions and contradictions in the larger racial order. In this respect, the silence—from the dominant group as well as from Mexican Americans themselves—about the reverse one-drop rule for Mexicans helped perpetuate the subordination of blacks, even as it promoted a state of permanent insecurity as "off-white" for Mexican Americans. Multiple examples show how this insecurity played out to cramp the legally based civil rights strategies of Mexican Americans in the post–World War II period by putting Mexican American plaintiffs in the awkward (and legally less viable) position of arguing that they faced discrimination in educational and criminal justice contexts—discrimination they could not name as racial for fear of jeopardizing their contingent "white" status.[8]

When, instead of ignoring it, we examine closely the reverse one-drop rule, the American racial system seems far more fluid and malleable than typically portrayed. Instead of a racial system that consists of hard, closed categories (such as the hypodescent rule operating to define who is black), we see the contours of an American racial system in which mobility regularly occurred at both the individual and group levels. It allows us to see with more clarity the movement of other off-white groups into the white category in the early and middle twentieth century. Mexican access to the white category promised an easier path into whiteness for other groups. (For information on Jewish, Irish, and Italian movement into the white category, see Brodkin [1998] and Jacobson [1998].) Until recently, scholars have tended to describe these patterns in "ethnic" rather than racial terms, and that tendency has prevented us from fully understanding American racial dynamics. Yet these dynamics tell us a great deal about the U.S. racial order; by continuing to uncritically reproduce the standard account of race in the United States as only about white-over-black subordination we may inadvertently reinforce white supremacy.

Notes

1. Two book-length examples by prominent publishers are Skerry (1993) and Skrentny (2002).

2. For critical reviews of the literature comparing the United States and Latin America, see Telles (2004), Sawyer (2006), and de la Fuente (2001).

3. This summary is based on Gómez (2007:22–25, 41–45).

4. The 1850 U.S. Census showed that New Orleans had 116,375 residents and was the fifth-largest U.S. city, after New York, Baltimore, Boston, and Philadelphia (in order of population).

5. For a discussion of naturalization cases involving the determination of the applicant's racial status, see Ian Haney López's (1996) book, *White by Law*.

6. Plessy is commonly referred to as the "plaintiff" in the litigation, but in actuality he was a criminal defendant who was appealing his conviction by challenging the constitutionality of the law he was convicted under.

7. For examples of how this process played out in nineteenth-century New Mexico, where Mexican Americans controlled the territorial legislature, see chapter 3 of *Manifest Destinies: The Making of the Mexican American Race* (Gómez, 2007:81–116).

8. There is a robust literature analyzing these mid-twentieth-century legal strategies and cases. For two recent sources that will lead readers to the full literature, see Olivas (2006) and Haney López and Olivas (2008).

References

Brodkin, Karen. 1998. *How Jews Became White Folks and What That Says About Race in America*. New Brunswick, NJ: Rutgers University Press.

Cornell, Stephen, and Douglas Hartmann. 1998. *Ethnicity and Race: Making Identities in a Changing World*. Thousand Oaks, CA: Pine Forge Press.

de la Fuente, Alejandro. 2001. *A Nation for All: Race, Inequality, and Politics in Twentieth-Century Cuba*. Chapel Hill: University of North Carolina Press.

Elliott, Mark. 2006. *Color-Blind Justice: Albion Tourgée and the Quest for Racial Equality from the Civil War to* Plessy v. Ferguson. Oxford: Oxford University Press.

Esquibel, José Antonio. 2006. "The Formative Era for New Mexico's Colonial Population, 1693–1700." Pp. 64–79 in Claire Farago and Donna Pierce (eds.), *Transforming Images: New Mexican Santos In-Between Worlds*. University Park: Penn State University Press.

Gómez, Laura E. 2007. *Manifest Destinies: The Making of the Mexican American Race*. New York: New York University Press.

Haney López, Ian. 1996. *White by Law: The Legal Construction of Race*. New York: New York University Press.

Haney López, Ian, and Michael A. Olivas. 2008. "The Story of *Hernandez v. Texas*: Jim Crow, Mexican Americans, and the Anti-Subordination Constitution." Pp. 197–220 in Devon W. Carbado and Rachel F. Moran (eds.), *Race Law Stories*. New York: Foundation Press.

Harris, Cheryl I. 2004. "The Story of *Plessy v. Ferguson*: The Death and Resurrection of Legal Formalism." Pp. 181–222 in Michael C. Dorf (ed.), *Constitutional Law Stories*. New York: Foundation Press.

Horsman, Reginald. 1981. *Race and Manifest Destiny: The Origins of American Racial Anglo-Saxonism*. Cambridge, MA: Harvard University Press.

Jacobson, Matthew F. 1998. *Whiteness of a Different Color: European Immigrants and the Alchemy of Race*. Cambridge, MA: Harvard University Press.

Martínez, Oscar J. 1975. "On the Size of the Chicano Population: New Estimates, 1850–1870." *Aztlán* 6:43–65.

Menchaca, Martha. 2001. *Recovering History, Constructing Race: The Indian, Black, and White Roots of Mexican Americans*. Austin: University of Texas Press.

Montejano, David. 1987. *Anglos and Mexicans in the Making of Texas, 1836–1986*. Austin: University of Texas Press.

Ngai, Mae M. 2004. *Impossible Subjects: Illegal Aliens and the Making of Modern America*. Princeton: Princeton University Press.

Olivas, Michael A. (ed.). 2006. *"Colored Men" and "Hombres Aquí"*: Hernandez v. Texas *and the Emergence of Mexican-American Lawyering*. Houston: Arte Público Press.

Rodriguez, Gregory. 2007. *Mongrels, Bastards, Orphans, and Vagabonds: Mexican Immigration and the Future of Race in America*. New York: Pantheon Books.

Rosen, Deborah A. 2007. *American Indians and State Law: Sovereignty, Race, and Citizenship, 1790–1880*. Lincoln: University of Nebraska Press.

Sánchez, George J. 1993. *Becoming Mexican American: Ethnicity, Culture, and Identity in Chicano Los Angeles, 1900–1945*. New York: Oxford University Press.

Sawyer, Mark Q. 2006. *Racial Politics in Post-Revolutionary Cuba*. Cambridge, UK: Cambridge University Press.

Skerry, Peter. 1993. *Mexican Americans: The Ambivalent Minority*. New York: Free Press.

Skrentny, John D. 2002. *The Minority Rights Revolution*. Cambridge, MA: Harvard University Press.

Telles, Edward E. 2004. *Race in Another America: The Significance of Skin Color in Brazil*. Princeton: Princeton University Press.

Telles, Edward E., and Vilma Ortiz. 2008. *Generations of Exclusion: Mexican Americans, Assimilation, and Race*. New York: Russell Sage Foundation.

White, Richard. 1991. *"It's Your Misfortune and None of My Own": A New History of the American West*. Norman: University of Oklahoma Press.

CHAPTER 6

Racializing the Language Practices of U.S. Latinos

Impact on Their Education

Ofelia García

All human beings, regardless of race, gender, or ethnicity, use language to communicate. It is perhaps because of our familiarity with language that we often do not recognize its discursive power and how we use it to construct ideologies. This chapter examines how U.S. schools perpetuate educational inequities between U.S. Latinos and others by racializing[1] the ways in which they speak. Bonnie Urciuoli (1996:15) explains the concept of racialization as follows: "[W]hen people are talked about as a race, ... the emphasis is on natural attributes that hierarchize them." The Spanish language and bilingualism have become markers of being nonwhite, of being "out of place," thus minoritizing the position of U.S. Latinos and excluding them. The objective of the present chapter is to reveal how this racialization has impacted the education of U.S. Latinos through history and continues to do so today.

This chapter reviews the negative characteristics that have been assigned to both U.S. Spanish and bilingualism in the United States, preventing them from being used as a negotiable resource. The insistence on assigning negative static characteristics to a language, instead of acknowledging its use in social negotiations with others, is one way in which many nation-states have constructed imagined[2] national, ethnic, and linguistic identities, while protecting the legitimacy of the dominant group. This chapter uses the theoretical framework of linguistic ideology to link the characteristics assigned to U.S. Spanish and its speakers to broader sociopolitical goals of U.S. nationhood.[3]

DEBASING U.S. SPANISH AND BILINGUALISM: THE ROLE OF SCHOOLS

The Beginnings: Spanish as the Language of the Conquered and the Colonized

The 1848 Treaty of Guadalupe Hidalgo, which ended the Mexican-American War, ceded nearly half of the Mexican territory to the United States (what today is California, Arizona, Texas, Nevada, New Mexico, Utah, and parts of Colorado and Wyoming). The language people spoke, Spanish, was slowly eradicated from the territory, especially in schools.[4] California became a state in 1850 and five years later, in 1855, English was declared the only language of instruction in schools (Castellanos, 1983:18). In 1850, the territory of New Mexico (including present-day Arizona and New Mexico) was added to the Union. When thirteen years later Arizona and New Mexico were separated as territories, around 50 percent of the population of New Mexico spoke Spanish. New Mexico was not admitted to statehood until 1912, when more Anglos had moved in and the majority spoke English. The pressure to linguistically assimilate was carried out, in part, by repressing schooling in Spanish and replacing it with schools in English only. For example, in 1874, 70 percent of the schools taught in Spanish, 33 percent were bilingual, and only 5 percent were conducted in English only. Fifteen years later, in 1889, 42 percent of the schools were taught in English only, whereas only 30 percent of the schools were conducted in Spanish, and 28 percent remained bilingual (Del Valle, 2003). By 1891 a New Mexico statute required all schools to teach in English only.

No longer just the language of the conquered, Spanish became the language of the colonized. When Puerto Rico was occupied as a result of the Spanish-Cuban-American War in 1898, an English-only rule was imposed in Puerto Rican schools. Eighteen years later, Spanish was allowed only during the first four years of school. This education policy was in effect for thirty-two years until 1948, when Spanish was reestablished as a medium of instruction in Puerto Rico, after the massive failure of English-language instruction of Puerto Ricans had been acknowledged (García, Morín, and Rivera, 2001).

This view of Spanish as the language of conquered Mexicans and colonized Puerto Ricans and its exclusion from education contrasts sharply with the tradition of teaching Spanish as a foreign language to Anglos in the United States (for more on this, see García, 1993 and 2003). The elite Spanish teaching tradition focusing on the reading of the literature of Spain started at Harvard University in 1813 with George Ticknor and was continued by such well-known American *literati* as Henry Wadsworth Longfellow and Washington Irving. Its aim was not bilingualism but merely literary understandings of the Hispanic heritage.

In 1917, the American Association of Teachers of Spanish (now the American Association of Teachers of Spanish and Portuguese, or AATSP) was established. As German was excluded from schools after World War I, Spanish started to be taught at the secondary level. Yet, the first AATSP president, Lawrence Wilkins, prevented the inclusion of Spanish in the elementary school curriculum and the hiring of U.S. Latinos, whom he viewed as "foreign" teachers. Spanish was taught at the secondary level in the same way that it had been previously taught at the university—that is, with an emphasis on reading and without regard to the Spanish spoken in the American Southwest (García, 1993, 2003).

The first editor of the AATSP's journal *Hispania,* Aurelio M. Espinosa, was of Hispanic descent, yet he was opposed to the hiring of native speakers and the teaching of a Latin American variety of Spanish. In an article titled "Where Is the Best Spanish Spoken?" Espinosa wrote, "The best modern Spanish ... is that spoken by the educated people of Old and New Castile" (Espinosa, 1923:244). In another article, he wrote, "American teachers must do in the future 99 percent of the teaching of Spanish" (Espinosa, 1921:281), thus again showing his aversion to hiring teachers of U.S. Hispanic background. The model of Spanish to be taught in U.S. high schools and universities had little to do with the Spanish of its citizens. Castilian Spanish became the preferred variety to be taught to Anglos, while the Spanish of the new U.S. territories was relegated to an inferior position and restricted in all educational enterprises.

The Mid-Twentieth Century: Enter the Immigrants

The Bracero Program was established in 1942 to bring short-term Mexican contract laborers to the United States for agricultural work. Mexican children continued to be placed in segregated schools that used English as the only language of instruction. Reports on the education of Mexican Americans noted that Spanish-surnamed children were three years behind their Anglophone counterparts (Castellanos, 1983). Many were placed in special-education classes meant for disabled students. And yet, Spanish continued to be excluded from U.S. classrooms.

With the help of the Ford Foundation, the first bilingual program after World War II was set up in 1963 in Dade County, Miami, at the Coral Way Elementary School. Spanish, alongside English, was then used to educate the children of Cuban refugees who were thought to be in the United States only temporarily. At the same time, other bilingual schools in the Southwest were developed in order to educate children who were failing in the nation's schools— two in Texas and two in the San Antonio Independent School District in 1964, another in New Mexico and Texas in 1965, yet another in San Antonio, and two in Texas in 1966. Also in 1966, two bilingual schools were established in California and one in Arizona, followed by another in New Mexico in 1967 (Castellanos, 1983).[5] The renaissance of bilingual education to educate U.S. Latinos was a result of the Civil Rights Era—and it started, as Diego Castellanos (1983) has remarked, without any federal involvement.

In 1968, the U.S. Congress passed Title VII of the Elementary and Secondary Education Act—the Bilingual Education Act. Sponsored by Senator Ralph Yarborough of Texas, this act defined its goal as the quick acquisition of English and limited its participation to poor students. The situation was dire. In the Southwest, Chicano children had, on average, only a seventh-grade education. In Texas, the high school dropout rate for Chicanos was 89 percent. Less than a half percent of college students at the University of California campuses were Chicanos (Mackey and Beebe, 1977:6). In 1960, of all Puerto Ricans twenty-five years of age and older in the United States, 87 percent had dropped out without graduating from high school and the dropout rate in eighth grade was 53 percent (Castellanos, 1983). The use of U.S. Spanish in bilingual education was thus a tool to improve the education of children of Mexican and Puerto Rican descent. It would soon be otherwise.

In 1965, the Immigration and Naturalization Services Act of 1965 (also known as the Hart Celler or the INS Act of 1965) abolished the national-origin quotas[6] that had been established by the National Origins Act of 1924 (also known as the Johnson-Reed Act). As a result, an unprecedented number of immigrants from Latin America (as well as Asia and other non-Western nations) entered the United States, where they joined Latinos of Mexican and Puerto Rican descent.

Table 6.1 shows the number of immigrants who entered the United States between 1910 and 2000, according to the U.S. Census.[7] The number of immigrants from Latin America rose sharply after 1970, when they accounted for one-fifth of all immigrants in the United States; by 2000, they constituted more than one-half of the total (51.7 percent). According to the 2000 census, there were 16,916,416 foreign-born Latin Americans in the United States, and approximately 15 million of them spoke Spanish.

As a result of this marked increase in the number of Spanish-speaking immigrants, Spanish began to be characterized as the language of foreigners. By 1974, when Title VII was reauthorized, bilingual education was defined as "transitional," meaning that Spanish could be used only temporarily and that students needed to be transitioned to English-only classes.

The words of Samuel Huntington (2004:30, 45) reflect the racialized portrayal of Latinos as foreign Spanish-speaking immigrants outside of U.S. society:

Table 6.1 Region of Birth of Foreign-Born Population in the United States, 1910–2000 (in Percentages)

	1910	1930	1960	1970	1980	1990	2000
Europe	87.4	83.0	75.0	61.7	39.0	22.9	15.8
Asia	1.4	1.9	5.1	8.9	19.3	26.3	26.4
Africa	—	0.1	0.4	0.9	1.5	1.9	2.8
Oceania	0.1	0.1	0.4	0.4	0.6	0.5	0.5
Latin America	2.1	5.5	9.4	19.4	33.1	44.3	51.7

Source: U.S. Census Bureau, Population Division No. 29 and Summary File 3.

The persistent inflow of Hispanic immigrants threatens to divide the United States into two peoples, two cultures, and two languages. Unlike past immigrant groups, Mexicans and other Latinos have not assimilated into mainstream U.S. culture, forming instead their own political and linguistic enclaves—from Los Angeles to Miami—and rejecting the Anglo-Protestant dream.... There is no *Americano* dream. There is only the American dream created by an Anglo-Protestant society. Mexican Americans will share in that dream and in that society only if they dream in English.

As Spanish started to be recognized as only the language of immigrants, its status as the language of original settlers and even as the language of those who had been conquered and colonized was minimized or erased.[8] As a consequence, bilingual education—specifically the use of U.S. Spanish in educating Latinos—came under increasing attack.

By the 1980s, the English-only movement had gathered force. (For more on this, see Crawford, 2004.) In 1981, Senator Samuel Hayakawa introduced the first constitutional amendment to make English the official language of the United States. With Dr. John Tanton, Hayakawa founded the organization "U.S. English" in 1983. Tanton had also established the Federation for American Immigration Reform. U.S. English was thrown into disarray when an internal memo authored by Tanton was circulated in 1988. In the memo Tanton wrote about the "threats" of U.S. Latinos, which he said included their tradition of the *mordida* (bribery), their Catholicism, their "low educability," and their high birthrates.

Into the Twenty-First Century: Erasing Bilingualism and Blaming Spanish for Poverty

In a recent tabulation of Latinos at mid-decade, the Pew Hispanic Center (2006) reported 41,926,302 Latinos in the United States—that is, one out of every seven residents.[9] Of these, 26,784,268, or 64 percent, are of Mexican descent. Twenty-five million U.S. Latinos are native-born, whereas 17 million, or 40 percent, are foreign-born. But are all these Latinos speakers of Spanish?

The language shift among U.S. Latinos has been widely documented and continues at an unrelenting pace even today (e.g., Alba and Nee, 2003; Portes and Rumbaut, 2001). According to the 2000 U.S. Census, 16 percent of Latinos born in Latin America are already monolingual speakers of English. For the most part, third-generation Latinos speak English only, and the second generation shows a strong preference for English over Spanish. According to the 2000 census, 22 percent of U.S. Latinos over five years of age, numbering almost 7 million, are English monolinguals. The remaining 25 million also speak Spanish. But is Spanish *the* language of U.S. Latinos?

Although Spanish is *a* language of Latinos, it is not *the* language of Latinos. Indeed, Spanish-English bilingualism is the predominant form of communication among Latinos. The U.S. Census asks those who speak Spanish how well they speak English. As shown in Table 6.2, the 2000 census indicates that 70 percent of U.S. Latinos over the age of five are bilingual.[10]

**Table 6.2 English Proficiency of U.S. Latino Spanish Speakers
(over Five Years of Age)**

	Number	*Percent*	*Number*	*Percent*
Speak English "very well"	11,874,405	48		
Speak English "well"	5,323,330	22		
Bilingual			17,197,735	70
Speak English "not well"	4,675,560	19		
Speak English "not at all"	2,762,920	11		
Monolingual Spanish speaker			4,675,560	30

Source: 2000 U.S. Census, Summary File 3 and Table PCT11.

Almost 13 percent of all U.S. schoolchildren speak Spanish at home, and Spanish represents almost 70 percent of all languages other than English spoken by U.S. students aged five to seventeen. In California and Texas, one in three children—and in Arizona and New Mexico, one in four children—speaks Spanish at home. In Florida and New York, one in six children speaks Spanish at home. And one in seven children speaks Spanish at home in Illinois and New Jersey. Ignoring the Spanish that these children speak at home robs educators of the ability to build on the children's strengths and use an important pedagogical tool—the language spoken at home. It also removes from immigrant Latino parents the possibility of helping their children with homework. And yet, Spanish is excluded from most U.S. classrooms.

Spanish is used in bilingual education only in cases where the children are "limited English proficient" (LEP) or "English language learners" (ELLs). This naming practice is evidence of racializing language ideologies, for it denies that in learning English these students are "emergent bilinguals" (see García, Kleifgen, and Falchi, 2007). It is also important to note that most U.S. Latino schoolchildren who speak Spanish at home are proficient in English. As shown in Table 6.3, 30 percent of all Latino schoolchildren are already English monolinguals or at least speak English only at home. The remaining 70 percent speak Spanish at home. Adopting a broad definition of bilingualism that includes all those who speak English "very well" and "well," we find that 85 percent of all the schoolchildren who speak Spanish at home are also bilingual.[11] And by including those who speak English only at home, we learn that 90 percent of all Latino schoolchildren are proficient in English, although the great majority of these are bilingual.

Although we have information about the English spoken by U.S. Latinos, we know little about their Spanish, for the U.S. Census never asks about the degree of proficiency with which that language is spoken, as it does for English. Spanish-English bilingualism is typically portrayed as a "problem" rather than as a resource. Bilingualism is thus never assessed and Spanish-language education policies and practices, even those relating to bilingual education, often work against the development of that bilingualism.

In fact, it is precisely through erasure of bilingualism's potential that Spanish is racialized and constructed as the language of poverty. For example,

Table 6.3 U.S. Latino Schoolchildren (Five to Seventeen Years Old): Home Languages and Number of English Proficient and Emergent Bilinguals

	Number	Percent
Speak English only	2,590,250	30
Speak Spanish	6,005,055	70
Speak English "very well"	3,699,841	62
Speak English "well"	1,410,526	23
Bilinguals	5,110,367	85
English proficient	7,700,617	90
Speak English "not well"	693,051	12
Speak English "not at all"	201,637	3
Emergent Bilinguals	894,688	15
Non–English proficient	894,688	10

Source: 2000 U.S. Census, Summary File 3 and Table PCT62H.

although Spanish-English bilingualism characterizes the language use of most U.S. Latinos, research on language and income for U.S. Latinos focuses primarily on English-language ability or on Spanish monolingualism, without considering the impact of their bilingualism. The National Commission for Employment Policy (NCEP) has sponsored economic research since 1980 on the relationship between English-language ability and income differentials for Latinos. All of the NCEP studies reiterate that a deficiency in English-language abilities is one of the primary roadblocks for Latinos in the labor market. The gap in income differentials between Spanish monolinguals and English-speaking Latinos, despite comparable levels of education and experience, was also the subject of a study by David Bloom and Gilles Grenier (1996), who found that compared to English speakers, Spanish monolingual Latinos suffered income penalties of 8–15 percent in the case of men and 6 percent in the case of women.

These disparities in income when comparing Spanish monolinguals with those who speak English, as if they were two opposing categories, promote the gradual construction of English as the language of economic opportunity and of Spanish as one of limited opportunity and poverty. But most important, this comparison makes Spanish-English bilingualism nonexistent as a category of analysis, thus excluding the possibility of its use as a resource, whether at the individual or societal level.

Altogether different findings have been generated by scholars who consider bilingualism a valid variable in the relationship between language and income. For example, in a 1995 study, Ofelia García found that English monolingualism had no effect whatsoever on income, especially for Cuban Americans in Miami-Dade County, where Spanish had negotiated for itself a role not just for communication but also for economic value (García, 1995). These findings were confirmed by Thomas Boswell, who claimed that, for both Florida and Miami-Dade County, "Hispanics who speak English very well and speak Spanish have higher incomes, lower poverty rates, higher educational attainment, and better-paying jobs than Hispanics who only speak English. The differential in mean income is especially apparent" (2000:422). In Miami-Dade County, Spanish-English bilingualism has begun to emerge as a valuable economic resource.

April Linton (2003:24) has also documented a "positive relationship between upward mobility and bilingualism." The development of this positive relationship is explained by Alejandro Portes and Rubén Rumbaut's (1996, 2001) theory of "selective acculturation," which refers to the ability of people to adapt to the majority culture while holding on to elements of their origin. According to this model, when ethnic networks and strong communities (such as that of the Cuban American population in Miami-Dade County) support children in their efforts to deal with prejudice, navigate the education system, and find a place in the labor market for their ethnic language, bilingualism can bring equal, if not greater, benefits to them. Affirming the value of Spanish-English bilingualism, Douglas Massey (1995:648) has written: "Increasingly the economic benefits and prospects for mobility will accrue to those able to speak both languages and move in both worlds."

Conflating Language and Ethnicity and Blaming Spanish for Poverty and Educational Failure

Another way in which Spanish is constructed as the language of poverty is through the conflation of ethnicity and language (see del Valle, 2006). For example, in 2005 the median income of U.S. Latinos was $36,000, compared to $50,000 for white non-Latinos—and the implication, according to many, is that Spanish is to blame for this lower income (and that Latinos are nonwhites). But native-born U.S. Latinos, all of whom are presumably English speakers, also fare much worse than white non-Latinos. In fact, in 2005 the median income of native-born U.S. Latinos, all English speakers, was $39,000, higher than that of foreign-born Latinos ($34,000) but much lower than that of white non-Latinos (Pew Hispanic Center, 2006).

The Swiss economist François Grin (2003) has argued that when one language is promoted to prominent status, its native speakers will have social and economic advantages precisely because of their competence in the prestigious language. The racialization of Spanish and the erasure of Spanish-English bilingualism do indeed appear to have privileged white English monolinguals while excluding U.S. Latinos. Moreover, U.S. schools have played an important part in both that construction and that racialization process. U.S. education circles promote the idea that the problem with the education of U.S. Latinos is the large number of "limited English proficient" students, but as Table 6.3 shows, only 10 percent of U.S. Latino schoolchildren do not speak English or speak it less than well. In light of these data, one wonders about the plight of the other 90 percent who are English proficient—and, even more seriously, about that of the 2,590,250 U.S. Latino schoolchildren who are English monolinguals.

According to the 2000 U.S. Census, only 64 percent of Latinos between the ages of eighteen and twenty-four have completed high school, compared to 92 percent of white non-Latinos and 84 percent of black non-Latinos in the same age group. While the dropout rate for sixteen- to twenty-four-year-olds who are out of school and do not have a high school or GED diploma is 7 percent for whites and 13 percent for black non-Latinos, the percentage for Latinos is greater than the combined total for their white and black peers—28 percent. But because it is nearly impossible to differentiate among U.S. Latinos who are English mono-linguals, those who are bilinguals, and those who are Spanish monolinguals, Spanish is made the culprit even though other factors, primarily the racialization of language ideologies in the United States, are responsible for the inequities in the education of U.S. Latinos. (For more on "emergent bilinguals," see García, Kleifgen, and Falchi, 2007.)

Another example of how the conflation of Spanish language and Latino ethnicity hides other factors is the way in which the status dropout rate[12] is estimated. The 2000 U.S. Census reported that the status dropout rate for Latinos sixteen to twenty-four years old was 28 percent, significantly higher than the 7 percent dropout rate for white non-Latinos and the 13 percent rate for black non-Latinos. Breaking down these figures further, and considering only Latinos born in the United States who are all English speakers, we still find that the status dropout rate is higher than that for both whites and blacks. Second-generation Latinos have a 15 percent dropout rate, compared to 16 percent for those in the third generation. Clearly something is happening here besides the Spanish language, since even those U.S. Latinos born in the United States who speak English are doing worse than white and black non-Latinos. The racialization of U.S. Latinos, and not the Spanish language itself, largely explains the educational inequities to which they are subjected.

Erasing Spanish and Bilingualism in Education Today

No longer viewed as the language of original settlers, or even of the conquered and colonized who might be entitled to language and civil rights, but character-ized as the language of foreign immigrants, often undocumented, and blamed for the poverty and the low level of education of U.S. Latinos, Spanish is held in contempt in political and educational circles. The language Latinos speak is often characterized as *Spanglish,* a debased and mixed-contact variety (Stavans, 2003). The words of comic character Dame Edna in an advice column reflect this position: "Forget Spanish. There's nothing in that language worth reading except *Don Quixote.* . . . There was a poet named García Lorca, but I'd leave him on the intellectual back burner if I were you. As for everyone's speaking it, what twaddle! Who speaks it that you are really desperate to talk to? The help? Your leaf blower?" (quoted in Stavans 2003:116).

Kept on the back burner by those who refuse to understand that Spanish is a global language (for more on Spanish as a global resource, see Mar-Molinero and Stewart, 2006), that it is a valuable resource and economic commodity for many in the United States (see Carreira, 2000; García, 2007; García and Mason, forthcom-ing; Villa, 2000), and that bilingualism, in our globalized world, is an asset not to be ignored, U.S. Latinos are robbed of the possibility of nurturing their bilingualism and becoming educated Spanish speakers capable of competing in the global market. U.S. schools have been the battleground on which the struggle for control over language, and the resources it can accrue, has been settled. By establishing a clear linguistic hierarchy with English on top, Spanish at the bottom, and bilingualism as nonexistent, U.S. educational policy ensures that educational privilege continues to be in the hands of English monolinguals. The battle has been fierce.

Spearheaded by Ron Unz, a Silicon Valley software millionaire, Proposition 227 (California Education Code, Section 305–306)—introduced as "English for the Children"—was passed in California in 1998, eliminating bilingual education in that state. Massachusetts and Arizona have also declared bilingual education illegal. In 2001, Title VII of the Elementary and Secondary Education Act (the Bilingual Education Act) was eliminated as part of the authorization of No Child Left Behind (NCLB). The silencing of the word "bilingual" from U.S. discourse is readily noticeable. Figure 6.1 displays some of the wording changes that have been made to erase what James Crawford (2004) calls "the B-Word."

The high-accountability measures of NCLB require mandatory, high-stakes tests in English for all children (Menken, 2008; Wiley and Wright, 2004). As Crawford (2004:332) has noted: "In the name of 'accountability,' [the law] created new carrots and sticks that may ultimately prove more powerful than Unz' initiatives in pressuring schools to adopt all English instruction."

The attacks on the use of Spanish in teaching at the elementary and secondary levels of bilingual education have been curiously correlated with a growing

Figure 6.1 Changes in Naming and Silencing of the Word "Bilingual"

Office of Bilingual Education and Minority Languages Affairs (OBEMLA) →	Office of English Language Acquisition, Language Enhancement and Academic Achievement for LEP students (OELA)
National Clearinghouse for Bilingual Education (NCBE) →	National Clearinghouse for English Language Acquisition and Language Instruction Educational Programs (NCELA)
Title VII of Elementary and Secondary Education Act: The Bilingual Education Act →	Title III of No Child Left Behind, Public Law 107-110: Language Instruction for Limited English Proficient and Immigrant Students, 2001

attention to the teaching of Spanish to bilingual U.S. Latinos at the secondary and tertiary levels (e.g., Roca and Colombi, 2003; Valdés, 1997). And yet, as Guadalupe Valdés and his colleagues (2006) make clear, theories concerning the teaching of Spanish to U.S. bilinguals remain underdeveloped, while teaching programs themselves, especially at the secondary level, are almost nonexistent. For example, according to James Draper and June Hicks (2002), programs of Spanish for Spanish speakers in the United States had 141,212 students during the fall of 2000, making up only 1.9 percent of secondary school students enrolled in Spanish courses. This is a minuscule figure compared to the number of children five to seventeen years of age who claim to speak Spanish at home—5,970,217. The U.S. school system is clearly not developing the potential for bilingualism that the sheer number of Latino students should otherwise make possible.

CONCLUSION

This chapter has shown how U.S. policy has racialized U.S. Latinos, specifically by assigning negative characteristics to their variety of Spanish and bilingualism. Even more important, it has described how education—even when Spanish is used in teaching—has been instrumental in that racialization, inasmuch as it perpetuates the stereotype that the language practices of Latinos reflect their supposed intellectual deficits and inferiority as a people and race.

From its earliest contacts with the conquered inhabitants of the Southwest to its dealings with the colonized people of Puerto Rico, the U.S. government has maintained a policy of eradicating Spanish by encouraging a shift to English. It has done so by adopting a policy of debasing and racializing Spanish, linking it to subjugated populations, immigration, poverty, and lack of education. One result has been schools' infrequent use of U.S. Spanish to educate meaningfully those who speak it. Only in the period immediately after the Civil Rights Era was Spanish used to educate equitably. But this period was short-lived. And in the twenty-first century, as the number of U.S. Latinos grows and as Spanish attains for itself a competitive global position both in the United States and throughout the world, the battle over U.S. Spanish is being waged ever more fiercely. Bilingual education has suffered great losses, except when it is two-way and includes English-speaking children, and when its activities are concealed behind another label—"dual language." Classes of Spanish for native speakers have also not reached their potential.

The racialization of Latino ways of using language and the resulting inequities in their education have taken place, many times, with the consent of the U.S. Latino population. Pierre Bourdieu's concept of *habitus* as "a system of dispositions common to all products of the same conditionings" (1991:59) is important in understanding how U.S. Latinos themselves have acquired, as a result of socialization in U.S. schools, ways of viewing and accepting English monolingualism as if it were second nature. Many Latino schoolchildren have been led to believe that they deserve the unequal treatment they encounter in U.S. schools—poorer teachers, narrow pedagogical approaches, crumbling school buildings—because invalid high-stakes tests tell them that they are inferior, and that they do not meet academic proficiency levels. (For more on the inequities surrounding high-stakes tests for U.S. Latinos, see García, Kleifgen, and Falchi, 2007.) The racialization of the language practices of U.S. Latinos has been most successful, convincing many that only standard English monolingualism is normal and that Latino language practices are a mark of intellectual and racial inferiority, and thus a reason for exclusion from educational and social opportunities.

NOTES

1. The "racialization" of language practices refers to assigning negative characteristics to ways of using language, and transferring those characteristics to those who speak in these ways. Tove Skutnabb-Kangas (2000) has referred to this process as "linguicism." See also Urciuoli (1996).

2. For discussion of the concept of the "imagined," see Anderson (1991).

3. The assigning of negative characteristics to minority languages is always ideological and enmeshed in social systems that reproduce inequities (see Gal, 1989; Irvine and Gal, 2000; Woolard and Schieffelin, 1994).

4. See also García, 2008. As a reminder, note that Spanish came into the territories of Latin America as a language of conquest.

5. A list of these schools appears in Castellanos (1983:73).

6. As early as 1890, 2 percent of the total number of nationals were already in the United States.

7. Census data are based on self-report and may not be reliable. Undercounting of the undocumented also occurs.

8. Erasure is one of three semiotic processes of linguistic ideology (Irvine and Gal 2000:36).

9. Background information on this section can be found in García and Mason (forthcoming).

10. This analysis considers those who self-report as "speaking English very well or well" to be bilingual. The federal government, and specifically NCLB, calculates the number of "limited English proficient" students as all who speak English less than very well. I remind the reader that this information is based on self-evaluation.

11. See note 10 for explanation.

12. The status dropout rate refers to those who are out of school and have not earned a high school diploma or GED.

REFERENCES

Alba, Richard, and Victor Nee. 2003. *Remaking the American Mainstream: Assimilation and Contemporary Immigration.* Cambridge, MA: Harvard University Press.

Anderson, Benedict. 1991. *Imagined Communities: Reflections on the Origin and Spread of Nationalism,* rev. ed. London: Verso.

Beacco, Jean-Claude. 2005. *Languages and Language Repertoires: Pluralism as a Way of Life in Europe.* Strasbourg, France: Council of Europe.

Bloom, David, and Gilles Grenier. 1996. "Language, Employment, and Earnings in the United States: Spanish-English Differentials from 1970 to 1990." *International Journal of the Sociology of Language* 121:45–68.

Boswell, Thomas D. 2000. "Demographic Changes in Florida and Their Importance for Effective Educational Policies and Practices." Pp. 406–431 in Ana Roca (ed.), *Research on Spanish in the United States: Linguistic Issues and Challenges.* Somerville, MA: Cascadilla Press.

Bourdieu, Pierre. 1991. *Language and Symbolic Power.* Cambridge, MA: Harvard University Press.

Carreira, María. 2000. "Validating and Promoting Spanish in the U.S.: Lessons from Linguistic Science." *Bilingual Research Journal* 24:333–352.

Castellanos, Diego. 1983. *The Best of Two Worlds: Bilingual-Bicultural Education in the U.S.* Trenton: New Jersey State Department of Education.

Crawford, James. 2004. *Educating English Learners: Language Diversity in the Classroom,* 5th ed. Los Angeles: Bilingual Educational Services.

Dame Edna [Barry Humphries]. 2003. "Ask Dame Edna." *Vanity Fair* (February):116.

del Valle, José. 2006. "U.S. Latinos, *la hispanofonía,* and the Language Ideologies of High Modernity." Pp. 27–46 in Clare Mar-Molinero and Miranda Stewart (eds.), *Globalization and Language in the Spanish-Speaking World.* New York: Palgrave Macmillan.

Del Valle, Sandra. 2003. *Language Rights and the Law in the United States.* Clevedon, UK: Multilingual Matters.

Draper, James B., and June H. Hicks. 2002. *Foreign Language Enrollments in Public Secondary Schools, Fall 2000: Summary Report.* Retrieved March 15, 2008. (www.actfl.org/files/public/Enroll2000.pdf)

Espinosa, Aurelio M. 1921. "On the Teaching of Spanish." *Hispania* 4(6):269–284.

———. 1923. "Where Is the Best Spanish Spoken?" *Hispania* 6(4):244–246.

Gal, Susan. 1989. "Language and Political Economy." *Annual Review of Anthropology* 18:345–367.

García, Ofelia. 1993. "From Goya Portraits to Goya Beans: Elite Traditions and Popular Streams in U.S. Spanish Language Policy." *Southwest Journal of Linguistics* 12:69–86.

———. 1995. "Spanish Language Loss as a Determinant of Income Among Latinos in the United States: Implications for Language Policy in Schools." Pp. 142–160 in James W. Tollefson (ed.), *Power and Inequality in Language Education.* Cambridge, UK: Cambridge University Press.

———. 2003. "La enseñanza del español a los latinos de los EEUU: Contra el viento del olvido y la marea del inglés." *Ínsula* 679–680:9–12.

———. 2005. "Positioning Heritage Languages in the United States." *Modern Language Journal* 89(4):601–605.

———. 2007. "Lenguas e identidades en mundos hispanohablantes: Desde una posición plurilingüe y minoritaria." Pp. 377–400 in Manuel Lacorte (ed.), *Lingüística aplicada del español.* Madrid: Arco.

———. 2008. *Bilingual Education in the 21st Century: A Global Perspective.* Malden, MA: Blackwell.

García, Ofelia, Joanne A. Kleifgen, and Lorraine Falchi. 2007. *Equity in the Education of Emergent Bilinguals: The Case of English Language Learners.* New York: Teachers College, Columbia University, Campaign for Educational Equity.

García, Ofelia, and Leah Mason. Forthcoming. "Where in the World Is U.S. Spanish? Creating a Space of Opportunity for U.S. Latinos." In Wayne Harbert, Sally McConnell-Ginet, Amanda Miller, and John Whitman (eds.), *Language and Poverty.* Clevedon, UK: Multilingual Matters.

García, Ofelia, José Luis Morín, and Klaudia Rivera. 2001. "How Threatened Is the Spanish of New York Puerto Ricans? Language Shift with Vaivén." Pp. 44–73 in Joshua A. Fishman (ed.), *Can Threatened Languages Be Saved? Reversing Language Shift Revisited.* Clevedon, UK: Multilingual Matters.

Grin, François. 2003. *Language Policy Evaluation and the European Charter for Regional or Minority Languages*. New York: Palgrave Macmillan.

Hernández-Chávez, Eduardo. 1993. "Native Language Loss and Its Implications for Revitalization of Spanish in Chicano Communities." Pp. 45–47 in Barbara J. Merino, Henry T. Trueba, and Fabián A. Samaniego (eds.), *Language and Culture in Learning: Teaching Spanish to Native Speakers of Spanish*. London: The Falmer Press.

Huntington, Samuel P. 2004. "The Hispanic Challenge." *Foreign Policy* (March/April). Retrieved September 1, 2006. (http://www.foreignpolicy.com)

Irvine, J. T., and Susan Gal. 2000. "Language Ideology and Linguistic Differentiation." Pp. 34–84 in Paul B. Kroskrity (ed.), *Regimes of Language: Ideologies, Polities, and Identities*. Santa Fe, NM: School of American Research Press.

Kloss, Heinz. 1977. *The American Bilingual Tradition*. Rowley, MA: Newbury House.

Linton, April. 2003. *Is Spanish Here to Stay? Contexts for Bilingualism Among U.S.-Born Hispanics*. San Diego: Center for Comparative Immigration Studies, Summer Institute.

Mackey, William F., and Von Nieda Beebe. 1977. *Bilingual Schools for a Bicultural Community: Miami's Adaptation to the Cuban Refugees*. Rowley, MA: Newbury House.

Mar-Molinero, Clare, and Miranda Stewart (eds.). 2006. *Globalization and Language in the Spanish-Speaking World: Macro and Micro Perspectives*. New York: Palgrave Macmillan.

Massey, Douglas S. 1995. "The New Immigration and Ethnicity in the United States." *Population and Development Review* 2(3):631–662.

May, Stephen. 2001. *Language and Minority Rights: Ethnicity, Nationalism, and the Politics of Language*. Essex, UK: Pearson Education.

Menken, Kate. 2008. *English Language Learners Left Behind: Standardized Testing as Language Policy*. Clevedon, UK: Multilingual Matters.

National Commission for Employment Policy. 1982. *Hispanics and Jobs: Barriers to Progress*. Washington, DC: National Commission for Employment Policy.

Pew Hispanic Center. 2006. *A Statistical Portrait of Hispanics at Mid-Decade*. Retrieved March 15, 2008. (pewhispanic.org/files/other/middecade/complete.pdf)

Portes, Alejandro, and Rubén G. Rumbaut. 1996. *Immigrant America: A Portrait*, 2nd ed. Berkeley: University of California Press.

———. 2001. *Legacies: The Story of the Immigrant Second Generation*. Berkeley: University of California Press.

Roca, Ana, and M. Cecilia Colombi (eds.). 2003. *Mi Lengua: Spanish as a Heritage Language in the United States—Research and Practice*. Washington, DC: Georgetown University Press.

Ruiz, Richard. 1984. "Orientations in Language Planning." *NABE Journal* 8(2):15–34.

Skutnabb-Kangas, Tove. 2000. *Linguistic Genocide in Education—or Worldwide Diversity and Human Rights?* Mahwah, NJ: Lawrence Erlbaum.

Stavans, Ilan. 2003. *Spanglish: The Making of a New American Language*. New York: Rayo.

Urciuoli, Bonnie. 1996. *Exposing Prejudice: Puerto Rican Experiences of Language, Race, and Class*. Boulder, CO: Westview Press.

U.S. Census Bureau. 2000. *U.S. Census Bureau Report 2000*. Washington, DC: U.S. Government Printing Office.

Valdés, Guadalupe. 1997. "The Teaching of Spanish to Bilingual Spanish-Speaking Students: Outstanding Issues and Unanswered Questions." Pp. 263–282 in M. Cecilia Colombi and Francisco X. Alarcón (eds.), *La enseñanza del español a hispanohablantes*. Boston: Houghton Mifflin.

Valdés, Guadalupe, Joshua A. Fishman, Rebecca Chávez, and William Pérez (eds.). 2006. *Developing Minority Language Resources: The Case of Spanish in California*. Clevedon, UK: Multilingual Matters.

Villa, Daniel. 2000. "Languages Have Armies, and Economies, Too: The Presence of

U.S. Spanish in the Spanish-Speaking World." *Southwest Journal of Linguistics* 19: 143–154.

Wiley, Terrence G., and Wayne E. Wright. 2004. "Against the Undertow: Language Minority Education Policy and Politics in the 'Age of Accountability.'" *Educational Policy* 18(1):142–168.

Woolard, Kathryn A., and Bambi B. Schieffelin. 1994. "Language Ideology." *Annual Review of Anthropology* 23:55–82.

CHAPTER 7

English-Language Spanish in the United States as a Site of Symbolic Violence

Jane H. Hill

> The propensity to reduce the search for causes to a search for responsibilities makes it impossible to see that *intimidation,* a symbolic violence which is not aware of what it is (to the extent that it implies no *act of intimidation*), can only be exerted on a person predisposed (in his habitus) to feel it, whereas others will ignore it. It is already partly true to say that the cause of the timidity lies in the relation between the situation or the intimidating person (who may deny any intimidating intention) and the person intimidated, or, rather, between the social conditions of production of each of them. And little by little, one has to take account thereby of the whole social structure.
> —*Pierre Bourdieu (1991:51)*

Pressure against the public—and even private—use of Spanish in the United States is intense. Campaigns for English as the exclusive "official" language of government proliferate. Employers, often supported by the courts, try to create English-only workplaces. Public schools retreat to English monolingualism, with bilingual education now sharply restricted in California and Arizona and threatened in several other states, and the right of students to speak Spanish even in the halls and on the playground is under renewed attack in some districts (Reid, 2005).

These initiatives cannot be driven by a genuine concern for the status of English, unquestionably the dominant language in the United States and the single most important language in the world, with more second-language speakers than any other language. Instead, they are shaped almost entirely by racist hysteria over an imagined influence of populations whose heritage language is Spanish. The goal of the present chapter is to argue that those who defend U.S. Spanish, both as a national resource for all Americans and as a vital heritage for historically Spanish-speaking communities, should attend not only to these very obvious initiatives but also to less salient ways that the status of Spanish is eroded and that speakers of Spanish are "intimidated" in the United States today. The "official-English" and "anti-bilingual-education" movements are unquestionably part of the "whole social structure" to which Bourdieu draws our attention in the epigraph to this chapter. But this structure includes as well the "linguistic appropriation" of Spanish by English speakers in everyday practices among Americans of English-language heritage across a wide front.

Borrowing from Karl Marx's idea of capitalist appropriation, I define "linguistic appropriation" as a process with two dimensions. First, symbolic materials from the donor language are adopted by speakers of the target language, who benefit from them. Taken alone, such practices are benign. Nothing is lost to anyone when an English speaker learns enough Spanish to become a more knowledgeable tourist in Spain or Latin America, or a more comprehending audience for Spanish-language writers and performers. However, following Marx's insight, linguistic appropriation contains a second dimension, the denial of the resources thus recruited to members of the donor language community. The official-English movement is a very obvious example of such denial, and it emboldens extremists who apply active pressure against Spanish speakers in many informal ways, as when they interrupt speakers using Spanish in contexts ranging from public talks to private conversations with the exhortation "This is America, speak English!" However, these are not the only kinds of denial that occur. More subtle manifestations of what Bourdieu called "intimidation" can be explored in their larger context, as one face of a set of processes that include the recruitment of symbolic goods, the reshaping of their meaning to new purposes, and the way that these reshaped meanings can then be turned against the sites of their origin.

"Mock Spanish" (Hill, 1998), a set of tactics through which symbolic values from Spanish are incorporated into American English, is an important site of linguistic appropriation. In Mock Spanish, Spanish-origin elements are assigned new pronunciations and new meanings. Mock Spanish forms add value to an English-speaking "American" identity, creating for Americans what I have called a "desirable colloquial persona" that is humorous, easygoing, and cosmopolitan. Simultaneously, however, they assign Spanish to a zone of foreignness and disorder, and reproduce denigrating stereotypes of these communities where the language is used. Mock Spanish includes the use in English of tokens thought by speakers to be "Spanish" in expressions such as "No problemo," "Hasta la vista, baby," "la vida loca," and "Zip, zero, nada," and in single words such as "mañana," "siesta," "cerveza," and "cojones." In the present chapter I will briefly review the history of Mock Spanish, discuss the major linguistic tactics by which it is produced, and then show how its functions work by the semiotic process of social indexicality.

MOCK SPANISH IN AMERICAN ENGLISH: A BRIEF HISTORY

Spanish-language loanwords appear in English at least by the seventeenth century. The oldest token I have identified is "peon," pronounced ['pijan], first attested in 1634 (in the *Oxford English Dictionary;* note that throughout this chapter "real" Spanish items are indicated in italics in standard Spanish orthography, while "Mock" Spanish items, in roman letters, lack acute accent marks). Tokens appear in American English at an early date; for instance, a jail could be called "calaboose," a bold mispronunciation (see below) of Spanish *calabozo,* by 1792 (Cassidy, 1991:508). "Adios" appears in the sense of a hostile dismissal by 1837 (Cassidy, 1991:13). "Vamos" as a command meaning "get out of here" (usually "vamoose") appears by 1900 (Parker, 1902, cited in Bagley, 2002:67; Parker reports the utterance from an incident in 1857). The full flowering of Mock Spanish as it is used today is evident by the middle of the twentieth century. Hollis Gray and his colleagues (1949) report on a rich array of Mock Spanish usages among English-speaking students at the University of Arizona in that period; these include "bold mispronunciations" (see below) in salutations such as "hasty lumbago" and "buena snowshoes." Another source that dates the emergence of something like the modern form is a text in a Raymond Chandler mystery novel, *The Long Goodbye,* of 1953. Chandler is noted for his loving depictions of postwar Los Angeles, but no Mock Spanish appears in the earlier books. In *The Long Goodbye* an evil doctor threatens to beat up Chandler's detective Philip Marlowe. As Marlowe turns to leave, "Dr. Vukanich" says, "Hasta luego, amigo. Don't forget my 10 bucks. Pay the nurse" (Chandler, [1953] 1981:131).

A veritable explosion of Mock Spanish dates from the 1980s and 1990s, a period for which I have documented Mock Spanish forms appearing in every type of media, from major Hollywood film and television productions to minor sites of mass reproduction such as T-shirts, greeting cards, and dog dishes. Interestingly, this period coincides with the rise of the "official-English" movement and with heightened panic over the impact of immigration by Spanish speakers. Mock Spanish during this period became a device that could lend colloquial flair to English at every level of usage, from representations of vulgar street talk in films to political oratory at the highest level. Also during this period, probably influenced by Hollywood films, Mock Spanish spread around the English-speaking world; I have identified examples from Scotland, Ireland, England, and Australia. An item in my collection attesting to the internationalism of Mock Spanish, and to its presence in elite usage, is an envelope that contained information on how to subscribe to the upscale British literary magazine *Granta.* The come-on on the envelope reads "Carpe dinero!"

TACTICS OF INCORPORATION IN MOCK SPANISH

Mock Spanish is constituted by a set of well-established ways of borrowing Spanish-language items, assimilating their pronunciation to English (often in a "hyper-Anglicized" or boldly mispronounced form), shifting the meanings of these items, and using them while speaking English to signal that the speech or text thus embellished is colloquial and informal—often very colloquial and informal, ranging down to the extremes of vulgarity. Both the grammar and pronunciation of Mock Spanish are English. While nonce borrowings occasionally appear in Mock Spanish usage, I would be surprised if its core vocabulary is larger than 100 words. Occasionally new forms enter Mock Spanish from popular culture. For example, in the early 1990s Camel cigarettes advertised in Spanish-speaking neighborhoods with billboards containing a picture of the character "Joe Camel" over the caption "*Un tipo suave*" (a cool guy). I spotted a tip jar in a coffee shop with a handwritten label, "El tip-o suave." Ricky Martin's 1999 hit song "Livin' la Vida Loca" contributed this expression to Mock Spanish. However, as Mock Spanish can successfully deploy only the "Spanish" that is intelligible to monolingual speakers of English, its lexicon is relatively closed.

I have identified four major tactics used to create Mock Spanish. The first is semantic pejoration. Spanish words of neutral or even positive meaning are shifted in Mock Spanish into a semantic space that ranges from the merely jocular to the deeply negative and insulting. Important examples here are expressions of leave-taking, like "Adios" and "Hasta la vista," that can function as insulting or threatening dismissals. Mock Spanish "Adios" has a wide range of meanings. It can be used as a signal of southwestern warmth and authenticity, as when the *Arizona Daily Star* headlines its sports section at the end of a successful University of Arizona basketball season with "Adios to Wildcat seniors." But insulting usages are far more common. For example, a bus-bench advertisement—in an exclusive, upscale Anglo neighborhood—for a Tucson pest-control firm declared "Adios, cucaracha." Such usages are by no means limited to the U.S. Southwest; the *New York Post* editorial for December 21, 2006, observed that New York State comptroller Alan Hevesi was about to plead guilty to a felony under the headline "Adios, Alan." In my collection is a nationally marketed Hallmark greeting card in the "Shoebox" line (on recycled paper) that bears a little figure in serape and sombrero saying "Adiós" (complete with accent mark). Inside, the card reads, "That's Spanish for sure, go ahead and leave your friends, the only people who really care about you, the ones who would loan you their last thin dime, give you the shirts off their backs, sure, just take off!" "Hasta la vista" became a national catchword after the line was uttered by Arnold Schwarzenegger in the 1992 blockbuster film *Terminator 2: Judgment Day*. In the film, Schwarzenegger says "Hasta la vista, baby," just before pulling the trigger on a powerful gun to blow an enemy to pieces. Schwarzenegger has continued to use the tag line in his political career; in California in 2004, when he ran against Gray Davis in a recall election for governor, his supporters sold T-shirts and bumper stickers that read "Hasta la vista, Davis."

Spanish-language terms of address and titles are important objects of semantic pejoration. Thus "amigo" can be used insultingly, as can "Señor" or "Señorita." Another widely used object of semantic pejoration is "nada," which in Spanish means, simply, "nothing," but in Mock Spanish means "absolutely nothing." Spanish *pronto* means merely "soon," but Mock Spanish "pronto" is used imperatively to subordinates, to mean "immediately." Spanish *¿Comprende?* means "Do you understand?" while Mock Spanish "Comprende?" (sometimes pronounced "Comprehende?" [Cassidy, 1991:745]) can be a threat that means something like "Do you understand, stupid?" The use of a Spanish monetary term such as "dinero" or "pesos" means that the items thus priced are, at best, bargains and, at worst, dirt-cheap sleaze. Famous examples of pejorated items are "macho" (which in Spanish includes the simple meaning "male" and need not convey masculine sexual excess or male chauvinism) and "mañana" (which in Spanish means "morning" or "tomorrow" and need not connote procrastination or laziness). Spanish food terms are uniquely available to form colloquialisms, as with "the big enchilada," "the big taco," "the whole enchilada," "a few frijoles short of a burrito" (meaning "stupid," as in "a few bricks short of a load"), and "hot tamale" (an attractive Latina). The mayor of Scottsdale, Arizona, recently objected to the name of a new chain restaurant called "The Pink Taco" in her town; she said the name was offensive since it referred to female genitalia, but the name, an excellent example of semantic pejoration, was not changed (Finnerty, 2006). Regardless of the specific tactic used, all Spanish items that appear in Mock Spanish are eligible as targets for semantic pejoration. They need not be insults, but they cannot be in any way formal or serious.

The second tactic for constructing Mock Spanish is that of euphemism: borrowing Spanish words that are insulting, lewd, or scatological even in their original meaning and using these instead of English words of equivalent meanings. "Loco" (especially in the fixed expression "loco in the cabeza") is old and very common. A very good example of a scatological usage is the Spanish nursery word "caca" as a euphemism for English "shit." A coffee cup in my collection (purchased at a nice gift shop near the University of Arizona several years ago) reads "Caca de toro," and might be used on a desk in a place of employment where English "Bullshit" would be unacceptable. For several years a bumper sticker reading "Caca pasa" (for English "Shit happens") was ubiquitous in Tucson. A usage that is especially offensive to Spanish speakers is "cojones" (pronounced /kə ˈhowniyz/ and often misspelled as "cajones"). Speaking as U.S. ambassador to the United Nations, former Secretary of State Madeleine Albright used the term in an address to the Security Council, arguing that a Cuban pilot who had shot down a spy plane from Florida had shown "not cojones, but cowardice" (Gibbs, 1996). *The Economist,* the upscale British weekly magazine addressed to the international Anglophone business community, once featured on its cover an image of U.S. President George W. Bush with an arrow pointing to his crotch bearing the legend "No cojones on Palestine and Israel" (*The Economist,* April 3–9, 2004).

The third tactic for constructing Mock Spanish is to add Spanish morphology, especially the definite article "el" and the suffix "-o," to English words.

Here the most widely used example is "No problemo," derived from English "No problem." Note that the Spanish word is *problema*. A second example of -o suf-fixation is "mucho," as in "Sell mucho book-os," overheard in the University of Arizona bookstore, or "Happy Birthday to a guy who's moo-cho terrifico," on a greeting card with a picture of a cow. (Note that "mucho," accessible because it is clearly related to English "much," is the only adverb available in Mock Spanish; Spanish *muy* almost never appears.) A recent addition to the universe of -o suf-fixed Mock Spanish items is the travel website www.eurocheapo.com. An excellent example of the addition of "el" is a screensaver from the early 1990s, an image of a fish swimming in an aquarium marketed under the name "El Fish." This was a pun on "Electronic Fish," but it worked nicely since something called "El Fish," within the semantically pejorated universe of Mock Spanish, is something less than a real fish. "El" and "-o" are often found together, forming locutions like "el cheapo" and "el foldo" (e.g., "So the generals have done the big el-foldo [sic] and are signing on to the McCain escalation plan" in a recent blog commentary on the Iraq war [Digbysblog, 2006]).

The "el . . . -o" frame can be used for any reference that the speaker or writer wishes to locate within a jocular colloquial register. For instance, teenagers in La Jolla, California, referred to a popular hangout area, La Jolla Cove, as "El cove-o." My husband used to refer to the major network evening news programs as "el news-o." Suffixation with "-o" can proliferate through an utterance or a text, as in this example from the personal-ad section of the student newspaper at the University of California at San Diego (for which I thank Kathryn Woolard): "Don Thomas! Watcho your backo! You just mighto wake uppo con knee cappo obliterato. Arriba!" The content of this personal ad suggests that a sort of Mafia imitation might have been intended, but the "Arriba!"—a usage made famous by the Warner Brothers' cartoon character Speedy Gonzalez—seems to clinch a diagnosis of Mock Spanish. The frame "numero X-o" is especially productive. "Numero Uno" is common, but constructions like "numero Two-o" and "numero Eleven-o" also appear, and are key components of a "down-home" colloquial style (as in the political commentary of the late Molly Ivins).

The last major tactic for Mock Spanish is hyper-anglicization and the closely related tactic of "bold mispronunciation." Note that all Mock Spanish tokens are anglicized; one cannot speak Mock Spanish while using any pronunciation that even remotely approximates Spanish phonology. Thus orthographic stops like "d" and "g" are pronounced as English stops, not as Spanish spirants. Coronals like "t" and "d" are pronounced as alveolars, not as dentals. Both orthographic "r" and "rr" are pronounced as the English approximant [R], and never as a tap or trill, even when orthographic "t" is pronounced as a flap [ɾ] by Americans. The sequence /pwe/ as in "puente" and "pueblo" sometimes becomes /pjuˈwɛ/. Vowels also have English pronunciations, being either simple lax or offglided tense depending on environment, and unstressed vowels are centralized. Vowels change their qualities to fit the English canon. Thus Spanish "e" in final posi-tion, as in "adobe," becomes /iy/ rather than /ey/, since English does not have the latter in stressed word-final position in native vocabulary. Under stress, it remains /ey/, as in [howˈzey] "Jose."

However, many Mock Spanish words—and some important words that are not really Mock Spanish, such as place-names of Spanish origin—are not merely anglicized, they are "hyper-anglicized" in a way that goes beyond normal anglicization to suggest a stance of maximal distancing from the Spanish pronunciation. For instance, even though Spanish stressed "a" is often approximated with the longer and laxer English /a/ as in "father" in Mock Spanish words such as "caca" and "mañana," in place-names Spanish stressed "a" nearly always appears as /æ/, the vowel of "cat." Some place-names are variable; I have heard ['lows 'garows] and ['lows 'gærows] for "Los Gatos," a community on the peninsula south of San Francisco. Place-names with Spanish *San,* meaning "saint" or "holy," are almost invariably realized as [sæn], even though first-language English permits [..an] as in the name "Don," or, indeed, in [hwan] from Spanish "Juan." An example noticed by Fernando Peñalosa (1981) is ['sæn 'piydRow] "San Pedro" instead of ['san 'peydRow], which would be a normal Anglicization. The more important the place-name, the more likely it is to be hyper-anglicized. Two interesting cases are "Tucson" and "Los Angeles." In English the first is pronounced /'tuwsan/, where Spanish is /tuk'son/ (from seventeenth-century Tohono O'odham *tuk son* "black base"). English /'las 'ænjələs/ "Los Angeles" is of interest because the pronunciation /las/ for "Los" is almost invariant, whereas other California and southwestern place-names with "Los" often appear in English as /lows/. Place-names can be subjected to further hyper-anglicizations, as in clipped "San Antone" from "San Antonio" and clipped and boldly mispronounced "San Berdoo" from "San Bernardino."

Bold mispronunciation, a subclass of hyper-anglicization, is quite old; for instance, the pronunciation of Spanish /o/ as Mock Spanish /uw/ rather than /ow/ is attested in "calaboose" from 1792, noted above, and continued in Cowboy Spanish items like "vamoose" from *vamos* and "buckaroo" from *vaquero.* Today this tactic yields bilingual puns like "Fleas Navidad," which shows up every year on humorous Christmas cards, and another hardy perennial, "Grassy-Ass" for "Gracias" (diversely realized in images on humorous greeting cards). "Mucho" spelled as "Moo-cho" with a picture of a cow is very popular. A whole set of jocular leave-takings formed with "hasty" as a bold mispronunciation of "hasta" (realized as "hasty") uses this technique: hasty lumbago, hasty banana, and so on.

THE FUNCTIONS OF MOCK SPANISH

Mock Spanish has at least two major functions. The first is the construction of a light, jocular, humorous stance that signals that the speaker possesses a desirable colloquial persona that is peculiarly "American." The second is the assignment of reimagined "Spanish" to a zone that is disorderly and "un-American," along with the reproduction of negative stereotypes of the Spanish language and Spanish-language-heritage populations. These functions emerge within layers of meaning of Mock Spanish that are not referential. Instead, they are constituted by the semiotic process known as "indexicality."

"Indexicality" is one of the three major relationships between the sign and its object distinguished by the American philosopher Charles S. Peirce; the others are "iconicity" and "symbol." An "indexical" sign is grounded in its object by proximity, contiguity, or necessity. Examples of Peircean "indexes" are a weathervane, which indexes the direction of the wind; smoke, which indexes fire; and symptoms such as hives or fever, which index physiological disorder or illness. "Iconic" signs are grounded in their objects by resemblance; for instance, a map resembles the territory for which it stands. "Symbols" are grounded by convention: "Cat" is a sign referring to the animal because the English-speaking community is committed to this denotation.

Peirce's idea of indexicality was adapted in linguistics by Roman Jakobson (e.g., 1971) and his student Michael Silverstein (e.g., 1976, 1979) in order to investigate "shifters" such as "this, that," "here, there," "yesterday, today, tomorrow," the pronouns "I" and "you," and tense markers. Just as with the classical Peircean examples of indexical signs, the meaning of shifters inheres in the larger context in which they are manifested. To assign reference to them, one must know when the utterance occurred (for temporal expressions and tense markers), where it occurred (for the deictics "this, that, here, there"), and who was speaking (for the discourse-participant pronouns "I" and "you"). Silverstein (1976) distinguished these "referential indexicals" from the "social indexicals," such as polite *vous* versus intimate *tu* in French, or terms of address in English (e.g., first name versus title plus last name). The interesting property of the social indexicals is that they are "creative": They produce or entail their context rather than being determined by it. That is, the relationship between people who use first names to one another has no logical or referential status comparable to, for instance, "a time before the moment of utterance" in the case of the English past tense or "the person who is speaking" in the case of English "I." Instead, the relationship is continually entailed precisely by the usage itself. "Mock Spanish" items are "social indexicals." Just as the use of nickname as a term of address signals a speaker's stance toward her interlocutor—that is, her assessments or hopes about their relationship—Mock Spanish items entail the speaker's "stance" toward interlocutors and topics within the context of utterance, and define thereby the nature of that context.

Silverstein (1979) observed that such social-indexical meanings could rise to the level of what he called "metapragmatic" awareness. For instance, when a young dental assistant, getting the information from a chart, uses first name as a term of address for a middle-aged woman who is a new patient, the patient might understand the usage as "disrespectful." When a high school student uses orthography common in text messaging (e.g., "2" for "too") in an assigned composition task, a teacher might understand the usage as "inappropriate." Many speakers have strong views on such issues and can discuss these with great fluency. However, other indexical dimensions of language may operate below the level of metapragmatic awareness, at least for some speakers and listeners. For instance, Scott Kiesling (2004) has argued that "dude" as a term of address is favored by young American men because its history makes it appropriate for signaling a stance of "cool solidarity" required by conflicting standards that favor profound male homosocial intimacy but simultaneously insist on strict heterosexuality. The use of "dude" manages this dilemma by being intimate—but not too intimate. Many speakers have strong views on "dude" and people who use it, but unless they have read Kiesling they are almost certainly unaware of the way that the usage works to uphold a heteronormative socio-sexual order.

Users of Mock Spanish exhibit this kind of split in metapragmatic awareness. They usually have a high level of metapragmatic awareness of the first set of functions. When asked to comment on tokens of Mock Spanish, English-heritage speakers suggest that they are humorous and colloquial. They often believe that their Mock Spanish usages show that they "know a little Spanish." That is, such persons are not only entertaining, they are cosmopolitan. However, I have never met a speaker from an English-language-heritage background who has realized that anyone might object to Mock Spanish, or who has been able—or willing—to admit to the functions of Mock Spanish in denigrating Spanish and its speakers, without extensive exposure to data and analysis of the type presented here. In contrast, many members of Spanish-language-heritage communities find Mock Spanish objectionable. Sometimes they object to it simply because it is mispronounced, or ungrammatical, or distorts the meaning of words, and therefore violates canons of purism that are very important to many Spanish speakers in the United States, who must struggle to maintain grammatical standards in a context with almost no support for their efforts. Sometimes they are able to articulate this as "disrespectful" of the Spanish language. And often (as, for instance, by Peñalosa [1981] in his classic *Chicano Sociolinguistics*), they are able to identify it as racist, especially when Mock Spanish usages emanate from, or are accompanied by (as they often are), racist imagery such as the Frito Bandito or the cartoon character Speedy Gonzalez.

The function of Mock Spanish in creating, for English-heritage speakers, a "desirable colloquial persona" is very easy to illustrate. Mock Spanish is so important in this function that being able to use it is a vital part of the rhetorical skill set of someone who aspires to a prototypical "American" identity—which is, of course, male, although women use Mock Spanish too. Mock Spanish use by African Americans is a very important phenomenon that illustrates its broader connotation of "Americanness" rather than merely of "whiteness" (unfortunately, attention to this topic is beyond the scope of this chapter). My favorite example of this function is from the film *Terminator 2: Judgment Day*. In the film the superstar actor Arnold Schwarzenegger plays a hero machine, a "Terminator," sent from the future to defend a child, John Connor, who will grow up to save humanity by defeating an army of evil machines. Consider the following dialogue, which occurs as John Connor and his mother are fleeing the forces of evil in a car driven by Schwarzenegger as the "Terminator."

> MOTHER: Keep it under sixty-five. We don't want to get pulled over.
> TERMINATOR: Affirmative (in machine-like voice, with German accent).
> JOHN CONNOR: No no no no no no. You gotta listen to the way people talk! You don't say "Affirmative," or some shit like that, you say "No problemo." And if

somebody comes off to you with an attitude, you say "Eat me." And if you want to shine them on, you say "Hasta la vista, baby."

TERMINATOR: Hasta la vista, baby (still in machine-like voice).

JOHN CONNOR: Yeah, later, dickwad. And if someone gets upset, you say "Chill out!" Or, you can do combinations.

TERMINATOR: Chill out, dickwad (in machine-like voice).

JOHN CONNOR: That's great! See, you're gettin' it!

TERMINATOR: No problemo (in nearly normal voice).

In this crucial dialogue sequence the famous tag "Hasta la vista, baby" is introduced for the first time—Schwarzenegger's good terminator will use it again in a scene where he destroys an evil terminator. In his final utterance, the Mock Spanish tag "No problemo," the terminator's voice is heard as fully human for the first time in the film. In short, it is through the use of Mock Spanish that Schwarzenegger's terminator moves from being a machine, a symbol of fascist foreignness amplified by his German accent, to being a sympathetic protagonist. The English tags that accompany the Mock Spanish in this little language lesson—"Eat me," "dickwad"—work to define the vulgar lower limits of the register of "colloquialism" constructed by Mock Spanish. Note that in the most recent Terminator film, *Terminator 3: Rise of the Machines,* released in 2003, Schwarzenegger's character does not use Mock Spanish. Indeed, the John Connor character in that film, who has grown into an adult, tries to elicit it from him. Schwarzenegger's character is given the line "That was the other T-2-100." By the time of the final edit of the film, Schwarzenegger was already planning his run for governor in a heavily Hispanic state as a "middle-of-the-road" Republican, seeking crossover Democratic votes.

In *Terminator 2: Judgment Day,* the Terminator becomes not merely human but "American." This use of Mock Spanish to construct an explicitly "American" voice appears in other films as well. In 2006, the film *Talladega Nights: The Ballad of Ricky Bobby* was an enormous hit for the comedian Will Ferrell; the DVD of the film, which appeared in time for Christmas, was prominently marketed by all major retail chains as appropriate family entertainment for the holiday season. Ferrell plays Ricky Bobby, a NASCAR racing champion who hits hard times when his preeminence is challenged by Jean Girard, a French driver from the Formula One circuit. Jean Girard is not only French (and effete to the highest degree, in contrast to Ricky Bobby's down-home style) but also gay (this antithesis of all that is "American" is played to over-the-top perfection by the great comedian Sacha Baron Cohen). Ricky Bobby's first confrontation with Jean Girard comes in a bar when the French driver switches the jukebox from country music to cool jazz. As Ricky Bobby reaches back to punch out the French interloper, he says, "Welcome to America, amigo." Another plot twist is that, in his despair over his failures on the track, Ricky Bobby breaks up with his best buddy Cal Naughton. In the last moments of the film, Ricky and Cal reunite, and Mock Spanish plays a key role in this moment of tender all-American homosociality. Cal's track nickname is "Magic Man," and Ricky announces that finally he, too, has picked a perfect nickname: It is "El Diablo," which Ricky asserts "is like Spanish for a fighting chicken, with the claws, and the beak!" This clever touch, which shows that Ricky, typical of Mock Spanish users, knows nothing at all about Spanish, is part of the film's pointed satire of NASCAR-centered "Americanness," and the film's use of Mock Spanish, appearing at pivotal moments in plot transition, is very telling.

Mock Spanish nicknames are an important part of a certain kind of American masculinity. U.S. President George W. Bush is famous for giving nicknames to friends and subordinates. Among those recorded are "Pablo" for his first treasury secretary, Paul O'Neill; "Camarones" for Carl Cameron, a correspondent for Fox News; and "El Grande Jorge" for Congressman George Miller of California. Bush himself is often called "El Jefe" when bloggers and journalists seek a jocular tone, although within the Bush family this is the nickname for George H. W. Bush, the president's father. Another Mock Spanish nicknamer on the political right is radio personality Rush Limbaugh, who often refers to himself as "El Rushbo." The most elaborate Limbaugh nickname is probably "El loco poco Dicko" for former Democratic congressional leader and presidential candidate Dick Gephardt. However, the use of Mock Spanish is certainly not restricted to the political right, or to men. I have already mentioned its use by the columnist Molly Ivins, who is far to the left in American political terms, and another example is from the *Boston Globe*'s columnist Ellen Goodman: "But the sexier and racier question dominating the early chatter [about possible Democratic presidential candidates for 2008] is the possible mano-a-womano, black-and-white matchup that could be offered with Hillary Clinton or Barack Obama atop the national ticket" (Goodman, 2006). And Mock Spanish can appear even in intensely anti-Spanish contexts, as in an Internet image on the website www.illegalimmigrationbumperstickers.com, where Congressman Tom Tancredo (R-CO), among the most vitriolically anti-Hispanic members of the U.S. Congress, is labeled "America's '*Numero Uno* Point Man!' in Congress on Illegal Immigration!" (italics and extra exclamation point in original).

In summary, Mock Spanish is a very important resource for American English speakers who wish to present a "desirable colloquial persona" that is humorous, laid-back, and colloquial and can even be vulgar when called for. It is crucial to be able to convey the stance associated with this style, not just in everyday interaction but in the highest levels of public life, and Mock Spanish is available as a ready-made to do this job. When Madeleine Albright said "cojones" in front of the Security Council of the United Nations, her image, which for many Americans had merged with Marx Brothers caricatures of a formidable older woman, was transformed into one of a tough, savvy, all-American broad who could be promoted with confidence to the exalted position of Secretary of State. Mock Spanish is always good for a laugh, for showing that, even in a formal context like Ellen Goodman's *Boston Globe* op-ed on the Democratic presidential candidates, the writer is serious, but not so serious that you wouldn't like her. President Bush's Mock Spanish nicknames work to challenge the idea that he might be "all hat and no cattle," a Yale fratboy cheerleader just masquerading as a tough Texas cowpoke. And for at least two decades scriptwriters have drawn endlessly on Mock Spanish tags to create characters like John Connor in

Terminator 2 and Ricky Bobby in *Talladega Nights,* who resonate as "real people" for an American audience.

If Mock Spanish is such a useful tool in creating a kind of stance, a kind of interlocutory persona, that many Americans find very desirable, what could possibly be wrong with it? How can it constitute a form of "symbolic violence"? Indeed, should we not think of Mock Spanish in precisely the opposite way, as making a continual display of the importance of the contribution of Spanish to the American language, and as showing American openness to and respect for this linguistic heritage? Regrettably, it is easy to show that this is not the case.

First of all, Mock Spanish associates the Spanish language irrevocably with the nonserious, the casual, the laid-back, the humorous. Spanish is available for joking and for insult; it is not available to lend gravitas or sophistication. Compare, for example, a case of "Mock German": the Internet marketing of an expensive computer keyboard, intended for programming specialists, under the name "Das Keyboard" (überGeeks only!). Here, the German definite article "Das" is intended to convey fine engineering and high-tech credibility. It is unimaginable that such a product could be called "El Keyboard." "El Keyboard" would be like "El Fish," a cheap imitation, or, at best, a way of joking about something familiar and not terribly special.

Second, Mock Spanish, with its relentlessly anglicized phonology and grammar, assigns native Spanish fluency to the realm of the "un-American." A speaker of American English who pronounces Spanish place-names or the names of public figures with any approximation of native Spanish-language phonology risks being accused of being stuffy, effete, even ridiculous. A Spanish speaker who insists on such pronunciations, even one who pronounces his or her own name with Spanish phonology, is seen as making a highly marked political gesture (Louisor-White and Valencia Tanno, 1994). In the early 1990s, a *Saturday Night Live* television skit made this very clear. The skit includes the usual *SNL* cast of Anglos, along with Puerto Rican actor Jimmy Smits as a guest performer. All the Anglo characters make themselves ridiculous (I draw this judgment from having shown the skit many times in talks and to classes—and also from a line given to the Smits character: "If you don't mind my saying, sometimes when you take Spanish words and kind of over-pronounce them, well, it's kind of annoying") by insisting on phony-sounding hyper-Hispanicized pronunciations of everyday Spanish forms like "Nicaragua," "San Diego," the Denver football team, the "Broncos," and names for Mexican food. A running joke involves the name of Smits's character, Antonio Mendoza, an economics consultant, who keeps insisting that he prefers that his name be pronounced just /mɛnˈdowzə/, and not /menˈdoθa/ or /menˈdosa/. I take this as an important part of the construction of a desirable identity for the Smits character, who is displayed in the skit as the only person present who is unpretentiously comfortable in a genuine, all-American skin.

Third, Mock Spanish, with its utter neglect of Spanish grammar (consider, for instance, "Nuevo Catholics," which appeared in the *New York Times*), creates a linguistic space for what I have called "orderly disorder" (Hill, 1998)—"orderly" because it is part of a larger, cultural order where Spanish has been assigned a particular, nonserious space. Within this space, even serious messages involving health and safety, where by law Spanish translations are required, are likely to be grossly ungrammatical. Nearly thirty years ago Peñalosa (1981) pointed out the presence in restrooms in Southern California of signs that said "Wash your hands/Lava sus manos" and noted that it was astonishing that three grammatical errors could be fitted into three words. As written, the sign can only be instructing the reader to wash the hands of some other, unnamed person; what is intended is "Lavarse las manos," with the infinitive being the appropriate choice of the verb form for public instructions (e.g., "*No fumar*" or "*No estacionarse*"). An especially astonishing example is a large sign on the Mexican side of the U.S.-Mexico border at the Mariposa crossing in Nogales. The sign reads, "All vehicles must stop/Todos vehiculos deben pararse," where the Spanish translation is an illiterate pidgin. A definite article is required before *vehículos* (note the accent mark on the "i"), *deben* is a curious choice of command form, and *pararse* is at best odd; normally "stop" (as of a car) is simply *parar,* and to at least some Spanish speakers of my acquaintance, *pararse* means "stand up."

Rusty Barrett (2006) studied uses of Mock Spanish–influenced utterances by Anglo wait staff to Spanish-speaking kitchen staff in a Mexican restaurant in Austin, Texas (the menu included many examples of Mock Spanish). One tactic of the English speakers was to use Spanish "nonce loans" from which all Spanish syntax and morphology were stripped, such as "Could you *hablar por telefono* and see if he can *trabajo?*" (Barrett, 2006:180, 185). Even written communications from management to Spanish-speaking staff used this kind of language. The predictable mix-ups and misunderstandings, which at best compromised the efficient running of the restaurant and at worst led to lapses in sanitary practice, were invariably blamed on the Spanish speakers. Barrett reports that, astonishingly, even a manager who spoke quite good Spanish nearly always used this kind of pidgin when she spoke to Spanish-speaking employees.

One case in my files of such Mock Spanish–influenced usage arguably led to the death of an American citizen. In April 2001, a Peruvian military pilot shot down a suspected drug-smuggling plane, only to discover that he had accidentally killed an American missionary and her infant daughter. Accompanying the Peruvian flight was an American spotter plane; one member of the crew tried to stop the Peruvian from firing by radioing these words: "Are you sure it's a bandido?" This was almost certainly pronounced [bænˈdiydow], which would be unintelligible to a Spanish speaker (*USA Today,* 2001).

The "orderly disorder" of Spanish for English speakers in the United States, which is taken for granted and even appreciated by these speakers, contrasts with the most acute anxiety among Spanish speakers, as documented by Bonnie Urciuoli (1996) for Puerto Ricans in the New York City area, that they must never mix the two languages, that even a slight Spanish accent in English is discreditable, and that to code-switch (a practice that decades of linguistic research has shown is an important part of linguistic order among bilinguals) is deeply compromising and suggests ignorance of English. This contrast, between the casual disorderliness of Spanish in white-dominated public space and the hypervigilance of linguistic boundaries within that space required for Spanish speakers, is a striking example of how practices associated with "whiteness" can become unmarked and unnoticeable, while very similar practices associated with "color" become the object of intense monitoring (Hill, 1998).

Finally, the connotations conveyed by the semantic pejoration of Mock Spanish vocabulary items constantly reproduce and reinscribe vulgar racist stereotypes of the Spanish language and of people of Spanish heritage. To find "mañana" entertaining, one must have access to the stereotype of "laziness." For "adios" and "hasta la vista" to function as hostile threats, one must have access to the stereotype of insincerity, of superficial politeness that is really only a thin veil for vicious motives. For a furniture store in Tucson to advertise a sale under the headline "Contemporary and Southwestern dining, for pesos!" makes sense only if speakers understand goods priced in pesos to be especially cheap, since the meaning is not literal; the store would never have accepted Mexican currency, which is almost impossible to exchange in Tucson.

Other Mock Spanish forms index stereotypes of dirt, disorder, and sexual looseness. I have done the most detailed work on "mañana" (Hill, 2005b) and on the ways that stereotypes of "political corruption" as typical of the Spanish-speaking world are reproduced in Mock Spanish. Here I treat briefly the latter case, which is conveyed by Mock Spanish uses of political titles like "el presidente" and "Generalissimo El Busho" (the latter a favorite of the leftist cartoonist Ted Rall, who draws Bush wrapped in an absurdly overdecorated military uniform with huge epaulettes and a high-peaked military cap covered in braid and insignia; the label is clearly a hit, since "Generalissimo El Busho" paraphernalia can be purchased on Rall's website). In order to "get the joke" of these usages one must have access to the stereotype of the corrupt "Banana Republic" politician. Occasionally the requirements of humor or rhetoric bring these stereotypes to the surface and show that the Mock Spanish form makes them readily available. For instance, in March 2001 the leftist magazine *The Nation* ran a contest in which readers were invited to submit an appropriate title for George W. Bush. The editors of *The Nation* suggested that "Mr. President" was awkward, since he had not really been elected (Bush was installed in office for his first term by a decision of the U.S. Supreme Court, which stopped a recount of votes in the state of Florida). Inevitably, one reader submitted "El Presidente." *The Nation* editors commented, "A Banana Republican, of course" (*The Nation,* 2001:5).

Another case where the denigrating connotations of borrowed Spanish political language surfaced was in a *New York Times* op-ed essay by Bill Keller, who deplored intemperate attacks on Bush. Keller observed that "I doubt anyone ever referred to his father as a 'chicken hawk' or to the first Bush administration as a 'junta.' These are insults, not arguments." (Keller, 2003). For readers who may be uncertain of this point, junta is a perfectly ordinary Spanish word for a unit of political governance such as a town council. My son, who plays the viola in a symphony orchestra based in Valladolid in Spain, collects his paycheck from La Junta de Castilla y León, the governing body of the autonomous region. The English loanword has been pejorated to refer to some sort of undemocratic cabal, as when several colonels rule a country after a military coup.

A fascinating irony of the "Banana Republic" stereotype is that the original "Banana Republic" was created not by Latin Americans possessed by some essential instinct for Ruritanian misrule but, rather, by Americans who installed a corrupt dictatorship in Honduras in 1910 to protect the interests of what eventually became the United Fruit Company. Similar American-assisted coups installed at least three other notorious military dictatorships: Rafael Trujillo in the Dominican Republic in 1930, Carlos Castillo Armas in Guatemala in 1954, and Augusto Pinochet in Chile in 1973. However, the stereotype is extraordinarily resilient. This pervasive resiliency, I believe, is at least partly due to the constant use of forms like "el presidente" as jokes and insults. The stereotype shapes relationships between the United States and Latin America at the highest level, when democratically elected heads of state like Hugo Chávez of Venezuela and Evo Morales of Bolivia are immediately assimilated by U.S. mass media to the stereotype of suspected corruption and misrule. Interestingly, these relationships are inflected not only by the suspicion of corruption but as well by the idea that Latin America is somehow a trivial part of the world that can be taken lightly, a position entirely consistent with the trivializing jocular stance constructed by Mock Spanish.

In the early months of his presidency, before 9/11, George W. Bush, who as a former governor of Texas had some notion of the importance of U.S. relations with Mexico, put Latin American policy very much on the front burner, and hoped to develop some solid agreements on trade and immigration. This initiative, however, was interpreted by critics as revealing his basic lack of gravitas and inexperience in foreign policy. Maureen Dowd of the *New York Times* commented, "W.'s advisers tried to make him look more impressive in his first forays into diplomacy by keeping the big world leaders at bay and letting him hang out with lesser leaders he could talk to in Spanish. So now we have a whole new alliance with Central and South American countries simply because W. feels more comfortable at what *USA Today* dubbed 'amigo diplomacy'" (Dowd, 2001).

CONCLUSION

The epigraph from Bourdieu that opens this chapter raises an important question: What roles do "responsibility," "intention," and "awareness" play in symbolic violence? I have found it helpful to understand linguistic appropriation and Mock Spanish within the larger sociocultural framework of white racism in the United States. Most people understand racism within the terms of a folk theory that insists that a "racist" must hold prejudiced beliefs and act intentionally upon these. When the components of "denial" that I have enumerated above for Mock Spanish are suggested to them, they vigorously reject these as impossible, because surely no racism is intended by such common and even entertaining and delightful usages. And, indeed, sometimes it is difficult to see why one would analyze Mock Spanish as in any way "violent," symbolically or otherwise. Consider the following exchange, which I overheard on a Sunday morning in March 2001 in the Elk City Cafe in Redway, California. Both speakers were Anglos.

COUNTER WAITRESS TO MALE CUSTOMER: How's it going?
 CUSTOMER: Oh, mas o menos.
 WAITRESS: Not so bueno, huh?

On its face, in isolation, this exchange is entirely benign. It is certainly inappropriate to accuse such speakers, in that moment, of "intending" a message of racist denigration. However, in following Bourdieu's instruction to "take account of the entire social structure" (or at least as much of it as I can in this space), I hope to have shown that this innocuous bit of chit-chat is part of a much larger system that is indeed a site of symbolic violence, that works to accomplish what Bourdieu would call "unification of the linguistic market." Under this system of unification, if Spanish is to be "American," it cannot sound like Spanish, it cannot have Spanish grammar or morphology, it cannot be serious. To become "American," Spanish words must be transformed into jokes and insults, and the speakers just quoted are participating in this transformation and in this unification of the market, which is accomplished not simply by pressure against Spanish in the public arena, but by the infinite repetition of unmarked appropriations of Spanish that range all the way from this exchange over Sunday morning pancakes in the Elk City Cafe to the language of the *New York Times* opinion pieces and high diplomacy. In their totality, these practices constitute a powerful system of "intimidation." In the face of such an all-pervasive set of cultural practices among speakers of American English, it would be absurd for us to try to decide whether any individual speaker, on any local occasion, "intends" the denigration of Spanish or its speakers. They are only doing what real "Americans" do. And what they do constitutes, at the larger structural level to which each individual moment of practice contributes, a clear case of ongoing symbolic violence against the Spanish language and people of Spanish-speaking heritage in the United States.

Against the background of what we can now see is a large and complex set of linguistic practices and politics, we can begin to understand the intensity of reaction when public uses of Spanish that violate this system of unification of the market occur. Consider, for instance, the extreme reaction in most English-language media in the United States to the release of "Nuestro Himno," an arrangement of "The Star-Spangled Banner" by several Latino artists, in April 2006. "Nuestro Himno" is moving and beautiful, serious to the highest degree, and its Spanish language is very fine. Appearing immediately after the massive nationwide demonstrations in March 2006 for recognition of the human rights of undocumented immigrants, "Nuestro Himno" explicitly asserted a place for the Spanish language in American public life, a place for Spanish in the expression of patriotism, and a claim on full "Americanness" for speakers of Spanish. The public reaction among Anglos was almost universally one of intense condemnation. Right-wing talk radio hosts and guests devoted endless hours and even days to vitriolic attacks on the arrangement, and President Bush stated in a press conference on April 28, 2006, that "I think people who want to be a citizen of this country ought to learn English. And they ought to learn to sing the anthem in English." In the climate of hysteria in this period, even a single word in public Spanish could trigger this kind of reaction. In a game against the New York Yankees on May 5, 2006, to celebrate the Cinco de Mayo holiday, the Texas Rangers wore uniforms with "Rangers" replaced by "Los Rangers." I would have recognized this as a colloquialism entirely within the overlapping ranges of Booster Regional Spanish (evoking the Texas "heritage") and Mock Spanish, but correspondents on the blog of right-wing commentator Michelle Malkin found the uniforms highly offensive and insulting, as "kowtow[ing] to their Mexican-American and Mexican illegal audience" (Malkin, 2005).

One element in my epigraph from Bourdieu is not completely appropriate to this discussion, and that is his claim that within such a system of unification, "timidity" will preclude deviations. While I have heard from U.S. Spanish speakers many anecdotes about a sense of intimidation, and while scholars like Urciuoli (1996) have carefully documented this phenomenon, works like "Nuestro Himno," the continuing production of Spanish-language and bilingual books and essays in the United States by courageous publishing houses and authors, and hundreds of small gestures of resistance, both against Mock Spanish and its relatives and in support of real Spanish, show that the Spanish-heritage community in the United States has not been completely intimidated. Symbolic violence against U.S. Spanish, like other hegemonic forms, ultimately fails as a totalizing effort, and we can hope that in the future such efforts will expand to yield an appropriate recognition of the worth of Spanish—real Spanish, with all its wealth of dialect and register diversity—as a form of expression that is recognized as a way of being American.

References

Bagley, Will. 2002. *Blood of the Prophets.* Norman: University of Oklahoma Press.

Barrett, Rusty. 2006. "Language Ideology and Racial Inequality: Competing Functions of Spanish in an Anglo-Owned Mexican Restaurant." *Language in Society* 35:163–204.

Bourdieu, Pierre. 1991. *Language and Symbolic Power.* Cambridge, MA: Harvard University Press.

Cassidy, Frederick (ed.). 1991. *Dictionary of American Regional English.* Volume I, *Introduction, and A–C.* Cambridge, MA: Harvard University Press.

Chandler, Raymond. [1953] 1981. *The Long Goodbye.* New York: Vintage Books.

Digbysblog. 2006. "Unhappy New Year." Retrieved May 1, 2007. (http://digbysblog.blogspot.com/2006_12_01_digbysblog_archive.html#116689902380404624)

Dowd, Maureen. 2001. "I Have a Nickname!!!" *New York Times,* April 29, Section 4, p. 17.

Finnerty, Megan. 2006. "Suggestive Name Puts Eatery, City at Odds." *Arizona Republic,* April 22. Retrieved May 6, 2006. (http://www.azcentral.com/ent/dining/articles/0422pinktaco.html)

Gibbs, Nancy. 1996. "An American Voice." *Time* 149(1):32–33.

Goodman, Ellen. 2006. "Hillary and Barack for Real, Despite Sexism and Racism." *Arizona Daily Star,* December 29, p. A 11.

Gray, Hollis, Virginia Jones, Patricia Parker, Alex Smith, and Klonda Lynn. 1949. "Gringoisms in Arizona." *American Speech* 24:234–236.

Hill, Jane H. 1998. "Language, Race, and White Public Space." *American Anthropologist* 100:680–689.

———. 2005a. "Borrowing as Appropriation: Indexicality and the Language of White

Racism in American English." Plenary Lecture, Annual Meeting of the Linguistic Society of America, Albuquerque, NM, January 6.

———. 2005b. "Intertextuality as Source and Evidence for Indirect Indexical Meanings." *Journal of Linguistic Anthropology* 15:113–124.

Jakobson, Roman. 1971. "Shifters, Verbal Categories, and the Russian Verb." Pp. 130–147 in *Selected Writings of Roman Jakobson,* vol. 2. The Hague: Mouton Press.

Keller, Bill. 2003. "Fear on the Home Front." *New York Times,* February 22, p. A35.

Kiesling, Scott. 2004. "Dude." *American Speech* 79(3):281–305.

Louisor-White, Dominique, and Dolores Valencia Tanno. 1994. "Code-Switching in the Public Forum: New Expressions of Cultural Identity and Persuasion." Paper presented to the Conference on Hispanic Language and Social Identity, University of New Mexico, Albuquerque, February 10–12.

Malkin, Michelle. 2005. "Los Rangers." Retrieved May 7, 2006. (http://michellemalkin.com/archives/005138.htm)

The Nation. 2001. "Name the President!" March 26, p. 5.

Peñalosa, Fernando. 1981. *Chicano Sociolinguistics.* Rowley, MA: Newbury House Press.

Reid, T. R. 2005. "Spanish at School Translates to Suspension." *Washington Post,* December 9, p. A03.

Silverstein, Michael. 1976. "Shifters, Linguistic Categories, and Cultural Description." Pp. 11–55 in Keith H. Basso and Henry A. Selby (eds.), *Meaning in Anthropology.* Albuquerque: University of New Mexico Press.

———. 1979. "Language Structure and Linguistic Ideology." Pp. 193–247 in Paul R. Clyne, William F. Hanks, and Carol L. Hofbauer (eds.), *The Elements: A Parasession on Linguistic Units and Levels.* Chicago: Chicago Linguistic Society.

Urciuoli, Bonnie. 1996. *Exposing Prejudice: Puerto Rican Experiences of Language, Race, and Class.* Boulder, CO: Westview Press.

USA Today. 2001. "Are You Sure It's a Bandido?" April 27–29, p. 1A.

CHAPTER 8

Racialization Among Cubans and Cuban Americans

Lisandro Pérez

> To be Cuban is to be more than white, more than mulatto, more than black.... [T]he affinity of character is more powerful than the affinity of color.... [I]n Cuba there will never be a race war.
> —*José Martí ([1893] 2001:299–300)*

José Martí was wrong in his analysis and prediction about race in Cuba. A romantic nationalist, gifted writer, and political organizer, he was largely responsible, in the late nineteenth century, for forging an idealistic vision of a sovereign Cuban nation. He attempted to implement that vision by organizing a broad-based movement among émigrés that culminated in the definitive war for the independence of the island. An unracialized Cuba was both an aspiration and a political necessity, as Martí sought to bring together the disparate sectors of Cuban society, in the island and abroad, in a determined push for nationhood. But before, during, and after Martí's time, the dream of a Cuba without racial differentiation was far from the reality. Even Martí's confident prediction that Cuba would never have a race war was proved wrong only seventeen years after his death.

But the history of Cuban race relations has been cyclical rather than linear. In some instances, political and economic conditions served as gravitational forces to minimize racial differentiation. In others, centrifugal forces served to increase racial differentiation.

The driving argument of this chapter is that currently the forces of racial differentiation are once again at work, not only in Cuba but also among Cubans in the United States. The specific conditions that have led to this upsurge in racialization differ between island and diaspora. Before we analyze those conditions, however, it is important to establish the broader context of Cuban race relations by examining the evolving racial demographics of the island and the historical and cultural antecedents of the current situation.

"He *Looks* White": Cuba's Racial Demographics

An often-told anecdote, which may or may not be historically accurate, illustrates the nature of Cuban racial dynamics. Commenting on the sudden rise to power in 1933 of a little-known army sergeant of mixed racial ancestry by the name of Fulgencio Batista, one white Cuban politician is said to have remarked to another, with some concern: "He looks black." His colleague sardonically replied: "No, he *looks* white." Although the retort was intended to place the upstart sergeant "in his place," it also shows the fluidity of Cuban racial categories, a fact that has tended to make imprecise and controversial any discussion of the island's racial composition.

Cuba is a good example of a country with what Charles Wagley (1965) described as the phenotypical pattern of racial categorization prevalent in Brazil and the Hispanic Caribbean—that is, a system in which social race is determined strictly by physical characteristics such as skin color, hair texture, and facial features. Unlike the arrangement in the United States, which, Wagley argues, uses ancestry to create a dichotomous classification system (black and white), the Brazilian and Caribbean system based on physical characteristics places race along a continuum, making distinctions that are relative and that have no clear dividing boundaries between the races (Wagley, 1965:541). Batista, as do most Cubans, fell somewhere in the middle of the "unmixed" extremes of the racial continuum, thus leading to questions as to how to racially categorize him.

The only source of comprehensive data on Cuba's racial composition is the series of modern population censuses that started in the postcolonial era and has continued into the twenty-first century. Those censuses, nine in all, were conducted under very diverse political conditions: from U.S. protectorate status, to governments of the Cuban Republic, to enumerations taken by the current socialist government (Pérez, 1984), with the latest one conducted as recently as 2002. Yet, all those censuses employed exactly the same methodology for ascertaining and categorizing race, a methodology that reflects the classification system described by Wagley. Three racial categories were used to tap into the continuum: white, black, and mixed. Furthermore, members of each household were placed into those three categories by the enumerator, who did not ask each person his or her race but, rather, simply made a judgment based on his or her visual perception. The system is therefore based, strictly speaking, on physical characteristics as perceived by the enumerator and not on self-perception or ancestry.

Table 8.1 presents the percent distribution, by race, for each census since 1899. The validity of these census figures has long been questioned because they appear to grossly overestimate the white population, a phenomenon explained by the tendency of enumerators to make judgments that favor the "whiter" end of the continuum (Moore, 1988:357–359). While that is a problem, these figures should not be disregarded. Their validity may certainly be questioned, especially the inflation of the "white" percentage, but their reliability appears quite good. They represent, after all, the collective judgments of hundreds of thousands of Cubans who served as enumerators over more than a century and who made those judgments reflecting prevailing cultural norms about racial categorizing. The census data, for example, are sensitive to known population trends, such as the massive immigration of Spaniards that increased the white percentage during the first few decades of the twentieth century. The figures also reflect the trends during the post-1959 period, after the 1953 census. The exodus of the upper sectors of Cuban society (more on this later) is reflected in the relative drop of the white percentage. The absence of modern-day migration from Africa and the Caribbean has led to a leveling and even a decline of the black percentage. The greatest relative growth has occurred in the "mixed" category. It has frequently been observed that the population of Cuba has turned "blacker" since 1959. "Darker" may be a more accurate term, although one could take the same ironic view of the politician who commented on Batista and say that now more Cubans "look" whiter. In any case, Alejandro de la Fuente has called this process the "mulattoization" of the Cuban population (de la Fuente, 2001:308).

FROM SLAVERY TO THE REPUBLIC

One of the many paradoxes of Cuba is that a strong and unitary national identity has coexisted with a marked cultural diversity. Cuba is one of the most "Spanish"

Table 8.1 Percent Distribution of the Population of Cuba, by Race, 1899–2002[a]

	1899	1907	1919	1931	1943	1953	1981	2002
White	66.9	69.7	72.2	72.1	74.3	72.8	66.0	65.0
Black	14.9	13.4	11.2	11.0	9.7	12.4	12.0	10.1
Mixed[b]	18.2	16.9	16.6	16.9	16.0	14.8	22.0	24.9

[a]A census was taken in 1970, but no data on racial composition from that census have been released.

[b]Figures on the Asian population (which comprises less than 1 percent of the total) have been included in the "mixed" category to make the data series consistent with the 2002 census, which for the first time did not list Asians separately.

Sources: Compiled and computed from Oficina Nacional del Censo, República de Cuba (n.d.:CVII); and Oficina Nacional de Estadísticas (2005).

countries of Latin America, largely because of the lateness of its independence from Spain and the massive migration of Spaniards to the island during the first decades of the twentieth century. Paradoxically, Cuba is also one of the most "African" countries of Spanish America. The culture of the African slaves has shown an extraordinary resilience and remains a vital and integral part of the island's cultural and social landscape. It is a culture that clearly manifests its African lineage. The explanation lies in the size and timing of the arrival of major waves of African slaves to Cuba. With the possible exception of Brazil, nowhere in the Western Hemisphere did Africans arrive as massively and as late in the nineteenth century as they did in Cuba. Cuba's sugar revolution, arguably the most significant economic event of the island's colonial era, did not start in earnest until the early 1800s.

By the end of slavery late in the nineteenth century, Cuba had hundreds of thousands of first- and second-generation Africans, among whom African cultural influences remained strong. The impact of this influence on the modern culture of Cuba cannot be understated. The music that Cubans created during the first half of the twentieth century, a result of the syncretism of African and European cultural elements and instrumentation, serves as the best example of this influence.

The struggles for independence that started in 1868 "freed slaves, made them soldiers, and called them citizens" (Ferrer, 1999:3). Free men of color assumed positions of responsibility, including command positions as commissioned officers, and led a truly multiracial independence army (Ferrer, 1999:3). Liberation from Spain promised a new beginning for race relations because the rhetoric of independence, advanced primarily by Martí, promulgated racelessness (Ferrer, 1999:3; 2000:60–61).

Unquestionably, the Cuban Republic (1902–1958) failed to meet those expectations. Things got off to a dismal start soon after its establishment in 1902. Afro-Cubans were largely marginalized from political life and therefore excluded from participation in what became the vehicle for social mobility for many Cubans in the aftermath of the devastating struggles for independence: the money to be made, legitimately and illegitimately, in the wake of the massive U.S. investments and franchises in the island. Exclusion from the government, run largely by the white veterans of the war for independence, meant exclusion from the institution that pulled the levers that channeled those investments and contracts (Pérez, 2006:160–168). This exclusion led to an armed rebellion by Afro-Cubans, a rebellion that was ruthlessly quashed by the Cuban army during the brief race war of 1912 (Helg, 1995:193–226).

Just how much the Cuban Republic failed to meet the expectations of an unracialized Cuba and what the extent of racism and discrimination was prior to the 1959 Revolution have been topics of considerable debate. Tomás Fernández Robaina (1990:148–189) and Jorge Ibarra (1998:141–151) have argued that institutional discrimination remained strong throughout the Republic, pointing to evidence of racism and racial stratification in the occupational and economic structure. Jorge Castellanos and Isabel Castellanos (1990:331–429) and Alejandro de la Fuente (2001:17–255), while not disagreeing that discrimination persists, document the progress in race relations, especially in juridical terms and after the Revolution of 1933. That progress, however, fell woefully short of the antiracist and raceless rhetoric that fueled the participation of Afro-Cubans in the independence movement. Martí's lofty vision for the Cuban nation drove the stated agenda of every political movement in the twentieth century, both inside and outside of Cuba. Reaching the high bar that Martí set as national ideals was a difficult task, not only in terms of race but also with respect to areas such as sovereignty and social justice. The omnipresence of his social thought in Cuban political discourse has served to accentuate the gap between aspirations and reality, creating an ethos of failure and frustration that helped to fuel the turbulence that characterized twentieth-century Cuba. By the 1950s attaining Martí's social agenda was one of the banners around which coalesced a successful revolutionary movement.

RACE AND REVOLUTION

From the time it rose to power in 1959 to the present, the current government of Cuba has exhorted the population to unite behind a revolutionary project that claims socioeconomic equality as both a goal and an accomplishment. Universal public health and education have been the underpinnings of an agenda that started with wide-ranging programs of social redistribution. Those programs are summarized as follows by Carmelo Mesa-Lago (2000:179): "increases in overall wages, the minimum wage in agriculture, and minimum pensions, . . . reduction of electricity rates and urban housing rent by as much as 50 percent, . . . expansion of free education and health care and subsidized public housing, . . . [and] expansion in social services." The result, indicates Mesa-Lago, was a decrease in income differentials. De la Fuente (2001:316) notes that largely through generous spending, the government created "unprecedented opportunities for mobility and minimized competition," so the revolution that brought Castro to power "had been fairly successful in eliminating inequality."

Since nonwhite Cubans were more likely than whites to be concentrated near the bottom of the pre-revolutionary class system, they benefited disproportionately from the sweeping changes enacted by the new government. Most saw their life chances significantly enhanced by the social programs of the revolution (Sawyer, 2006:57–58). The ideology and programs of the revolution also led to a greater integration of Cuba's nonwhite population into the life of the nation. Indeed, the revolution served, at least initially, to create among Afro-Cubans a sense of enfranchisement in the goals of the national revolutionary program.

As recently as 2001, in a comparative study of patriotism in Cuba, the Dominican Republic, and Puerto Rico, Mark Sawyer, Desilenis Peña, and Jim Sidanius (2002) concluded that their Cuban respondents showed a tendency that ran counter to the findings among the other two nationality groups: Cuban blacks were more likely than Cuban whites to express "patriotic" sentiments of national attachment and identification with their country. The researchers suggest that "the rhetoric and policies of the Cuban revolution may have had a broad effect on Cuban racial attitudes and rendered Cuba quite an exceptional case" (Sawyer, Peña, and Sidanius, 2002:22).

At the other (upper) end of the pre-revolutionary class system, however, many whites saw their life chances and opportunities limited by the new order. The contentious transition from capitalism to socialism negatively affected, first and foremost, the upper sectors of Cuban society (Grenier and Pérez, 2003:23). Consequently, another dimension of the impact of the revolution on Cuba's racial dynamics was the overwhelming overrepresentation of whites in the ensuing exodus from the island. This was especially true during the early 1960s, when the impact of those redistribution programs was most acutely felt among those who had occupied the upper sectors of pre-revolutionary society. The racial selectivity of the migration continued into the 1970s when preference was given to family reunification in granting exit permits and visas. The Memorandum of Understanding between the United States and Cuba that established the Airlift, which lasted from 1965 to 1973 and to date has been the longest and largest of all the migration waves from Cuba, gave priority to those in the island who were "claimed" by their relatives in the United States, thus favoring for emigration the family members of the predominantly white population that had arrived earlier (Aguirre, 1976:112). No doubt a contributing factor to the low levels of emigration among blacks was the depiction by the Cuban government of the United States as a racist society (Aguirre, 1976:113). The Mariel boatlift, which occurred in 1980, has been the only migration wave from Cuba in which persons with African ancestry constituted a visible component. In the 2000 U.S. Census, nearly 20 percent of those arriving through Mariel indicated they were nonwhite, and even that figure is likely to be an underestimate.

According to the same census, nearly 90 percent of the Cuban-origin population identified as being "white," a profile very different from that of the island's population—and, in turn, a contrast that cannot be explained by the use of different racial classifications systems in the U.S. and Cuban censuses (Pérez, 2007:395). The 2004 American Community Survey, conducted by the U.S. Bureau of the Census and analyzed by the Pew Hispanic Center (2006:3), placed the proportion of "whites" among U.S. Cubans at 86 percent, a much higher share of whites than was reported for all other Latino groups. Race, therefore, has been a major selectivity factor in the migration from Cuba since 1959.

"A GOOD PRESENCE": THE RISE OF RACIALIZATION IN CUBA

The current government's irrefutable accomplishments in the area of racial equality have largely been limited to those sectors in which the redistribution efforts have had the greatest impact: education, health care, and, to some extent, employment. Some progress has also been made in placing Afro-Cubans in leadership positions (Sawyer, 2006:69).

The redistribution program has fallen short, however, in the area of housing, where pre-revolutionary race and class distinctions have persisted (Alvarado

Ramos, n.d.:12; Sawyer, 2006:69). Although many nonwhites now live in sections of major cities that were once all-white, socioeconomic differentials between neighborhoods are still evident and have undercut some of the gains in education and perpetuated de facto residential segregation and the association of race with crime. The government recognized in 1986 that the "heritage of racism had not been totally eliminated under Cuba's socialism" (de la Fuente, 2001:315–316).

These enduring racial differentials were aggravated by the crisis that Cuba faced in the 1990s with the fall of the Berlin Wall and the loss of economic support, especially subsidized trade, from the former Soviet bloc. Labeled the "Special Period in Peacetime," it was a time when Cubans faced unprecedented austerities. It became imperative for Cuba to try to insert itself into the world market, raise domestic production, and improve consumption levels. The leadership, however, was unwilling to implement far-reaching market reforms for fear of losing political control. But in 1993 it was forced to adopt three market-oriented reforms that had the effect of deepening the extent of racial differentiation: (1) fiscal measures intended to reduce the budget deficit, thereby curtailing state spending on public social programs; (2) expansion of currency remittances from Cubans living abroad through the legalization of the possession and circulation of hard currency (e.g., dollars) and greater flexibility in visits to Cuba by relatives; and (3) an expanded foreign investment law that resulted in development of the tourism industry, specifically by attracting foreign firms to that sector (Mesa-Lago, 2000:293). These were colorblind measures, but because of existing racial socioeconomic differentials they had a disproportionate impact on the nonwhite population.

With those new measures, the advances that had been made toward social (and racial) equality stagnated. The economy of the Special Period made the acquisition of dollars the key to a household's welfare. Remittances and access to employment in tourism became critical to acquiring those dollars. Yet the availability of both of those mechanisms was heavily marked by race. As noted previously, Cubans living abroad are overwhelmingly white. Those living in the island who receive remittances (as well as visits from relatives) are therefore likely to be white (Sawyer, 2006:110–111). Furthermore, some evidence suggests that nonwhites are heavily underrepresented in the tourism industry (Alvarado Ramos, n.d.:14). Because of its desirability, employment in that industry is highly competitive, and many blacks feel that they do not have the same opportunities as whites for jobs in hotels, restaurants, and other tourist facilities. De la Fuente (2001:319–320) cites a 1994 survey conducted by researchers in Havana and Santiago that confirms the perception that prejudice and discrimination are present in the tourist sector. Sawyer's (2006:109) research in Cuba also confirms that blacks are at a disadvantage in obtaining jobs in tourist-oriented facilities. Employment in those facilities is highly competitive, and notions of "aesthetics" and "good culture" play a role in hiring decisions, with an emphasis, de la Fuente (2001:320) notes, on a "good presence"—a construct that is frequently racialized in a prejudicial way and discriminates against blacks. Even if the government had the best intentions of ensuring that discrimination is not practiced, the hiring in the tourist sector is usually done by the managers of foreign investors. De la Fuente (2007:138) cites cases in which black Cubans filed complaints against employers for racial discrimination in the hotel industry.

Without equal access to remittances and the tourism industry, the only alternative open to the nonwhite population for acquiring dollars is self-employment in myriad activities in the informal sector, many of which are marginal, at best, and illegal in many instances. Aside from the manufacture and sale of crafts to tourists (a legal activity), many activities in the informal sector involve the theft or, as it is referred to in Cuba, the "diverting" of state goods and resources for processing and resale. Tobacco, gasoline, leather, and other such goods sold in the informal sector can only have originated in a state enterprise because the government controls all production. The best example, and the one most evident to a visitor to Havana, is the illegal street selling of cigars, a trade in which nonwhites appear to be disproportionately involved—not surprisingly, given their limited access to legitimate sources of dollars. The same can be said of prostitution (known locally as *jineterismo*), which also increased during this period. This sort of marginal or illegal activity reinforces the long-standing connection between race and urban crime in Cuba (Sawyer, 2006:114).

Another dollar-generating activity that is largely unavailable to nonwhites is the operation of a *paladar,* a restaurant in one's home catering to foreign visitors and Cuban customers with dollars. Given the likelihood, indicated earlier, that nonwhites are more likely to live in substandard housing, this is not a viable alternative for many of them (de la Fuente, 2001:321).

Since the 1990s, then, racialization has increased markedly, as a result of changing economic conditions in Cuba. As de la Fuente (2001:318) has observed, "under the so-called Special Period, racial inequality and racially defined social tensions have increased substantially." The backing the revolution received from the black population was now questionable: "[W]hat was once a dependable corps of revolutionary support has now been eroded by the island's economic catastrophe and a lingering whiff of institutional racism in what is supposed to be a classless society" (Whitefield, 1993:1-A).

CUBAN IN CUBA, BLACK IN THE UNITED STATES: RACIALIZATION AMONG CUBAN AMERICANS

In the year 2000, the *New York Times* ran a series of in-depth articles on "How Race Is Lived in America," which won the Pulitzer Prize for National Reporting. One of the articles in the series, written by Mirta Ojito of the *Times* staff, focused on two friends, one white, one black, who now live in the United States but had once been close friends in Cuba (Ojito, 2000). Joel Ruiz, who is black, and his white friend, Achmed Valdés, met in middle school in Cuba and maintained a very close friendship until 1994, when they both left, in separate rafts, for the United States. Both settled in Miami, only about a fifteen-minute drive apart, but they now rarely see each other. They inhabit two different worlds in a highly segregated city. In Cuba, race was not unimportant, but "it was not what defined them. Nationality, they had been taught, meant far more than race. They felt, above all, Cuban" (Ojito, 2000:A1).

In Miami, Ruiz went to work and live in the same neighborhood where his uncle, who had arrived earlier, had settled. He noticed that everyone there, unlike Cuba, was black—without exception. Valdés, on the other hand, settled in a white Cuban neighborhood where blacks are viewed with suspicion, and he learned that "American blacks ... are to be avoided because they are delinquent and dangerous and resentful of whites" (Ojito, 2000:A20). A victim of such suspicions, Ruiz learned to avoid white Cuban neighborhoods, especially Cuban restaurants, where he'd had an unpleasant experience. Both former best friends were now living in a society where "skin color easily trumps nationality" (Ojito, 2000:A20). Ojito (2000:A1) quotes Ruiz, referring to his old friend: "I am here and he is over there ... and we can't cross over to the other's world."

Residential segregation is the most evident manifestation of the sharp racial differentials that have arisen among Cubans in the United States. That is true not only within Miami but also more broadly in the settlement patterns of Cubans throughout the country. Whereas white Cubans prefer Florida and New Jersey, nonwhite Cubans are more likely to have settled in New York (Dixon, 1988:235).

Black Cubans who have made Miami their home are likely to have the same experience as Ruiz, who found a physical, as well as social, barrier separating him from his friend. This city, where more than 60 percent of the Cuban-origin population of the United States have chosen to live, is one of the most segregated metropolitan areas in the country, especially in terms of the distance between Hispanics and blacks. Douglas Massey and Nancy Denton (1987) computed probabilities of residential contact in 1970 and 1980 between blacks, Hispanics, Asians, and Anglos in sixty metropolitan areas. Miami had one of the lowest probabilities of contact between blacks and Hispanics of all the cities studied (Chicago, Los Angeles–Long Beach, Miami, New York, and San Francisco–Oakland), with relatively little change registered during that decade (Massey and Denton, 1987:807).

The 2000 U.S. Census data on residential segregation analyzed by John Logan of the Lewis Mumford Center at SUNY-Albany confirmed the continuation of the trend first described by Massey and Denton (Logan, 2008). Of the 331 metropolitan areas in the study, Miami ranked fourth in its black/Hispanic dissimilarity score, the measure of residential segregation between the two groups. Logan considered a score of 60 or above "very high." Miami had a score of 80.8, even higher than its score for segregation between whites and blacks, and considerably higher than its score for whites and Hispanics.

Although during much of its early history Miami was a winter resort for vacationers from the north, especially New Yorkers, it had the racial dynamics typical of a southern city, with segregated schools, public facilities, and housing. The core of the black community was Overtown, a vibrant black enclave adjacent to the northern portion of the central business district. In the late 1950s, the construction of Miami's expressway system virtually destroyed Overtown when the system's major interchange, the intersection of I-95 and SR-836, was placed directly in that enclave, leveling thousands of homes and displacing tens of thousands of its residents (Dunn, 1997:156). The center of Miami's black community shifted north to the neighborhood known as Liberty City.

By the early 1960s, Cubans started arriving in larger numbers and were settling in the Shenandoah area, a former white middle-class neighborhood that had deteriorated, directly west and south of the central business district. It became known as Little Havana. With greater numbers of Cubans arriving in the 1960s and 1970s through the Airlift, the predominantly Cuban neighborhoods of the city grew, as the new arrivals pushed into the southern and western portions of the metropolitan area, along the corridors of two principal east-west arteries: Flagler Street and S.W. 8th Street. Cubans also settled in large numbers in Hialeah, a traditionally white blue-collar incorporated area in the northwestern part of the county.

These settlement patterns resulted in African American and Cuban communities that were physically very distant from each other, with Cubans occupying the southern and western portions of the metropolitan area and blacks concentrated in the north-central and northeastern areas. Marking and accentuating that separation is SR-836, the East-West (Dolphin) Expressway, which in effect functions as a racially significant barrier.

Faced with intense racial segregation in Miami, most black Cubans found themselves in the same situation as Ruiz, with race trumping nationality: They settled in predominantly black areas of Miami, as the predominantly Cuban areas remained primarily white. The data from the 2000 U.S. Census of the Population clearly show the racial divide.[1] In that year only 30,074 persons in Miami-Dade County were classified as black Hispanics/Latinos—that is, persons who indicated on question five of the census form that they were of "Spanish/Hispanic/Latino origin or descent," but who also indicated they were "black, African American, or Negro" in question six. That figure amounted to 1.3 percent of the total population of the county and 2.3 percent of the Hispanic/Latino population. Because that figure includes several nationalities, the black Cuban population is smaller.

The five census tracts in the Miami metropolitan area with the largest number of black Hispanics/Latinos are all located in the north-central part of the city, north of SR 826 and either embedded or adjacent to predominantly African American areas. In contrast, the most "Cuban" of the census tracts in Miami—that is, the eleven census tracts with 70 percent or more of their populations classified as being of Cuban origin or descent—are either south of SR 826 in the Flagler/8th Street corridor or in Hialeah. All of those census tracts are more than 90 percent white. The entire incorporated area of Hialeah, with more than 226,000 inhabitants, is 88 percent white.

Physical separation is a fundamental division between black and white Cubans in Miami, but it is only the beginning. The much-touted benefits of the Cuban enclave in Miami for successful economic adjustment do not appear to apply to Afro-Cubans. In 1990, one Miami journalist found cause to label Afro-Cubans in Miami "the lost people" (Hamaludin, 1990:6A). Occasional news stories have portrayed Afro-Cubans in the United States as a marginal group, struggling on the fence between two cultures and encountering prejudice and discrimination, even from their white conationals (Goldfarb, 1991; Lee, 1987; Nordheimer, 1987; Prout, 1981).

Data from the Children of Immigrants Longitudinal Study (CILS), conducted in the 1990s among second-generation youth in Miami, point out the increasing stratification among Cubans in Miami, especially between the earlier and later arrival waves, a distinction that is racially significant (Pérez, 2001; Portes and Rumbaut, 2001). As the Cuban population becomes more economically heterogeneous, defying the earlier stereotype of uniform economic success, there will be a greater bifurcation, with many Cuban families, especially nonwhites, falling into the secondary labor market. We still lack, however, a comprehensive and detailed study focusing on the experience of black Cubans in the United States.

MAIDS AGAIN? A LOOK AT THE FUTURE

It is probably easier to predict the future of racial differentiation in the diaspora than in Cuba. Nevertheless, there is every reason to believe that racialization will persist in the island as well as among Cubans in the United States. If most black and white Cubans living in the United States, and especially in Miami, continue to be on opposite sides of a segmented labor market, then it is likely that there will be intergenerational consequences of the current racialization that characterizes the Cuban American population and that such differentiation based on race will persist into the future. White Cuban Americans are more likely to continue to make strides on the road to structural assimilation, while black Cuban Americans will continue to lag, with proportionately greater numbers than white Cubans joining the urban underclass (Dixon, 1988:236).

The outlook for the island is more complicated. Socialist systems that combined strong political control with centrally planned economies were able to integrate and hold together nation-states with severe regional, religious, or ethnic fissures. The onset of a market economy and the relaxation of political controls allowed those cleavages to surface and assert themselves. In some cases, acute internal strife was the result. In others, entire nations subdivided or even atomized, and international boundaries were redrawn.

Cuba has historically had a strong unitary national consciousness and has never exhibited such deep fissures in its national landscape. Despite a past characterized by periodic upsurges in racialization, and even racial strife, it is not a racially disjointed society.

Nevertheless, the recent increase in racialization discussed in this chapter provides cause for concern about the future. If one assumes (as many do) that Cuba's future will, sometime and somehow, involve the introduction of significant market-oriented reforms, then race may be a fissure point. The implementation of even very limited market reforms has already led to an increase in social and racial tensions. An intensification of those tensions can be expected when more profound market mechanisms are implemented and competition becomes a guiding feature of the system. Such an increase in tensions is consistent with the experience of many post-socialist nations.

In addition to the anticipated economic reforms, it is generally expected (though not necessarily inevitable) that a future Cuban political system will be characterized by greater freedom of expression and association. Such a system would presumably permit the mobilization of racially based groups to respond to what will surely be a growing sense of disenfranchisement or alienation in the face of the dismantling of a system that had made great strides in racial equality. Although that system has a long way to go in achieving such equality, many Afro-Cubans will see its demise as a step in the opposite direction.

The seriousness of racial divisions in the future may well be a function of the nature and rate of change in the country. A slow and peaceful evolutionary transition toward a market system, one that would allow greater political freedoms, would conceivably allow for the negotiation of political and economic formulas that could minimize and perhaps resolve problems that might lead to racial tensions and conflicts. In the best of all scenarios, progressive social change would be managed within a national consensus that would involve Afro-Cubans and their concerns. And Afro-Cubans will have concerns. As de la Fuente (2007:144) notes: "Afro-Cubans will enter a post-Castro Cuba with specific grievances and needs that they will likely translate into concrete economic, social, and political demands."

The worst scenario would be the opposite one: a violent and sudden rupture in the country's institutions. This model of change would increase the possibility of the imposition of political and economic models that would stem not from a national consensus but from the need to bring peace and stability to the country. Such a scenario would also increase the likelihood of foreign intervention or meddling to resolve the crisis. An active U.S. military and/or political role at the time of a Cuban crisis would certainly not be without historical precedent. The report of the Commission for Assistance to a Free Cuba, a State Department document adopted in 2004 by the president of the United States as part of U.S.-Cuba policy, is in effect a blueprint for an active U.S. role in the reconstruction and development of a post-socialist Cuba.

A U.S. presence would have implications for racial tensions. The current Cuban government has cast the U.S. government and the Cuban émigré community as proponents of turning back the clock on the social progress achieved by blacks during the revolution by calling for the return of a market economy and the settlement of claims for compensation or restitution of property expropriated by the Cuban government. A great deal of the discourse emerging from both Washington and Miami, as well as the experience of Cuban Americans in race relations, tends to reinforce that image.

It may well be that a profound change in Cuba will eventually mean a better life for all Cubans, including Afro-Cubans. But the future is always uncertain, and as the Cuban nation looks ahead to what may happen when true change comes to the island, blacks have even more reason to be apprehensive than whites. This point is poignantly underscored by the following anecdote recounted by de la Fuente (2001:1):

More than thirty years had passed when, in the summer of 1993, a white, upper-class Cuban-American woman from Miami returned to the island for a visit. She was greeted there by her former maid, now retired, a black woman and the mother of two children: an engineer and a medical doctor. It was an emotional encounter, full of common memories and mutual happiness. But when the unavoidable issue of a post-Communist Cuba came up during the conversation, the black ex-maid asked: "Will my children be maids again?"

NOTE

1. All data from the 2000 U.S. Decennial Census were compiled and computed from the U.S. Bureau of the Census website (http://factfinder.census.gov/home/saff/main.html), using the Census 2000 Summary File 1 (SF1) 100-Percent Data. Since most of the data presented here are for small intra-urban geographic areas, either for census tracts or places, the data from this source do not permit identifying black Cubans separately from black Hispanics/Latinos. It is also important to keep in mind that Hispanics/Latinos may be of any race, since the data are derived from two separate items in the census. It is therefore possible to conclude that a census tract is, say, more than 70 percent Cuban and also more than 90 percent white.

REFERENCES

Aguirre, Benigno E. 1976. "Differential Migration of Cuban Social Races: A Review and Interpretation of the Problem." *Latin American Research Review* 11:103–124.

Alvarado Ramos, Juan Antonio. N.d. "Relaciones raciales en Cuba." Cuban Transition Project, University of Miami.

Castellanos, Jorge, and Isabel Castellanos. 1990. *Cultura afrocubana*. Vol. 2: *El negro en Cuba, 1845–1959.* Miami: Ediciones Universal.

de la Fuente, Alejandro. 2001. *A Nation for All: Race, Inequality, and Politics in Twentieth-Century Cuba.* Chapel Hill: University of North Carolina Press.

———. 2007. "Race, Culture, and Politics." Pp. 138–162 in Marifeli Pérez-Stable (ed.), *Looking Forward: Comparative Perspectives on Cuba's Transition.* Notre Dame, IN: University of Notre Dame Press.

Dixon, Heriberto. 1988. "The Cuban-American Counterpoint: Black Cubans in the United States." *Dialectical Anthropology* 13:227–239.

Dunn, Marvin. 1997. *Black Miami in the Twentieth Century.* Gainesville: University Press of Florida.

Fernández Robaina, Tomás. 1990. *El negro en Cuba, 1902–1958: Apuntes para la historia de la lucha contra la discriminación racial.* Havana: Editorial de Ciencias Sociales.

Ferrer, Ada. 1999. *Insurgent Cuba: Race, Nation, and Revolution, 1868–1898.* Chapel Hill: University of North Carolina Press.

———. 2000. "Rethinking Race and Nation in Cuba." Pp. 60–76 in Damián J. Fernández and Madeline Cámara Betancourt (eds.), *Cuba, the Elusive Nation: Interpretations of National Identity.* Gainesville: University Press of Florida.

Goldfarb, Carl. 1991. "Prejudice Felt by Latin Blacks." *Miami Herald,* June 30, pp. 1B, 2B.

Grenier, Guillermo, and Lisandro Pérez. 2003. *The Legacy of Exile: Cubans in the United States.* Boston: Allyn and Bacon.

Hamaludin, Mohamed. 1990. "Black Cubans Are Getting Ready to Be More Visible." *Miami Times,* November 15, pp. 1A, 6A.

Helg, Aline. 1995. *Our Rightful Share: The Afro-Cuban Struggle for Equality, 1886–1912.* Chapel Hill: University of North Carolina Press.

Ibarra, Jorge. 1998. *Prologue to Revolution: Cuba, 1898–1958.* Boulder, CO: Lynne Rienner.

Lee, Felicia. 1987. "Black Cubans in U.S. Battle Against Stigmas." *Miami Herald,* December 3, p. 19A.

Logan, John. 2008. "Metropolitan Ethnic and Racial Change." Lewis Mumford Center for Comparative Urban and Regional Research, University at Albany, SUNY. Retrieved March 2, 2008. (http://mumford.albany.edu/census/data.html)

Martí, José. [1893] 2001. "Mi raza." *Patria,* April 16. Pp. 299–300 in José Martí, *Obras completas.* CD-ROM edition. Havana: Centro de Estudios Martianos.

Massey, Douglas S., and Nancy A. Denton. 1987. "Trends in the Residential Segregation of Blacks, Hispanics, and Asians: 1970–1980." *American Sociological Review* 52(December):802–825.

Mesa-Lago, Carmelo. 2000. *Market, Socialist, and Mixed Economies: Comparative Policy and Performance—Chile, Cuba, and Costa Rica.* Baltimore: Johns Hopkins University Press.

Moore, Carlos. 1988. *Castro, the Blacks, and Africa.* Los Angeles: Center for Afro-American Studies, University of California at Los Angeles.

Nordheimer, Jon. 1987. "Black Cubans: Apart in Two Worlds." *New York Times,* December 2, p. D26.

Oficina Nacional de Estadísticas. 2005. *Censo de población y viviendas: Cuba, 2002. Informe nacional.* Retrieved August 2, 2008. (http://www.cubagob.cu/otras_info/censo/tablas_pdf/informe_nacional.pdf)

Oficina Nacional del Censo, República de Cuba. N.d. *Censo de población y viviendas, 1981,* vol. 16. Havana: Comité Estatal de Estadísticas.

Ojito, Mirta. 2000. "Best of Friends, Worlds Apart." *New York Times,* June 5, pp. A1, A20.

Pérez, Lisandro. 1984. "The Political Contexts of Cuban Population Censuses, 1899–1981." *Latin American Research Review* 19(2):143–161.

———. 2001. "Growing Up in Cuban Miami: Immigration, the Enclave, and New Generations." Pp. 91–126 in Rubén G. Rumbaut and Alejandro Portes (eds.), *Ethnicities: Children of Immigrants in America.* Berkeley: University of California Press and Russell Sage Foundation.

———. 2007. "Cuba." Pp. 386–398 in Mary C. Waters and Reed Ueda (eds.), *The New Americans: A Guide to Immigration Since 1965.* Cambridge, MA: Harvard University Press.

Pérez, Louis A., Jr. 2006. *Cuba: Between Reform and Revolution,* 3rd ed. New York: Oxford University Press.

Pew Hispanic Center. 2006. "Fact Sheet: Cubans in the United States." Retrieved March 3, 2008.

Portes, Alejandro, and Rubén G. Rumbaut. 2001. *Legacies: The Story of the Immigrant Second Generation.* Berkeley: University of California Press/Russell Sage Foundation.

Prout, Linda R. 1981. "Racism, Cuban Style." *Village Voice* 26(36), September 2–8, pp. 14–15. (pewhispanic.org/files/other/middecade/complete.pdf)

Sawyer, Mark Q. 2006. *Racial Politics in Post-Revolutionary Cuba.* New York: Cambridge University Press.

Sawyer, Mark Q., Yesilenis Peña, and Jim Sidanius. 2002. "Cuban Exceptionalism: Group-Based Hierarchy and the Dynamics of Patriotism in Puerto Rico, the Dominican Republic, and Cuba." Working Paper No. 190. New York: Russell Sage Foundation.

Wagley, Charles. 1965. "On the Concept of Social Race in the Americas." Pp. 531–545 in Dwight B. Heath and Richard N. Adams (eds.), *Contemporary Cultures and Societies of Latin America.* New York: Random House.

Whitefield, Mimi. 1993. "Blacks Support for Castro Erodes Along with Economy." *Miami Herald,* August 9, pp. 1A, 12A.

CHAPTER 9

Racializing Miami

Immigrant Latinos and Colorblind Racism in the Global City

Elizabeth Aranda, Rosa E. Chang,
and Elena Sabogal

The transitions enveloping the city of Miami in recent decades have captured the attention of scholars, the media, and policymakers alike. Since the 1960s, the constant influx of Cuban refugees has altered the city's ethnic makeup; more recent migrations from other Latin American countries have further diversified its ethnic canvas (U.S. Census Bureau, 1990, 2000b). In Miami, Spanish and English are commonly used interchangeably in everyday life, and the prevalence of ethnic businesses has made the city into what Alex Stepick and his colleagues (2003) have referred to as the "capital of Latin America."

While the outmigrations of both white and black natives have been steady since the 1990s, new immigrant groups continue to arrive, increasing the foreign-born concentration of the region (Frey 1996, 2004, 2005). Unclear, however, is how Miami's immigrants see themselves, other immigrants, and the place they have chosen to settle in. In this chapter we examine interviews and focus-group data with Latin American and Caribbean immigrants to explore their perspectives on Miami, particularly in juxtaposition to the spread of nativism throughout the country; we pay specific attention to the role of race, class, ethnicity, and legal status in shaping immigrants' constructions of themselves and their compatriots;

and we extend contemporary theories of racism to the case of Miami and its multiethnic diversity.

MIAMI AS A GLOBAL CITY

Miami is among the seven most popular destinations for immigrants in the United States, especially for Caribbean and Latin American immigrants (Portes and Rumbaut, 2006). Miami-Dade County's population grows by 2.7 percent every year due to migration (Henderson, 2003). While this region has been experiencing the flight of both white and black natives for some time now (Alba, Logan, and Stults, 2000; Frey, 1996, 2004), this population loss is counteracted by new immigrants coming to Miami. Since the 1990s, Miami has been the destination for Colombian asylum-seekers, Peruvian professional visa-overstayers, Puerto Rican middle-class migrants, and a bifurcated community of poor and wealthy Mexicans as well as Cuban and Haitian legal and undocumented immigrants. Miami-Dade County itself has the highest proportion of foreign-born individuals of any U.S. metropolitan area (U.S. Census Bureau, 2002). Additionally, the county became the first and only county in Florida to have a Latino majority (57 percent). The majority Latino group is Cuban, but the Latino groups that experienced the greatest growth from 1990 to 2000 in Miami-Dade County were Venezuelans (119 percent), Mexicans (65 percent), Argentineans (55 percent), Dominicans (55 percent), and Hondurans (48 percent).

These demographic shifts and their implications regarding interethnic and race relations are of particular importance because they are occurring within the context of an ever-increasing globalized city (Grosfoguel, 2003; Sassen, 1998). Miami went from being a tourist and retirement destination for northerners to the center of international trade and finance for the Caribbean (Grosfoguel, 2003), an emerging hub for multinational corporations' Latin American headquarters. The need for direct supervision over capital investments has grown, rendering cities such as New York obsolete in terms of their ability to closely manage Caribbean investments. As an alternative to New York, Miami has become "the core city of the entire region," or, in Ramón Grosfoguel's words, "the capital of the Caribbean" (2003:87). Underlining the role of the Cuban exile community in this process, Grosfoguel further argues that Miami emerged as the antithesis to Communist Cuba, promoting the success of American capitalism and democracy through uninhibited economic growth.

Miami's "growth machine" (Nijman, 1997:164) has become a "strategic terrain for a whole series of conflicts and contradictions" (Sassen, 1998:xxv). Saskia Sassen's work on global cities illustrates how they have become the "sites for the overvalorization of corporate capital and the further devalorization of disadvantaged economic actors, both firms and workers ... and many of the disadvantaged workers in global cities are women, immigrants, and people of color" (1998:xx–xxi). It is the combination of geography, the intensification of capital, and the vulnerable pool of laborers in Miami that has enhanced its visibility as a hemispheric hub. This became evident when Florida's former governor,

Jeb Bush, and the mayors and commissioners of Greater Miami mobilized to make Miami the Permanent Secretariat of the Free Trade Areas of the Americas (FTAA). The board of directors of Florida FTAA (2007) wrote in their proposal that "Miami, Florida is unique in the Western Hemisphere for its geographical, physical, demographic, and technical assets. As a global business center, Miami, Florida is ideally positioned as the most convenient location to headquarter the Permanent Secretariat of the FTAA."

Endemic to the global city and its economic prosperity is the polarization of income and wealth, a trend that has increased in Miami in recent decades. According to the Brookings Institution Center on Urban and Metropolitan Policy (Frey, 2004:14), the richest 20 percent of the population made twenty times more than the poorest quintile, a much larger inequality gap than the nation's, in which the top income quintile earned 14.6 times more than the bottom quintile. The median household income in Miami-Dade County in 2000 was $35,966; 18 percent of households were poor, earning only $18,497 or less; and about 35 percent of the population earned over $50,000. Moreover, the city has one of the highest median house prices ($372,000) in the country and the highest proportion of renters and homeowners who spend 30 percent or more of their pay on housing (Padgett, 2006).

Given global cities' large concentration of highly skilled professionals (many of whom are members of elite Latin American families who initially traveled to the United States to get their university degrees and later settled in Miami), serving classes of people are sought to fill the jobs that cater to these professionals, or globalization's elite classes. Miami's growth, however, has not reached all segments of the population; it is the third-poorest city in the United States (U.S. Census Bureau, 2004). In short, Miami embodies contradictions that are the hallmarks of the global city's social structure. It is in this context that the middle class has become increasingly segmented.

As these economic transformations accelerate, newly arrived immigrants along with native and foreign-born Miamians are left to make sense of the impact of the global economy on their individual opportunities. Although studies such as those by Alejandro Portes and Alex Stepick (1993) and Stepick and his colleagues (2003) reveal much about race relations among whites, blacks, and Latinos in Miami, these studies generally skip over differences within immigrant populations, particularly Latinos, and how new forms of racism pervade social contact among Miami's newest arrivals. This is important in light of continuing demographic changes and the growing internationalization of the city.

Given this gap in the literature, we argue that racialization is not just a triangular dynamic involving whites, blacks, and "Latins," as the dominant accounts of Miami have depicted. As the populations of whites and African Americans decline, immigrants, both Cuban and non-Cuban, are taking up new positions in the local system of racial stratification in this new economic regime, characterized by a growing polarization between rich and poor. Moreover, the squeeze on the middle class, in combination with the growing segregation of Latino Miami from the rest of the country, has led to racially charged characterizations of Miami and ethnic hostilities with anti-immigrant overtones. We seek to understand the racial dimensions of this discourse.

THE RACIALIZATION OF MIAMI

Among the prevailing racial characterizations about the effects of increasing immigration to the United States are warnings of the challenges Hispanics, in particular, pose for America (Huntington, 2004). Samuel Huntington has argued that a large number of immigrants can dominate cities such as Los Angeles and Miami, causing a "cultural division between Hispanics and Anglos" that could become "the most serious cleavage in U.S. society" (2004:32). Patricia Zavella (1997) has written about how global economic restructuring led to similar characterizations of California and to a sense of "paradise lost" among white citizens. Similarly, as Nicholas De Genova (1998) and De Genova and Ana Yolanda Ramos Zayas (2003) have shown in their case studies, Chicago, an urban space that continuously produces and reproduces itself through the many contradicting struggles involving immigrants, resembles Miami in terms of its ongoing struggles.

While numerous scholars have challenged Huntington's work (see Bonilla-Silva, 2006; Centeno, 2005; Gaudio and Bialostok, 2005; and Portes and Rumbaut, 2006), his nativistic cries resonate throughout the United States at many levels. At the policy level, legislation has been enacted to continue to add to, in the words of Juan Gonzalez (2000), the U.S. version of the Great Wall of China on the U.S.-Mexico border (see also Jonas, 2006). U.S. nativism is also propagated at the individual level, as evidenced by the plethora of policymakers and media pundits who continuously portray immigration as one of the principal threats to the United States. Even members of Congress have reinforced fears of "cultural invasions," as Republican Tom Tancredo did when he stated that an immigrant-receiving area such as Miami "has become a Third World country." According to Tancredo, "the sheer size and number of ethnic enclaves devoid of any English and dominated by foreign cultures is widespread" and "until American gets serious about demanding assimilation, this problem will continue to spread" (Clark, 2006).

Questions remain about the nature of contemporary U.S. nativism. Is it a manifestation of global economic restructuring? Is it an expression of racism? What does the contemporary anti-immigrant discourse reveal about the state of race relations in the United States? We aim to address all of these issues in the present chapter.

Theoretical Background

Recent claims that Miami resembles "a Third World country," as well as claims that immigrants are eroding the national fabric that weaves the country together, are rooted in modern forms of racialization. According to Laura Gómez (2007:2), racialization refers to "how groups come to be identified and to identify themselves in racial terms and learn their place as deserving or undeserving in the racial category." Moreover, as race is given meaning through the interactions of individuals, the notions about a racial group take shape within the social and historical context they occupy (Omi and Winant, 1994). Racialization thus encompasses not only the physical outlook of racial groups but also impressions of how each group behaves. Contained within each racial category are expectations of behaviors attached to it. These sets of impressions and expectations are adopted as societal ideologies, creating a racial system of oppression that gives rise to myths regarding the inferiority and superiority of particular racial groups.

In the case of modern-day immigration debates, individual immigrants are blamed for perceived losses in national unity. Moreover, immigrants' perceived actions, such as the notion that immigrants will not and do not intend to assimilate, place the causal variable of perceived national demise on the shoulders of newcomers. Perceived consequences of immigration such as the devolution of society into an underdeveloped entity emerge from the association of "the other" with uncivilized and inferior peoples wreaking havoc on "our" way of life. These arguments, which in the past were primarily associated with right-wing politics, have increasingly come to dominate the center, becoming part of mainstream American discourse. They are manifestations of what Grosfoguel (2003) has called "cultural racism."

After World War II, the "global racial/colonial formation" shifted from a biologically based racist discourse to a culturally based one in which "the culture of groups is naturalized in terms of some notion of inferior versus superior nature" (Grosfoguel, 2003:195). Grosfoguel asserts that cultural racism is "articulated in relation to poverty, labor market opportunities, and marginalization," such that the immigrant "problem" is "constructed as a problem of habits or beliefs, that is, a cultural problem, implying cultural inferiority and thus naturalizing/ fixing/essentializing culture" (2003:195). We believe that cultural racism is also expressed in relation to assimilation and allegations that immigrants will disrupt national unity and undermine American culture through their alleged refusal to learn "American ways." Examples of this type of racism are characterizations of undocumented immigrants as criminals who do not respect U.S. laws.

The discourse on illegal immigration, however, is packaged in language that is not overtly culturally racist. By constructing undocumented immigrants as criminals that undermine the American system of democracy and justice, anti-immigrant sentiment rooted in cultural racism is expressed using colorblind racial discourse, thereby not appearing racist at all. The acute turn against immigrants in recent years leads us to argue that contemporary nativism embodies expressions of what Eduardo Bonilla-Silva (2003) has called "colorblind racism," or the "new racism."

Bonilla-Silva argues that the "new racism" is based on a racial ideology that combines liberalism with anti-minority beliefs and has replaced Jim Crow, allowing for the reproduction of the current racial order without appearing racist. We argue that the linchpin of the "new racism" toward immigrants is the notion of the illegal subject. In this discourse, justice and equality are used to reinforce a system of institutionalized racism, in which citizenship shapes who belongs and who remains outside the margins of the nation. In the United States, this nation, as Grosfoguel argues, is imagined as the "equivalent to 'white' middle-class values and behavior" (2003:195, 197).

Citizenship sediments the boundaries of the nation; the hierarchies of stratification it creates are legitimated through policies that aim to enforce the law. Hence, allowing undocumented immigrants to legalize their status or to access services is seen as a form of reverse discrimination, in which individuals are constructed as gaining a "leg up" through unfair means. The mode of entry to the country trumps hard work, and even productive and moral individuals are consequently cast as criminals for having broken the laws of entry. No consideration is given to the historical roots of undocumented migration or to the role of the United States in originating and sustaining flows of workers across the border. Thus, the racial marginalization of Mexicans and other Latin Americans now viewed as threats to national security is cemented and justified through principles of liberalism, democracy, and justice, thereby ensuring the healthy reproduction of global racial inequality while casting all immigrants as suspect.

The American nation's romanticized self-conception as a nation of immigrants and opportunity for all is invoked to counter the impression of a nativist nation. Drawing distinctions between past and current immigrants helps to shape the social construction of the good and bad immigrant, bypassing any mention of race but implying that actions related to culture often serve as one of the contrasting elements between generations of immigrants. In this sense, portraying immigrants as being disinclined to learn English and to embrace U.S. culture euphemistically refers to racial fears of a darkening nation and "funny accents."

The definition and the elements of the "new racism" concur with the sociological notion that race is socially constructed. Race relations are defined through group and individual practices that encourage Jim Crow–like racist behaviors guised in the discourse of justice and national security. In this chapter we examine these forms of colorblind racism, focusing on immigrants in Miami, a city whose racial configuration has become complicated by high levels of ethnic, racial, and class diversity.

Data and Methods

The data cited in this chapter come from a study of Latin American immigrants in South Florida (Aranda, Sabogal, and Hughes, 2003). This study explores patterns of adaptation among immigrants settled in Miami, interethnic relations as perceived by each particular immigrant, and the extent to which immigrants are engaged in both sending and receiving societies. In-depth, open-ended interviews were conducted with immigrants from Peru, Colombia, the Dominican Republic, Puerto Rico, Mexico, and Cuba. The sample comprised 102 face-to-face interviews and 15 focus groups that included 108 participants. The numbers of men and women were almost equally divided; the average age of the participants was thirty-eight. In terms of occupation, about 12 percent were in managerial or executive positions, 24 percent were in professional jobs, 28 percent were in sales and services positions, 6 percent were homemakers, and 10 percent were students. About 19 percent of the participants provided no information about their occupation, and the remaining 7 percent worked in miscellaneous occupational categories such as farming, precision, and administrative positions.

Data collection also involved focus groups in which members of each ethnic group were interviewed together. Two or three focus groups were held with members of each ethnic group, which in turn contained from six to fourteen people. Within these focus groups, participants were asked about their reasons for migration and their perceptions and experiences with members of other racial and ethnic groups; additionally, these focus groups allowed for the exploration of ethnic media use and perceptions regarding how the media portray members of each immigrant group.

The immigrant groups interviewed in this study were chosen for several reasons. Some of the groups represented Latino groups with the largest presence in South Florida (e.g., Cubans), and whose share of the Latino population has been increasing (e.g., Dominicans, Colombians). Others represented contrasting cases with regard to citizenship status, occupational niche in South Florida, as well as maturity of the immigrant flow (e.g., Peruvians, Puerto Ricans, Mexicans). Most of the immigrants recruited for the study arrived in the United States after 1986. Participants were recruited through snowball sampling of friendship and occupational networks. This sample was not meant to be statistically representative of Miami's population, as it was a convenience sample in which efforts were made to recruit immigrants from diverse social class backgrounds. The final ethnic breakdown of our sample was as follows: Peruvians, 19.3 percent; Mexicans, 18 percent; Colombians, 16.9 percent; Puerto Ricans, 15.7 percent; Dominicans, 14.5 percent; and Cubans, 14.5 percent.

Each interview and focus-group exchange was transcribed verbatim. All data were coded and entered into NVIVO, a qualitative analysis software package. The coding scheme was tied to the questionnaire. For this chapter, all excerpts related to race and ethnic relations were pulled from the transcripts and analyzed for recurring themes. The quotes used in this chapter were translated into English for publication.

COLORBLIND DISCOURSE

Even though perceptions of immigrants as cultural threats reverberate in national debates on immigration policies, cultural diversity is part of the mainstream discourse regarding those aspects of Miami that the city's dominant groups identify to make the city more attractive to investment (Nijman, 1997). This contradiction indicates that cultural diversity is tolerable as long as there is still a dominant white majority. Since this is not the case in Miami, the city itself becomes a racialized entity from the perspective of the white minority within the city and the white majority outside of the city. From the vantage point of Miami's immigrants, however, the cultural diversity they encounter is one of the city's greatest assets.

Consider the following example provided by Luz, a Puerto Rican professional woman who, during our interview with her, highlighted the positive aspects of life in Miami in comparison to other areas in the United States: "Unlike any other state in the United States, you feel like home [referring to Miami]. Whatever mood strikes you, you can speak either Spanish or English. You can have *parrandas* [parties] during the Christmas season without having to explain its meaning. The people [in Miami] do not look at you as if you're crazy because they understand the Latino culture. So, it is positive in that aspect."

Language and cultural familiarity is part of what makes an area feel like home. Additionally, being part of the majority culture (in Miami, Latino culture) reduced feelings of cultural alienation among many in our sample. After experiencing discrimination in other parts of the United States, Luz now appreciates living in the familiar cultural context that Miami provides. Luz's preference for a social context that enhances feelings of belonging could be taken as an indicator that a multicultural context allows for cultural citizenship. William Flores and Rina Benmayor (1997) have conceptualized cultural citizenship as a series of activities that involve claiming space and rights, thereby leading to the empowerment of marginalized individuals and groups. While Latino culture might make Miami a strategic site for cultural citizenship, Flores and Benmayor (1997:15) argue that the dominant society "finds such space 'foreign' and even threatening."

How does the discourse of cultural diversity become racialized? Although our interviewees acknowledged the cultural differences shaping Miami's sociocultural context, they did not question the city's level of development as others have done with their use of the "Third World country" metaphor. This metaphor is revealing of the perceptions of Latino culture—the culture itself is equated to an "inferior" level of development, casting suspicion on the city as a whole, even though it is an American city. This expression of cultural racism represents the discourse of colorblind racism (Bonilla-Silva, 2003), given that the discourse of national unity and identity is used to subvert multicultural projects in the global city. It also assumes that Latinos and American culture are mutually exclusive, reinforcing Latinos' position as outsiders to the nation. In this sense, the discourse based on colorblind assumptions reinforces the racial subordination of Latinos in the United States.

Colorblind discourse identifies racism that has gone "underground," yet is still rampant in today's society and perhaps more damaging than the more overt kind, given that it allows for maintenance of the racial status quo and is much more difficult to identify. In an era of increasing immigration and global integration, the racialization of Miami represents an effort to increase the social distance between the American collective imagination and a city that mirrors what the country may look like in decades to come (versus how it should be in the minds of conservative whites—that is, a predominantly white, English-speaking country). This social distance, in turn, increases fears of immigrants, which we argue are also reproduced among immigrants themselves. As Bonilla-Silva (2003) has argued, among Latinos in the United States, elite members become part of the "hegemonic whiteness" and lower-class Latinos belong to the "collective blacks."

Thus, while immigrants hail cultural diversity in the city, social class and race, among other factors, shape the racialization of immigrant others.

COLORBLIND RACISM AMONG LATINOS

In our sample, immigrants' discourses did not come without their own boundaries of exclusion. Their views of Miami and other immigrants were full of contradictions that, we argue, convolute the development of a racial consciousness and awareness of subjugation. These contradictions were most apparent when participants noted that what gave Miami its unique character was also its greatest source of conflict. Amalia, a Colombian professional, illustrated this point: "Well, the negative aspects, let's say the idea of the American Dream, which for me there never really has been an American Dream.... So many persons have come chasing the American Dream that there are not as many opportunities as there were before. It is so overpopulated, so many immigrants."

In suggesting that the American Dream is increasingly unattainable because of declining opportunities, Amalia implied that immigration is the key culprit preventing Miamians from getting ahead. In particular, she conceived of their presence in the city as creating an overpopulated effect, for which the presumed solution is greater immigration control. The irony is that Amalia is an immigrant herself. Caitlin Killian and Cathryn Johnson (2006:75) argue that immigrant "disidentification" allows for the construction of a positive identification "of someone who is well-adjusted, at ease, and/or doing reasonably well economically (not poor)." However, this resistance may serve the purpose of reifying the hierarchical positioning of native and immigrant groups, reinforcing the negative stigmas that immigrants are trying to deflect (Killian and Johnson, 2006). This leads to the question of whether there are layers to the cultural diversity discourse, such that some immigrants and the diversity they bring are perceived as benign while other immigrants and other diversity pose more of a burden. Such cleavages in the immigrant population can be found in the following example. David, a Cuban professional, stated:

> The positive aspect about Miami is that it is a diverse city; the negative aspect about Miami is that it is a diverse city.... I believe that being a diverse city is positive because it offers us the opportunity to embrace our own culture and understand the splendor found in diversity.
>
> The negative aspect of a diverse Miami is that this diversity does not allow the community to develop as other communities around the country have. Programs become difficult. We have to take into consideration the meaning behind a "diverse culture." How we approach the Haitian community may not be the same as how we approach the Mexican community or the Guatemalan or Venezuelan communities. I believe it is difficult.

As this quote indicates, David believes that Miami's diversity is both its best and its worst quality. Much like the anti-immigrant discourse that alleges that multiculturalism fractures national unity, David perceives that the city's celebrated diversity impedes the development of community. Interestingly, David points to some immigrant groups (Haitians, Mexicans, Guatemalans, and Venezuelans) as requiring different approaches, implying that they pose a challenge to community building. David's observation could be taken as a response to immigrant diversification, since many of the groups he mentions are poor and nonwhite in an area that has historically received most Cuban immigrants. In other words, the diversity that he hails is the contribution that Latino culture brings to a city that used to be composed primarily of whites and blacks. It is the presence of newly arrived immigrants from other Latino and Caribbean cultures that, in his view, seems to pose the greatest challenges.

As a professional, David identifies the poorer groups (with the exception of the Venezuelans, who may threaten Cubans' position as "golden exiles") as the source of community challenges. One could argue that the association of certain groups such as Mexicans, Haitians, and other Central Americans such as Hondurans with groups who are poor or in need of government services is an outcome of colorblind discourses in which low social class is a racializing mark. These groups, who represent recent immigrants who came to Miami out of economic need, stand in opposition to others who are there because they have fled Communism and embraced capitalism (the opposing image of someone who needs services), resulting in a discourse that posits "deserving" immigrants versus those perceived as "undeserving." We believe that the construction of these categories is rooted in systemic racism (Feagin, 2006), and that the social class and culture of immigrants, in addition to race, play into the racial formation process. In short, not all immigrants occupy the same position in the imagination of white America. Current colorblind discourses racialize immigrants into dichotomized categories consisting of those who are deemed deserving of entry and membership and those who are not.

"DESERVING" AND "UNDESERVING" IMMIGRANTS

De Genova and Ramos-Zayas's (2003:57) account of divisions between Mexicans and Puerto Ricans in Chicago illustrates how the politics of citizenship shape the "ideologies of work and worth" among Latinos. As U.S. citizens, Puerto Ricans can claim welfare benefits, their access to which invokes a racialized stigma of laziness that shapes how they are perceived by fellow Latinos. Yet the image of the illegal Mexican worker is also a racialized construct, whereby Mexicans are deemed to be exploitable and thereby submissive, helpless, and lacking dignity. These hegemonic discourses invoke questions of "deservingness or competence for U.S. citizenship" (De Genova and Ramos-Zayas, 2003:82).

The notion of deservingness—a topic that came up among the participants in our sample—is shaped by the politics of migration and race. The construct of the undeserving immigrant, the one whose presence must be limited if not stopped altogether, is the figure blamed for the plights of the "good," deserving immigrants. This socially created construct is tied to the image of the Latino male illegally crossing the border, or the immigrant woman abusing the welfare system because of her high fertility, viewed as a sign of her "primitive" culture. Both images are racialized and represent threats to American safety and culture.

The good immigrant is the one who comes by legal means, works hard, and becomes as close to white as possible. This process of amalgamation suggests that the normative course of incorporation involves assimilation into white American society. Assimilation, in turn, involves acquiring the values of the Protestant ethic and illustrating these values at work through the accumulation of capital and goods. Thus, the good immigrant embraces Western values of success and modes of achieving these (i.e., independence and individualism)—values that comprise the tenets of Western capitalism. In short, the good immigrant embraces neoliberalism and succeeds in the "market." Older generations of Cuban refugees are examples of good immigrants, for they fled Communist Cuba in search of market forces. In contrast, today's Cuban immigrants—who have been exposed to and are assumed to have internalized Communism—are constructed as undeserving, particularly when their economic prospects after migration are bleak.

While these assumptions about the distinctions between good and bad immigrants shape immigrant discourses, what turns both deserving and undeserving immigrants into bad immigrants is their clamoring for rights; good immigrants should remain invisible, even though they may be among the "deserving." After all, "ideal" immigrants are those who do not "burden the system" or request help. The corollary is the presumption of success in the market. Even though fighting for civil rights is an American value, it is posited against America's own myths about equal opportunity and not needing one's civil rights if one properly embraces the Protestant ethic. Both good and bad immigrants, however, are visible, and visibly disenfranchised; as such, they challenge the country's cultural myths about being a nation of immigrants and a nation of equal opportunity. Becoming American in the post–Civil Rights Era has thus become a process in which the social construction of the immigrant's image can marginalize immigrants from themselves. This process of marginalization unfolds as an immigrant's time in the United States increases (presumably bringing more and more experiences with blocked opportunities and/or discrimination). Ultimately, many tenured immigrants assimilate the view from the outside and treat new immigrants as they were treated.

For the "undeserving" immigrant, the discourse of illegality is used to turn low-wage laborers into a suspicious class of people. The construct of illegal people creates a new hierarchy where undocumented immigrants cannot clamor for rights, for they need to remain in the shadows of their employers. The following quote by Guillermo, a Peruvian, illustrates this emerging form of stratification:

> I believe that the Hispanic is underneath the Mexicans and even underneath the people who are black. In the United States there's still a lot of ill-treatment toward the Hispanics, it should've changed already. It should not be that as an immigrant ... maybe to receive the same help as other immigrants, or people who have legal status in this country. And I think that sometimes they block you just because you are Hispanic. Well, I believe that I have ... that I need to improve [my situation] in this country.

Legal status (e.g., whether one has legal status, is a citizen, or is undocumented) has become a marker of racialization. It is interesting to observe how Guillermo identifies the Miami racial hierarchy, implying that those without "papers" are beneath the historically marginalized groups of Mexicans and African Americans. In this sense, the invisibility of being undocumented immigrants could just as well be a racial marker that, in their view, places a group at the bottom of the racial hierarchy, without access to rights or resources to help improve their condition. Moreover, Guillermo believes that his status as a "Hispanic" makes it more difficult to acquire a legal immigration status, illustrating the multidimensional nature of racialization as it unfolds in the global city. In other words, ethnicity and legal status combine to form new layers of stratification among immigrants and among Latinos. Some of the negative views toward immigration expressed in our sample suggest a social distancing from these stigmatized identities.

The resulting dynamics that trickle down into the realm of interpersonal relations are rooted in legacies of colonization reproduced within the global city; these dynamics are whitewashed in the discourse of colorblind racism, resulting in a dichotomization of the immigrant image. Within this context, immigrant disidentification reinforces colorblind racism, which results in negative views toward other immigrants. Even though all the participants in this study were recent immigrants, the data suggest that they were already adopting contradicting U.S. discourses—the hallmark of colorblind racism.

In the case of Miami, where about half of all Latinos are Cuban, their status as historically "golden exiles" and, more recently, as *balseros* (rafters) determines not just their placement in the ethnic and racial queue but also how others perceive them. Given that Miami has the highest metropolitan immigration rate, there is a palpable resentment on the part of non-Cuban immigrants toward Cuban Americans, whom they perceive to be the gatekeepers of opportunities. José, a Colombian man, expressed his feelings regarding this issue:

> You feel the rivalry among the many nationalities [in Miami], it feels like if sometimes we generalize about others ... for instance, that "the Nicaraguans are too complicated"; that "Cubans are this and that." So there's always this rivalry just to end up saying that our own country is the best. The Cubans say that everything from Cuba is the best, the Nicaraguans say ... you understand? It's like a rivalry.... So there are conflicts. So, in general terms, no, people do not get along very well when they are from different countries. For instance, if you and I work together and I am not from Peru and you ask me if I am Colombian, this interaction already starts something, this is just an example, a hypothetical story, because if I am also from Peru you will respond differently and say that you will put in a good word for me with the boss, but also it could also be that you are from a different region in Peru.... Sometimes the rivalries get to the point in which, without any doubts, the Cubans are the majority, they have most of the benefits and those from other nationalities, it is a little bit more difficult to obtain things because they have less influence. I also agree, sorry if there's anyone from Central America here, I apologize [laughs] but I think that people ... and I say it literally ... they are from the lower class, in my opinion ... I don't know if I am offending anyone here ... they come from the segment that is less educated, they don't

know how to express themselves correctly, they are not respectful, they don't ask for permission, let's say they are [sic].

In addition to resentment toward Cuban American gatekeeping practices, José discusses resentment among different immigrant groups in Miami. As Noah Lewin-Epstein and Asaf Levanon (2005:93) argue, new immigrants might pose not only an economic threat to the dominant ethnic group but also "an economic and cultural threat to subordinate ethnic groups." At the same time, there is evidence of colorblind racism in this quote, particularly when we hear how José regards Central Americans. As critical as he is of the rivalries, his own derision of other "classes" of immigrants reinforces ethnic animosities.

Like people elsewhere in the country, Miamians are thus faced with con-tradictions, and the ways in which they deal with these reveal the predominant racial ideology of the region. One outcome of such dynamics, however, is the sedimentation of hegemony that ultimately pits immigrants against themselves. This is evident not just when immigrants blame other immigrants but also when immigrants internalize these notions and blame themselves for their lack of success in the global city. Indeed, the American Dream and individualistic ideologies became so internalized that immigrants sometimes blame themselves for their lack of social mobility rather than faulting the social structure that limited their life chances.

Carolina, a Dominican immigrant, said this about the American Dream:

> The only good thing that I see in this country is that all your dreams, if you work hard for them, can be achieved. If you work really hard, and have a lot, you have to have a strong will. It is not easy here, to achieve a dream here. But there are a lot of opportunities. There are good people, there are bad people, but if you really set your mind to it, if you really fight, if you go to school and work, you can achieve it.

In discussing her own situation, she blamed her imperfect English for her per-ceived status:

> The only negative aspect is if you do not speak English well and, for instance, if you want to do something grand in this country then you have to speak English well. That is the negative aspect but if you lean more toward Spanish, because everything here [in Miami] is Spanish, then we have no problem. However, [in the rest of the country] if you want to obtain a good job then you need to speak English well and sometimes people get comfortable. I am comfortable; at home I don't talk to my children in English and my son tells me, "But mom, I can help you," and the thing is, I don't know. I don't seem to be able to speak to my son in English; I am already so used to speaking to him in Spanish. Sometimes we do converse in English and everything, but he tells me "*Mami*, what you need is to focus more on your writing and watch more TV in English." I never had time to watch TV but I have more free time now and I watch, and I believe I am going to go to school. I think I am going to school for one year to learn only English. That is the only thing . . . but here if you have a dream you can achieve it if you fight for it.

In his work on global racial ideologies, Howard Winant (2001:8) argues that the "talisman of the current 'color blind' discourse about race in the U.S.... has been the resurgence of faith in doctrines of individualism and meritocracy." Bonilla-Silva (2006) similarly asserts that the discourse of modern-day racism revolves around the fictive notion of equality of opportunity. And both scholars argue that, given the inequality of results among U.S. race/ethnic groups, color-blind racism allows dominant group members to blame "the victims" while not "sounding racist." Those who tout the openness of the American socioeconomic structure often claim that people who do not succeed are solely responsible for their conditions. In doing so, they explain away racial inequalities by citing individualistic causal factors and ignoring larger structural sources of constraint. This discourse appears to have shaped the way Carolina views her own situation in Miami. It also lies at the heart of the contradictions that emerged in immigrants' assessments of Miami that centered more on the ideology of the American Dream and the U.S. meritocracy than on the reality of their experiences and that of their fellow immigrants.

Some Latinos have indeed adopted U.S. racism and blended it within their own ideological frameworks. To recognize that the American system is not really open, and that the meritocracy is a fallacy, is to realize that one's own migration was perhaps in vain, thus diminishing any and all sacrifices made to undertake the journey. Conversely, holding on to the American Dream helps give meaning to one's migration, even if the dream remains elusive.

CONCLUSION

In this chapter we examined patterns of racialization among Latino immigrants in Miami. In problematizing issues of class, race, legal status, and immigration politics, our analysis focused on how various discourses are reconfiguring themselves in the global city. In an era of increasing immigration and globalization yet greater scrutiny of immigrant and racial minorities, we show how the racialization of Miami as a "foreign" city in the United States' collective imagination is appropriated by immigrants and projected onto others through the discourse of colorblind racism.

The dominant discourse about immigrants encapsulates more than competition-induced perceptions of threat. The social construction of the immigrant "problem" is rooted in systemic racism and emerging ideologies nourished by mainstream hype regarding the cultural threats that immigrants pose to the United States' national identity and hence its security. These threats are refracted at multiple levels onto the immigrant landscape in Miami. Latinos living in the city are threatened because they fear being associated with the stigma attached to new immigrants in today's highly charged anti-immigrant climate. Moreover, the diversification of the Latino and immigrant populations in South Florida as well as the dichotomization of immigrant images into "deserving" and "undeserving" has led to an environment in which cultural racism and the discourse of colorblind racism are thriving. As levels of income inequality rise and neoliberal policies of global cities lead to a contraction of public services and of the social infrastructure that traditionally has served disadvantaged populations, immigrants themselves blame other immigrants using the discourse of colorblindness rather than recognizing the structural sources of their struggles. Not readily aware that they are integrating into what Sassen (1998) calls a "new economic regime," they transplant their frustrations with their own barriers to mobility upon more recent immigrants, or groups they perceive to be powerless and undeserving. Indeed, the contradictions revealed in the data above—whereby immigrants are attracted to a Latino cultural environment but also repelled by aspects of their own culture—indicate that they have largely adopted the interpretations of dominant-group members toward their own entry into the country, causing resentment and "rivalry" among different immigrant groups.

Contradicting discourses of colorblindness stem from hemispheric racial ideologies, but they are also influenced by the United States' mainstream discourse on immigration. Bonilla-Silva (2006) predicts that the system of race relations in the United States will come to resemble that in Latin America, where colorblind racism has defined racial politics for centuries. These racial politics are manifested in multiple ways, depending on the country. The unifying theme is that of privileging whiteness; however, the way in which blackness, or racial otherness, is constructed also draws upon U.S. colorblind discourses about deserving and undeserving immigrants, which, in turn, are rooted in class, race, cultural, and status hierarchies. These hierarchies sort immigrants into various categories that yield different levels of acceptance or disdain. In this way, power relations have become more complicated in a city that until recently has been considered a city of whites, blacks, and Cubans.

REFERENCES

Alba, Richard D., John R. Logan, and Brian J. Stults. 2000. "The Changing Neighborhood Contexts of the Immigrant Metropolis." *Social Forces* 79(2):587–621.

Aranda, Elizabeth, Elena Sabogal, and Sally Hughes. 2003. "The 'Other' Latin Americans: Identity, Assimilation, and Well-Being Among Transnational Immigrants." Proposal submitted to the National Science Foundation, June.

Bonilla-Silva, Eduardo. 2003. *Racism Without Racists: Color-Blind Racism and the Persistence of Racial Inequality in the United States.* Lanham, MD: Rowman & Littlefield.

———. 2006. *Racism Without Racists: Color-Blind Racism and the Persistence of Racial Inequality in the United States,* 2nd ed. Lanham, MD: Rowman & Littlefield.

Centeno, Miguel. 2005. "Who Are You?" *Contexts* 4(1):56–57.

Clark, Lesley. 2006. "Congressman Calls Miami a 'Third World Country.'" *Miami Herald,* November 27. Retrieved February 6, 2007. (http://www.miami.com/mld/miamiherald/16110727.htm)

De Genova, Nicholas. 1998. "Race, Space, and the Reinvention of Latin America in Mexican Chicago." *Latin American Perspectives* 25(5):87–116.

De Genova, Nicholas, and Ana Yolanda Ramos-Zayas. 2003. *Latino Crossings: Mexicans, Puerto Ricans, and the Politics of Race and Citizenship.* New York: Routledge.

Feagin, Joe R. 2006. *Systemic Racism: A Theory of Oppression.* New York: Routledge.

Flores, William V., and Rina Benmayor. 1997. *Latino Cultural Citizenship: Claiming Identity, Space, and Rights.* Boston: Beacon Press.

Florida FTAA, Inc. 2007. "Miami's Proposal for the Future Home of FTAA." Retrieved December 4, 2007. (www.floridaftaa.org)

Frey, William H. 1996. "Immigration, Domestic Migration, and Demographic Balkanization in America: New Evidence for the 1990s." *Population and Development Review* 22(4):741–763.

———. 2004. *The New Great Migration: Black Americans' Return to the South, 1965–2000.* Center on Urban and Metropolitan Policy. Washington, DC: The Brookings Institution.

———. 2005. *Immigration and Domestic Migration in U.S. Metro Areas: 2000 and 1990 Census Findings by Education and Race.* Report 05-572. Ann Arbor: Population Studies Center, University of Michigan, Institute for Social Research. Retrieved February 6, 2007. (http://www.psc.isr.umich.edu/pubs/pdf/rr05-572.pdf)

Gaudio, Rudolf P., and Steve Bialostok. 2005. "The Trouble with Culture: Everyday Racism in White Middle-Class Discourse." *Critical Discourse Studies* 2(1):51–69.

Gómez, Laura. 2007. *Manifest Destinies: The Making of the Mexican American Race.* New York: New York University Press.

Gonzalez, Juan. 2000. *Harvest of Empire: A History of Latinos in America.* New York: Penguin Books.

Grosfoguel, Ramón. 2003. *Colonial Subjects: Puerto Ricans in a Global Perspective.* Berkeley: University of California Press.

Henderson, Tim. 2003. "Highest Immigration Rate Belongs to Dade." *Miami Herald,* May 21.

Huntington, Samuel. 2004. "The Hispanic Challenge." *Foreign Policy* (March/April): 30–45.

Jonas, Susanne. 2006. "Reflections on the Great Immigration Battle of 2006 and the Future of the Americas." *Social Justice* 33(1):6–20.

Killian, Caitlin, and Cathryn Johnson. 2006. "'I'm Not an Immigrant!' Resistance, Redefinition, and the Role of Resources in Identity Work." *Social Psychology Quarterly* 69(1):60–80.

Lewin-Epstein, Noah, and Asaf Levanon. 2005. "National Identity and Xenophobia in an Ethnically Divided Society." *International Journal on Multicultural Societies* 7(2):90–118.

Nijman, Jan. 1997. "Globalization to a Latin Beat: The Miami Growth Machine." *ANNALS, AAPSS* 551(May):164–177.

Omi, Michael, and Howard Winant. 1994. *Racial Formation in the United States,* 2nd ed. New York: Routledge.

Padgett, Tim. 2006. "There's Trouble—Lots of It—in Paradise." *Time,* November 19. Retrieved February 2, 2007. (http://www.time.com/time/magazine/article/0,9171,1561128,00.html)

Portes, Alejandro, and Rubén G. Rumbaut. 2006. *Immigrant America,* 3rd ed. Berkeley: University of California Press.

Portes, Alejandro, and Alex Stepick. 1993. *City on the Edge: The Transformation of Miami.* Berkeley: University of California Press.

Sassen, Saskia. 1998. *Globalization and Its Discontents: Essays on the New Mobility of People and Money.* New York: The New Press.

Sohmer, Rebecca, Alan Berubé, Steven Bowers, David Jackson, Damon Jones, Bruce Katz, Amy Liu, Christopher Lyddy, Mark Muro, Audrey Singer, and Thacher Tiffany. 2004. *Growing the Middle Class: Connecting All Miami-Dade Residents to Economic Opportunity.* Center on Urban and Metropolitan Policy. Washington, DC: The Brookings Institution.

Stepick, Alex, Marvin Dunn, Max J. Castro, and Guillermo Grenier. 2003. *This Land Is Our Land: Immigrants and Power in Miami.* Berkeley: University of California Press.

U.S. Census Bureau. 1990. *1990 Summary Tape File 3 (STF 3)—Sample Data.* Retrieved March 28, 2008. (www.census.gov)

———. 2000a. *Census 2000 Summary File 1 (SF 1) 100-Percent Data.* Retrieved March 28, 2008. (www.census.gov)

———. 2000b. *Census 2000 Summary File 3 (SF 3)—Sample Data.* Retrieved March 28, 2008. (www.census.gov)

———. 2002. *American Community Survey.* Retrieved March 28, 2008. (www.census.gov)

———. 2004. *American Community Survey.* Retrieved March 28, 2008. (www.census.gov)

Winant, Howard. 2001. *The World Is a Ghetto: Race and Democracy Since World War II.* New York: Basic Books.

Zavella, Patricia. 1997. "The Tables Are Turned: Immigration, Poverty, and Social Conflict in California Communities." Pp. 136–161 in Juan F. Perea (ed.), *Immigrants Out! The New Nativism and the Anti-Immigrant Impulse in the United States.* New York: New York University Press.

CHAPTER 10

Blacks, Latinos, and the Immigration Debate

Conflict and Cooperation in Two Global Cities

Xóchitl Bada and Gilberto Cárdenas

In this chapter we analyze the connections between the immigration debate and black-Latino conflict and cooperation. In particular, we examine the different perceptions that leaders, the media, academics, ethnic organizations, and the public have crafted regarding the impact of Latino immigrants on blacks and the possibilities for building bridges between these communities. To illustrate the dynamics of the debate, we focus on the cases of Latino-black relations in Los Angeles and Chicago, cities with large immigrant populations that have been experiencing dramatic demographic shifts since the 1990s.

On December 16, 2005, the U.S. House of Representatives passed the Border Protection, Antiterrorism, and Illegal Immigration Control Act of 2005 (a.k.a. H.R. 4437 or the Sensenbrenner bill). The bill stirred a national immigration debate that concentrated on the management of population flows, national security, and the presence of undocumented immigrants. As in the past, public opinion on immigrants as reflected in polls and media coverage was divided in its attitudes toward the presence of an estimated 11.5 million undocumented immigrants and future flows.

As a direct consequence of the Immigration Reform and Control Act (IRCA) of 1986, coupled with the dynamics of global economic restructuring, the United States has received a steady supply of immigrant workers that includes vast numbers of undocumented immigrants. Many of the workers who have crossed the border illegally come from Latin America and tend to have low levels of education. Latinos constitute the majority of undocumented immigrants in the United States. Due to their vulnerability and low levels of education, it is remarkable that during the spring of 2006, an estimated 3–5 million immigrants—most of them Latinos—took by surprise hundreds of cities throughout the United States and staged peaceful demonstrations to protest H.R. 4437.

Between February and April of 2006, large marches were organized in Chicago, Dallas, Houston, and Los Angeles. Millions of Latinos participated in 259 different marches in 43 states. They rallied in the streets and downtowns of more than 158 cities, carrying the important message that civic participation is exercised not only through voting booths. In these marches, one of the most popular slogans read: "Today we march, tomorrow we vote." This is how these seemingly disenfranchised dwellers expressed themselves and demanded respect for their rights. The cities of Chicago and Los Angeles set attendance records, with estimated crowds ranging from 400,000 to 750,000 marchers in the biggest events. In these and other cities, such as San Jose and Fresno, California, the pro-immigrant marches were historic, becoming the largest demonstrations staged in a very long time.

During the marches, national media and conservative commentators such as Lou Dobbs and Bill O'Reilly kept inflaming the public with criticism against the marchers. As a result of the overwhelming media attention, along with the precarious economic situation faced by many middle-class Americans, it is no surprise that current immigration has stirred public debate about its effects on the native-born. The discussion has included nativist concerns (cultural changes, linguistic fears); environmental factors (increased pollution, environmental exhaustion); labor market concerns (wage decreases in the service sector, interethnic competition); and national budget concerns (drains on state-sponsored health services, public education, and welfare provisions).

During the marches, many Latino leaders compared the new movement with the Civil Rights Era, arguing that whereas in the 1940s blacks were politically disenfranchised and endured a long struggle to end racial discrimination, the new immigrant movement was fighting for recognition of Latino contributions to U.S. society. At the same time, Latino leaders argued that theirs was a fight on behalf of all immigrants who cannot vote but who have internalized the aspirations of a democratic society that values freedom. After all, the marchers were using many of the same tools that civil rights leaders used in the 1960s. Unfortunately, African Americans did not overwhelmingly welcome the comparison. While some black leaders supported the movement, others insisted that they had to endure tremendous violence during their civil rights struggles. Many blacks were prompted to recall the era of enslavements, lynchings, and rapes before they were able to march peacefully. To answer those concerns, some Latino leaders reminded blacks that Jim Crow laws did not spare Mexican Americans from discrimination and school segregation.

In fact, Latinos in the Southwest were among the pioneers in the struggle against school desegregation. For instance, the precedents of *Mendez v. Westminster* in California and *Delgado v. Bastrop* in Texas were very important for the eventual success of *Brown v. Board of Education*. In 1968, Rodolfo "Corky" Gonzales led the southwestern contingent at the Poor People's March on Washington. This was part of the unfinished legacy of the Civil Rights Movement after the assassination of Martin Luther King Jr.—a collaboration suggesting that King supported all people suffering from poverty in the late 1960s. Moreover, Chicanos marched and boycotted when they had to endure precarious working conditions in the fields of California and Texas in the 1960s, and some of these struggles were organized through black-Latino coalitions. During the 1970s in Los Angeles, the Third World Left movement worked in solidarity with Latinos, blacks, and Asians.

DYNAMICS OF LATINO-BLACK INTERGROUP RELATIONS

With the exception of educational attainment, Latinos have fared slightly better than blacks on several socioeconomic measures, such as residential integration and socioeconomic status, at least when considered nationally and as a homogeneous population. However, national measures present several problems due to the diverse racial and socioeconomic composition of Latino groups. For example, Puerto Ricans continue to be residentially segregated in the United States, a situation that is even worse for black Puerto Ricans.

Within the last decade, the demographic profile of the Latino population has changed substantially. The 2006 Latino National Survey (LNS) found the following self-identified racial distribution among Latinos: nearly 23 percent white, 0.8 percent black, and more than 67 percent some other race. Most significantly, over 51 percent of the Latino respondents said that Latino/Hispanic is a distinct race and over 87 percent identified strongly or very strongly with terms like "Latino" and "Hispanic," an important increase compared to the 1989 LNS, in which Latinos were more likely to identify with their national origin.

Overall, these new trends are certainly good news for the possibility of minority coalitions between blacks and Latinos, as they suggest that Latinos are increasing their belief in a linked fate as a minority group and a decline in their identification as whites. This development in racial identification of Latinos is not surprising, considering that a significantly larger proportion of newer immigrants from Latin America is indigenous and of African descent. They will certainly take longer to integrate into the ethnic American political landscape, where group identification could mean either upward mobility or downward assimilation, depending on the feasibility of their racial options. For black Americans, the options are reduced as skin tone is not as easily masqueraded as for some Latinos.

In the United States, the acceptance of immigrant groups who arrived after the original British colonizers has been sinuous and paradoxical. For nineteenth-century Irish immigrants it took a long period of time, and a number of loyalty demonstrations, to "become white" and to be seen as such by the white majority. For instance, some Irish Americans in Philadelphia, who lived side by side with blacks and shared the same class difficulties, aligned themselves with the existing racial framework and behaved as anti-black to demonstrate their right to belong to the American Republic. However, not all immigrant groups can escape the "nonwhite" identification assigned to them by the white majority. In a recent questionnaire applied to 151 white college students, an overwhelming majority classified all Latino groups as not white.

Nonetheless, the immigration debate in the United States is quintessential to the foundation of the Republic and has experienced different waves of inclusion-exclusion of certain immigrant groups. Tense interethnic relations have focused not just on skin color but also on language or perceived cultural inferiority. Italian, Irish, and Eastern European peasant immigrants had to prove their whiteness. Latinos and Mexicans, in particular, have long been identified by their racially distinct attributes, real or imagined. Even Germans had to endure language discrimination and were subjects of suspicion. In the mid-1700s, Benjamin Franklin wrote: "[W]hy should the Palatine Boors be suffered to swarm into our Settlements, and by herding together establish their language and manners to the exclusion of ours? Why should Pennsylvania, founded by the English, become a Colony of Aliens, who will shortly be so numerous as to Germanize us instead of our Anglifying them, and will never adopt our Language or Customs, any more than they can acquire our Complexion?"

Today, the United States is far from achieving the full integration and economic advancement of all ethnic groups, especially the most disadvantaged people of color. The conditions that still lead many minorities to marginalization are caused by multiple variables. It would be all too easy to choose among racism, undocumented immigration, economic restructuring, or the culture of poverty as the sole culprits of this problem. The dynamics that have perpetuated the social exclusion of people of color are far more complex.

Historically, new immigrant groups have been held responsible for the economic suffering of more established groups. Eastern Europeans in the early twentieth century were blamed for stealing jobs from the native-born and accepting low wages. During the great migration from the American South, black workers were accused of displacing whites in the midwestern meatpacking industries and were called scabs. The same fate happened to Mexican immigrants who were working in the fields during the organizing drives of the National Farm Workers Association (NFWA), because organizers believed that undocumented migrants were driving down wages and bringing unfair labor competition. It did not matter that most of the workers had ethnic roots in common with the immigrants.

Intergroup and intragroup racial perceptions have received scant scholarly attention. Few comprehensive studies address the topic of interracial relations beyond the reductionist black and white dichotomy. Although Latinos are the new largest minority, they have varied ethnic ancestries, such as African, Asian, and indigenous. Therefore, the white-on-black racial framework for understanding discrimination needs to be modified to unveil the deeper causes leading blacks and Latinos to fare poorly in terms of social mobility.

For instance, the special needs of Latinos are still not well recognized in the national political arena. There is a need to overcome the barriers of symbolic inclusion and obtain more concrete inclusion in national debates. The African American community has fared much better in terms of political representation, partly as a result of the demographic profile of the Latino population, which is newer and less homogeneous and tends to have lower levels of naturalization. So far, the Latino population has made good progress in achieving political representation in states where it has traditionally concentrated—mainly California, Texas, and Illinois. However, the political impact and visibility of Latinos, as well as their most famous struggles, have largely been isolated to those states. César Chávez and Dolores Huerta, two of the most important Latino fighters for social justice, have not had national notoriety. In contrast, African American leaders such as Martin Luther King, Al Sharpton, and Jesse Jackson have gained wide national recognition.

Another problem that has prevented the forging of stronger alliances between Latinos and blacks is the ambiguity of racial identification among Latinos. This has been reinforced by the Negrophobic and anti-Indian education they receive in the United States and the stereotypically negative portrayals of African Americans in the national mass media. In an effort to belong to the most acceptable racial category, many Latinos have chosen to identify themselves as whites, thus undermining the possibilities for a united front among people of color. For example, "nearly 50% of all US Hispanics who answered the 2000 Census chose to call themselves 'white,' thus declining to classify themselves in a manner that would distinguish them from the dominant majority." According to the 2006 LNS, however, Latinos' identification with the white label is decreasing.

On the other hand, the idea of identifying with a mestizo (mixed) race to find a common root among all Latinos has gained some credence among academic circles, although it remains a foreign concept that does not permeate public life in the United States. Even if mestizaje were to establish a wider following among Latinos, the concept does not necessarily include Afro-descendants. Mestizaje, as the Mexican philosopher José Vasconcelos imagined it, represented the fusion of the Indian race (preferably Aztec) and the Spanish blood. Therefore, it is important to offer new panethnic identifications that bring back to the surface the black roots of Latinos, which have been present since Mexicans stayed after the U.S. annexation of Texas and have continued to be replenished with Afro-Caribbean and Mexican migrants from nontraditional southern places of origin in the last two decades.

By and large, Latinos need to be more aware of their ethnic racial origins: African-descended, Amerindian, and Asian-descended, in addition to their diverse national ancestries. At the same time, more public attention needs to be invested in overcoming the lack of knowledge about Latinos' diverse racial backgrounds and the ways in which this interferes with their ability to build bridges with the African American community. And Latinos themselves need to acknowledge their reluctance to accept that their panethnic identity also comprises blacks. This denial is partly explained by the fact that social discrimination is still commonly experienced by blacks living in Mexico, Colombia, Brazil, and other Latin

American countries. Moreover, instead of concentrating on the common issues affecting the two largest minorities in the country, much of the public attention to the demographic explosion of Latinos has focused either on the discontent of African Americans who must share their power to accommodate Latinos or on their concerns that the massive flows of unskilled Latino immigrants are undermining access to entry-level jobs in the low-wage service sector for the most disadvantaged members of the African American community.

African Americans and Latinos in the Labor Market: Academic and Media Debates

Illegal workers supplant native-born ones, foreign-born workers drive wages down, and immigrants steal jobs away from African Americans. These are some of the most common depictions behind the headlines that have sprawled in mainstream and ethnic media outlets during intense immigration debates over the last twenty years. Simultaneously, the media have noted the lack of support for a nationwide pattern of displacement of American workers that can be correlated with immigrant employment outcomes. More detailed academic studies scrutinizing cities, metropolitan areas, and economic sectors have not found conclusive evidence that immigrant workers are the primary cause for labor displacement, labor market segmentation, or generalized unemployment among the foreign-born.

The state of California has been examined closely as a magnet for undocumented immigration and one of the most rapidly changing states in its demographic composition; but no conclusive evidence demonstrates a correlation between immigration and higher levels of unemployment among native-born minorities. For instance, Manuel Pastor and Enrico Marcelli (2004:108) attempted to measure the impact of the labor force competition between undocumented Mexicans and African Americans, and found mixed results: "[T]he geographic pattern suggests that there are few displacement effects but an occupational analysis does suggest some competition when there are exceptionally high numbers of undocumented migrants in the same field."

More recently, the Pew Hispanic Center addressed the question of whether above-average growth in the foreign-born population was associated with worse-than-average employment outcomes for the native-born population. The study found no consistent national pattern in the relationship between those two variables. However, other national labor indicators seem to put some blame on the immigrants when measuring the fate of blacks. In a *New York Times* article published a few days after the May 1 marches of 2006, the director of the African American Leadership Institute at the University of Maryland noted that, in 2004, 72 percent of black male high school dropouts in their twenties were jobless, compared with 34 percent of white dropouts and 10 percent of Hispanic dropouts. Harvard University professor George Borjas, one of the most interviewed authors for this debate, has argued that the average annual wage loss for all American male workers from 1980 to 2000 was $1,200, or 4 percent, and nearly twice that, in percentage terms, for those without a high school diploma.

He has further claimed that the impact was disproportionately high on African Americans and Hispanic Americans (Borjas, 1998).

On the other hand, Earl Ofari Hutchinson, one of the most consistent pro-immigrant black commentators, in expressing surprise at the old civil rights groups' lack of support for the 2006 immigrant movement, made the following remarks:

> [I]llegal immigration is not the prime reason so many poor young blacks are on the streets. A shrinking economy, sharp state and federal government cuts and the elimination of job and skill training programs, failing public schools, a soaring black prison population, and employment discrimination are the prime causes of the poverty crisis in many inner city black neighborhoods. The recent studies by Princeton, Columbia and Harvard researchers on the dreary plight of young black males reconfirmed that chronic unemployment has turned thousands of young black males into America's job untouchables.

The African American community appears to have ambivalent positions over immigration. A recent poll by the Pew Hispanic Center found that nearly 80 percent of African Americans said that immigrants from Latin America work very hard and have strong family values, but nearly twice as many blacks as whites said that they or a family member had lost a job, or not gotten a job, because an employer hired an immigrant worker. Blacks were also more likely than whites to feel that immigrants take jobs away from American citizens.

Despite such ambivalence, African Americans have been more sympathetic toward immigrants than their white counterparts. A 2003 Gallup poll found that 20 percent of blacks and 11 percent of whites were in favor of an increase in immigration. The poll also found that income is a significant predictor of a more sympathetic attitude toward immigration, with 75 percent of those with incomes exceeding $75,000 agreeing that immigration is good for the country, compared to only 46 percent of those with incomes below $30,000. Considering that African Americans are overrepresented at the bottom end of the income distribution, the individual support is very surprising.

Another factor that has contributed to negative stereotypes toward immigrants of color is their portrayal by the mass media. The vast majority of white-dominated media in the United States have always promoted a negative racial framing toward immigrants of color. Leo Chavez (2001) has demonstrated the virulence of negative stereotyping in his analysis of seventy-six immigration-related covers appearing on ten popular magazines from 1965 to 1999. During that period, he documented forty-nine alarmist covers, nineteen affirmative covers, and eight neutral covers. The affirmative ones were mostly printed around the fourth of July to celebrate the immigrant heritage of the United States. Therefore, fully 64.4 percent of the covers displayed immigration-related issues using narratives and iconographies that framed the debate mostly in alarmist terms. The most frequently used iconographies and narratives were marine references (water, floods), martial references (time bombs, battleground), and crisis (Mexican immigrants portrayed as masses and multitudes).

Overall, African American and Latino leaders have shown differential capabilities for reaching out to their own constituencies regarding Latin American immigration and interethnic conflict and cooperation. Sometimes the leadership has failed to communicate effectively with relevant audiences; on other occasions their success has been only moderate, especially in comparison to the massive engagement achieved by the dominant mass media.

The fledging multiracial coalitions formed around immigrant rights in the spring of 2006 suggest some hope for the future, but it is still too early to predict the long-term consolidation of sustained mutual support. It took some time for civil rights lobbyists to speak up in favor of the marches, and most of them offered their full endorsement only during the last wave of events. This attitude is related to the lack of effective outreach from the Latino community toward the African American grassroots. The feeling of being left out was common among some organizations, especially in Los Angeles, where endorsements from the African American community took longer to arrive than in Chicago. Although some African American organizations were divided in their endorsement of the movement, most supported the immigrant rights movement, including, among many others, the National Association for the Advancement of Colored People (NAACP), the Congressional Black Caucus, the Rainbow/PUSH Coalition, Mothers on the Move (MOM) in New York, several state chapters of the Association for Community Organizations for Reform Now (ACORN), the Nation of Islam and the Council of Islamic Organizations in Chicago, and the Industrial Areas Foundation in North Carolina.

AFRICAN AMERICAN–LATINO IMMIGRANT COALITIONS IN LOS ANGELES

The contemporary history of Latino-black relations in Los Angeles is a mixed account of conflict and cooperation. The conflict episodes tend to be localized in places where both populations share space at least in equal numbers, often as a result of a rapid increase in the immigrant Latino population and immigrants' birth rates. The exodus of middle-class African Americans and whites from Los Angeles into smaller cities in California or to southern states has left mostly low-income black and Latino minorities sharing the space in decaying urban spaces, where residents are struggling to survive in the midst of deindustrialization, coupled with an increase in the mostly low-income service sector. Moreover, ethnic conflict in Los Angeles has been mostly related to concentration and class effects. Therefore, Latinos and African Americans have shown the highest degree of tension, compared to black and white intergroup conflict.

According to the 2005 American Community Survey, Los Angeles County had 4.6 million Latinos and 0.9 million blacks (including 24,526 Afro-Latinos), with a total population of 9.7 million (U.S. Census Bureau, 2006). Therefore, in this metropolitan area, the once traditional minorities have acquired a combined majority status. But the numeric expansion of the Latino community has not been accompanied by proportional political representation. Approximately 2.1

million Latinos living in the area are foreign-born, and many of those are legal permanent residents unable to vote. Nevertheless, their electoral disenfranchisement has not prevented them from participating in other areas of civic life that do not require formal citizenship.

For instance, interracial labor coalitions have been possible among African Americans and Latino migrants with and without legal residence. A good case in point was the 2002 Los Angeles bus riders' strike, when Latinos made common cause with unionized African Americans to save the work contracts of bus drivers. The success of this coalition kept public transportation for Latin American migrant workers and other low-income minorities as a viable option for commuting to work. The support of Miguel Contreras, the first Latino head of the Los Angeles County Federation of Labor, was very important. He came to the drivers' defense as soon as the strike started. This broke long-established political relationships for the labor movement, because the Metropolitan Transportation Authority directors were supported by county supervisors, Latina Gloria Molina and African American Yvonne Braithwaite-Burke, both Democrats who had decided to make common cause with Los Angeles's Republican mayor against the unions.

On the other hand, the conflict over staff hiring at Los Angeles county hospitals, the frequent interracial riots in overcrowded state prisons, and the violence in the town of Inglewood over Black History Month celebrations in past decades need to be contextualized within the dramatic population shifts. For example, the violence in Inglewood that led to the cancellation of Black History Month at Inglewood High School in 1999 can be traced to the resentment of Latino teens over the celebration of black culture for an entire month. Moreover, between 2000 and 2005, Inglewood experienced rapid change in the composition of its population. In 2000, African American residents constituted 47 percent of the population and Latinos 46 percent. By 2005, Latinos made up 57 percent of the population while blacks had decreased in number to 39 percent. This demographic change did not come with more proportional representation in city government. In 2006, the Inglewood City Council had only one Latino member, who was elected in 2003. Nevertheless, in this middle-class community, the conflict has lately been contained and Latinos have expressed an interest in accepting the historical influence that African Americans had on this town and are willing to find a common ground.

Recently, Local 1877 of the Service Employees International Union (SEIU) in California became more inclusive of African Americans. Their "Justice for Janitors" campaign added special provisions for African American janitors, who had felt largely displaced since the arrival of new immigrant populations to this industry. The union negotiated higher wages and its largely Latino members are now planning to seek contractual language guaranteeing African Americans at least 12 percent of janitorial jobs, reflecting their presence in the population. The hotel workers' union negotiated similar guarantees for black workers in 2005. In 2006, the SEIU conducted a unionization drive for security guards nationwide, including Los Angeles, where the industry's employees are more than 50 percent African American.

These are contemporary examples of fledging labor collaborations between Latinos and African Americans. However, the newly gained visibility of the Latino population through massive protests against the Sensenbrenner bill in Los Angeles culminated many years of grassroots organizing and coalition building among various ethnic groups. For instance, during the 1960s and 1970s, at the height of leftist and revolutionary politics, Chicanos formed the Brown Berets as a result of their contacts with the Black Panthers, and Puerto Ricans formed the Young Lords. Although not all interethnic coalitions have worked closely together, the relationship between the Brown Berets and the Black Panthers was exceptional in Southern California, especially in support of César Chávez's movement with the National Farm Workers Association. Some of the social movements around those decades emerged in parallel. Just five years after the Watts riots, Chicano high school students staged walkouts to demand better schools in East Los Angeles in 1968, the same year in which Martin Luther King was assassinated. Many Latinos, including Mexican Americans, attended King's memorial at the Los Angeles Coliseum shortly after his death.

The issues that have united Latino and African American communities have been mostly related to economic disparities, social exclusion, and labor rights. In the twenty-first century, the dire economic and social situation of low-income and ethnic minorities helps explain why the city of Los Angeles experienced a series of protests that went from a weeklong student walkout movement to several pro-immigrant rallies and marches from March to May of 2006. Although Latinos were the most visible ethnic group during the marches, many others joined the protests, such as Koreans, Chinese, and African Americans.

Whereas most local African American leaders endorsed the movement, African Americans did not march in large numbers in defense of immigrant rights. This reflected the lack of solid preexisting coalitions among grassroots organizations that included immigrant rights as part of their agenda. The organization of the marches caught many Latino leaders by surprise and they have accepted that they did not reach out for the solidarity of African American labor leaders, who largely felt excluded from the movement's leadership. This has been corrected in subsequent events such as the National Latino Congress. Held on September 6–10, 2006, this conference was conceived as an event for people of color, where both African American and Latino communities could discuss their most pressing issues and pledge to make long-lasting coalitions around common interests. The mutually agreed agenda included topics such as public education improvements, fighting against U.S. foreign policy that simultaneously favors job losses in the United States and more immigration from the South to the North, voter registration among minorities, electoral redistricting, and labor rights for all workers, regardless of their immigration status.

Most liberal African American leaders publicly supported the pro-immigrant movement during the two-month period between the 2006 marches, while expressing concern for the plight of low-income African Americans, the ones most likely to feel the impact of increasing immigration of low-skilled workers. Aside from opposing voices on African American radio stations and some small protests organized by the Minutemen that attracted African American followers, the overall response of the organized African American community toward immigrant rights was positive. The common ground has been the acknowledgment that the Civil Rights Movement does not belong exclusively to African Americans and that Latinos deserve the support of the black community, in exchange for a more stable cooperation between the two communities on issues that affect them equally.

AFRICAN AMERICAN–LATINO IMMIGRANT COALITIONS IN CHICAGO

In Chicago, the building of alliances between different Latino groups in contemporary history can be traced to the successful political coalition between Puerto Ricans and Mexicans in the 1970s. Under the leadership of Puerto Rican activist Hector Franco—who had previously participated in Latino-black coalitions such as the Allies for a Better Community (ABC) in Chicago's Westtown—twenty-three Mexican American and Puerto Rican organizations came together to fight for immigrant rights and equal access to job opportunities, among other social-justice issues. Through their newly found panethnic identity, members of these organizations realized that they faced similar issues that prevented both communities from attaining equal access to housing, jobs, and education. A decade later, this type of multiethnic coalition would bear fruit again when the first black mayor of Chicago was elected.

Harold Washington's election in 1983 is an excellent example of the possibilities of successful rainbow coalitions. Washington owed his victory in the primary election to the overwhelming turnout of African American voters, 15 percent of the white independents, and 13 percent of the Latino vote, which increased to an impressive 75 percent during the general election. This happened because multiethnic coalitions such as the Independent Political Organization (IPO) of Little Village, a Latino organization, had been actively working with the African American community in the same area. Moreover, the IPO, whose main objective was to engage in the electoral arena, did not limit membership to U.S. citizens or legal permanent residents. Everyone, regardless of immigration status, was invited to participate in the organization. The idea that civic participation had to engage all residents of a neighborhood was very well understood by Mayor Washington during his tenure. As María de los Ángeles Torres (2004:92) has documented, Washington knew the importance of including different sectors within the minority population.

Considering that Chicago's Latino population is new compared to the Latino population in Los Angeles, this multiethnic coalition success represents an important lesson for understanding the particular needs of mixed neighborhoods in urban areas. For example, the city of Compton, in Los Angeles County, has a Latino majority population (57 percent) but zero representation in the city council. Here we observe a new racial dynamic, whereby lack of understanding of the unique needs of mixed-status immigrant populations prevents power sharing between blacks and Latinos. Conflict between African Americans and Latinos in Compton stems from multiple factors: residential transition, access to scarce social services for children of undocumented immigrants, and lack of visible civic engagement from the Latino community, as well as misunderstandings about bilingual education coupled with low-quality public education. Therefore, conflict over political power has been difficult to overcome and African American politicians have not reached out to the Latino population, arguing that it is overwhelmingly composed of noncitizens. In 1994, Mayor Omar Bradley declared to the *Los Angeles Times:* "What does the African American do to empower them [Latinos] when it's constitutionally illegal [for noncitizens to vote]?" Bradley apparently thought that the only way to empower a citizen is to make him or her a voter. If Latinos were given the opportunity for political representation, the dialogue for building successful coalitions among immigrant communities, legal Latino residents, and African Americans could start. In Chicago, all residents have the opportunity to vote in school councils, regardless of their immigration status. This has proven to be a very positive step toward inclusion of all parents' voices in the educational debate.

As we have seen, Latinos in Chicago have a historical record of establishing multiethnic minority coalitions that include immigration issues. This favorable context helped to consolidate the more recent pro-immigrant movement forged in the city—specifically, in 2006. For instance, the March 10 movement—one of the most important umbrella coalitions established to defend immigrant rights in Chicago—was a response to the Sensenbrenner bill approved in January 2006. This movement started as a coalition among unions, grassroots groups, churches, and immigrant-led organizations with the common goal of preparing a massive pro-immigrant march. The movement's leaders quickly understood that their demands needed the support of other minorities. In Cook County, which includes the city of Chicago, Latinos represent 22.5 percent of the population, African Americans 25.8 percent, and Asians 5.4 percent. Together, the three communities capture slightly over half of the total population in the county (U.S. Census Bureau, 2006). The Latino leadership knew that it was very important to bring together all these minorities to have a successful and representative protest. Indeed, the March 10 movement was able to reap the benefits of this positive environment. The city had already staged a large pro-immigrant rally in the year 2000, bringing 10,000 participants downtown—a large crowd that had not been seen in Chicago since the Harold Washington era. However, the endorsement of the African American community had been more timid then, with the Association of Community Organizations for Reform Now (ACORN) and the African Diaspora bringing the majority of black participants to the September 2000 march.

In 2006, the March 10 movement was much more successful in engaging the African American community and inviting important black leaders as participants to the planning meetings in the Pilsen neighborhood, a largely Latino immigrant neighborhood. The organizers knew that they had a language challenge when they planned for their meetings with the Asian and African American communities, but they managed to bring simultaneous translators to the planning sessions. Thanks to the engaged participation of several labor leaders, the organizers were able to establish broader networks with the African American leadership.

However, several obstacles had to be overcome. Among these was the fact that the Latino leadership had to work with the African American community less than a year after the negative remarks made by former Mexican president Vicente Fox about blacks' work ethic. The *Chicago Defender,* a prominent African American newspaper in Chicago, paid much attention to President Fox's unfortunate remarks, publishing nine commentaries on them. Some commentators stressed that the positive aspect of this incident was that it forced African Americans to find a common base with Latinos, but others dismissed the president's attitude, even after he agreed to meet with African American leaders in Mexico City.

In order to heal the crack created by President Fox, the Latino leadership was helped by an initiative of the Mexican Fine Arts Museum in Pilsen, which inaugurated an exhibit on the African Presence in Mexico in February 2006. The exposition was positively reviewed in African American newspapers and got excellent attendance from the African American community. However much or little the exhibition's timing affected the success of the black-Latino coalition for the pro-immigrant rally in March, it undoubtedly helped to instill a sense of commonality between the two groups. That some veterans of the Young Lords— which had included Puerto Ricans, African Americans, and Mexican Americans in the 1960s—were among the organizers of the March 10 movement contributed to the building of credibility with African Americans.

The Latino Chapter of the Chicago Rainbow/PUSH Coalition had also been doing some modest work since 1983. More recently, the Latino Chapter has focused on bilingual education, trying to convince black parents of the benefits of teaching a second language to their children. In the words of the president of the Latino Chapter: "I always tell black parents that I would love it if their kids can do business in immigrant Latino barrios and vice versa. I always tell them that if they speak Spanish, they can do business with Latin America. It is a win-win situation. I want Latino kids to learn English, but I also think that black kids can benefit from learning Spanish through good quality bilingual education" (personal interview, August 12, 2006). Other issues that have attracted black-Latino common platforms have been minority access to higher education, fighting against police brutality, and supporting unity candidates for Police Commander positions in some districts.

Jesse Jackson spoke at Casa Michoacán in Pilsen during one of the organizing meetings for the May 1 March in 2006. (Casa Michoacán is the headquarters of the Illinois Federation of Michoacano Hometown Associations, a migrant-led grassroots organization emphasizing civic binational organizing.) Jackson had committed to speak at the May 1 rally in New York City, so he gave his public endorsement for the march in late April. In his speech, he said: "There is real fear among blacks about the loss of jobs. But it's not ... the undocumented workers that are the cause. It's cheaper wage jobs." He further argued that the struggle for decent pay was related to the exodus of manufacturing jobs, which are being exported overseas to avoid labor rights and living wages. The turnout of African Americans at the May 1 march was modest but inspiring. According to a study conducted by researchers at the University of Illinois in Chicago, an estimated 3 percent of the May 1 marchers in downtown Chicago were African American.

Among the most visible organized groups with large African American constituents were ACORN and Student/Tenant Organizing Project (STOP), a housing activists' movement against gentrification from the city's South Side.

However, not all Chicago-based African American organizations and leaders rallied in favor of immigrants during the spring of 2006. Notable exceptions include the Reverend Anthony Williams, an African American pastor of St. Stephens Lutheran Church, who led a coalition to oppose the hiring of undocumented immigrants. His coalition included Black Minutemen and a group called Voices of the Ex-Offender (VOTE), an African American organization that suggested that an amnesty for felons should be considered as seriously as an amnesty for undocumented immigrants. Williams even attacked Jesse Jackson for his unconditional defense of undocumented immigrants.

CONCLUSION

Contemporary pro-immigrant marches should be understood in terms of human and workers' rights, which are universal and can resonate among all disadvantaged minorities in the United States. Blacks, Latinos, and other minorities have many commonalities with the immigrant rights struggle, which is mainly a labor rights issue. Although not comparable to the slavery suffered by African Americans for centuries, the current conditions of some immigrant workers in agriculture and the low-paying service sector throughout the United States have been brought to trial, in Florida and elsewhere in the country, as cases of modern-day slavery.

To build successful coalitions, Latinos and African Americans should focus on unifying themes, such as labor discrimination and racially motivated labor segregation. Latinos need to challenge employers in ethnic firms who prefer undocumented immigrants over blacks because they believe the former to be more docile and less likely to demand better work conditions or denounce irregularities. Some employers recruit through preexisting networks among employees, which results in further discrimination against blacks. Blacks should also be aware that many white employers still prefer to hire nonblack workers, arguing "customer preferences," as is the case in some sectors of the restaurant industry. This has more to do with the remnants of a racist society than with a deliberate attempt by immigrants to trump up African American social mobility.

Likewise, blacks have made major inroads in government employment and Latinos should not waste time in lawsuits disputing those historic gains. Latino immigrants are demanding the opportunity to work for wages that are not artificially lowered because of the constant threat of employers to denounce their illegal status to authorities. Blacks have much to gain in this fight. If all jobs were offered in a leveled playing field, employers would have to provide better wages and blacks would be more attracted to those jobs, thus producing a more equitable competition in the job market.

Most African American civic, political, religious, and grassroots organizations have supported the immigrant rights struggle. We still need to know more about the internal dynamics that have propelled this support, despite the African American voices that have demanded a restrictionist immigration policy. We believe that black-Latino coalitions hold great promise in finding a niche "somewhere over the rainbow." African Americans and Latinos share multiple economic goals, including higher levels of employment, higher wages and other standards at the bottom of the labor markets, and better education and job training to increase their human capital. Attaining such goals requires overcoming inevitable conflicts, such as differential access to state resources and employment, funds for bilingual education, and immigration flows themselves. However, the art of coalition building involves finding reasonable trade-offs in the spirit of mutual support.

REFERENCES

Avila, Oscar, and Michael Martínez. 2006. "Immigrants at Crossroads: Stakes Are High for Legalization Campaign." *Chicago Tribune,* May 1, p. 89.

Ayi, Mema. 2006. "Jackson: We're All in This Immigration Battle Together." *Chicago Defender,* April 26. Retrieved March 25, 2008. (https://www.highbeam.com)

Bada, Xóchitl, Jonathan Fox, and Andrew Selee (eds.). 2006. *Invisible No More: Mexican Migrant Civic Participation in the U.S.* Washington, DC: Woodrow Wilson Center for International Scholars. Retrieved March 25, 2008. (www.wilsoncenter.org/topics/pubs/Invisible%20No%20More.pdf)

Bailey, Thomas R. 1987. *Immigrant and Native Workers: Contrasts and Competition.* Boulder, CO: Westview Press.

Borjas, George J. 1998. "Do Blacks Gain or Lose from Immigration?" Pp. 51–74 in Daniel S. Hammermesh and Frank D. Bean (eds.), *Help or Hindrance? The Economic Implications of Immigration for African Americans.* New York: Russell Sage Foundation.

Chavez, Leo R. 2001. *Covering Immigration: Popular Images and the Politics of the Nation.* Berkeley: University of California Press.

Feagin, Joe R. 2006. *Systemic Racism: A Theory of Oppression.* New York: Routledge.

Flores-González, Nilda, Amalia Pallares, Herring Cedric, and Maria Krysan. 2006. *UIC Immigrant Mobilization Project: General Survey Findings.* Washington, DC: Woodrow Wilson Center for International Scholars. Retrieved March 25, 2008. (http://www.wilsoncenter.org/news/docs/uicstudy.pdf)

Fraga, Luis R., John A. García, Rodney E. Hero, Michael Jones-Correa, Valerie Martinez-Ebers, and Gary M. Segura. 2006. *Latino National Survey.* University of Washington Institute for the Study of Ethnicity, Race, and Sexuality (WISER). Retrieved March 25, 2008. (http://depts.washington.edu/uwiser/LNS.shtml)

García, Michelle 2006. "A Bronx Tale." *The Nation,* June 19. Retrieved March 25, 2008. (http://www.thenation.com/doc/20060619/garcia)

Ginsberg-Jaeckle, Matt. 2006. "Unity in the Community: Housing Activists March for Immigrants' Rights." *Fight Back!* (July/August). Retrieved March 25, 2008. (http://www.fightbacknews.org/2006/03/unitycommunity.htm)

Greenberg, Brad A. 2006. "Racial Generation Gap Grows Here, Study Says; Latinos Inhabiting Untraditional Areas." *Daily News of Los Angeles,* March 7, p. N1.

Greenhouse, Steven. 2006. "Borrowing Language of Civil Rights Movement, Drive Is On to Unionize Guards." *New York Times,* July 26. Retrieved March 25, 2008. (http://www.nytimes.com/2006/07/26/us/26guards.html)

Hernández, Tanya Kateri. 2003. "'Too Black to Be Latino/a': Blackness and Blacks as Foreigners in Latino Studies." *Latino Studies* 1(1):152–159.

Hutchinson, Earl Ofari. 2006. "Old Civil Rights Group MIA on New Civil Rights

Movement." *The Buffalo Criterion Online,* March 30. Retrieved March 25, 2008. (www. econ.brown.edu/.../teaching/Ec%20137/Ec%20137%20new%20material/blacks%20vs%20immigrants.pdf)

Ignatiev, Noel. 1995. *How the Irish Became White.* New York: Routledge.

Kochhar, Rakesh. 2006. *Growth in the Foreign-Born Workforce and Employment of the Native Born.* Washington, DC: Pew Hispanic Center. Retrieved March 25, 2008. (http://pewhispanic.org/reports/report.php?ReportID=69)

Konkol, Mark J. 2006. "Chicago Immigration March Gets PUSH Support: Jackson Pledges Participants, Says Blacks Need Not Fear." *Chicago Sun Times,* April 26, p. 48.

Lantigua, John. 2003. "Labor Under Lock and Fist." *Palm Beach Post,* December 7. Retrieved March 25, 2008. (http://www.palmbeachpost.com/hp/content/moderndayslavery/reports/slave1207.html)

Massey, Douglas S., and Nancy A. Denton. 1993. *American Apartheid: Segregation and the Making of the Underclass.* Cambridge, MA: Harvard University Press.

Massey, Douglas S., Jorge Durand, and Nolan J. Malone. 2002. *Beyond Smoke and Mirrors: Mexican Immigration in an Era of Economic Integration.* New York: Russell Sage Foundation.

Menchaca, Martha. 2001. *Recovering History, Constructing Race: The Indian, Black, and White Roots of Mexican Americans.* Austin: University of Texas Press.

Morales Almada, Jorge. 2006. "El Congreso Latino promoverá el voto." *La Opinión,* September 8. Retrieved March 25, 2008. (http://www.laopinion.com/primerapagina/?rkey=00060907220242623831)

Moreno, Rubén. 2006. "Inglewood apuesta por la diversidad." *La Opinión,* February 6. Retrieved March 25, 2008. (http://www.laopinion.com/archivo/index.html)

Padilla, Felix M. 1985. *Latino Ethnic Consciousness: The Case of Mexican Americans and Puerto Ricans in Chicago.* Notre Dame, IN: University of Notre Dame Press.

Pastor, Manuel, Jr., and Enrico A. Marcelli. 2004. "Somewhere over the Rainbow? African Americans, Unauthorized Mexican Immigration, and Coalition Building." Pp. 107–135 in Steven Shulman (ed.), *The Impact of Immigration on African Americans.* New Brunswick, NJ: Transaction Publishers.

Patterson, Demetrius. 2006. "Black, White Laborers United to Oppose Hiring of Illegal Immigrants." *Chicago Defender,* May 3. Retrieved March 25, 2008. (http://www.jobbankusa.com/News/Hiring/laborers_unite_oppose_hiring_illegal_immigrants.html)

Pulido, Laura. 2006. *Black, Brown, Yellow, and Left: Radical Activism in Los Angeles.* Berkeley and Los Angeles: University of California Press.

Simon, Rita James, and Susan H. Alexander. 1993. *The Ambivalent Welcome: Print Media, Public Opinion, and Immigration.* Westport, CT: Praeger.

Stevens, Gillian. 1999. *The Ideology of Language and the Incorporation of Immigrants in the United States, 1965–1995.* Paper 8 in Negotiating Difference Series. New York: International Center for Migration, Ethnicity, and Citizenship.

Suárez Orozco, Marcelo, and Mariela M. Páez. 2002. "Introduction: The Research Agenda." Pp. 1–37 in Marcelo Suárez Orozco and Mariela M. Páez (eds.), *Latinos: Remaking America.* Berkeley: University of California Press.

Swarns, Rachel L. 2006. "Growing Unease for Some Blacks on Immigration." *New York Times,* May 4, p. 1.

Torres, María de los Ángeles. 2004. "In Search of Meaningful Voice and Place: The IPO and Latino Community Empowerment in Chicago." Pp. 81–106 in Gilberto Cárdenas (ed.), *La Causa: Civil Rights, Social Justice, and the Struggle for Equality in the Midwest.* Houston: Arte Público Press.

Torres-Saillant, Silvio. 2003. "Inventing the Race: Latinos and the Ethnoracial Pentagon." *Latino Studies* 1(1):123–151.

U.S. Census Bureau. 2006. *2005 American Community Survey.* Retrieved March 25, 2008. (http://factfinder.census.gov)

Vaca, Nick Corona. 2004. *The Presumed Alliance: The Unspoken Conflict Between Latinos and Blacks and What It Means for America.* New York: Rayo.

Valenzuela, Abel, Jr. 1997. "Compatriots or Competitors? Job Competition Between Foreign- and U.S.-Born Angelenos." Pp. 287–314 in Darrell Y. Hamamoto and Rodolfo D. Torres (eds.), *New American Destinies: A Reader in Contemporary Asian and Latino Immigration.* New York: Routledge.

Waldinger, Roger David, and Michael Ira Lichter. 2003. *How the Other Half Works: Immigration and the Social Organization of Labor.* Berkeley: University of California Press.

Washington, Laura S. 2006. "Solidarity from Barrio to Barbershop." *In These Times,* April 25. Retrieved March 25, 2008. (http://www.inthesetimes.com/article/2620/)

Watanabe, Teresa. 2006. "The State: L.A. Workers Join Fierce Debate over Immigration." *Los Angeles Times,* February 28, p. A1.

CHAPTER 11

Central American Immigrants and Racialization in a Post–Civil Rights Era

Nestor P. Rodriguez and Cecilia Menjívar

CENTRAL AMERICAN IMMIGRATION IN A POST–CIVIL RIGHTS ERA

The U.S. immigration wave that is continuing into the twenty-first century is reproducing structures of racial and ethnic relations.[1] Central American immigration, which accounts for over 50,000 new legal immigrants annually and for over 1 million of the unauthorized migrants in the country (Jefferys and Rytina, 2006: table 3; Hoefer, Rytina, and Campbell, 2006: table 3), is a major example of this development. In many U.S. metropolitan areas, Central Americans constitute large populations (see Table 11.1). Coming from a region that was incorporated into the modern world-system through domestic structures of rigid racial stratification, Central American immigrants arrive in metropolitan areas and other U.S. localities where social relations are changing through matrices associated with new social-spatial boundaries and shifting social identities (Lamphere, 1992). Moreover, the settlement of Central American immigrants is occurring in the temporal context of what we call the Post–Civil Rights Era—a new social and political period in which major inequalities among racially defined populations persist but the policymaking sectors of U.S. society no longer feel pressured to address such inequalities.

Table 11.1 Top Five Central American Populations, and Other Selected Populations, in U.S. Metropolitan Areas, 2005

Metropolitan Area	Total	Central Americans	Non-Hispanic Whites[a]	African Americans	Latinos[b]	Asians	Native Americans
Los Angeles	12,703,423	684,888	4,225,707	914,183	5,576,583	1,746,622	63,361
New York	18,351,099	377,032	9,453,182	3,212,619	3,871,522	1,649,502	52,938
Miami	5,334,685	263,842	2,103,014	1,075,174	2,013,725	111,196	10,582
Washington, DC	5,119,490	249,433	2,684,362	1,329,389	577,445	425,378	17,525
Houston	5,193,448	192,882	2,313,993	840,219	1,686,048	293,763	22,526

[a]The frequencies listed for Non-Hispanic whites as well as for African Americans, Asians, and Native Americans represent persons who did not specify more than one race. Less than 3 percent of each of the populations in the five metropolitan areas reported more than one race.

[b]Includes Central Americans.

Source: U.S. Census Bureau (2005).

Central American immigrants also are arriving at a time when, with the exception of "anti-illegal immigrant" policies, the most blatant forms of racism are not publicly acceptable and therefore sometimes public officials and policymakers shroud their views and attitudes behind benevolent rhetoric (Menjívar and Kil, 2002). This form of discrimination is pernicious and becomes a moving target that is sometimes difficult to pinpoint, resulting in insidious forms of rights violations. This new context has important implications for the insertion of Central Americans in the racialized social structures of the locales where they settle.

CENTRAL AMERICAN RACIAL BACKGROUND

Central American immigrants are coming from a region in which European colonization historically imposed rigid social boundaries that depended significantly on a social construction of race, which included physical appearance, ancestry, and sociocultural criteria, to use Charles Wagley's (1968) definition of "social race." With variations across local areas, in the early stages of the incorporation of the region into the developing modern world-system, around the seventeenth century, race became a means to develop hierarchical divisions of labor (Wade, 1997). As in other peripheral regions, in the colonial economies of Central America the masses of racialized indigenous populations performed the most labor-intensive and low-status work and usually survived only in conditions of poverty (Guzmán Böckler and Herbert, 1970). Today, the indigenous population of over 5 million in Guatemala continues to live in these circumstances (Loucky and Moors, 2000a), and that of El Salvador, though not as visible in official statistics, also continues to live among the poorest of the poor. Although the peace accords that ended the Guatemalan civil war in 1996 proposed more rights for the indigenous population, the large Ladino population (people of mixed European and indigenous origins) of the country did not give wide support to this reform (Jonas, 2000).

With the growth of mestizo populations, racial boundaries in the region that was to become Central America became less polarized between European and indigenous but did not disappear, especially concerning the categories of indigenous and whites. In local areas, the intermarriage of African-origin and mestizo peoples with others resulted in new categories (e.g., mulatto), but in terms of identity, the fast-growing mestizo population became mainly a category of what they were not—neither indigenous nor white. That is to say, "mestizo" did not develop into a popular self-concept; consequently, the self-designations that mestizos adopted were usually regional and, later, national or Ladino in cultural identity. With the exception of Guatemala and other local areas populated by Black Caribs or aboriginal groups, mestizos in Central America became the new masses of peasants and other low-status workers who often lived in poverty (Wade, 1997).

In many Latin American regions, mestizos constitute the dominant population, but in some areas the so-called mestizos are actually indigenous populations that have been coerced into abandoning their original cultural expressions. This happened after the Matanza (massacre) of 1932 in El Salvador, where the killings of thousands of indigenous people in the name of an "anti-Communist" offensive sent many expressions of indigenous culture to clandestinity and invisibility. Thus, many indigenous people were forced to take on a mestizo identity. Jeffrey L. Gould (1998) refers to this condition as the "myth of mestizaje" in his research on Nicaragua. At the urging of the UN International Convention on the Elimination of All Forms of Racial Discrimination, El Salvador's 2007 census of population included a question about ethnic identity that was supposed to make possible the official recognition of indigenous populations. However, the question was asked in such a way that it generated results that simply corroborate the "myth of mestizaje," which contributes to the erroneous claim that El Salvador's indigenous population is tiny or nonexistent: Eighty-six percent reported that they were mestizos, 13 percent whites, and only 1 percent indigenous (Tenorio and Huezo Mixco, 2008).

As mestizaje became the master narrative for the vast majority of populations in the Central American region, old and new forms of racialization coalesced. In some areas of Central America—such as Guatemala—the descendants of European settlers (e.g., German coffee plantation owners) still survive in higher-status conditions (Adams, 1970; Perea, 1997), and new white settlers continue to arrive to operate foreign-owned businesses. Moreover, in Guatemala Mayans continue to be identified as distinct, lower-status populations (Carmack, 1992), as are significant numbers of other native groups (e.g., Miskitu, Guaymí, Chiriquí, and Kuna) in the lower half of the isthmus (Bourgois, 1989).

It is hard to escape the conclusion that race played a role in the "scorched-earth" campaign that the Guatemalan army implemented in the Mayan highlands at the start of the recent Guatemalan civil war (Jonas, 1991). The Guatemalan military used a devastating level of violence against many Mayan communities, representing a deliberate strategy of genocide (Falla, 1994; Jonas, 1991). It is also hard to escape the conclusion that in the adjacent civil war in El Salvador the decisions of the U.S.-supported military to attack peasant communities with complete disregard for human life were partly facilitated by the mestizo identities of these communities. Indeed, arguments about the "ethnic roots" of the Salvadoran civil war (and not just those that place the conflict in a more simplistic Marxist-Leninist framework) are popular (Tenorio and Huezo Mixco, 2008).

In 1932 the Salvadoran government, in an attempt to establish "order" and extinguish an alleged Communist rebellion, suppressed an uprising with unprecedented ferocity. The government army set out to annihilate all vestiges of Communism, including some 30,000 people, the overwhelming majority of whom were indigenous. Approximately 28.6 percent of the population in the western regions, where the massacre took place and where most residents were indigenous, met with their deaths (Montes, 1987:19). The slaughter, known as La Matanza, weakened and discarded indigenous social and cultural institutions, and had significant social and demographic effects for generations to come (Anderson, 1992; Montes, 1987). Until recently, indigenous peoples were forced to live clandestine lives because any indication of indigenous culture—such as language or dress—could be interpreted as subversive (Menjívar, 2000).

Evolving Central American Intergroup Experiences in the United States

For many Central Americans, new racial experiences are transpiring in the United States. In the span of just a couple of decades, thousands of Central Americans have been introduced to the racial and ethnic matrices of U.S. society at various social, cultural, and economic levels. The integration of Central American newcomers into the U.S. racialized social structure also creates consequences for later immigrant generations.

Racial, Ethnic, and Panethnic Identities

Despite their increasing presence in the United States, Central Americans have remained relatively invisible. As the Guatemalan scholar Arturo Arias observes, Central Americans are hidden "within the imaginary confines of what constitutes the multicultural landscape of the United States" (2003:170). Only in prominent destination areas of Central American immigration, notably Los Angeles, San Francisco, Washington, D.C., and Miami, are they recognized as distinct from the major Latino groups. Within the racial landscape of the United States, Central Americans are often a "minority within a minority," a situation that Arias (2003) links to a colonial history in which Central America was considered inferior to Mexico.

As members of a larger minority population, many Central Americans adopt multiple strategies to navigate the racial-ethnic landscape in the United States. Sometimes they opt to "pass" for Mexicans. For example, as revealed by one of Cecilia Menjívar's (2007) studies in Phoenix, where Mexicans make up three-quarters of the Latino foreign-born population, Salvadorans and Guatemalans were likely to adopt Mexican sayings, accent, and dress styles. For the Salvadoran and Guatemalan newcomers, these conscious efforts facilitated their adaptation in the United States. A twenty-four-year-old Salvadoran man, for instance, spoke with a Mexican accent and wore western boots and a hat in the style of a *norteño*— that is, a Mexican from northern Mexico, the region from which most of the people he works and lives with originate. In his words, "It's easier this way. I have learned to dance *quebraditas* [a Mexican dancing style], to appreciate their music, even to sing their songs. It makes life easier if you don't look different. Even to find a girlfriend. It's much easier if I act Mexican than if I act Salvadoran because all the girls are Mexican and they wouldn't want to go out with a guy who's so different, so foreign [laughs]" (personal interview, 2004). In the same vein, his mother explained why she uses "Mexican words," as she puts it, in her everyday speech: "I don't want to explain myself all the time. At work, for instance, I prefer to speak like a Mexican than to try to explain what I mean by a particular term. It's just easier to use the words that the Mexicans use, and then of course, you get used to that. It just makes life easy. If you live here [in the United States] long enough, little by little you become more and more Mexican. Sounds funny, no?"

This invisibility has also tended to have a homogenizing effect for Central Americans. Often they have been simply labeled as "other Latinos," "other Hispanics," or, at best, "Central Americans." Such labeling has occurred despite the wide variety of languages, ethnicities, histories, and cultures present in this group, although not all Central Americans identify themselves in the same racial terms. For instance, according to the U.S. Census of 2000, 36 percent of Salvadorans living in the United States identified themselves as white, compared to 38 percent of Guatemalans, 43 percent of Hondurans, and 54 percent of Nicaraguans. And whereas 5 percent of Hondurans and 2 percent of Nicaraguans identified themselves as black, fewer than 1 percent of Salvadorans and 1 percent of Guatemalans chose this category. Although an estimated 50 percent of Guatemalans are of Mayan descent, only 1.5 percent of that nationality identified as American Indian in the census. This low self-identification rate, however, might be due to a bureaucratic misunderstanding rather than to an absence of American Indians among Central Americans. In addition, more than 50 percent of Salvadorans and Guatemalans, 42 percent of Hondurans, and 36 percent of Nicaraguans identified themselves as "other race." Between 7 and 8 percent of the people in each group marked some combination of two or more races (U.S. Census Bureau, 2000). This racial heterogeneity among Central Americans is not readily apparent to non-Latinos; consequently, they are more likely to be perceived by non-Latinos as a single group, as Latinos or Hispanics, than as a heterogeneous community. But Central Americans are not alone in this respect, as the clustering of different groups into a single "panethnicity" has been a common approach to dealing with diverse groups in the United States.

A shy Guatemalan boy in Los Angeles, for example, was placed in a group of predominantly Central American kids at school—mainly Salvadorans and Mayan, and non-Mayan Guatemalans—because the teachers wanted him to feel more welcome. However, the boy could not communicate with them because he did not speak Spanish or Quiché, the Mayan language that the other Mayan students spoke. Eventually he managed to learn enough Spanish to be able to feel "Central American" (Menjívar, 2002b:546).

The racial self-identification of a person from any one group is not simply an individual decision; it also reflects the social construction of race and ethnicity in a particular society. In addition, racial and ethnic identity differs by generation and subgroup. In the case of Central Americans, their identity or self-classification is very much linked to how the U.S. government has received them—that is, as refugees or as unauthorized migrants. Government labeling has shaped many aspects of life among the various groups. Such identifications affect intragroup relations as well, particularly between groups that have little linguistic and cultural common ground, and they shape whether and how Central Americans carve out spaces within the larger Latino mosaic in the United States.

It is important, however, to note that relations among the different Central American groups, as well as between them and the larger Latino groups, have included many instances of collaboration, particularly in campaigns to promote issues of social justice. Interestingly, the classification of the Central American groups within larger panethnic categories (e.g., Mexican, Latino, Hispanic) has had important consequences for political mobilization and empowerment. The perception by Central Americans and other Latino groups that they share common ground and ancestry (including indigenous descent or black heritage) has contributed to the development of political agendas focused on common interests and goals. Time will tell if these intragroup dynamics translate into more political power for Latinos more generally.

Guatemalan Maya

Mayans represent a significant number of racially distinct migrants from Guatemala to the United States. One might expect that this migration would liberate them from the racial stratification and subordination that many Maya encounter in Guatemala. These conditions range from being denied entrance into certain social spaces to being relegated mainly to inferior, low-paying work and kept away from major positions of power in core institutions. Yet, this is not a permanent exclusion for all Maya, as the definition of "Maya" is conveyed heavily along cultural traits, especially since the physical characteristics of group difference vis-à-vis mestizos occur across a continuum rather than across a discrete division of body features. A Mayan can conceivably end her or his social definition of being Maya by abandoning Mayan cultural practices (and moving to a new community), as many Maya and Ladinos are physically indistinguishable (Wagley, 1968).

After arriving in the United States, many Maya fade into the large mass of Latino immigrants. Their presence is known only to themselves and to the Latino immigrants who emigrated from regions with an indigenous presence. To others, a Mayan is just another Latino immigrant. Yet, Mayan migrants, as part of the larger indigenous migration from Latin America, traverse through historical and racial dimensions that most mestizo/Ladino migrants do not share. While both populations of migrants may travel along identical roads north, their journeys represent anthropologically distinct experiences. The Maya are retracing the original migrations of the ancestors of their ancestors (Carmack, 1981) and moving away from a racially based, colonized history, while the mestizos and Ladinos have little or no ancestral connection to the northern destination and are moving within working-class social strata not historically weighed down by ascribed status.

In the United States, many Guatemalan Mayan migrants have continued their participation in rural economies as farmworkers, somewhat similar to what they did back in Guatemala (Burns, 1993; Loucky and Moors, 2000b). But, as described by Jacqueline Hagan (1994), in Houston, a large number of Maya who initially immigrated without visas from the Guatemalan department of Totonicapán experienced major economic mobility after locating jobs in a high-end supermarket chain in the early 1980s (before the 1986 Immigration Reform and Control Act [IRCA] outlawed the employment of unauthorized workers). As the Totonicapán Maya climbed up the occupational ladder of the supermarket chain over the years of their employment, some became crew leaders and supervisors in various sections of the stores. A few even became assistant managers. In these positions, some Mayans became managers and supervisors of Guatemalan migrant workers who in Guatemala identified as Ladinos, a social category defined as higher status than Mayan.

This Houston case illustrates that the social, hierarchical configurations in Guatemala dealing with racial and intergroup relations do not necessarily transfer to U.S. society. Yet, this observation may not have much external validity outside workplaces (e.g., the high-end supermarkets), where U.S. norms regulate behavior among workers. It is possible that in workplaces of the secondary labor market, where work regulations are informal, Guatemalan norms of relations between Mayans and Ladinos may have more play. For instance, a fifty-year-old indigenous woman in Los Angeles, when asked if she includes Ladinas in her web of friends and acquaintances from whom she can obtain medical-related assistance, put it bluntly: "No, I don't have Ladina friends because they were not my friends back in Guatemala either. I have black, Chinese, Salvadoran, Honduran, all sorts of friends but not Ladinas. It's more difficult to be friends with them. Of course, if I ever need medical advice I would not even dream of talking with a Ladina because I don't know any" (Menjívar, 2002a:451).

The migration process, however, may create an exceptional experience captured in the migrant role and identity that alters established intergroup relations of the home country, especially as the social privileges at stake in racialized environments back home are not present for Ladinos in the United States. A Guatemalan Mayan girl in Los Angeles reflected as follows on her perception of her identity in the United States versus Guatemala: "My mother says that here we [indigenous people] have more opportunities than in Guatemala. Here I can be a doctor if I want to, there I can't do it because they don't like us.... They don't like Mayans ... or something like that.... That's what my mother says, I don't know. So it's better that I live here, right?" (Menjívar, 2002b:541).

Regardless, established intergroup attitudes and norms of the home country did not disappear in the first stages of the Totonicapán Mayan immigration. With the amnesty and legalization provided by the IRCA, Guatemalan Mayans traveled freely to visit families and hometowns in Guatemala. In one of these early trips, a Mayan migrant from Totonicapán helped a reporter and photographer of the *Houston Chronicle* to travel to Guatemala to do stories on the migrants' community of origin and their relocation to the United States. The stories ran on the front page and a special insert of a Sunday edition of the newspaper. Immediately after, Mayan migrants called the migrant who assisted the newspaper crew to leave messages complaining about the stories and pictures. The angry callers complained that the stories and pictures would cause others to identify them as indigenous people and subject them to racial prejudices and discrimination. However, this fear is only one of several different attitudes demonstrated by Mayan immigrants concerning intergroup relations in their new U.S. settlements. Across the country, including Houston, some Maya have developed various events and festivals to promote their indigenous culture (Fink, 2003; Hagan, 1994).

Garífuna

A common perception of Central American immigration is that it consists of people who are racially classified as white (Hispanic) in the United States. Yet, an important black migrant stream flows from Central America to the United States. It concerns the Black Caribs—Garífuna—primarily from Honduras and Belize, with a small number also emigrating from other areas on the Central American Caribbean coast (Rodriguez, 1987).

Historically employed in Central American plantations and coastal industries, Garífuna men started migrating to the United States as early as the 1940s, and women in the 1960s. In Central America, the Garífuna are generally poor, with low levels of literacy, and usually participate in the lower levels of major institutions in Central America society (England, 2006). Larger numbers of Garífuna joined the migrant streams radiating out of Latin America to the United States in the 1980s. Although the number of Garífuna migrants was very small vis-à-vis other Central Americans, they represented a greater mixture of Amerindian and African origins. Together with migrants from the Caribbean, they have increased the number of people of African origin in the United States.

While it may take other Latino immigrants some time before they grasp the nature of racism in the United States, the Garífuna, as a black group, comprehend it quickly. Having originated in Central American countries dominated by mestizos/Ladinos and other nonblacks, the Garífuna are very much aware of the prejudices associated with their racial identity (Rodriguez, 1987). While their Spanish fluency (or English fluency for Garífuna from Belize) helps to bridge inter-Latino distances, the Garífuna always face potential negative experiences with other Latinos because of their black racial identity.

In the 1980s, Garífuna migrants settled across various U.S. localities but particularly in the urban centers of New York (Bronx), Los Angeles, Houston, and New Orleans (England, 2006). Many Garífuna stayed connected in the United States through family and friendship networks, and for some men through soccer leagues that interacted across cities, such as between New Orleans and Houston (Rodriguez, 1987). Garífuna identity became a source for organizing a variety of Garífuna organizations and cultural events, but always nearby the Garífuna kept Honduran flags to symbolize the national origins of their group (England, 2006; Rodriguez, 1987).

CONTRASTING PRE– AND POST–CIVIL RIGHTS CONTEXTS

Large-scale Central American immigration, starting in the early 1980s, developed across a social environment significantly different from just two decades earlier. Even into the 1970s, rigid racial and ethnic segregation characterized many U.S. communities. The dominant white society maintained racial and ethnic segregation across workplaces, schools, places of worship, entertainment centers, hospitals, restaurants, train and bus stations, cemeteries, and many other places of social interaction. While primarily geared toward African Americans, the legal and normative segregation, and the accompanying prejudice and discrimination, also separated other populations of color from whites (Feagin and Feagin, 1993). These populations of color included Mexican Americans and other Latin American–origin groups. In the Southwest, many Mexican Americans also separated themselves from African Americans, either because they shared the practices of racial division or because they feared attacks from whites if they themselves did not discriminate against African Americans (Mindiola, Niemann, and Rodriguez, 2002). Oppressed groups did not take their oppression passively.

The Black Movement, the Chicano Movement, the Civil Rights Movement—all were part of the social struggle that ended the Pre–Civil Rights Era of rigid racial and ethnic segregation in the United States.

While in the Pre–Civil Rights Era Latinos generally did not experience the same degree of racist oppression faced by African Americans, in some settings they came very close to doing so. In southern Texas, for example, white residents treated Mexican Americans as a sort of third race, subjecting them to social and economic subordination and political exclusion (Feagin and Feagin, 1993). Sometimes the brutal tactics of social repression used against African Americans in the South were also used against Mexican Americans in the Southwest. In the early 1900s in Texas, these tactics included raids by Ku Klux Klan riders against Mexican American rural camps and campaigns by white lawmen (Texas Rangers) to kill Mexicans in areas near Mexico (Feagin and Feagin, 1993).

In the post–World War II setting, the large-scale overt violence against Latinos subsided, except for mounting cases of police brutality (Feagin and Feagin, 1993). Eventually civil rights legislation provided some opportunities for more inclusion of Latinos in core institutions (political, educational, etc.), but it did not end high rates of poverty and other major institutional disadvantages, such as limited access to health care, among African Americans and Latinos. Civil rights legislation, however, did promote the value of equality. Affirmative action measures, for example, pressured some employers to consider more minority job applicants, even if they did not hire them. While many minorities remained skeptical of the impacts of governmental programs to promote equality, many whites felt that the programs had made great progress to eliminate racial discrimination and provide equal opportunities (Feagin, Vera, and Batur, 2001). According to this latter perspective, lasting problems of racial and ethnic inequality are due to minority cultural disadvantages and not to structural barriers.

We call the racial conditions that evolved in the 1980s and 1990s the "Post–Civil Rights Era." The major feature of the Post–Civil Rights Era is continuing racial and ethnic inequality with a prevailing attitude among many whites that all the legislative measures needed to deal with this condition have already been implemented. A defining moment of the Post–Civil Rights Era was the Supreme Court decision in the *Hopwood v. Texas* case in 1996, which ruled that an institution of higher education could not use race as a factor in its admission policy. While in some sectors (professional sports, public health agencies, etc.) minorities gained substantial social mobility, whites usually remain dominant at the very top echelons, especially in the private sector (Feagin, Vera, and Batur, 2001). With a declining concern for racial and ethnic equality, many office workplaces take on color divisions, with whites dominating the higher job ranks and African Americans and Latinos concentrated in the lower ranks. In the lower-paying job market, and especially in the informal economic sector, these divisions become even more striking, as African American and Latino men and women, including Central American immigrants, represent a disproportionate majority.

An advantage for Central American immigrants arriving in the Post–Civil Rights Era is that they do not face the rigid segregation of the Pre–Civil Rights Era. The disadvantage, however, is precisely that they have arrived during an era in which major racial and ethnic inequalities persist in a social atmosphere in which the government is not only hesitant to act but is actually prevented by a Supreme Court ruling from acting directly on issues of racial inequality. By the mid-1990s another major disadvantage surfaced—a nativist movement that amounts to a new racism, this time particularly targeting Latino immigrants.

NEW RACISM—"IMMIGRANTS OUT!"

The nativist movement that strengthened in the 1990s is the focus of Juan F. Perea's (1997) edited volume *Immigrants Out!* As Joe Feagin (1997) reports in the volume, modern nativism has deep, historical roots; one by one, new immigrant groups that do not fit the mold of white Anglo-Saxon Protestants—that is, groups seen as "uncivilized savages" or "inferior races"—have been subjected to attacks. According to Feagin, nativism always existed as racist nativism, even in the launching of racist attacks by whites of northern European origin against immigrants from other European regions.

The new nativism, which solidified in the 1990s, targets not a specific nationality but primarily Latino immigrants in general, and it is disguised as targeting unauthorized Latino immigrants. This is the current context facing Central Americans, along with other Latino immigrants. Nativistic and restrictionist voices claim that high rates of Latino immigration and uncontrolled unauthorized migration threaten the United States in several ways: Immigrants supposedly stress the carrying capacity of the nation; promote overcrowding; create intergroup division and strife; displace U.S. workers; overwhelm public welfare; educational and health institutions; increase crime rates; endanger U.S. border security; and so forth (Feagin, 1997; Johnson, 1997).

The noted Harvard political scientist Samuel P. Huntington articulated the fears of the impact of Latino immigrants in his article "The Hispanic Challenge." According to Huntington (2004:1), "The persistent flow of Hispanic immigrants threatens to divide the United States into two peoples, two cultures and two languages." Moreover, according to Huntington (2004:1), in contrast to earlier immigrants, "Mexicans and other Latinos have not assimilated into mainstream U.S. culture, forming instead their own political and linguistic enclaves." In his view, Latino cultural elements are at such variance with "the Anglo-Protestant values that built the American dream" that they threaten the very survival of U.S. society. In his mind, the consistency and force of Latino, and particularly Mexican, immigration are so great that to ignore them creates a huge societal risk. Huntington's alarm over Latino immigration echoes CIA director William Colby's warning during the Cold War that Mexican immigration was the greatest threat facing the United States, even greater than the threat from the Soviet Union (cited in Cornelius, 1983:389–390).

Huntington's thesis of the imminent dangers of Latino immigration contrasts sharply with conclusions publicized a year earlier by two major scholars of U.S. immigration, Richard Alba and Victor Nee (2003), in their book *Remaking the American Mainstream*. According to Alba and Nee, Latinos and other new immigrants are still experiencing the historical process of assimilation, albeit into a society affected by immigrant contributions. In contrast to Huntington, Alba and Nee envision a more socially integrated future in U.S. society, as institutional changes facilitate the social incorporation of new groups and their subsequent generations, diminishing the boundaries among the major population groups.

In the mid-1990s, public sentiments to exclude unauthorized immigrants (particularly Latinos) went from rhetorical expressions to legislated measures. One drastic example was Proposition 187, passed by voters in California in 1994. Measures of the law, which was largely invalided later in federal court, barred unauthorized immigrants from most public services (including public health programs for pregnant women) and even from public education (Johnson, 1997). The law also required several enforcement activities, essentially turning the state into a social dragnet for unauthorized immigrants. In 2004, Arizona voters approved Proposition 2000 (also called "Protect Arizona Now" or "Arizona Taxpayer and Citizen Protection Act"), supposedly to protect the state from abuses by immigrants. The new law requires proof of eligibility to receive social services and requires state and local workers to report immigration violations to federal authorities in writing. In addition, the law requires voters to document their U.S. citizenship when registering to vote and when voting.

By the middle of the first decade of the twenty-first century, several local governments across the country passed ordinances to penalize landlords who rented to unauthorized migrants and to make English the official language of the area. In Hazleton, Pennsylvania, for example, following a murder committed by an unauthorized immigrant, the city council passed the Illegal Immigration Relief Act to suspend the licenses of businesses that employed unauthorized migrants, levy a fine of $1,000 a day on landlords who rented to illegal immigrants, and require that city business be conducted only in English (Barry, 2006). This local governmental action to exclude unauthorized immigrants was repeated in New Jersey, Texas, and California.

State and local laws passed to exclude unauthorized migrants pressure all Latinos, immigrants or not, by subjecting them to suspicion and scrutiny. Such laws create a climate of fear for immigrants, even for legal residents, since Latino immigrant families sometimes have members in irregular or unauthorized status. Even Latinos who are U.S. citizens are targeted because of stereotypical appearance, as has happened in recent immigration raids throughout the country. Moreover, these laws, and the polemics of their proponents, can promote vigilantism, leading to assaults by individuals or groups against persons assumed to be foreign-born. The most recent U.S. crime statistics indicate that in 2005, 722 Hispanics reported being victims of hate crimes (U.S. Department of Justice, 2006: table 1).

It is likely that the new government measure of constructing a wall along the U.S.-Mexico border will reinforce the public image of Latino immigrants as deviants and a danger to the United States. By emphasizing the construction of the border wall as the major means to control unauthorized immigration (and not going aggressively after all nationalities of visa overstayers), the public image of "illegal" immigration is likely to become based solely in terms of

Latino unauthorized migrants. Central American immigrants, therefore, do not enter a context in which race does not matter; they enter a different system of race relations and classification. Indeed, as Douglas Massey (2007:146) notes, Latino immigrants today live in a context of "postmodern racism," facilitated by the government and by pundits and politicians, where immigrants become dehumanized and are perceived as having no rights, and which "opens the door to the harshest, most exploitative, and cruelest treatment that human beings are capable of inflicting on one another" (Massey, 2007:150).

THE "LATINO EXCLUSION ACT"

More than local measures of exclusion, the Illegal Immigrant Reform and Immigrant Responsibility Act (IIRIRA) of 1996 created a new atmosphere of exclusion that had not been felt by Latino immigrants since the federal roundup of over a million Mexicans during Operation Wetback in the 1950s. IIRIRA substantially tightened earlier immigration and asylum measures and dramatically increased deportations, including cases where immigrants are questionably classified as "criminal aliens" (Rodriguez and Hagan, 2004).

Before the implementation of IIRIRA, deportations annually reached about 44,000, but after the law took effect the numbers climbed dramatically, reaching 208,521 in fiscal year 2005 (U.S. Department of Homeland Security, 2006: table 41). While Mexicans account for the majority of deportations, the 2005 figure included 36,032 deportations to Central American countries, with the three largest numbers deported to Honduras (14,556), Guatemala (12,529), and El Salvador (7,235). Given that 96 percent of the deportees are Latinos and that almost six out of ten are deported for "noncriminal" reasons, it may not be far-fetched to call IIRIRA the "Latino Exclusion Act."

Another factor that shapes the exclusion of Central American immigrants, particularly Guatemalans and Salvadorans, is their legal reception. For reasons linked to the key role the United States played in the armed conflicts in the region, many Guatemalans and Salvadorans, and to a certain extent Nicaraguans, have been left in "permanent temporariness" (Bailey et al., 2002) or in a "legal limbo" (Menjívar, 2006) for more than two decades. Their uncertain status—not fully documented or undocumented but often straddling both—permeates many aspects of these immigrants' lives and delimits their range of action in various spheres, from job market opportunities and housing to family and kinship, from the place of the church in their lives and their various transnational activities to artistic expressions (Menjívar, 2006). It also shapes these immigrants' long-term incorporation, citizenship, and belonging, and creates multiple forms of exclusion. As Kitty Calavita (1998:530) observes, immigration law "actively 'irregularizes' people by making it all but impossible to retain legal status over time." In the process, immigration law creates and re-creates an excluded population by establishing gray areas of incertitude, with the potential to affect broader issues of citizenship and belonging (Menjívar, 2006). Moreover, this graying of social incorporation for many immigrants from Central America has taken place within the stiffer and more exclusionary measures of IIRIRA. Consistent with immigration reforms that focus on barring immigrants from resources and benefits in society, ever more restrictive immigration laws seek not only to reduce the number of immigrants entering the country but also to keep more of them in undetermined legal statuses that facilitate exploiting them in multiple ways while they are in the country. In short, these laws work to exclude certain immigrants and to curtail their rights as members of society.

The legal dispensations conferred to Salvadorans and Guatemalans—such as Temporary Protected Status (TPS) to the former group and modified Nicaraguan Adjustment and Central American Relief Act (NACARA) benefits and the opportunity to resubmit asylum applications to both groups—create the conditions for the uncertain legal status of many of these immigrants. Thus, the hallmark of the U.S. government response to Central American massive migrations has been temporary and tenuous at best. The federal government seems to have gone to great lengths to keep these groups in a marginal legal position, to institutionalize legal obstacles that prevent these immigrants from becoming full members of society. Indeed, these permits and convoluted application procedures represent legal reminders that these immigrants do not fully belong.

RACISM AND RACIAL FORMATION IN THE CONTEXT OF GLOBALIZATION

It would be nearsighted to conclude that racist nativism affects immigrants from Central American countries solely from the standpoint of contemporary U.S. society. As Feagin (1997) argues, and as others have documented (e.g., Jones, 1992), since the founding of the country, racist nativism has risen with immigration flows that originate outside northern Europe. From this perspective, immigrants from Central America join Asian Indians, Vietnamese, Muslims from the Middle East and Central Asia, and other non-European newcomers as the most recent targets of racist nativism. They represent the present-day "impossible subjects" that Mae Ngai (2004) describes as legally impossible, without rights, excluded, and stigmatized by negative racial stereotypes as dangerous.

At the base of the racist nativism against Latinos and other newcomers is a major transformation in which once-distant populations now appear in the domestic scene in large numbers. This transformation is the process of globalization, which also includes the world transfers of capital and cultural symbols. If the social movements of the 1960s created fear among many whites of losing their social dominance, large-scale immigration since the 1980s may create even greater fears for them of unwanted social change, since the perceived agents of domestic social change are foreign-born peoples, or so-called aliens.

As Michael Omi and Howard Winant (1994) theorize through the concept of racial formation, individuals and groups develop, change, and destroy racial categories and their significance. Prior to World War II, for example, Asians were considered racially inferior and excluded from U.S. society, but today they are viewed across several sectors as a model group for their high educational and income achievements and their disproportionate representation in professional and high-tech occupations. It remains to be seen whether Central Americans will experience a similar transition in public perception—that is, whether they will have access to the resources needed for social mobility. If the conditions they face today do not change, their prospects do not look auspicious.

Immigrating in a Post–Civil Rights Era, Central Americans are settling in social settings that continue to be racialized, in an atmosphere in which the government has retreated from directly tackling social problems of race and is even contributing to the persistence of these problems. Central American immigrants face at least two alternatives in their new society. One is a future as new fodder for the reproduction of racialized social structures in U.S. society. A second possibility is developing social relations with other Latinos and other historically subordinated groups to help change the U.S. history of social and racial inequality. The vigorous actions and mobilization that Central American men and women across the United States have undertaken to organize their immigrant communities and to unionize low-wage immigrant workers suggest that Central Americans will be valuable actors in this struggle.

NOTE

1. We would like to thank Vanessa Tucker and Christy Garcia at Arizona State University for their first-rate research assistance. The usual disclaimers apply. Direct correspondence can be sent to Nestor Rodriguez (nrodriguez@uh.edu) or Cecilia Menjívar (menjivar@asu.edu).

REFERENCES

Adams, Richard Newbold. 1970. *Crucifixion by Power: Essays on Guatemalan National Social Structure, 1944–1966.* Austin: University of Texas Press.

Alba, Richard, and Victor Nee. 2003. *Remaking the American Mainstream: Assimilation and Contemporary Immigration.* Cambridge, MA: Harvard University Press.

Anderson, Thomas P. 1992. *Matanza: The 1932 "Slaughter" That Traumatized a Nation, Shaping U.S.-Salvadoran Policy to This Day,* 2nd ed. Willimantic, CT: Curbstone Press.

Arias, Arturo. 2003. "Central American Americans: Invisibility, Power, and Representation in the US Latino World." *Latino Studies* 1(1):168–187.

Bailey, Adrian J., Richard A. Wright, Alison Mountz, and Ines M. Miyares. 2002. "(Re)producing Salvadoran Transnational Geographies." *Annals of the Association of American Geographers* 92(1):125–144.

Barry, Ellen. 2006. "City Vents Anger at Illegal Immigrants." *Los Angeles Times,* July 14, p. A1.

Bourgois, Philippe. 1989. *Ethnicity at Work: Divided Labor on a Central American Banana Plantation.* Baltimore: Johns Hopkins University Press.

Burns, Allan F. 1993. *Maya in Exile: Guatemalans in Florida.* Philadelphia: Temple University Press.

Calavita, Kitty. 1998. "Immigration, Law, and Marginalization in a Global Economy: Notes from Spain." *Law and Society Review* 32(3):529–566.

Carmack, Robert M. 1981. *The Quiché Maya of Utatlán: The Evolution of a Highland Guatemala Kingdom.* Norman: University of Oklahoma Press.

Carmack, Robert M. (ed.). 1992. *Harvest of Violence: The Maya Indians and the Guatemalan Crisis*. Norman: University of Oklahoma Press.

Cornelius, Wayne A. 1983. "America in the Era of Limits: Migrants, Nativists, and the Future of U.S.-Mexican Relations." Pp. 389–390 in Carlos Vásquez and Manuel García y Griego (eds.), *Mexican-U.S. Relations: Conflict and Convergence*. Los Angeles: UCLA Chicano Studies Center Publications and Latin American Studies Publications.

England, Sarah. 2006. *Afro-Central Americans in New York City: Garífuna Tales of Transnational Movements in Racialized Space*. Gainesville: University Press of Florida.

Falla, Ricardo. 1994. *Massacres in the Jungle: Ixcán, Guatemala, 1975–1982*. Boulder, CO: Westview Press.

Feagin, Joe R. 1997. "Old Poison in New Bottles: The Deep Roots of Modern Nativism." Pp. 13–43 in Juan F. Perea (ed.), *Immigrants Out! The New Nativism and the Anti-Immigrant Impulse in the United States*. New York: New York University Press.

———. 2006. *Systemic Racism: A Theory of Oppression*. New York: Routledge.

Feagin, Joe R., and Clairece Booher Feagin. 1993. *Racial and Ethnic Relations*, 4th ed. Englewood Cliffs, NJ: Prentice-Hall.

Feagin, Joe R., Hernán Vera, and Pinar Batur. 2001. *White Racism*, 2nd ed. New York: Routledge.

Fink, Leon. 2003. *The Maya of Morgantown: Work and Community in the Nuevo New South*. Chapel Hill: University of North Carolina Press.

Gonzalez, Nancy L. 1988. *Sojourners of the Caribbean: Ethnogenesis and Ethnohistory of the Garífuna*. Urbana: University of Illinois Press.

Gould, Jeffrey L. 1998. *To Die in This Way: Nicaraguan Indians and the Myth of Mestizaje, 1880–1965*. Durham, NC: Duke University Press.

Guzmán Böckler, Carlos, and Jean-Loup Herbert. 1970. *Guatemala: Una interpretación histórico-social*. Mexico City: Siglo XXI.

Hagan, Jacqueline Maria. 1994. *Deciding to Be Legal: A Maya Community in Houston*. Philadelphia: Temple University Press.

Hoefer, Michael, Nancy Rytina, and Christopher Campbell. 2006. "Estimates of the Unauthorized Immigrant Population Residing in the United States: January 2005." Washington, DC: Office of Immigration Statistics, Department of Homeland Security. Retrieved May 14, 2008. (http://www.dhs.gov/xlibrary/assets/statistics/publications/ILL_PE_2005.pdf)

Huntington, Samuel P. 2004. "The Hispanic Challenge." *Foreign Policy* 141 (March/April):1–12. Retrieved May 14, 2008. (http://www.foreignpolicy.com/)

Jefferys, Kelly, and Nancy Rytina. 2006. "U.S. Legal Permanent Residents: 2005." Washington, DC: Office of Immigration Statistics, Department of Homeland Security. Retrieved May 14, 2008. (http://www.dhs.gov/xlibrary/assets/statistics/publications/USLegalPermEst_5.pdf)

Johnson, Kevin R. 1997. "The New Nativism: Something Old, Something New, Something Borrowed, Something Blue." Pp. 165–189 in Juan F. Perea (ed.), *Immigrants Out! The New Nativism and the Anti-Immigrant Impulse in the United States*. New York: New York University Press.

Jonas, Susanne. 1991. *The Battle for Guatemala: Rebels, Death Squads, and U.S. Power*. Boulder, CO: Westview.

———. 2000. *Of Centaurs and Doves: Guatemala's Peace Process*. Boulder, CO: Westview Press.

Jones, Maldwyn Allen. 1992. *American Immigration*, 2nd ed. Chicago: University of Chicago Press.

Lamphere, Louise (ed.). 1992. *Structuring Diversity: Ethnographic Perspectives on the New Immigration*. Chicago: University of Chicago Press.

Loucky, James, and Marilyn M. Moors. 2000a. "The Maya Diaspora: Introduction." Pp. 1–10 in James Loucky and Marilyn M. Moors (eds.), *The Maya Diaspora: Guatemalan Roots, New American Lives.* Philadelphia: Temple University Press.

Loucky, James, and Marilyn M. Moors (eds.). 2000b. *The Maya Diaspora: Guatemalan Roots, New American Lives.* Philadelphia: Temple University Press.

Massey, Douglas S. 2007. *Categorically Unequal: The American Stratification System.* New York: Russell Sage Foundation.

Menjívar, Cecilia. 2000. *Fragmented Ties: Salvadoran Immigrant Networks in America.* Berkeley: University of California Press.

———. 2002a. "The Ties That Heal: Guatemalan Immigrant Women's Networks and Medical Treatment." *International Migration Review* 36(2):437–466.

———. 2002b. "Living in Two Worlds? Guatemalan-Origin Children in the United States and Emerging Transnationalism." *Journal of Ethnic and Migration Studies* 28(3):531–552.

———. 2006. "Liminal Legality: Salvadoran and Guatemalan Immigrants' Lives in the United States." *American Journal of Sociology* 111(4):999–1037.

———. 2007. "Central Americans." Pp. 278–282 in John H. Moore (ed.), *Encyclopedia of Race and Racism.* Farmington Hills, MI: Macmillan.

Menjívar, Cecilia, and Sang Kil. 2002. "For Their Own Good: Benevolent Rhetoric and Exclusionary Language in Public Officials' Discourse on Immigrant-Related Issues." *Social Justice* 29 (1–2):160–176.

Mindiola, Tatcho, Yolanda Niemann, and Nestor Rodriguez. 2002. *Black/Brown Relations and Stereotypes.* Austin: University of Texas Press.

Montes, Segundo. 1987. *El compadrazgo: Una estructura de poder en El Salvador.* San Salvador: UCA Editores.

Ngai, Mae N. 2004. *Impossible Subjects: Illegal Aliens and the Making of Modern America.* Princeton: Princeton University Press.

Omi, Michael, and Howard Winant. 1994. *Racial Formation in the United States: From the 1960s to the 1990s.* New York: Routledge.

Perea, Juan F. (ed.). 1997. *Immigrants Out! The New Nativism and the Anti-Immigrant Impulse in the United States.* New York: New York University Press.

Rodriguez, Nestor. 1987. "Undocumented Central Americans in Houston: Diverse Populations." *International Migration Review* 21 (Spring):4–25.

Rodriguez, Nestor, and Jacqueline Hagan. 2004. "Fractured Families and Communities: Effects of Immigration Reform in Texas, Mexico, and El Salvador." *Latino Studies* 2(3):328–351.

Tenorio, María, and Miguel Huezo Mixco. 2008. "Talpajocote." Retrieved May 30, 2008. (http://talpajocote.blogspot.com)

U.S. Census Bureau. 2000. *2000 Census of the Population.* Summary File (SF 3)—Sample Data, Custom Table: Race by Hispanic or Latino by Specific Origin. Retrieved August 1, 2008. (http://www.census.gov/main/www/cen2000.html)

———. 2005. *2005 American Community Survey.* Custom Table: Metropolitan Statistical Area by Hispanic or Latino by Specific Origin. Washington, DC. Retrieved August 1, 2008. (http://www.census.gov/acs/www/)

U.S. Department of Homeland Security. 2006. *Yearbook of Immigration Statistics: 2005.* Washington, DC: Office of Immigration Statistics. Retrieved May 14, 2008. (http://www.dhs.gov/xlibrary/assets/statistics/yearbook/2005/OIS_2005_Yearbook.pdf)

U.S. Department of Justice. 2006. "Hate Crime Statistics 2005." Federal Bureau of Investigation. October release date. Retrieved May 14, 2008. (http://www.fbi.gov/ucr/hc2005/table1.htm)

Wade, Peter. 1997. *Race and Ethnicity in Latin America.* London: Pluto Press.

Wagley, Charles. 1968. *The Latin American Tradition: Essays on the Unity and the Diversity of Latin American Culture.* New York: Columbia University Press.

CHAPTER 12

Agency and Structure in Panethnic Identity Formation

The Case of Latino Entrepreneurs

Zulema Valdez

Do Latinos constitute a racial group?[1] According to Michael Omi and Howard Winant (1994:55), the formation of racial groups is socially constructed, a "socio-historical process by which racial categories are created, inhabited, transformed, and destroyed." Unlike traditional racial groups (i.e., whites or blacks), Latinos are not recognized as a distinct racial group by America's mainstream institutions, such as the U.S. federal government. Instead, Latinos are defined as a panethnic group—a social group identity that combines multiple ethnic subgroups whose ethnic identities are circumscribed by distinct national-origin boundaries (Padilla, 1985), and that collectively are perceived to share certain homogeneous characteristics and features (Lopez and Espiritu, 1990). Latinos include persons of "Mexican, Puerto Rican, Cuban, Central or South American or other Spanish culture or origin, *regardless of race*" (Office of Management and Budget, 1997; emphasis added).

Nevertheless, a closer examination of Latinos' racial group identity reveals the complexity involved in determining this diverse group's racial classification, even by the members themselves. For example, the 2000 census officially identified four racial groups: American Indian or Alaskan Native, Asian or Pacific Islander, black, and white. Among Latino respondents, 48 percent self-identified racially as white and 2 percent as black. Six percent reported belonging to two or more racial groups.

Yet, fully 42 percent self-identified as "some other race." Of these respondents, the overwhelming majority reported a panethnic or national-origin identity rooted in Latin America (e.g., Latino/Hispanic, Salvadoran) (Swarns, 2004).

Additionally, the 2007 Latino National Survey included questions that replicated the U.S. census categories as well as questions on Latinos' "primary identity." Notably, the majority of Latino respondents identified their racial group (according to U.S. census categories) as white. When asked to identify their "primary identity," however, 44 percent of Latinos identified themselves panethnically (i.e., Latino or Hispanics), while 47.2 percent identified themselves nationally (i.e., Mexican, Cuban, etc.). To a separate question that asked whether Latinos constitute a racial group, roughly half of all survey respondents answered "yes," regardless of their reported racial or primary identity (Valdez, 2008). Clara Rodríguez and Héctor Cordero-Guzmán (1992) have argued that the selection of "some other race" in the census among Latinos suggests that ethnicity/national origin and culture provide the basis for the emergence of a new racial group, distinct from the traditional (white/black) American racial classification system. Valdez's (2008) findings evince support for this contention, as fully half of those surveyed believe that Latinos form a distinct racial group.

In this chapter, I explore national-origin, panethnic, and racial group identity among Latinos who live and work in Little Latin America, a geographically concentrated Latino enclave in Houston, Texas. In particular, I investigate the conditions under which Latino immigrants identify themselves or others by national origin or panethnically, and whether or to what extent panethnic identity is invoked to represent a racial identity. My findings reveal that Latino business owners overwhelmingly self-identify by national origin, or what Joan Moore (1990) refers to as an "anchoring" identity. In contrast, panethnic identity is generally reserved for non-co-national others. Specifically, my findings indicate that Latino business owners identify others panethnically under certain conditions: (1) to stereotype or express bias against Latinos, (2) to distance their own ethnic identity from the negative stereotypes or prejudices associated with Latinos, and (3) to communicate social interactions between Latinos and members of traditional racial groups. In this way, Latinos' contingent use of national and panethnic identity, the latter invoked to impose a racial identity among non-co-nationals, exposes the dynamic process of identity formation and racialization.

NATIONAL, PANETHNIC, AND RACIAL IDENTITY

In their respective home countries, would-be migrants might identify with reference to their city, region, state, or other markers of common history or customs. Upon their arrival in the United States, however, national origin often becomes a primary, "anchoring" identity among immigrant co-nationals in the United States (Itzigsohn and Dore-Cabral, 2000; Moore, 1990). For immigrants, the use of national identity over other home-country identities facilitates a sense of belonging and homogeneity among co-nationals, whose origins lie within a common circumscribed territory. National identity is distinguished as a primary identity and is generally self-defined (Conner, 1978). Moreover, research reveals that one's national identity often takes precedence over other socially constructed "secondary" identities (Itzigsohn and Dore-Cabral, 2000; Moore, 1990).

In contrast, racial identity is characterized as a secondary form of group identity that is externally imposed and other-defined (Bonilla-Silva, 1997; Feagin, 2006). Research on racial identity formation commonly focuses on the unavoidable and compulsory placement of individuals into racial groups based on socially constructed ascribed characteristics, such as skin color or ancestry, regardless of self-identification. This process of race-making relegates those individuals who are recognized as members of a given racial group to that group's positioning along the U.S. racial hierarchy (Bashi, 1998; Bonilla-Silva, 1997; Cornell and Hartmann, 1998; Feagin, 2006). In a society where race matters, racial classification is nontrivial; in fact, it is structurally important, as it confers greater or lesser privileges and facilitates or constrains members' life chances.

Joe Feagin (2006) offers some insight into this process. He argues that the American social structure is organized along a racial hierarchy, with whites at the top, blacks at the bottom, and other groups (e.g., Latin American national-origin groups) in between. This structural hierarchy is shaped and maintained by the white racial frame, the "organized set of racialized ideas, stereotypes, emotions, and inclinations to discriminate" (Feagin, 2006:25). Under conditions of (largely unacknowledged) systemic racial oppression, power and privilege are ascribed to those at the top of the racial hierarchy, while oppression and disadvantage are ascribed to those at the bottom. As Feagin states:

> The U.S. racial continuum runs from the privileged white position and status at the top to an oppressed black position and status at the bottom, with different groups of color variously positioned *by whites* between two ends of this central racial-status continuum. Firmly at the top of the U.S. racial hierarchy are individual whites of all backgrounds and their families. They, as a group, hold the top position in terms of racialized privileges and power. Below whites in this racial hierarchy is the large class of men and women of color and their families. (2006:21–22; original emphasis)

Correspondingly, Omi and Winant maintain that panethnicity emerges in response to the racialization process, although they do not specify when or how panethnic identity is invoked over distinct national-origin or racial identities (Omi, 2001:247; Omi and Winant, 1994).

Drawing from the work of Feagin (2006), I argue that the emergence of panethnicity requires first and foremost a social context where race matters. That is, for panethnicity to arise as a meaningful category of human social grouping, a society must be organized *a priori* along a racial hierarchy. It is only under these conditions that the practice of compressing distinct national-origin groups into one "panethnic" group makes (common) sense. In other words, the emergence of panethnic categories reflects the individual and collective responses to structural forces that constrain each and every member of our society to identify racially.

This process of Latino racialization constitutes a recent transformation of American race relations in the contemporary post-1965 period, following immigration policy reforms that substantially increased U.S. migration from Latin American sending countries. Since power and privilege are conferred to whites who enjoy the top position of the U.S. racial hierarchy, it is unlikely that non-European, Latin American national-origin immigrants and their descendants would be allowed to encroach upon this privileged position and "become white." On the other hand, nonwhites are likely to resist structural incorporation into the other available racial category, black, and the consequent oppression that such a racial classification confers. Nor would they "fit" easily into the American race relations conception of who is white or black, with respect to phenotypical characteristics and features that are commonly ascribed to those traditional racial groups. Since nonwhite, nonblack groups do not correspond to preconceived notions, and since these groups are likely to resist ascription as racially oppressed blacks, the development of additional racial categories to situate these newer immigrants of color within the American racial hierarchy is warranted. Ultimately, I argue that under these conditions, panethnicity may serve to connote a racial identity for Latinos. In this way, it resolves Latinos' positioning within the U.S. racial hierarchy.[2]

LITTLE LATIN AMERICA, HOUSTON, TEXAS

Located in Houston, Texas, Little Latin America[3] (population 49,691) is approximately three square miles in size. This community, like many others in the southwestern United States, has undergone a demographic transition that reflects the restructuring of the U.S. economy and a substantial increase in immigration. Formerly known (somewhat infamously) as a haven for white middle-class singles, Little Latin America was dramatically transformed by the oil bust of the 1970s. White unemployment increased and forced an exodus from this area, as whites searched for available good-paying jobs, preferably located in predominately white suburbs (Shah, 2005). At the same time, legal and illegal immigrants, mostly from Mexico and other countries of Latin America, took advantage of vacant apartments, helped along by desperate landlords who sought to fill their large and increasingly dilapidated complexes (Shah, 2005). In contrast to the national average of 66.2 percent, only 6.1 percent of Little Latin America's population currently own homes. The vast majority of residents (93.9 percent) rent.

Today, Little Latin America is overwhelmingly Latino (71 percent), followed in descending order by non-Hispanic whites (14 percent), blacks (9 percent), and Asians (4.7 percent) (U.S. Bureau of the Census, 2000). Of the Latino national-origin population, 41 percent are of Mexican descent and 29 percent are Central and South American immigrants and their descendants. More than half of the Little Latin America community is foreign-born, of whom 86 percent originate from Mexico or other Latin American countries. Not surprisingly, three-fourths of the Little Latin America community speak a language other than English at home (65 percent of whom speak Spanish).

More than 63 percent of the working-age population is employed, a figure close to the national average (63.9 percent). Of this population, approximately 95 percent are wage and salary workers. Only 5 percent are self-employed, which is about average for the U.S. Latino population as a whole. Little Latin America can be characterized as a working-poor community, since most adult neighborhood residents work; however, almost 30 percent of families fall below the poverty line (compared to the neighborhood national average of 9.2 percent). Like many urban areas in the racially segregated United States, Little Latin America is a Latino-concentrated community, sandwiched between an upper-middle-class white community, "Houston Heights," and a lower-class black community, "Southwest Central."

THE SAMPLE

My sample consists of ten Latino restaurants from which twelve restaurant owners were interviewed (in two of these restaurants, co-owner spouses partici-pated). This sample was drawn from fifteen restaurants, or half the number of full-service restaurants in the three-square-mile radius of Little Latin America. Although the owners of five restaurants refused to be interviewed, the sample of ten restaurants represents two-thirds of the original sample size and one-third of the total restaurant population (N=30). I personally visited each restaurant twice, the first time to introduce myself and drop off an information sheet (in English and Spanish) regarding my study of Latino entrepreneurs in the area, and the second time (with third, fourth, or fifth visits if necessary) to conduct the interview. The restaurateurs represent a diverse mix of Latino national origins and gender: a Chilean woman, a Cuban man, a Honduran woman, a Peruvian woman, a non-Hispanic white woman (the spouse of the Cuban man), three Mexican men, three Salvadoran men, and a Salvadoran woman (the spouse of one of the Salvadoran men). The restaurateurs who refused to be interviewed or could not be reached after several in-person attempts and repeated phone calls include two Mexican women (refused), two Salvadoran man (refused), the owner/s of a Salvadoran restaurant (could not be reached), and the owner/s of a Honduran restaurant (could not be reached). I conducted all but two of the interviews in English; the remaining two were conducted in Spanish by a female graduate research assistant. (I was also present during these latter interviews.)

SELF-DEFINED NATIONAL IDENTITY

When asked about their "background" and "ancestry," all of the Latino restaurant owners identified themselves based on their national origin, as these examples illustrate:

- "I'm 100 percent Mexican."—José
- "I consider myself to be Cuban … Cuban American."—Rubén
- "My parents were from Chile, I'm Chilean."—Carla

Moreover, business owners often expressed the importance of their national origin in establishing their businesses. José, a Mexican business owner, expressed a typical sentiment among business owners:

> ZULEMA: How important is your ancestry, your background, to your business?
> JOSÉ: Well, actually, it's very important. The ideas that I have here, we have them all over Mexico. This kind of business is all over Mexico. This idea comes from Mexico.

Martín, a self-identified Salvadoran and an owner of two restaurants in the area, likewise indicated the importance of his national origin in shaping his work ethic:

> ZULEMA: Earlier, you said that your background is Salvadoran. How important is your Salvadoran background to your business?
> MARTÍN: It's important because the people from El Salvador are used to working hard. I would say it's very important.
> ZULEMA: Do you feel that you are more Salvadoran or American?
> MARTÍN: I think I'm both. I love this country. Here you have opportunities. I have the same love for both countries.

The owner identified himself as Salvadoran and, when probed, as American as well. He said that he "loves" El Salvador and the United States equally; however, he implied that being Salvadoran has helped him in his business because Salvadorans "are used to working hard."

OTHER-DEFINED RACIAL IDENTITY

Statements about the benefits of being a member of a specific national-origin group, however, were sometimes combined with negative expressions directed at the business practices or lifestyles of other (non-co-national) Latinos. In these instances, business owners often invoked a panethnic label to identify the offending members' group. Martín provided an example when, immediately following from the above exchange, he volunteered a comparison between Salvadorans and "Latin people" more generally:

> MARTÍN: I can say, though, that the Latin people, in general, don't have loyalty with anyone. If someone gives them good service, good food, or a good price, they will buy from the Chinese, they will buy from Middle Easterners. They will buy from any nationality. They don't care what nationality you are from. They don't have loyalty to anyone. Latin people are like that. For example, there are many people who have meat markets. The owners of the Mexican meat markets are Chinese. The Latin people go and buy from them. On the other hand, the Chinese don't. They don't buy from anyone that's not Chinese. The Middle Easterners, the same. They are faithful to their own people. Latin people *do buy* from people who are not Latin. The Latin people are not faithful to anyone.

In the context of an explicit discussion about the benefits of being Salvadoran, the owner offered a contrasting group, "Latin people," and expressed prejudice against this non-co-national group. By suggesting that "Latin people . . . will buy from any nationality . . . from people who are not Latin," he characterized "Latin people" as lacking in solidarity. Furthermore, he implied that the Mexican-origin population not only lacks social capital but is also non-entrepreneurial, since "Mexican meat markets," which presumably should be owned by *Mexicans,* are actually owned and operated by *Chinese* entrepreneurs. (Notably, a Mexican-owned restaurant and a Mexican-owned bakery are within walking distance from this Salvadoran restaurant.) The Salvadoran business owner expressed prejudice against "Latin people" in general and stereotyped "Mexicans" in particular. However, he did not ascribe such negative characteristics to Salvadoran co-nationals. When these comments are viewed through the lens of the U.S. racial hierarchy, the white racial frame is exposed, as panethnicity in this "externally imposed" context captures the process of racialization that reduces specific national-origin groups to one subordinate racial group—"Latin people." Furthermore, the owner's perceived benefits of being Salvadoran when contrasted to the detriments of being Latin suggest not only a contestation of his own membership in the panethnic group but also an attempt to exclude Salvadorans from "Latin people's" subordinate placement within the racial hierarchy.

Panethnic labeling to racialize non-co-nationals was employed by all of the Latino business owners, albeit to a greater or lesser degree. For example, Carla, a fifty-four-year-old self-identified Chilean woman, attributed her business acumen to her Chilean identity. She explained that when she moved to Little Latin America from New Jersey in the mid-1980s, it was a Mexican ethnic enclave in transition, as many Salvadorans and other Central Americans were beginning to migrate to the area. She opened a Salvadoran restaurant to cater to the newly arrived Salvadoran immigrant community and readily identified her business, staff, and customer base with respect to national origin (Salvadoran). However, she specifically invoked the panethnic identity, Hispanic, when contrasting her "clean" restaurant with other restaurants in the area:

> Zulema: You are Chilean, but the food is Salvadoran?
> Carla: Yes. It's business [laughing].
> Zulema: It's a business decision?
> Carla: Yes, because in 1986 when we [Carla, her mother, and her brother] came here, there were only Mexican restaurants. When I saw the area, there's a lot of Salvadorans. . . . So we decided to make it a Salvadoran restaurant. All of the cookers, all the employees, except us, are Salvadoran. But this question, everyone asks. Sometimes Salvadorans are surprised. They say this is the best! This is the best Salvadoran restaurant in all of Houston.
> Zulema: Why do you think that is?
> Carla: For the quality of the food . . . the way we treat the customers . . . and the cleaning. Do you see that? [points to the kitchen] My pots. Tell me if they have any black stuff on them? On the bottom.
> Zulema: Uh . . . you mean those pots on top of the stove and refrigerator? No, I don't see any black stuff anywhere.

> CARLA: I keep my restaurant clean. You know, you can go to many Hispanic restaurants around here and the pots are all black. I don't like any of that! I'm not like that!

In short, the use of a panethnic identity, "Hispanic," was invoked by this Chilean restaurateur to negatively stereotype (non-Chilean) Hispanic-owned restaurants as unclean.

In these accounts, the use of the panethnic terms "Latin people" and "Hispanic" served to racialize and subordinate non-co-ethnic Latino national-origin groups. This process of "othering" neutralizes the distinct group differences that exist across national-origin subgroups. At the same time, it ranks one's national origin as decidedly superior to the subordinate and racialized panethnic group. This contingent use of panethnicity essentially equates panethnic identity with racial identity. Notably, the development of panethnic identity is possible only in societies that are structured racially—that is, where race relations matter. In the U.S. context, panethnic identities constitute *racial* categories inasmuch as they are associated with inferior or subordinate characteristics and features, when compared against those associated with (superior) national-origin groups. Because panethnicity serves the same function as race, panethnic groups are incorporated into the white racial hierarchy. Moreover, whether distinct national-origin group members "naturally" fit into specific panethnic groups owing to presumed sociocultural similarities (e.g., "Latinos" all speak Spanish) is beside the point; rather, these ethnic group members are thought to be distinct from white or black racial group members. In these instances, panethnic identity does *not* serve as a mediating, alternative, or intermediate nonracial category of classification (Diaz McConnell and Delgado-Romero, 2004; Lopez and Espiritu, 1990; Oboler, 1992, 1995; Omi, 2001; Omi and Winant, 1994; Portes and Macleod, 1996; Rodríguez and Cordero-Guzmán, 1992) but, instead, arises to provide *additional racial groups* with which to classify those who do not easily fit into preexisting racial categories.

EXPOSING THE WHITE RACIAL FRAME: WHITE SUPREMACY

As I mentioned above, my interview questions were originally constructed to gather information on Latino business practices and experiences within Little Latin America. Therefore, it is not surprising that the vast majority of the respondents' intergroup interactions featured mentions of co-nationals and/or non-co-national Latinos. That said, non-Hispanic whites comprise the second-largest population in Little Latin America. When this racial group was referenced by respondents, the superior position of whites within the American racial hierarchy was implicitly and sometimes explicitly acknowledged.

Martín, for example, revealed his understanding of Salvadorans' subordinate position relative to "Anglos." When comparing his customer base in the two restaurants he owns in the area, he clearly identified the superior position of "Anglos" when compared to "regular" Salvadorans:

ZULEMA: Now I'd like to ask you about this restaurant. It's Salvadoran as well....

MARTÍN: Yes, it's a Salvadoran restaurant, but it's not like the other one. This one is for a high-class clientele. The other one is like a café, with counters only. It has loud music, it's full of men, *machos* [tough guys]. Regular Salvadoran people ... *this* restaurant is nicer. I can bring my American friends in and show them this is a nice place, with good Salvadoran food. They always ask, "take me to a good Salvadoran restaurant," and before I was embarrassed ... ashamed ... there was no place to go. Now I can take them here.

ZULEMA: So this is a nicer place than your other restaurant?

MARTÍN: Yes, this is a nice restaurant that I can bring visitors, Anglos, to and show them what a high-class Salvadoran restaurant looks like.

Martín made a distinction between his two restaurants by saying they target different clienteles. He characterized one of his restaurants as serving "regular Salvadoran people" and the other restaurant (in which this interview took place) as serving his "American friends" and "Anglos." This "Anglo" Salvadoran restaurant is located in a new strip mall. It is painted bright yellow and decorated with several paintings on every wall (mostly oil paintings of birds and landscapes in bright primary colors, painted by his daughter); the floors are covered in Spanish tile; an unopened bottle of red wine sits on every table; and piped-in music (Spanish classical guitar) can be heard in the background. At the time of this interview, a young white man and woman were in the restaurant and another white couple entered as I left. A young, light-skinned Salvadoran waiter was working (note: no relation to the owner).

It is significant that Martín expressed his own "embarrassment" and "shame" at the prospect of taking "Anglos" to the "regular Salvadoran restaurant." What this account makes clear is that Martín recognized (consciously or not) the superior position of whites within the racial hierarchy, which he situates above his own group. Notably, however, Martín made an allowance for some Salvadorans to raise their position by introducing class to his Salvadoran customer profile. Although "regular Salvadorans" were not included alongside whites, there was room for "high-class" Salvadorans to join Anglos in frequenting the "nicer" restaurant. A class distinction was never introduced by Martín or anyone else in discussions that invoked panethnic groups, thus underscoring their perceived homogeneity. Martín's account highlights the implicit (and sometimes explicit) recognition of whites at the top, and the subordinate position held by nonwhite groups reveals a clear understanding of the U.S. racial hierarchy.

Rubén, a fifty-seven-year-old Cuban restaurateur, likewise revealed his knowledge of the racial hierarchy in a brief discussion about voluntary segregation by Hispanics from "Anglos" (notably, not the other way around). In this account, Rubén highlighted the demographic changes that have taken place in Little Latin America—specifically, the transition from a working- and middle-class (white) community to a well-known area of Salvadoran immigrant settlement:

RUBÉN: The thing is that when I started in this area, this area was completely different. All of this was white-collar and blue-collar workers. All of these houses were well-kept.

ZULEMA: When did people start moving out? Was this around the time of the oil bust?

RUBÉN: I would say it was more toward the end of the '90s. No, it was more like the '80s, when things started changing. It was a lot of immigration from Salvadorans. Over here, they called it Little Central America [laughing]. That's why you see so many Salvadoran-related businesses. I don't know whether the owners are Salvadoran or not. You also have a lot of Anglos who come here. From Houston Heights. I got to tell you, about 95 percent of my clientele are Anglo. You see the Anglos coming in for lunch during the work week. They all work around here [points in the direction of Houston Heights]. But, you know, the weekend comes and it's all Hispanic. The Hispanics don't like to be around the Anglos, it makes them uncomfortable, but on the weekends, when they want to relax and have a nice meal, then you see the people from around here.

In discussing Little Latin America's transition from a (white) working- and middle-class community to one of new immigrant settlement, Rubén did not hesitate to identify these new immigrants by their Salvadoran national origin, and he implied that the Little Latin America community is now majority Salvadoran. (At 29 percent it is decidedly not—Mexicans still make up the largest group, 41 percent.) However, when he discussed the interracial tension between whites and the rest of the community, he identified the community as "Hispanic" rather than Salvadoran. The panethnic identity "Hispanic" was invoked to equate and racialize distinct Latino national-origin groups, who were then compared to whites. Additionally, Rubén discussed the discomfort that Hispanics feel in the presence of whites, which suggests that Hispanics recognize their subordinate position to whites. A cursory look at the customers on this Thursday afternoon supported Rubén's statement, as the vast majority appeared to be well-dressed and office-attired, non-Hispanic whites. Although I did not have another chance to drop by Rubén's restaurant on the weekend, I noticed that most of the restaurants in Little Latin America were very busy during weekends and that the vast majority of their customers appeared to be Latinos.

EXPOSING THE WHITE RACIAL FRAME: BLACKS AT THE BOTTOM

In only one instance did a business owner specifically discuss blacks. Toward the end of a two-hour interview, Miguel, a forty-five-year-old Mexican business owner, asked me why I was interested in Little Latin America. I responded that I was interested in how immigrants "make it" in America, especially Spanish-speaking immigrants who often have to settle in high-poverty or high-crime areas in the United States. I also mentioned that some Houston organizations I had talked with recommended the Little Latin America area as a good place to start this research. Miguel then replied:

MIGUEL: We have had windows broken and things like that. People trying to get in, but nothing bad. You know, many people have a very bad perception of this area. It's in the apartments. They have crime. If you really think about it, it's crimes of passion. You see all these killings. It's somebody who doesn't like somebody killing each other. It's not like they're going and robbing somebody. I read the newspaper. I read it constantly and I'm always reading those sections. I live two minutes away from here. I live in Houston Heights. It's not any different than living in this area. I've been there for eighteen years in that house. I don't even know anybody in that street being broken in. So the bad people are not here. They don't live here. You see people walking down the street. These people are not wealthy. They take the bus, they have a job and they're hardworking.

ZULEMA: They're just poor. . . .

MIGUEL: They're not walking around because they're trying to get into trouble. I would say that is west of here more so than here. I would say in that black neighborhood . . . I have never been, well, I was robbed here one time at gunpoint. I was at a bank and it was a couple of black men that did it. I was at a bank two or three miles away from here. They were waiting for someone to come out with a bank bag. I had a bank bag full of coins when they saw me. And I ran errands for about forty-five minutes until I got here. These guys followed me from this bank. That was the only incident that we had and I've been here for twenty-four years.

Houston Heights is a predominately white, middle- and upper-class area adjacent to Little Latin America. Miguel lives in Houston Heights and works in Little Latin America. He acknowledged the occurrence of crime in the area but made a distinction between murder that is committed as a "crime of passion" and that which is committed in the commission of a robbery. In addition, while acknowledging that "crimes of passion" occur in Little Latin America, he maintained that the community, albeit a poor one, is hardworking and that "the bad people are not here. They don't live here." Following this exchange, Miguel offered a contrasting example of a community with residents who "get into trouble." He not only characterized Southwest Central as a black community plagued by crime but offered a personal example of getting robbed at gunpoint by two black men who came into Little Latin America from Southwest Central to commit the robbery. In this account, the white racial frame is confirmed through a negative characterization of the black community and a rationalization of those who live in Little Latin America as poor but good, and even in some ways comparable to whites.

CONCLUSION

Upon arrival, immigrants and their descendants are embedded in the social structure of American society. Hence, they are exposed to the white racial frame that structures the U.S. racial hierarchy. As they adapt and integrate into American society, they also tend to adopt the white racial frame. In this context, the panethnic identity, Latino, is transformed into a racial identity, one that is sometimes invoked by the members themselves as they negotiate, resist, and construct Latinos' placement within the American racial hierarchy.

This chapter has explored the use of national, panethnic, and racial identities among Latino business owners who live and/or work in Little Latin America.

My findings reveal that Latino business owners consistently identified themselves nationally ("I'm 100 percent Mexican") and that Latino business owners invoked a panethnic label to classify non-co-nationals under certain conditions: (1) to stereotype or express bias against Latinos ("Latin people aren't loyal to anyone"); (2) to distance their own ethnic group from the negative stereotypes or prejudices associated with Latinos ("You can go to many Hispanic restaurants around here and the pots are all black . . . I'm not like that" [stated by one owner who associated "cleanliness" with being Chilean]; and (3) when discussing social interactions or relationships with traditional (white/black) racial groups (i.e., "Hispanics don't like to be around Anglos, it makes them uncomfortable"). My findings also demonstrate that Latinos engage in boundary maintenance and social closure by externally imposing the panethnic category "Latino" from *within*. From this perspective, self-identifying nationally may represent an attempt to resist or contest panethnic classification, which constitutes the process of racialization. This strategy of national self-identification and panethnic other-identification was employed by all of the Latino entrepreneurs I interviewed, regardless of national origin. Moreover, their use of panethnic categories to negatively stereotype or express bias exposed the white racial frame, which places Latinos in a subordinate position relative to whites within the U.S. racial hierarchy.

Overall, this exploratory research reveals the process of racialization inherent in a society where race matters. Although agency is revealed in individual or collective action—for example, in one's ability to self-identify nationally—the racialized social structure prevents actors from being identified "nationally" only: The imposition of race is always required; it is not an option. The development and contingent use of panethnicity serve this purpose, as panethnicity provides additional racial categories for groups who do not easily correspond to the traditional white/black racial classification system, such as Mexicans, Salvadorans, and Hondurans. The pattern of resisting, creating, and reproducing racial categories underscores the interdependence of agency and structure. Agency is shown in the attempt by individuals to resist the process of racialization and in the creation of new racial categories; and structure, in the reproduction of the racialized social structure as well as in the in-between positioning of nonwhite and nonblack Latino/as within the racial hierarchy.

NOTES

1. Direct comments can be sent to Zulema Valdez, Department of Sociology, Texas A&M University, 4351 TAMU, College Station, Texas 77843-4351 (zvaldez@libarts.tamu.edu). I would like to thank Wendy Leo Moore and participants of the 2007 Race and Ethnicity Working Group at Texas A&M University for helpful comments and insights. This research was funded by fellowship support from the ASA/NSF Fund for the Advancement of the Discipline (FAD) Grant, 2005–2007.

2. In the U.S. context, whether this racial identity is constructed as white, black, biracial, multiracial, or, as argued here, panethnic (i.e., Latino or Asian) may be somewhat negotiable; that one possesses a racial identity is not.

3. "Little Latin America" is a pseudonym, as are the names of other communities and individuals presented in this study.

REFERENCES

Bashi, Vilna. 1998. "Racial Categories Matter Because Racial Hierarchies Matter: A Commentary." *Ethnic and Racial Studies* 21(5):959–969.

Bean, Frank, and Marta Tienda. 1987. *The Hispanic Population in the United States.* New York: Russell Sage Foundation.

Bonilla-Silva, Eduardo. 1997. "Rethinking Racism: Toward a Structural Interpretation." *American Sociological Review* 62:465–480.

———. 1999. "Comment and Reply: The Essential Social Fact of Race." *American Sociological Review* 64(6):899–906.

Campbell, Mary E., and Christabel L. Rogalin. 2006. "Categorical Imperatives: The Interaction of Latino and Racial Identification." *Social Science Quarterly* 87:1030–1052.

Conner, Walker. 1978. "A Nation Is a Nation, Is a State, Is an Ethnic Group, Is a…." *Ethnic and Racial Studies* 1(4):379–388.

Cornell, Stephen, and Douglas Hartmann. 1998. *Ethnicity and Race: Identities in a Changing World.* Thousand Oaks, CA: Pine Forge Press.

Diaz McConnell, Eileen, and Edward A. Delgado-Romero. 2004. "Latino Panethnicity: Reality or Methodological Construction?" *Sociological Focus* 37(4):297–312.

Feagin, Joe R. 2006. *Systemic Racism: A Theory of Oppression.* New York: Routledge.

Feagin, Joe R., Hernán Vera, and Pinar Batur. 2001. *White Racism: The Basics,* 2nd ed. New York: Routledge.

Itzigsohn, José, and Carlos Dore-Cabral. 2000. "Competing Identities? Race, Ethnicity, and Panethnicity Among Dominicans in the United States." *Sociological Forum* 15(2):225–247.

Jones-Correa, Michael, and David L. Leal. 1996. "Becoming 'Hispanic': Secondary Panethnic Identification Among Latin American–Origin Populations in the United States." *Hispanic Journal of Behavioral Sciences* 18(2):214–254.

Lopez, David, and Yen Le Espiritu. 1990. "Panethnicity in the United States: A Theoretical Framework." *Ethnic and Racial Studies* 13(2):198–224.

Moore, Joan. 1990. "Hispanic/Latino: Imposed Label or Real Identity?" *Latino Studies Journal* 1:33–47.

Nagel, Joanne. 1994. "Constructing Ethnicity: Creating and Recreating Ethnic Identity and Culture." *Social Problems* 41:152–176.

Oboler, Suzanne. 1992. "The Politics of Labeling: Latino/a Cultural Identities of Self and Other." *Latin American Perspectives* 19:18–36.

———. 1995. *Ethnic Labels, Latino Lives: Identity and the Politics of (Re)Presentation in the United States.* Minneapolis: University of Minnesota Press.

Office of Management and Budget. 1997. *Federal Register Notice, October 30, 1997.* Washington, DC: OMB Publications Office.

Omi, Michael. 2001. "The Changing Meaning of Race." Pp. 243–263 in Neil J. Smelser, William J. Wilson, and Faith Mitchell (eds.), *America Becoming: Racial Trends and Their Consequences.* Washington, DC: National Academy Press.

Omi, Michael, and Howard Winant. 1994. *Racial Formation in the United States: From the 1960s to the 1990s.* New York: Routledge.

Padilla, Felix. 1985. *Latino Ethnic Consciousness.* Notre Dame, IN: University of Notre Dame Press.

Portes, Alejandro, and Dag Macleod. 1996. "What Shall I Call Myself? Hispanic Identity Formation in the Second Generation." *Ethnic and Racial Studies* 19(3):539–595.

Rodríguez, Clara E., and Héctor Cordero-Guzmán. 1992. "Placing Race in Context." *Ethnic and Racial Studies* 15(4):523–542.

Shah, Yaksha. 2005. "History of Gulfton." Unpublished manuscript.

Swarns, Rachel L. 2004. "Hispanics Resist Racial Grouping by Census." *New York Times*, October 24. Retrieved June 11, 2008. (http://www.nytimes.com/2004/10/24/national/24census.html)

U.S. Bureau of the Census. 2000. *American FactFinder*. Retrieved June 11, 2008. (http://factfinder.census.gov)

Valdez, Zulema. 2008. "The Effect of Group Identity and Group Consciousness on Latinos' Political Participation in the U.S." Unpublished manuscript.

Yancey, William, Eugene Erikson, and Richard Juliani. 1976. "Emergent Ethnicity: A Review and Reformulation." *American Sociological Review* 41:391–403.

CHAPTER 13

Racializing Ethnicity in the Spanish-Speaking Caribbean

A Comparison of Haitians in the Dominican Republic and Dominicans in Puerto Rico

Jorge Duany

According to Howard Winant's (1994:59) classic definition, racialization is "the extension of racial meaning to a previously racially unclassified relationship, social practice, or group."[1] More specifically, racialization involves imputing a hereditary origin to an individual's intellectual, emotional, or behavioral characteristics based on group membership. For example, many Americans believe that Asian Americans are mathematically inclined, African Americans are musically gifted, and Latinos are family-oriented. Such traits are supposed to be natural, involuntary, and enduring. In principle, any "ethnic" group (whether defined by national origin, language, religion, or some other cultural variable) can be racialized. Under some circumstances, a group's phenotypical characteristics (particularly skin color, hair texture, and facial features) are construed as primordial and socially significant. Once groups are racialized, they develop distinct patterns of occupational specialization, educational achievement, residential segregation, marriage, cultural representation, and legal treatment by the dominant society.

The thesis of this chapter is that the precarious status of Haitians in the Dominican Republic and of Dominicans in Puerto Rico is primarily due to their racialization. The public perception of both groups as black hampers their full socioeconomic incorporation and externalizes racial prejudice and discrimination to foreign "others." As a result, immigrants from Haiti as well as from the Dominican Republic are largely excluded from dominant discourses of national identity in the Dominican Republic and Puerto Rico. Until now, such discourses have been primarily oriented toward white and European elites and their Creole descendants, despite growing racial awareness among African-descended populations in Latin America, including the Dominican Republic and Puerto Rico (see Dzidzienyo and Oboler, 2005). In both places, blackness is still generally perceived as a minor component in the islands' demographic histories and contemporary cultures.

DISTANT NEIGHBORS:
HAITIANS IN THE DOMINICAN REPUBLIC

The literature on ethnicity and race in the Dominican Republic has been primarily concerned, perhaps even obsessed, with Haitian immigrants. Most scholars agree that Haitians and their descendants face strong prejudice and discrimination in the Dominican Republic (e.g., Dore Cabral, 1995; Torres-Saillant, 1999). Extensive research on Haitian cane cutters in the Dominican sugar industry (especially in the *bateyes,* the company workers' towns) has documented their miserable living conditions, economic exploitation, social exclusion, and legal disenfranchisement (Báez Evertsz, 1986; Grasmuck, 1983; Lozano, 1992; Martínez, 1995; Moya Pons, 1986b; Murphy, 1991; Pascual Morán and Figueroa, 2005). However, scholars disagree about the precise nature, historical origins, and popular diffusion of anti-Haitian ideas and practices among Dominicans. Some writers have traced the tensions between Haitians and Dominicans to the Haitian occupation of Santo Domingo (1822–1844), often referred to as the "black years" in Dominican history (Moya Pons, 1986a; Murphy, 1991). Others go back even further to the enmity between French and Spanish settlers on the island of Hispaniola (Sagás, 2000; San Miguel, 1997). Most analysts, however, concur that it was the large-scale migration of Haitian cane cutters to the Dominican Republic since the beginning of the twentieth century that intensified local resentment. The climax of *antihaitianismo* was the 1937 massacre of at least 15,000 Haitians along the Dominican border by Rafael Trujillo's military forces (Turits, 2002).

Ernesto Sagás (2000) has emphasized the elaboration of an anti-Haitian ideology by the Dominican elite that celebrates the Hispanic legacy and downplays African influences in Dominican culture, particularly during the Trujillo dictatorship (1930–1961). Sagás underlines border disputes since colonial times as a constant source of friction between French Saint-Domingue and Spanish Santo Domingo. Others have observed that such antagonism has taken place within a broader context of reciprocal influence and interdependence between the two nations (Baud, 1996; Martínez, 2003b; Matibag, 2003; Moya Pons, 1986a; Silié et al., 2002). Strong cultural links between Haiti and the Dominican Republic are prominent in folk religion, music, and dance (Austerlitz, 1997; Davis, 1987). A relatively peaceful coexistence between the two peoples has characterized daily life along the Haitian-Dominican border and even in the infamous *bateyes* (Derby, 1994; Moya Pons, 1986b; Silié and Segura, 2002).

A recurrent theme in the bibliography is that Dominican national identity was historically constructed and consolidated in direct opposition to Haiti. Thus, Dominican elites traditionally deemed the Dominican Republic essentially as a white, Hispanic, and Catholic country, whereas they disdained Haiti as a black, African, and Voodoo-practicing country (Howard, 2001; Moya Pons, 1986a; San Miguel, 1997). This antithesis between the races, cultures, languages, and religions of Hispaniola reached its zenith among Trujillo's intelligentsia, notably Joaquín Balaguer and Manuel A. Peña Batlle. Many Dominican writers traditionally shared a profound pessimism regarding the possibility of incorporating blacks (particularly Haitians) into their nation-building projects (Sagás, 2000). Less clear is the extent to which ordinary Dominicans embraced anti-Haitian ideas and practices, even under the Trujillo regime, when they became the dominant ideology. Some authors have argued that anti-Haitian feelings are widely shared by Dominicans today (Dore Cabral, 1995; Murphy, 1991; Onè Respe, 1994). Others have suggested that popular Dominican attitudes toward Haitians are much more tolerant than those of the ruling elite (Baud, 1996; Hernández and López, 2003; Torres-Saillant, 1998). In any case, most Dominicans seem to believe that Haitians are racially and culturally distinct from themselves. According to Lauren Derby (1994:521), "Dominicans and Haitians define their difference from one another through a wide range of bodily practices, including eating, procreating, washing, walking, sitting, and speaking (accent)."

Scholars have dwelled on the prevalent discourse that dubs most Dominicans *indios* (literally, "Indians"; figuratively, brown-skinned) (Candelario, 2007; Howard, 2001). During the late nineteenth century, according to Sagás (2000:35), "the Dominican people essentially dropped the words black and mulatto from their vocabulary and replaced them with the less traumatic and more socially desirable *indio*." The Trujillo regime converted the latter folk term into the official racial description for most Dominicans. Even today, very dark-skinned persons are characterized as *indio* or *india, oscuro* or *oscura*, and *quemado* or *quemada* on their government-issued identity cards; only Haitians are branded as *negros* or *negras* (or even *morados* or *moradas*—literally, purple). This practice has gained wide currency among Dominicans, as exemplified by the informants of a recent documentary who declared themselves to be *indios* rather than *negros* (Weyland, 2004). As Silvio Torres-Saillant (1998:139) has argued, "[E]thnically, the Indians represented a category typified by nonwhiteness as well as nonblackness, which could easily accommodate the racial in-betweenness of the Dominican mulatto." Thus, *indio* or *india* has provided a conceptual alternative to reconcile anti-black feelings with the racially mixed heritage of much of the Dominican population. Ginetta Candelario (2000:130) puts it well: "Rather than use the language of Negritude—*negro, mulatto,* and so forth—to describe themselves,

Dominicans use language which limits their racial ancestry to Europeans and Taino 'Indians.' ... The result is an ethno-racial Hispanicized Indian, or an Indo-Hispanic identity."

At the same time, the "indigenist" discourse has justified the mistreatment of Haitians, based on their supposedly different ancestry, physical type, culture, religion, and language. While most Dominicans identify themselves as "Indians," they associate Haitians with "Africans." In the Dominican Republic, Haitians have been stigmatized as primitive, backward, superstitious, destitute, dangerous, unhealthy, animal-like, and childlike creatures. In particular, Haitians have been commonly linked with witchcraft, black magic, and barbaric ritual practices such as slaughtering animals, eating children, and sucking human blood (Howard, 2001; Onè Respe, 1994; Sagás, 2000). According to Derby (1994:493), "the term, Haitian, is now a floating label of misconduct, improper behavior, or lack of civility" in Santo Domingo. In contrast, Dominicans tend to see themselves as the proud inheritors of Hispanic Catholic civilization, with a strong Amerindian legacy. In this regard, the popular use of the term *indio* has served to mask the pervasiveness of dark-skinned Dominicans of African or mixed origin, who would otherwise be practically indistinguishable from the despised Haitians.

Finally, the increasing Haitian presence in the Dominican Republic—no longer confined to the *bateyes* but also expanding in other agricultural areas, as well as in the cities—is a major source of public concern today (Ferguson, 2003; Lozano and Báez Evertsz, 1992; Silié, Segura, and Dore Cabral, 2002; Wooding and Moseley-Williams, 2004). Even when Haitians and Dominicans share the same poor urban communities, they tend to behave like distant strangers rather than close neighbors (Báez Evertsz, 2001). Haitian immigrants and their descendants are often denied basic social, educational, and medical services because of their tenuous legal status in the Dominican Republic. Many are literally stateless people without access to either Dominican or Haitian citizenship, and therefore without protection of their civil and human rights. Undocumented Haitians have long been easy scapegoats for the persistent socioeconomic problems of the Dominican Republic, including unemployment, poverty, crime, and public health issues such as the AIDS epidemic (Onè Respe, 1994). In short, the vast majority of Haitian immigrants occupy the lowest rung of an ethnic and racial hierarchy, erected over the last two centuries, that continues unabated today.

THE FAMILIAR OTHER: DOMINICANS IN PUERTO RICO

Research on Dominican migration to Puerto Rico has also documented its problematic incorporation into the receiving society (Duany, 1990; Duany, Hernández Angueira, and Rey, 1995; Martínez-San Miguel, 2003; Peralta, 1995). My own fieldwork, conducted together with Luisa Hernández, César Rey, and Lanny Thompson, has focused on the ethnic segmentation of the Puerto Rican labor market. In the urban center of Santurce, most Dominicans are employed in the service sector, many of them in the underground economy, such as domestic employees, itinerant sellers, security guards, beauty parlor attendants, and construction workers. In the inner highlands of Puerto Rico, undocumented Dominicans are replacing local agricultural workers in the coffee harvest, an economic activity increasingly dominated by Haitians in the Dominican Republic (Lozano and Báez Evertsz, 1992; Pascual and Figueroa, 2000). Dominicans in Puerto Rico typically toil for low wages, long hours, poor working conditions, and few or no fringe benefits. Their underprivileged socioeconomic position recalls that of Haitians in the Dominican Republic.

Traditionally, little animosity characterized the relations between Dominicans and Puerto Ricans. Historians have recorded the long-standing cultural, linguistic, and religious affinities between the Dominican Republic and Puerto Rico since the Spanish colonial period (Camuñas Madera, 1999; del Castillo, 1989; Pérez Memén, 1989; Rosario Natal, 1990, 1995). A small but constant flow of people in both directions occurred from the sixteenth to nineteenth centuries, including bureaucrats, soldiers, clerics, professionals, students, artisans, and slaves. During the nineteenth century, hundreds of exiles moved from Hispaniola to Puerto Rico, primarily as a result of political upheavals in French Saint-Domingue and Spanish Santo Domingo. Thousands of Puerto Ricans migrated to the Dominican Republic during the first three decades of the twentieth century, looking for agricultural jobs in the expanding sugar industry of the eastern provinces of San Pedro de Macorís and La Romana. Since the 1960s, the primary direction of the migrant flow was inverted, as thousands of Dominicans flocked to Puerto Rico. The links between the two countries have tightened through growing trade, investment, tourism, and migration.

Until 1970, most Dominican immigrants in Puerto Rico were relatively well-educated members of the middle class (Vázquez Calzada and Morales del Valle, 1979)—and probably light-skinned. Public expressions of an anti-Dominican bias in Puerto Rico began to be more noticeable during the 1970s, with increasing working-class migration, particularly undocumented migration, from the Dominican Republic (del Castillo, 1989; Romero Anico, 1984). Much of the prejudice has been due to the common association among low occupational status, dark skin color, foreign birth, and irregular legal status. In the 1990s, numerous studies confirmed the rising hostility toward Dominicans in Puerto Rico (Benítez Nazario, 2001; Cruz Caraballo, 1998; Duany, 1990; Iturrondo, 1993–1994; López Carrasquillo, 1999; Mejía Pardo, 1993; Ríos, 1992). This animosity now assumes various forms, ranging from ethnic jokes and graffiti to literary texts and the mass media (de la Rosa Abreu, 2002; De Maeseneer, 2002; Martínez-San Miguel, 2003). Regardless of their particular cultural medium, anti-Dominican attitudes and practices have become widespread among Puerto Ricans over the past three decades.

A recurrent theme in the scholarly literature is that Dominican origin is increasingly equated with blackness in Puerto Rico. Most Puerto Ricans on the island regard themselves as white, but define Dominicans as black or mulatto. Specifically, Puerto Ricans tend to depict Dominicans as darker-skinned than themselves and underline their Negroid facial features and hair texture (Cruz Caraballo, 1998; López Carrasquillo, 1999; Martínez-San Miguel, 2003). In turn, Dominicans tend to see themselves as lighter-skinned and having more Caucasian characteristics than their Haitian neighbors. (The 2000 Census of Puerto Rico confirmed the discrepancy in racial self-perceptions, with 81.3 percent of the Puerto Ricans classifying themselves as white, compared to only 36.2 percent of the Dominicans [Rivera-Batiz, 2004].) According to Yolanda Martínez-San Miguel (2003), Dominicans, not Americans, are now the main "others" against which Puerto Ricans identify themselves. Clearly, Dominicans in Puerto Rico are concentrated in lower-status occupations and largely segregated into poor inner-city neighborhoods such as Barrio Obrero in Santurce and Barrio Capetillo in Río Piedras (Denton and Villarrubia, 2007). As I have noted elsewhere (Duany, 1998, 2005), black Puerto Ricans are often mistaken for Dominicans (just as black Dominicans are taken to be Haitian in the Dominican Republic). Consequently, the dominant discourse of Puerto Ricanness has developed an adversarial relation to Dominican (as well as black) identity.

The growing number of Dominican residents of Puerto Rico, particularly in the San Juan metropolitan area, has fueled public tensions. Most commonly, Puerto Ricans complain that Dominicans are taking away their jobs and "invading" their neighborhoods. Popular jokes told by Puerto Ricans dwell on the immigrants' supposed lack of intelligence, nonstandard dialect, undocumented status, and low occupational prestige. Folk stories often ridicule Dominicans in Puerto Rico on the basis of their foreign accent, physical appearance, and cultural idiosyncrasies (Iturrondo, 1993–1994; López Carrasquillo, 1999; Mejía Pardo, 1993). Several popular radio and television programs have featured Dominicans as comic, ignorant, vulgar, and unruly characters (de la Rosa Abreu, 2002). Furthermore, Dominican immigrants have been blamed for an increasing crime rate, persistent unemployment, prostitution, and drug trafficking (Duany, 2005; Iturrondo, 2000). These are signs of the growing racialization of Dominicans in Puerto Rico as "needed but unwanted" immigrants, to use the title phrase of a recent monograph on Haitians in the Dominican Republic (Wooding and Moseley-Williams, 2004). Ironically, the prevailing images of Dominicans in Puerto Rico resemble those of Haitians in the Dominican Republic as well as Puerto Ricans in the United States.

THE SHARED MISERY OF A STIGMATIZED IDENTITY: COMPARING THE TWO CASES

Haitians in the Dominican Republic and Dominicans in Puerto Rico share surprising similarities. To begin with, a large proportion of both groups are undocumented immigrants and therefore lack legal protection by the receiving government. Second, ample sectors of the host populations, including many members of the working classes, state authorities, and intellectual elites, mistreat Haitians in the Dominican Republic and Dominicans in Puerto Rico. Third, public representations of both groups draw on analogous stereotypes, such as backwardness, filth, vulgarity, and immorality. Fourth, the two groups have confronted strong prejudice, discrimination, segregation, and exclusion from the receiving societies. Fifth, like Haitians in the Dominican Republic, Dominicans in Puerto Rico are objects of public scorn, folk humor, media misrepresentation, police brutality, and persecution by immigration authorities. Sixth, in Puerto Rico as well as in the Dominican Republic, popular and elite forms of culture—from songs to short stories—tend to shun the immigrants as alien to the national imaginary of the host society. Seventh, the two groups specialize in low-status occupational niches, such as agricultural labor, construction work, and domestic service, which native workers avoid because of low wages and poor working conditions.

Finally, both the Dominican Republic and Puerto Rico receive thousands of lower-class workers from neighboring countries, while simultaneously sending even more local workers to the United States. As Sherri Grasmuck (1983:166) noted more than two decades ago, Haitians and Dominicans, as well as Puerto Ricans, participate in a complex system of "international stair-step migration" in which "a labor force imported from a peripheral society occupies positions in a developed society which apparently are undesirable to the native working class, whereas the same peripheral society in turn imports part of its labor force from another peripheral society further down in the international economic hierarchy." To justify this ethnic division of labor, many migrant workers are racialized as black, as opposed to native workers, most of whom consider themselves to be white, "Indian," or at least not black.

At the same time, the two cases differ significantly on several counts. Haitians represent the longest and most massive migrant flow to the Dominican Republic, especially since the 1910s, whereas Dominicans are the most recent group to settle in large numbers in Puerto Rico, displacing Cubans in the 1970s. Haitians have traditionally concentrated in the rural areas of the Dominican Republic, particularly in the eastern sugar-growing provinces, whereas Dominicans cluster in the urban centers of Puerto Rico, especially in the San Juan metropolitan area. Anti-Haitian prejudice in the Dominican Republic dates back at least to the early nineteenth century, but anti-Dominican sentiment in Puerto Rico gained strength only in the 1980s. Whereas *antihaitianismo* became the official ideology of the Trujillo regime during the 1930s, the Puerto Rican government has never publicly espoused *antidominicanismo*. Arguably, xenophobia has not been institutionalized in Puerto Rico as extensively as in the Dominican Republic (García Cuevas, 1999).

Furthermore, many Dominicans have historically viewed Haitians as the main external threat to their national integrity, identity, and security, but Puerto Ricans have distinguished themselves primarily from Spaniards and later from Americans, and only recently from Dominicans. The Dominican Republic gained its independence from Haiti in 1844, whereas Puerto Rico remained under Spanish rule until 1898. While Haiti shares the island of Hispaniola with the Dominican Republic, including a much-disputed frontier until well into the twentieth century, the Dominican Republic and Puerto Rico are separated by a well-defined and uncontested maritime border, the Mona Passage. Puerto Rican animosity against Dominicans has not yet reached the level of symbolic or physical violence as anti-Haitian feelings in the Dominican Republic (as was evident in the 1937 slaughtering of Haitians under Trujillo). Many Dominicans perceive wider cultural disparities, particularly in language and religion, with Haitians than with Puerto Ricans. Instead, public references to "our Dominican brothers" are commonly heard in Puerto Rico.

Last but not least, the Haitian population in the Dominican Republic is much larger, in absolute and proportional terms, than the Dominican population in Puerto Rico. Informed estimates put the number of Haitians in the Dominican Republic at around half a million, compared to about 100,000 Dominicans in Puerto Rico (see Duany, 2005; Howard, 2001). The often expressed (but largely unfounded) fear of an "alien invasion" is therefore much more pronounced in the Dominican Republic than in Puerto Rico. Such a fear has led to periodic deportations of undocumented immigrants, more commonly in the former country than in the latter, although both have attempted to stem illegal entries into their territories. Together, these historical, geographic, and demographic factors help to account for the distinctive quality of intergroup relations in each society (see also Martínez, 2003a).

DENIGRATING THE OTHER: THE RACIALIZATION OF ETHNIC MINORITIES

I would argue that the basic explanation for the underlying parallels between Haitians in the Dominican Republic and Dominicans in Puerto Rico is their common racialization. As I noted before, Winant (1994) has approached "racialization" as the process of attributing biologically inherited origins to cultural practices, social groups, and human bodies distinguished by their physical types. Thus, racial meanings are assigned to a group's intellectual, emotional, and behavioral characteristics. As a result, groups are treated as if such characteristics were part of their essence—inherent, immutable, and fixed by nature. As José Cobas (personal communication, October 12, 2005) has argued, the basic purpose of racialization is to legitimate the treatment of "inferior" groups while maintaining an ideology that buttresses the supremacy of the white elite.

Haitians in the Dominican Republic and Dominicans in Puerto Rico have been racialized in Winant's sense. Many Dominicans believe that Haitians are savage, ugly, violent, and bloodthirsty because of their African ancestry, just as many Puerto Ricans feel that Dominicans are strange, dangerous, criminal, and sexually obsessed, largely because of their blackness. In both cases, many local people assume that they can identify foreigners based on their visible physical characteristics, such as skin color, hair texture, facial features, and even head shape (López Carrasquillo, 1999; Onè Respe, 1994). In addition, cultural differences such as "accent," dress, and body language are commonly invoked to distinguish natives from foreigners. Regardless of the actual differences between Haitian and Dominican immigrants, natives of their host societies often regard them as racially and culturally inferior. This discourse justifies that Dominicans in Puerto Rico and Haitians in the Dominican Republic usually hold the least attractive jobs and have lower standards of living than the native-born population. In contrast to the Lebanese in the Dominican Republic or Cubans in Puerto Rico, who are generally accepted as white, most Haitians and Dominicans are restricted to the lowest rungs of the labor and housing markets of both societies.

The racialization of Haitian and Dominican immigrants is extremely problematic for several reasons. One is that both the Dominican Republic and Puerto Rico are Afro-Caribbean societies with a high incidence of racial mixture and an important (though often underestimated) African heritage. The public image of Haitians in the Dominican Republic and of Dominicans in Puerto Rico as perennial outsiders reinforces the omission of blackness from the national imaginary of each society and projects blackness onto an external "other." Ironically, most Puerto Ricans as well as Dominicans in the United States are considered nonwhite, regardless of how they classify themselves. Hence, the racialization of Haitians in the Dominican Republic, Dominicans in Puerto Rico, and Puerto Ricans and Dominicans in the United States places all of these groups in a disadvantaged position vis-à-vis the "white" (or whitened?) majority of the host populations.

Comparing Haitian-Dominican relations and Dominican–Puerto Rican relations suggests that racialization can take place even in the absence of major historical, cultural, linguistic, and religious barriers. Different groups, such as Haitians or Dominicans, may be labeled similarly in different places, such as the Dominican Republic or Puerto Rico, if they perform similar economic functions, such as providing cheap labor, and occupy parallel social positions, such as undesirable aliens. Nor are phenotypical distinctions (including skin color, facial features, and hair texture) necessary for enduring prejudice and discrimination against a group. In both the Dominican Republic and Puerto Rico, the "imagined" differences in physical appearance between natives and foreigners are probably greater than the "real" ones, given their shared history of African slavery and racial mixture. Instead, the key issue is that blackness is constructed and represented outside the dominant discourses of national identity. Consequently, Haitians in the Dominican Republic as well as Dominicans in Puerto Rico are usually shunned as black "others" who threaten the presumed whiteness of the receiving societies.

Finally, the comparative analysis of the two groups indicates that the much vaunted myth of a "racial democracy" based on the ideology of mestizaje or mulataje (racial mixture) continues to subordinate blacks, mulattoes, and other "people of color" in the Spanish-speaking Caribbean. The proverbial ambiguity, flexibility, and fluidity of racial categories in the Dominican Republic and Puerto Rico collapse before the massive immigration of dark-skinned, lower-class workers, especially those without legal documentation. Unfortunately, the so-called racial continuum typical of the Spanish-speaking Caribbean lumps together all Haitians in the Dominican Republic and most Dominicans in Puerto Rico as black. For most practical purposes, the binary opposition between "us"—white or near-white natives—and "them"—black foreigners—overrides other social distinctions. This polarization is strangely reminiscent of Harry Hoetink's (1967) description of the northwest European variant in Caribbean race relations, even though it operates in two Spanish-speaking Caribbean islands. Perhaps, as Sidney Mintz (1996) has quipped, the fundamental division in both places continues to be white versus black, regardless of a person's ethnic identity. In any case, it does not bode well for immigrants whose skin tones approximate the darker hues of the color spectrum.

CONCLUSION

Both the Dominican Republic and Puerto Rico have become "international migrant crossroads"—to borrow Samuel Martínez's (2003a) apt phrase—as a result of massive movements of people between neighboring Caribbean countries, as well as even larger movements to and from the United States. The parallels between Haitians in the Dominican Republic and Dominicans in Puerto Rico are impressive. Although each situation has distinct historical roots and ramifications, both immigrant populations cluster at the bottom of the local ethnic and racial hierarchy. In both cases, the prevalent system of social stratification has not promoted warm, friendly, and personal contact between different groups, as proposed by Hoetink's classic model of the Iberian variant of race relations in the Caribbean. On the contrary, intergroup relations are often tinged with mutual suspicion, social distance, misunderstanding, antipathy, and even violence.

Under such circumstances, insisting on an ideal racial harmony or monolithic national identity, as many scholars and politicians have done in the past, is not an adequate solution to persistent ethnic and racial oppression. It seems more feasible to uncover and denounce the causes and consequences of social structures and cultural practices that continue to depreciate dark skin, manual labor, foreign birth, and "alien" values and customs. Unfortunately, such structures and practices—as the example of ethnic and racial humor illustrates—are all too common throughout the world. The racialization of Haitians in the Dominican Republic and of Dominicans in Puerto Rico follows a similar logic. Both groups are commonly identified by their real or imagined physical types, as if their bodies differed markedly from those of local populations. Cultural, linguistic, and even religious differences are naturalized in the process, neglecting the historical, economic, and political reasons for the massive movement of lower-class blacks and mulattoes from a poorer Caribbean country to a wealthier one. Here as elsewhere, racializing ethnicity serves to justify the ongoing exclusion of foreign "others" with dark skins and other physical characteristics associated with African descendants. As Michael Omi and Howard Winant (1994) argue, the extension of racial meanings to ethnic groups classified as black or even "nonwhite" tends to dehumanize them, deprive them of their citizenship rights, and marginalize them socially, economically, and culturally.

In closing, I would suggest four basic questions for further research. First, how exactly do current processes of racialization differ in the Dominican Republic, Puerto Rico, the United States, and elsewhere in the Caribbean? To what extent are such processes converging in all of these places? Second, why are certain ethnic minorities, such as the *cocolos* (descendants of English-speaking Caribbean immigrants) in the Dominican Republic or Cubans in Puerto Rico, better integrated than others into their host societies? How does social class correlate with different shades of skin color in producing such differences? Third, why are certain ethnic minorities, but not others, racialized as black and thereby excluded from dominant discourses of national identity? Finally, how do Caribbean immigrants, including Haitians, Dominicans, Puerto Ricans, and Cubans, interact in the United States? Do mutual stereotypes persist or decrease abroad? Are the immigrants and their descendants embracing a panethnic affiliation such as Hispanic, Latino, or Caribbean? The urgency of answering such questions confirms the pressing need for a comparative research agenda on contemporary ethnic and race relations in both the Caribbean and its diaspora.

NOTES

1. This chapter is an abridged and revised version of an article published in *Latin American and Caribbean Ethnic Studies* 1, 2 (2006):231–248. I would like to thank Jorge Giovannetti, Rhoda Reddock, Ernesto Sagás, Yolanda Martínez-San Miguel, José Cobas, and two anonymous reviewers for their insightful comments and suggestions on earlier drafts of the chapter.

REFERENCES

Austerlitz, Paul. 1997. *Merengue: Dominican Music and Dominican Identity.* Philadelphia: Temple University Press.

Báez Evertsz, Franc. 1986. *Braceros haitianos en la República Dominicana.* Santo Domingo: Instituto Dominicano de Investigaciones Sociales.

———. 2001. *Vecinos y extraños: Migrantes y relaciones interétnicas en un barrio popular de Santo Domingo.* Santo Domingo: Servicio Jesuita a Refugiados.

Bailey, Benjamin. 2002. *Language, Race, and Negotiation of Identity: A Study of Dominican Americans.* New York: LFB Scholarly Publishing.

Baud, Michiel. 1996. "'Constitutionally White': The Forging of a National Identity in the Dominican Republic." Pp. 121–151 in Gert Oostindie (ed.), *Ethnicity in the Caribbean: Essays in Honor of Harry Hoetink.* London: Macmillan Caribbean.

Benítez Nazario, Jorge. 2001. *Reflexiones en torno a la cultura política de los puertorriqueños.* San Juan: Instituto de Cultura Puertorriqueña.

Camuñas Madera, Ricardo. 1999. "Relaciones entre Santo Domingo y Puerto Rico: Una perspectiva histórica." Pp. 525–543 in Ramonina Brea, Rosario Espinal, and Fernando Valerio-Holguín (eds.), *La República Dominicana en el umbral del siglo XXI: Cultura, política y cambio social.* Santo Domingo: Centro Universitario de Estudios Políticos y Sociales, Pontificia Universidad Católica Madre y Maestra.

Candelario, Ginetta E. B. 2000. "Hair Race-ing: Dominican Beauty Culture and Identity Production." *Meridians: Feminism, Race, Transnationalism* 1(1):128–156.

———. 2007. *Black Behind the Ears: Dominican Racial Identity from Museums to Beauty Shops.* Durham, NC: Duke University Press.

Cruz Caraballo, Darwin. 1998. "Tú eres dominicano: Las interacciones entre adolescentes dominicanos y puertorriqueños." Unpublished manuscript, University of Puerto Rico, Río Piedras, May.

Davis, Martha Ellen. 1987. *La otra ciencia: El vodú dominicano como religión y medicina populares.* Santo Domingo: Editora Universitaria, UASD.

de la Rosa Abreu, Aida Liz. 2002. "La identidad cultural de la mujer dominicana de clase trabajadora en Puerto Rico: Su articulación en la comedia televisiva." M.A. thesis, University of Puerto Rico, Río Piedras.

del Castillo, José. 1989. "La inmigración dominicana en los Estados Unidos y Puerto Rico." Pp. 35–62 in Juan Hernández Cruz (ed.), *Los inmigrantes indocumentados dominicanos en Puerto Rico: Realidad y mitos.* San Germán, PR: Centro de Publicaciones, Universidad Interamericana de Puerto Rico.

———. [1981] 1990. "Las inmigraciones y su aporte a la cultura dominicana (finales del siglo XIX y principios del XX)." Pp. 169–210 in Bernardo Vega, Carlos Dobal, Carlos Esteban Deive, Rubén Silié, José del Castillo, and Frank Moya Pons (eds.), *Ensayos sobre cultura dominicana,* 2nd ed. Santo Domingo: Fundación Cultural Dominicana/ Museo del Hombre Dominicano.

De Maeseneer, Rita. 2002. "Sobre dominicanos y puertorriqueños: ¿Movimiento perpetuo?" *CENTRO: Journal of the Center for Puerto Rican Studies* 14(1):52–73.

Denton, Nancy A., and Jacqueline Villarrubia. 2007. "Residential Segregation on the Island: The Role of Race and Class in Puerto Rican Neighborhoods." *Sociological Forum* 22(1):52–77.

Derby, Lauren. 1994. "Haitians, Magic, and Money: *Raza* and Society in the Haitian-Dominican Borderlands, 1900 to 1937." *Comparative Studies in Society and History* 36(3):488–526.

Dore Cabral, Carlos. 1995. "Encuesta Rumbo-Gallup: La población dominicana es más antihaitiana que racista." *Rumbo* 29 (May):8–12.

Duany, Jorge. 1998. "Reconstructing Racial Identity: Ethnicity, Color, and Class Among Dominicans in the United States and Puerto Rico." *Latin American Perspectives* 25(3): 47–172.

———. 2005. "Dominican Migration to Puerto Rico: A Transnational Perspective." *CENTRO: Journal of the Center for Puerto Rican Studies* 17(1):243–268.

Duany, Jorge (ed.). 1990. *Los dominicanos en Puerto Rico: Migración en la semi-periferia.* Río Piedras, PR: Huracán.

Duany, Jorge, Luisa Hernández Angueira, and César A. Rey. 1995. *El Barrio Gandul: Economía subterránea y migración indocumentada en Puerto Rico.* Caracas: Nueva Sociedad.

Dzidzienyo, Anani, and Suzanne Oboler (eds.). 2005. *Neither Enemies nor Friends: Latinos, Blacks, Afro-Latinos.* New York: Palgrave Macmillan.

Ferguson, James. 2003. *Migration in the Caribbean: Haiti, the Dominican Republic, and Beyond.* London: Minority Rights Group International.

García Cuevas, Eugenio. 1999. *Mirada en tránsito (dominicanos, haitianos, puertorriqueños y otras situaciones en primera persona).* San Juan: Isla Negra.

Grasmuck, Sherri. 1983. "International Stair-Step Migration: Dominican Labor in the United States and Haitian Labor in the Dominican Republic." *Research in Sociology of Work: Peripheral Workers* 2:149–172.

Hernández, Ramona, and Nancy López. 2003. "The Dominican Republic." Pp. 73–86 in Alan West-Durán (ed.), *African Caribbeans: A Reference Guide.* Westport, CT: Greenwood.

Hoetink, Harmannus. 1967. *Caribbean Race Relations: A Study of Two Variants.* London: Oxford University Press.

Howard, David. 2001. *Coloring the Nation: Race and Ethnicity in the Dominican Republic.* Boulder, CO: Lynne Rienner.

Iturrondo, Milagros. 1993–1994. "San Ignacio de la Yola . . . y los dominicanos (en Puerto Rico)." *Homines* 17(1–2):234–240.

———. 2000. *Voces quisqueyanas en Borinquen.* San Juan: Ediciones Camila.

Itzigsohn, José, Silvia Giorguli, and Obed Vázquez. 2005. "Immigrant Incorporation and

Racial Identity: Racial Self-Identification Among Dominican Immigrants." *Ethnic and Racial Studies* 28(1):50–78.

López Carrasquillo, Alberto. 1999. "Prácticas de aceptación y rechazo de estudiantes dominicanos(as) en una escuela elemental en Puerto Rico." *Revista de Ciencias Sociales* (Nueva Época) 6:141–164.

Lozano, Wilfredo, and Franc Báez Evertsz. 1992. *Migración internacional y economía cafetalera: Estudio sobre la migración estacional de trabajadores haitianos a la cosecha cafetalera en la República Dominicana*, 2nd ed. Santo Domingo: Centro de Planificación y Acción Ecuménica, Santo Domingo.

Lozano, Wilfredo (ed.). 1992. *La cuestión haitiana en Santo Domingo: Migración internacional, desarrollo y relaciones inter-estatales entre Haití y República Dominicana*. Santo Domingo: FLACSO.

Martínez, Samuel. 1995. *Peripheral Migrants: Haitians and Dominican Republic Sugar Plantations*. Knoxville: University of Tennessee Press.

———. 2003a. "Identities at the Dominican and Puerto Rican International Migrant Crossroads." Pp. 141–164 in Shalini Puri (ed.), *Marginal Migrations: The Circulation of Cultures Within the Caribbean*. Oxford: Macmillan Caribbean.

———. 2003b. "Not a Cockfight: Rethinking Haitian-Dominican Relations." *Latin American Perspectives* 30(3):80–101.

Martínez-San Miguel, Yolanda. 2003. *Caribe Two Ways: Cultura de la migración en el Caribe insular hispánico*. San Juan: Callejón.

Matibag, Eugenio. 2003. *Haitian-Dominican Counterpoint: Nation, State, and Race on Hispaniola*. New York: Palgrave Macmillan.

Mejía Pardo, Diana. 1993. "Macroestructuras, superestructuras y proposiciones de opiniones en 17 relatos de puertorriqueños acerca de dominicanos." M.A. thesis, University of Puerto Rico, Río Piedras.

Mintz, Sidney W. 1996. "Ethnic Difference, Plantation Sameness." Pp. 39–52 in Gert Oostindie (ed.), *Ethnicity in the Caribbean: Essays in Honor of Harry Hoetink*. London: Macmillan Caribbean.

Moya Pons, Frank. 1986a. *El pasado dominicano*. Santo Domingo: Fundación J. A. Caro Alvarez.

Moya Pons, Frank (ed.). 1986b. *El batey: Estudio socioeconómico de los bateyes del Consejo Estatal del Azúcar*. Santo Domingo: Fondo para el Avance de las Ciencias Sociales.

Murphy, Martin F. 1991. *Dominican Sugar Plantations: Production and Foreign Labor Integration*. New York: Praeger.

Omi, Michael, and Howard Winant. 1994. *Racial Formation in the United States*, 2nd ed. New York: Routledge.

Onè Respe. 1994. *El otro del nosotros*. Santiago, Dominican Republic: Centro de Estudios Sociales Padre Juan Montalvo, S.J.

Pascual Morán, Vanessa, and Delia Ivette Figueroa. 2000. *Islas sin fronteras: Los dominicanos indocumentados y la agricultura en Puerto Rico*. San Germán, PR: CISCLA/Revista Interamericana.

———. 2005. "La porosa frontera y la mano de obra haitiana en la República Dominicana." *Caribbean Studies* 33(1):251–280.

Peralta, Reyna A. 1995. "Proyecto para la implantación de un Centro de Servicios Múltiples para Inmigrantes (CENSERMI)." M.A. thesis, University of Puerto Rico, Río Piedras.

Pérez Memén, Fernando. 1989. "Panorama histórico de las emigraciones dominicanas a Puerto Rico." Pp. 7–34 in Juan Hernández Cruz (ed.), *Los inmigrantes indocumentados dominicanos en Puerto Rico: Realidad y mitos*. San Germán, PR: Centro de Publicaciones, Universidad Interamericana de Puerto Rico.

Ríos, Palmira. 1992. "Acercamiento al conflicto domínico-boricua." *CENTRO: Journal of the Center for Puerto Rican Studies* 4(2):44–49.

Rivera-Batiz, Francisco. 2004. "Color in the Caribbean: Race and Economic Outcomes in the Island of Puerto Rico." Paper presented at the conference "New Directions in Social Science Research: Puerto Ricans on the Island and in the Mainland." Russell Sage Foundation, New York, May 21–22.

Romero Anico, Flavia A. 1984. "La migración dominicana: Sus implicaciones para Puerto Rico." M.A. thesis, University of Puerto Rico, Río Piedras.

Rosario Natal, Carmelo. 1990. "Para la historia de las relaciones intermigratorias entre Puerto Rico y la República Dominicana: Primeras etapas." *Revista de la Universidad de América* 2(1):20–25.

———. 1995. "Puerto Rico y la República Dominicana: Emigraciones durante el período revolucionario 1791–1850." *Revista de la Universidad de América* 7(1):107–114.

Sagás, Ernesto. 2000. *Race and Politics in the Dominican Republic.* Gainesville: University Press of Florida.

San Miguel, Pedro. 1997. *La isla imaginada: Historia, identidad y utopía en La Española.* San Juan: Isla Negra.

Silié, Rubén, Carlos Segura, and Carlos Dore Cabral. 2002. *La nueva inmigración haitiana.* Santo Domingo: FLACSO.

Silié, Rubén, and Carlos Segura (eds.). 2002. *Una isla para dos.* Santo Domingo: FLACSO.

Torres-Saillant, Silvio. 1998. "The Tribulations of Blackness: Stages in Dominican Racial Identity." *Latin American Perspectives* 25(3):126–146.

———. 1999. *El retorno de las yolas: Ensayos sobre diáspora, democracia y dominicanidad.* Santo Domingo: Manatí/La Trinitaria.

Turits, Richard Lee. 2002. "A World Destroyed, a Nation Imposed: The 1937 Massacre in the Dominican Republic." *Hispanic American Historical Review* 82(3):589–636.

Vázquez Calzada, José L., and Zoraida Morales del Valle. 1979. "Características socio-demográficas de los norteamericanos, cubanos y dominicanos en Puerto Rico." *Revista de Ciencias Sociales* 21(1–2):1–34.

Weyland, Karin. 2004. *Congo pa' ti: Identidad afrolatina en la cultura dominicana.* Video. Santo Domingo: Fundación Melassa.

Winant, Howard. 1994. *Racial Conditions: Politics, Theory, Comparisons.* Minneapolis: University of Minnesota Press.

Wooding, Bridget, and Richard Moseley-Williams. 2004. *Needed but Unwanted: Haitian Immigrants and Their Descendants in the Dominican Republic.* London: Catholic Institute for International Relations.

CHAPTER 14

Transnational Racializations

The Extension of Racial Boundaries from Receiving to Sending Societies

Wendy D. Roth

Scholarship on the racialization of Latinos generally focuses on the United States. The guidelines for U.S. federal racial classification maintain that Hispanicity is an aspect of ethnicity and that Latinos may be of any race. Nonetheless, in their daily lives, U.S. Latinos are often treated as a separate, nonwhite racial group. The racialization of Latinos is commonly understood as a result of migration, an experience produced within the host society. However, I argue that the racialization of Latinos is not unique to host societies like the United States but is experienced within the sending societies as well. Focusing on Puerto Rican and Dominican nonmigrants—those who have not lived outside their countries of origin—I maintain that the global transmission of U.S. culture perpetuates the racialization of Latinos in the home countries, while supported by local cultural frames.

For many Latin Americans, ethnic identities frequently overlap with racial identities; part of the common ancestry, history, and sense of peoplehood they share derives from their definition of themselves as a racially mixed people. What it means to be Dominican or Puerto Rican—or, more broadly, Latino—is descent from the mixing of white, black, and indigenous races. While the recognition of themselves as a people who are distinct because of their racial mixture originates with the culture and history of the home countries, the adoption of this trait as a core aspect of Dominicans' and Puerto Ricans' identity is fostered by the comparison to other regions, particularly to the culturally, economically, and politically omnipresent United States. In their view, racial mixture is part of what distinguishes Latinos from Americans, whom they typically perceive as racially unmixed. A steady awareness of the United States in daily life is promoted by globalization as well as transnational connections to those who have migrated. This constant awareness reinforces social boundaries even for those who have never left their home country. Contact with and knowledge about the United States make those distinctions more salient on a daily basis, affecting conceptions of race in the sending societies.

The racial classifications applied to Latinos in the United States are communicated back to the home countries, where they conflict with a different, more continuous concept of race. While this Americanized view seldom replaces Puerto Rican and Dominican nonmigrants' categories of race, many of them adopt a secondary understanding of their racial identity—one that takes into account the way they are viewed beyond their national borders and situates their race on an international stage dominated by the United States.

In this chapter, I argue that an Americanized view of race extends from the United States to Puerto Rico and the Dominican Republic. The transnational communication of how Latinos are classified in the United States is a necessary step in this process, but it is the extension of racial boundaries within a transnational social field that leads nonmigrants to adopt a dual conception of their race at home and abroad. To support these claims, I rely on in-depth interviews with Dominican and Puerto Rican nonmigrants in Santo Domingo and San Juan, respectively.

CONSTRUCTING RACIAL BOUNDARIES

Racial scholars frequently highlight the different conceptions of race in the United States and Latin America. Compared to the United States, Latin America provides a sharp contrast with its continuous racial model and recognition of multiple intermediate categories between black and white. Historically, most Latin American countries did not place the same legal and social barriers on interracial relationships as did U.S. society, and widespread racial mixing, or mestizaje, in Latin America produced an extensive blending of physical traits and racial phenotypes. While racial mixing occurred in the United States as well—particularly through whites' sexual exploitation of their slaves—the emerging "one-drop rule" produced a sharp dichotomy of racial classification between whites and blacks. These differences create the potential for Latin American immigrants to find that the racial classification imposed on them in the United States is different from the way they identify.

The process of racialization involves "the extension of racial meaning to a previously racially unclassified relationship, social practice, or group." This racial meaning is communicated and maintained through the construction of racial boundaries. The role of social boundaries in constructing ethnic and racial identities and stratification has recently gained renewed focus. Frederik Barth was the first to adduce that ethnic groups are defined not by their cultural content but by the boundaries that they and others create. Many predicted that ethnic distinctions would disappear as isolated social groups came into greater contact; Barth recognized that such interaction reinforces ethnic distinctions rather than reducing them. Contrast to the outgroup provides each ingroup with a basis for constructing their sense of who they are and who they are not.

I situate the construction of racial boundaries within this framework. Not only ethnic distinctiveness but also racialized meaning is reinforced through group interaction. However, the precise nature of "group interaction" has been insufficiently theorized. In Barth's essay, it involves in-person contact between members of distinct groups. When his ideas are related to immigrant communities, they can be described in terms of personal interactions between foreign-born and native-born members of the receiving society. Today, however, the increased contact between groups that sustains ethnic boundaries occurs through globalization as well as migration. Distant societies can be brought into virtual contact with one another in a globalized world, and the types of boundaries described by Barth no longer need to be experienced through personal interaction.

A distant society will not become a relevant reference category for every foreign community exposed to its culture through globalization. For many Latin American societies, however—and for Puerto Ricans and Dominicans in particular—one aspect of globalization is the spread of transnational migration. Nina Glick Schiller, Linda Basch, and Cristina Blanc-Szanton have described transnationalism as "the processes by which immigrants forge and sustain multi-stranded social relations that link together their societies of origin and settlement." Once in their host society, many immigrants continue to orient themselves toward their home society by maintaining regular contact and a range of economic, political, or sociocultural involvements. When the duration, magnitude, and impact of ties between migrant communities and their communities of origin are particularly strong, they may develop into a transnational social field—a dense web of transnational connections that make each location a relevant field of reference for daily life in the other location. Transnational social fields stretch this frame of reference beyond individuals' own networks; awareness of a key site of immigrant settlement does not depend on having one's own personal contacts there, but extends to everyone in the community of origin.

Because of these transnational linkages, the influence of U.S. society permeates daily life in many Latin American nations, including Puerto Rico and the Dominican Republic. While this influence is particularly strong in Puerto Rico because of its long-standing colonial relationship with the United States, Americans have become a reference category for identity construction in both nations. Through these influences, I argue, racialized boundaries, largely constructed in the United States, are extended transnationally to influence nonmigrants' conceptions of race in the sending society.

METHODOLOGY

The data for this chapter are based on qualitative interviews conducted in 2003 with nonmigrants in San Juan, Puerto Rico, and Santo Domingo, Dominican Republic. I conducted thirty interviews with Dominican nonmigrants and thirty interviews with Puerto Rican nonmigrants as part of a larger comparative project with Dominican and Puerto Rican migrants in New York, but the present study focuses only on the nonmigrant samples. Adult nonmigrant respondents met the following criteria: They had not lived outside their home country for more than six months; they identified their parents as "both Dominican" or "both Puerto Rican"; they lived or worked in their nation's capital; and they did not know any of the other respondents. Each group was stratified by age, sex, occupational status, and skin color (see Table 14.1).

High occupational status includes managerial and professional specialty occupations. Medium occupational status includes technical, sales, and administrative support occupations. Low occupational status includes service occupations; production, craft, and repair occupations; operators; fabricators; and laborers. Respondents who were unemployed at the time of the interview were classified according to their most recent occupation. Homemakers were classified according to the occupation of their partner or spouse. Individuals on long-term disability or welfare receipt were classified as low status.

Here, respondents' color refers to their observed skin color, as I perceived it on a scale from 1 (lightest) to 10 (darkest). "Light" corresponded to my ratings 1–3; "medium," 4–6; and "dark," 7–10. To anchor how I applied the scale, I rated a series of photographs (described below) before the fieldwork began.

Table 14.1 Nonmigrant Sample Stratification

	Nonmigrant Puerto Ricans	Nonmigrant Dominicans
Age		
21–35	11	11
36–50	11	11
Above 50	8	8
Sex		
Male	15	15
Female	15	15
Occupational Status		
High	10	11
Medium	11	8
Low	9	11
Color		
Light	13	11
Medium	11	7
Dark	6	12
Total	30	30

Respondents were later asked to describe their own color using the same scale; I expected, and found, discrepancies in the ratings used by the respondents and myself; however, I used "observed skin color" rather than the respondents' self-assigned skin color in the sample distribution for the purposes of comparing across samples. Although every measure of appearance is contextual, this measure represents an approximate assessment of how the individuals might be viewed in the United States.

The samples were designed to qualitatively explore social processes related to these characteristics and develop theoretical explanations rather than to be statistically representative. The value of this approach is that it uncovers more mechanisms and deeper interpretive understandings of identification than is possible through large-scale surveys.

Samples were generated by combining several methods. I canvassed and passed out flyers in public locations, including malls, shops, and buses. In some neighborhoods, I knocked on doors and recruited people with whom I came into contact over the course of my daily interactions in restaurants, shops, and other public places. In other instances, respondents were referred by personal contacts—that is, either by my research assistants or by staff in the research institutes where I was affiliated. In order to find some respondents with high occupational status, I contacted professional organizations, which in turn contacted their members on my behalf.

Interviews were conducted in Spanish, with both myself and a native Spanish-speaking research assistant present. We varied who led the interview to test for American/native interviewer effects. I did not find any differences based on who led the interview. I believe this is because my presence in the interview was sufficient to determine the audience to whom the respondent was speaking and to raise awareness of a U.S. context in his or her responses.

It is likely that respondents' awareness of their racialization on a world stage would not have been revealed if only a native interviewer had been present. Yet the nature and depth of the respondents' comments reveal that they were not simply telling me what they thought I wanted to hear—many were quite critical of the United States and the way it classified them, and apologized to me for having to be so honest. But while nonmigrants might not always adopt an Americanized view of race in their daily lives, they tend to see themselves in those terms when a U.S. frame of reference is suggested. I return to these points in the analysis.

To further probe the role of context and interviewer identity, I discussed the interviews with my research assistants. This process provided information on the degree to which the responses resonated with the respondents' observations of their native society as well as on how the assistants felt the respondents' answers might have differed if I, as a white American, had not been present. I tape-recorded some of these discussions, which form some of the data I draw on in this chapter.

As part of the interview, I showed all respondents a photographic instrument of individuals representing the range of racial phenotypes typically found in the Hispanic Caribbean. These photos varied from light ("white") to dark ("black") and displayed various types of racial mixture, including different hair and facial features. I chose them to represent a range of the physical "types" between black and white that are recognized in the Hispanic Caribbean and listed in Table 14.2. The individuals in the photos either were Latino (mostly Dominican or Puerto Rican) or were identified by my research assistants as resembling one of the physical types listed. I selected the final group of photos for the instrument in consultation with a research assistant who is a Puerto Rican migrant and a Dominican migrant hired as a consultant for that purpose. I then asked respondents to identify the race of each person in the photographs in open-ended terms—whatever terms they would normally use. This led to an in-depth investigation of what those terms meant to them and how they understood those racial categories. I also asked respondents to identify their own race in open-ended terms, and to complete the race and Hispanic-origin questions from the 2000 U.S. Census.

Table 14.2 Racial Terms Used in Puerto Rico and the Dominican Republic

Term	Approximate Meaning
Negro	Black
Azulito	Blue-black; very dark with African features; used primarily in Dominican Republic
Prieto	Dark-skinned; usually derogatory
Grifo	Dark-skinned with kinky hair; usually derogatory
Moreno	Dark-skinned; usually dark mulatto
De color	Euphemism for black
Cenizo	Literally, ashy; skin that looks grey or faded, traditionally from deposits due to bathing in river; used primarily in Dominican Republic
Mulato	Mixed-race, frequently the mixture of black and white
Trigueño	Literally, wheat-colored or brunette; usually light mulatto
Mestizo	Mixed-race; traditionally the mix of white and Indian but also used as the mix of any two races
Indio	Literally, Indian; brown-skinned with straight hair
Piel canela	Literally, cinnamon skin; tan or brown-skinned
Café con leche	Literally, coffee with milk; tan or brown-skinned
Blanco con raja	Literally, white with a crack; white with some visible black features; used primarily in Puerto Rico
Jabao	Fair-skinned with curly or kinky hair
Colorao	Redheaded, reddish skin
Rosadito	White, with rosy cheeks or skin tone
Rubio	Blonde
Cano	Blonde or grey hair, fair-skinned
Jincho	Pale-skinned, lacking color; may imply illness or unattractiveness
Blanquito	Literally, little white; figuratively, elitist, upper-class
Blanco	White

Note: This table adds to Jorge Duany's (2002) list of major racial terms in Puerto Rico.

Other studies have used visual images to elicit popular perceptions of race among Latin Americans. For example, Marvin Harris in Brazil, and subsequently Clarence Gravlee in Puerto Rico, showed a series of thirty-six drawings of males and thirty-six of females representing all combinations of three skin tones, three hair types, two nose types, and two lip types to capture the range of color terms respondents assigned to the drawings. Ginetta Candelario showed color photocopies of images from hairstyle books to Dominican women at a beauty salon in New York to elicit their perceptions of attractiveness and understand how aesthetic preferences are connected to racial images. The purpose of photo elicitation in the present study was to evoke the racial categories that respondents use, without suggesting the types of terms they should apply, and to explore what they choose to focus on in attributing race. For this reason, photographs of real people whom individuals might see during the course of their day were deemed preferable to systematic drawings that might have directed attention to the particular characteristics that were varied from one drawing to another.

RACIALIZED IDENTITIES IN THE HOME COUNTRIES

The racialization of Latinos does not occur in the United States alone. Indeed, many Puerto Rican and Dominican nonmigrants view their national identity in racial terms, associated with the mixture of Spanish, African, and Taíno Indian heritage. This mixture is frequently described in terms of physical characteristics, not just cultural ones. When asked what race she considers herself to be, Dulce, a sixty-year-old Puerto Rican woman, explained:

> Many Puerto Ricans consider themselves ... [a] mixture of white, Indian, and black.... I consider myself a mixture of white, black, and maybe Indian.... I don't consider myself *mulatta*[1] because *mulatto* is white and black. I consider myself Puerto Rican, and the Puerto Rican is that.
>   QUESTION: Puerto Rican is white, black, and Indian?
>   Yes. I don't know if I have Indian race and I don't know if I have black race but if I look at myself in the mirror I think that, although I have, look, straight hair and I'm more white than black, but I'm a Puerto Rican. There is no way that I'm not Latina. (Dulce, Puerto Rican, arts administrator)

With her light skin and straight hair, Dulce could describe herself as white and says that many people see her this way. But she believes that racial mixture is visible in her features—her full lips and her nose, which is slightly wider than most Caucasians'. And yet despite the physical evidence of mixture, she cannot say what specific mixture makes up her heritage. She therefore represents this apparent but unspecified mixture with the racialized label "Puerto Rican."

In the Dominican Republic, many respondents identify their racial identity as "Dominican." Inés defines the Dominican race by the racial mixture it represents. She explains: "Race is your descent, whether it's black, white, Yellow [Asian] ... if I'm of Haitian race, of Dominican race, of Latino race. We

Dominicans have a lot of mixture, but we're Latinos.... 'Latino' means from our country, Latin America, and our race is Dominican.... We're Dominicans, but the race comes from a descent of many races, that comes from Spaniards, Haitians, African.... [Dominican] is a race, but we have a blend" (Inés, Dominican, beauty salon owner).

Inés describes her appearance as "more white than black," but in her view, her mixed origins are not something to be hidden behind a veil of claimed whiteness. Like many nonmigrants Inés is proud of her mixed racial heritage; however, since this combination of racial ancestries cannot be easily defined, she represents it with a national label.

Others adopt a panethnic label as their race, noting that not only their own national group but practically all Latin Americans display this racial mixture. Isandro identifies himself as Latino and described what this means in racialized terms rather than cultural ones.

> QUESTION: In your own words, could you tell me what race you consider yourself to belong to?
> To me, I'm Latino. A lot of people say that Latino doesn't exist as a race. In case that one day it's defined or it's excluded [as a race], then I'd be black. But I understand that I'm Latino because I'm ... neither white nor yellow. I'm Latino.
> QUESTION: And what is the Latino race? What does it include?
> Okay, the Latinos, I think ... they're not whites, but they would be something like the mix of maybe white and black. They tend to usually be shorter in height than the whites. They tend to have features ... that are more lengthened, features that are finer than those of blacks. There are of course exceptions, but they tend to [have], like people say, refined features.... In this case, we would be maybe of a [certain] color, of average height, and refined features, like lengthened, and with dark hair. And the hair can vary; it could be wavy or straight, but dark. (Isandro, Puerto Rican, income tax auditor)

In embracing and racializing a Latino identity, nonmigrants tend to draw physical commonalities between themselves and Latinos throughout Latin America and the United States.

There are two contrasting patterns in how nonmigrants tend to racialize their ethnic and panethnic identities. The first, what I call *(pan)ethnicity as middle race,* is represented by Isandro above. This approach visualizes all Latinos as a physically homogeneous group with a specific set of features between black and white. Here, the ethnic or panethnic group is understood as an intermediate racial category, whose members all resemble one another. Ramiro, a Dominican man with light skin and blue eyes, explained: "All of us Latinos look alike. For example ... if you see a Colombian, and you see a Cuban and you see me, another Latino, you can only distinguish us by the way we talk but we all look a lot alike.... I think that all Latinos, most of us, are *mulattos* ... because we're all mixed with the same society" (Ramiro, Dominican, *colmado* [grocery store] owner). This approach typically sees all Latinos as brown. It tends to ignore those who fall at the Caucasian or African extreme of the racial spectrum, or to define them as not Latino but as white or black.

In the second pattern, *(pan)ethnicity as undefined race,* the diversity of appearance itself is part of what defines group identity. Even though these respondents characterized their ethnic or panethnic identity in racial terms, many claimed that these races are not well "defined." There are too many colors and appearances to characterize all members of the group under any one physical description. But what unites them all is that practically no one is pure white or black. The concept of racial purity is often conveyed through repetition: *Blanco-blanco* implies someone who is completely white in color and features, while *negro-negro* indicates someone who is completely black.[2] A Puerto Rican woman in her early forties, Diana would appear black by American standards. But as she described, in Puerto Rico neither she nor others are *really* black:

> There isn't anyone *negro-negro,* there isn't anyone *blanco-blanco.* There isn't anyone completely mestizo because there could be someone whose complexion is less dark but whose features are a little different ... [Here] you can find any guy or girl around who is white with [African] features. At the same time, you can find a person who [has] completely refined features, with features like a thin nose, small lips, very marked eyes, and so since there's been a mix of races and of colors, [we're] very different.... The Puerto Ricans can't be defined with any specific color. (Diana, Puerto Rican, librarian)

To her, a "defined" race represents racial purity, so the Latino race is undefined. It is characterized not by a given appearance but by racial mixture, in any combination of features. In this view, simply being racially mixed draws Latinos together, fostering a coherent group identity as much as shared language, customs, or music.

THE GLOBALIZATION OF RACIAL BOUNDARIES

Where do these racialized identities come from? The idea of Puerto Ricans and Dominicans as racially mixed is clearly cultivated by local cultural frames about who they are as a people. Each national community takes pride in its heritage, and public discourse—from literature and music to public performance and newspaper editorials—emphasizes these mixed roots. The educational system also plays a role in fostering a particular kind of national identity. As Sofía, a Puerto Rican college student, explained: "I believe in the majority of the schools what they teach you from when you are small is that the Puerto Rican is the union of African, Spanish, and Indian. And they ask you, and you can answer it like a poem. 'What race are you?' 'I am a mix of three races: Indian, Spanish, and African.'" Even a sense of shared panethnicity, or *Latinidad,* stems in part from Latin America itself.

But such identities are also strongly promoted by the salience of ethnic and racial boundaries. These cultural frames gain prominence from the comparisons that Puerto Ricans and Dominicans draw to salient reference groups. In the case of Dominicans, highlighting their mixed racial origins helps them define themselves in opposition to neighboring Haitians and thereby avoid a black identity. The growing presence of Dominican immigrants in Puerto Rico has had a similar effect, leading many Puerto Ricans to define their identity partly in opposition to the phenotypically darker Dominicans. But increasingly for Dominicans—as has long been the case for Puerto Ricans—racial boundaries contrasting them to Americans play an important role in defining their own identity.

When respondents describe their identity as a racially mixed people, they often draw comparisons to Americans—both white and black—whom they see as more racially pure. Daniel, a light-skinned Puerto Rican in his twenties, identified his race as "Puerto Rican." But in explaining what his racial identity means to him, he referred explicitly to the boundaries between Puerto Rico and the United States: "The Puerto Rican race is easily differentiable because there's like a mix. . . . It's easily differentiated from the nearby islands and from the U.S. A native race was created. . . . I think the largest difference is that at the beginning the Spanish decided to mix with the blacks and the Indians. And in the U.S. they were more exclusive. They wanted to maintain the English blood" (Daniel, Puerto Rican, former medical technician).

Respondents with more visible African features emphasized their *Latinidad* to differentiate themselves racially, not just culturally, from African Americans. Despite significant racial mixture among African Americans, many Puerto Rican nonmigrants perceive them as less mixed than themselves because they view the United States as a society where sexual relationships between blacks and whites have not occurred. Pablo, a dark-skinned Puerto Rican, explained:

> When I think of the blacks from, Americans ... I've never lived in the United States, but how they present it over there, in the movies and that, I don't identify with them.
>   QUESTION: And why don't you identify with them? Is it that the culture is different or—?
>   Well, I don't know if the black Americans have maintained themselves purer in terms of the African race ... but we have other mixes. For example, I have a wide nose, big lips, and that's very much like a black, but I'm not like within the blacks when you sometimes see them with wide noses, it's different for some reason. Perhaps it could be that they have maintained the race purer in that sense, and we over here being mixed. Well, features are conserved but they're diluted. No, they mixed and something else came out. (Pablo, Puerto Rican, billing clerk)

Holding Americans up as a racial comparison group reinforces a Latino or racialized ethnic identity, as these latter categories come to incorporate the nature of the difference.

"LATINO BEFORE THE WORLD"

Dominicans and Puerto Ricans are exposed to ideas and cultural products from a range of nations. The media they watch have a heavy U.S. influence, but there are also programs from Mexico, Brazil, and throughout Latin America. In terms of cultural influence, however, nonmigrants feel the United States has the strongest impact. When I noted to Geraldo, a Dominican political campaigner, that Dominicans are exposed to many Latin American cultural products, he replied, "Of course, but the U.S. is the empire. Most people want to be like them. Nobody wants to be Puerto Rican or Haitian or Cuban." Benjamín, a Puerto Rican man in his seventies, felt that the U.S. influence leads many nonmigrants to see themselves as racially "Latino."

> QUESTION: How did you start to see Latinos as a race?
> Well, I don't know. For me it's always been a race.... Here, we don't pay it too much mind because we depend on the United States. We depend on the United States. The United States gives us everything here.
> QUESTION: Have you heard that people in the U.S. talk about or see the Latinos as a race?
> Well, because in the United States ... they try to put Latinos apart, you know. They want to keep their race apart. The part of [the race that's] the Anglo Saxon. There are a lot that don't but there are others that want to be apart. And what happens? My brother suffered a lot in the United States. You can't imagine what he suffered because of segregation. (Benjamín, Puerto Rican, retired factory worker)

The boundaries that separate migrants—such as Benjamín's brother—from Americans in the United States are felt in Puerto Rico, too.

Because the United States has such a strong influence on nonmigrants' lives, many who identify their race as Latino or by their nationality do so because of their awareness of how they are seen racially by people outside their country. Even those who adopt one racial identity may identify with another when viewing themselves in international comparison. Dulce, who identifies her race as Puerto Rican, explained why she also identifies with a panethnic identity:

> I think that the Hispanic [identity] ... is used when the Hispanic wants to excel, when the Latin American wants to go out, when he wants to be seen, when he wants to be felt, heard, when he excels.
> QUESTION: And here, do you think that people feel Hispanic? Is that an identity that is used here?
> It's used in that way. But no, you'll always be Puerto Rican, but yes, Hispanic. You'll feel Hispanic when they talk like on a global level. (Dulce, Puerto Rican, arts administrator)

Nonmigrants, especially Puerto Ricans, embrace a panethnic identity when the context evokes a "global level" of awareness, a reality larger than their own local society.

I discussed the tendency for Puerto Rican respondents to identify their race as Latino or Puerto Rican with Roberto, one of my research assistants. A nonmigrant who would have been eligible for the study himself, Roberto described his perspective on why nonmigrants adopt a Latino identity when everyone around them in Puerto Rico is also Latino.

> I think that the Puerto Rican says he's Latino because when he sees himself—worldly, on the outside—he doesn't have any other category. When a Puerto

Rican travels to the United States, he's not white, like the white Americans, the Anglo-Saxons. Nor is he black, like the black North Americans. Another category of people comes in that the Americans themselves classified as Latinos. The Latinos, the Latino minority, or their Latino music. Therefore, a Puerto Rican in the United States considers himself Latino before the world.

And in Puerto Rico, even though he knows he's Latino, he doesn't consider himself Latino, or doesn't commonly call himself Latino. Here, he does classify himself as white, black, *trigueñito, blanquito, cano,* but he only classifies himself in that way when he's with people like him, when he's with Puerto Ricans, when he's with Latinos. But when he exposes himself to a different reality than the one that's there in Puerto Rico, when he begins to live in the United States or in another part of the world, he already comes with his Latino race. Because it's like the only category that he's allowed to be in the United States....

The Latinos have almost two classifications and it's very difficult because of that. It's because if you're black, you say, "I'm black," and that's it. And if you're white, "I'm white," and that's it. But if you're Latino, you're Latino before the world. If they ask you, "What are you?," because it's not only the race that I'm going to be here in Puerto Rico, it's the race that I'm going to be if I travel, the race that if I'm in Japan, I say "I'm Latino," if I'm in the United States I say, "I'm Latino," that's like your race. But we also have another race within the Latino. (Roberto, Puerto Rican, recent college graduate)

Awareness of the U.S. racial classification system and of how Puerto Ricans are categorized within it causes many nonmigrants to adopt a dual consciousness of their race at home and abroad. Even when my Puerto Rican research assistants led the interview, many respondents answered the same way. The very fact that I was asking about their racial identity raised for them the context of a world stage, because in the local context everyone already knew their race and did not have to ask.

In the Dominican Republic, panethnic identities are less frequently adopted than in Puerto Rico, although most respondents recognize them and associate them with labels that Americans impose on those who migrate to the United States. Rodolfo, a Dominican who works part-time as a social work assistant, expressed this view, claiming, "When you go to a different country you're already Latino ... because here in my country I'm Dominican ... We're Dominicans." Alicia maintained that the Latino label exists to draw physical comparisons between Latinos (here understood in terms of the *[pan]ethnicity as middle race* perspective) and those who do not appear Latino.

The Latino race? No. It's not a common term.... Latino isn't used ... unless we're among a group of foreigners, like North Americans, Germans, French, Chinese, Italians, and that she's there and that someone says she's Latina ... [In the Dominican Republic, it's used] only in certain contexts, for example ... to differentiate the Latino, the one that has dark hair, "ordinary" features, from others that are not [Latinos], that are refined, straight nose, thin mouth, light eyes. So the one that doesn't seem like this is Latino. Like Jennifer Lopez, like that. That she seems Latina because she has the mouth like a Latina, the buns.

QUESTION: Is this term used also to refer to someone who seems Caucasian but is Dominican?

No. I don't hear it frequently to say that. If it's a white, blond person, seems Caucasian, light eyes, and is Dominican, he's a *blanquito*. But Latino isn't said here in our way of talking.

QUESTION: So where do you hear this word?

On television, in the entertainment news. Among the jet set of Latino origin [they say, for example], "she was born here but grew up over there, she's of Latino origin." Television, the entertainment press, in ... U.S., European movies, which have actors that are from around here.... The North Americans use that term a lot. Yes, the *gringos* say that. (Alicia, Dominican, teacher)

In Alicia's view, the term "Latino" is used primarily to reinforce racialized boundaries. This process comes to Dominicans and Puerto Ricans in part through U.S. sources such as the media.

For many respondents, contact with friends and relatives who have moved to the mainland United States provides another means of communicating the racial boundaries created there. Nonmigrants learn from their contacts abroad that in the United States, Latinos are seen as neither white nor black but as a separate racial group. From return migrants as well as through his own visits to see family and friends in the United States, Lucio has learned not only that the racial groups "white," "black," and "Latino" are mutually exclusive but also that the latter two are socially disadvantaged:

The people who've gone to live in the United States, where the races are very well established for them—the black, the white, the Latino—then when those people come [back] they already have a way of establishing that.... The concept that I have, the times I've been to the U.S., my friends or relatives have told me: "That area there is ugly, that's where the Latinos and blacks live." ... And you go there and it's horrible. Over there is pretty because that's where the Italians live, the Americans live there, the North Americans, and so it's more taken care of. (Lucio, Puerto Rican, surgical technician)

For Puerto Ricans, the island's colonial status makes the United States a strong presence in daily life, and nonmigrants regularly interact with many American institutions. Racial classifications do not simply remain on the mainland; they infiltrate the island society partly through these institutional structures. Many Puerto Ricans, for example, serve in the U.S. military. Daniel, a light-skinned Puerto Rican who served in the Army Reserve several years earlier, described the socializing role it played in helping him understand how Americans racialize Latinos.

What happens is that in the U.S.... you yourself can be white but if you're of Hispanic race, then you're not white.

QUESTION: And how did you learn this?

Oh, because of the army. Once they told the white people to get up, and I stood up, and they all started laughing. And that's when ... I realized it was different. I stood up, because I didn't know that it was because of blood, I thought it was the color. So I stood up and then when everyone started laughing, then I realized it was different. (Daniel, Puerto Rican, former medical technician)

During this training exercise, which was supposedly intended to start a dialogue on racism, Daniel learned that in the United States, Hispanics are racialized as nonwhite. Institutions like the Armed Forces communicate this classification system and reinforce the racial boundaries that dominate life in the United States.

Michèle Lamont and Virág Molnár distinguish between social and symbolic boundaries. In the mainland United States, interactions between Latinos and non-Latinos create social boundaries that affect migrants' lives and opportunities. As these boundaries are exported to the home countries, they become symbolic—a conceptual distinction used to categorize people and define reality. The imposition of the "Latino" label has little practical significance in the daily lives of many Dominican and Puerto Rican nonmigrants, but they are acutely aware of how they are symbolically racialized by Americans on a social stage that impinges upon their own.

CONCLUSION

The racialization of Latinos occurs not just in the United States itself. Indeed, the influence of processes that begin in the United States extends to nonmigrants in their societies of origin. Racialized boundaries between the sending societies and the United States are relevant in nonmigrants' lives, with the United States acting as a salient reference category within these transnational social fields.

Puerto Rican and Dominican nonmigrants do not all blindly accept U.S. categories even as they retain their own. Many are critical of the way new categories are being imposed from abroad and actively resist their imposition. However, much like migrants who live in the mainland United States, many accommodate this language of classification and adopt it when their consciousness of U.S. society is triggered, even if they do not fully internalize it. Their dual consciousness of their racial identity at both ends of this transnational social field challenges how we measure and understand racial classification, both in sending and receiving societies. Recent work has shown that many individuals hold not a single, static racial identity but, rather, multiple, fluid identities that are contextually specific. The issue for scholars of racialization is not whether migrants internalize the receiving society's standards so much as which identities they use in which contexts. Surveys that provide a single snapshot of racial self-classification present only the tip of the iceberg in a much more complex process of racial identification.

The globalization of racialized meaning to sending societies suggests that future generations of migrants may experience a smoother integration process to their host society. Newcomers will be less likely to experience the shock of racial reclassification upon arrival. But a smooth integration into an unjust society is hardly a desirable goal. The reception of Latino migrants in the United States demands our attention not just because of the way Latinos are racialized but also because of how they are excluded from opportunities on the basis of that classification. The symbolic boundaries that exist in the societies of origin are less likely to pose real barriers for Latinos' life chances there. But the extension of those racial boundaries beyond mainland U.S. borders presents a new front on which the fight against racial exclusion needs to be fought.

NOTES

1. Spanish racial terms are defined in Table 14.2.

2. Flores (2000) notes the use of word repetition for emphasis or to convey authenticity—for example, that *pueblo pueblo* could be translated as "real people." Similarly, *blanco-blanco* may indicate authentic or pure whiteness.

REFERENCES

Alba, Richard. 2005. "Bright vs. Blurred Boundaries: Second Generation Assimilation and Exclusion in France, Germany, and the United States." *Ethnic and Racial Studies* 28:20–49.

Barth, Fredrik. 1969. "Introduction." Pp. 9–38 in Fredrik Barth (ed.), *Ethnic Groups and Boundaries: The Social Organization of Culture Difference*. Boston: Little, Brown.

Candelario, Ginetta. 2000. "Hair Race-ing: Dominican Beauty Culture and Identity Production." *Meridians: Feminism, Race, Transnationalism* 1:128–156.

Davis, F. James. 1991. *Who Is Black? One Nation's Definition*. University Park: Pennsylvania State University Press.

Duany, Jorge. 1997. "The Creation of a Transnational Caribbean Identity: Dominican Immigrants in San Juan and New York City." Pp. 195–232 in Juan Manuel Carrión (ed.), *Ethnicity, Race, and Nationality in the Caribbean*. San Juan: Institute for Caribbean Studies, University of Puerto Rico.

———. 1998. "Reconstructing Racial Identity: Ethnicity, Color, and Class Among Dominicans in the United States and Puerto Rico." *Latin American Perspectives* 25:147–172.

———. 2000. "Nation on the Move: The Construction of Cultural Identities in Puerto Rico and the Diaspora." *American Ethnologist* 27:5–30.

———. 2002. *The Puerto Rican Nation on the Move: Identities on the Island and in the United States*. Chapel Hill: University of North Carolina Press.

Duany, Jorge (ed.). 1990. *Los dominicanos en Puerto Rico: Migración en la semi-periferia*. Río Piedras, PR: Ediciones Huracán.

Flores, Juan. 2000. *From Bomba to Hip-Hop: Puerto Rican Culture and Latino Identity*. New York: Columbia University Press.

Glick Schiller, Nina, Linda Basch, and Cristina Blanc-Szanton. 1992. "Transnationalism: A New Analytic Framework for Understanding Migration." *Annals of the New York Academy of Sciences* 645:1–24.

Godreau, Isar P. 2000. "Peinando diferencias, bregas de pertenencia: El alisado y el llamado 'pelo malo.'" *Caribbean Studies* 30:82–134.

Gravlee, Clarence C. 2005. "Ethnic Classification in Southeastern Puerto Rico: The Cultural Model of 'Color.'" *Social Forces* 83:949–970.

Grosfoguel, Ramón, and Chloé S. Georas. 1996. "The Racialization of Latino Caribbean Migrants in the New York Metropolitan Area." *CENTRO: Journal of the Center for Puerto Rican Studies* 8:191–201.

Guarnizo, Luis Eduardo. 1997. "The Emergence of a Transnational Social Formation and the Mirage of Return Migration Among Dominican Transmigrants." *Identities* 4:281–322.

Harris, David R., and Jeremiah Joseph Sim. 2002. "Who Is Multiracial? Assessing the Complexity of Lived Race." *American Sociological Review* 67:614–627.

Harris, Marvin. 1970. "Referential Ambiguity in the Calculus of Brazilian Racial Identity." *Southwestern Journal of Anthropology* 26:1–14.

Howard, David. 2001. *Coloring the Nation: Race and Ethnicity in the Dominican Republic.* Oxford: Signal Books.

Itzigsohn, José, and Carlos Dore-Cabral. 2000. "Competing Identities? Race, Ethnicity, and Panethnicity Among Dominicans in the United States." *Sociological Forum* 15:225–247.

Itzigsohn, José, Carlos Dore Cabral, Esther Hernández Medina, and Obed Vázquez. 1999. "Mapping Dominican Transnationalism: Narrow and Broad Transnational Practices." *Ethnic and Racial Studies* 22:316–339.

Jiménez Román, Miriam. 1996. "Un Hombre (Negro) del Pueblo: José Celso Barbosa and the Puerto Rican 'Race' Toward Whiteness." *CENTRO: Journal of the Center for Puerto Rican Studies* 8:9–29.

Lamont, Michèle, and Virág Molnár. 2002. "The Study of Boundaries in the Social Sciences." *Annual Review of Sociology* 28:167–195.

Levitt, Peggy. 2001a. "Transnational Migration: Taking Stock and Future Directions." *Global Networks* 1:195–216.

———. 2001b. *The Transnational Villagers.* Berkeley: University of California Press.

Mörner, Magnus. 1967. *Race Mixture in the History of Latin America.* Boston: Little, Brown.

Oboler, Suzanne. 1995. *Ethnic Labels, Latino Lives: Identity and the Politics of (Re)Presentation in the United States.* Minneapolis: University of Minnesota Press.

Padilla, Felix M. 1985. *Latino Ethnic Consciousness: The Case of Mexican Americans and Puerto Ricans in Chicago.* Notre Dame, IN: University of Notre Dame Press.

———. 1990. "Latin America: The Historical Base of Latino Unity." *Latino Studies Journal* 1:7–27.

Rodríguez, Clara. 1974. "Puerto Ricans: Between Black and White." *New York Affairs* 1:92–101.

———. 2000. *Changing Race: Latinos, the Census, and the History of Ethnicity in the United States.* New York: New York University Press.

Rodríguez, Clara, and Héctor Cordero-Guzmán. 1992. "Placing Race in Context." *Ethnic and Racial Studies* 15:523–542.

Roth, Wendy D. 2006a. "Caribbean Race and American Dreams: How Migration Shapes Dominicans' and Puerto Ricans' Racial Identities and Its Impact on Socioeconomic Mobility." Ph.D. dissertation, Harvard University.

———. 2006b. "Latino Before the World: Panethnicity, Race, and the Diffusion of Identity." Paper presented at the Latin American Studies Association International Congress, March 15–18, San Juan, Puerto Rico.

Sagás, Ernesto. 2000. *Race and Politics in the Dominican Republic.* Gainesville: University Press of Florida.

Seda Bonilla, Eduardo. 1961. "Social Structure and Race Relations." *Social Forces* 40:141–148.

———. 1972. "El problema de la identidad de los niuyorricans." *Revista de Ciencias Sociales* 16:453–462.

Torres, Arlene. 1998. "La Gran Familia Puertorriqueña 'Ej Prieta de Beldá' (The Great Puerto Rican Family Is Really Really Black)." Pp. 285–306 in Norman E. Whitten, Jr., and Arlene Torres (eds.), *Blackness in Latin America and the Caribbean: Social Dynamics and Cultural Transformations.* Bloomington: Indiana University Press.

Torres-Saillant, Silvio. 1998. "The Tribulations of Blackness: Stages in Dominican Racial Identity." *Latin American Perspectives* 25:126–146.

U.S. Office of Management and Budget. 1997. "Revisions to the Standards for the Classification of Federal Data on Race and Ethnicity." *Federal Register Notice,* October 30.

Wade, Peter. 1997. *Race and Ethnicity in Latin America.* Chicago: Pluto Press.

Waters, Mary C. 1999. *Black Identities: West Indian Immigrant Dreams and American Realities.* Cambridge, MA: Harvard University Press.

Williamson, Joel. 1980. *New People: Miscegenation and Mulattoes in the United States.* New York: The Free Press.

Winant, Howard. 1994. *Racial Conditions: Politics, Theory, Comparisons.* Minneapolis: University of Minnesota Press.

Zack, Naomi. 1993. *Race and Mixed Race.* Philadelphia: Temple University Press.

Contributors

Elizabeth Aranda is Associate Professor of Sociology at the University of South Florida. She is the author of *Emotional Bridges to Puerto Rico: Migration, Return Migration, and the Struggles of Incorporation* (2007). She has also published in the *American Behavioral Scientist,* the *Sociological Quarterly,* and *Gender & Society.* She is currently working on a book about ethnic and race relations in Miami.

Xóchitl Bada is Assistant Professor of Latin American and Latino Studies at the University of Illinois in Chicago. Her doctoral dissertation examines the civic, cultural, and political participation of Chicago-based Michoacano migrant hometown associations. Her most recent publication is *Invisible No More: Mexican Migrant Civic Participation in the United States* (2006), coauthored by Jonathan Fox and Andrew Selee.

Gilberto Cárdenas holds the Julian Samora Chair in Latino Studies at the University of Notre Dame. Professor Cárdenas has worked in the area of immigration for thirty years and is internationally recognized as a scholar in Mexican immigration. He is the editor of *La Causa: Civil Rights, Social Justice, and the Struggle for Equality in the Midwest* (2004).

William D. Carrigan is Associate Professor of History at Rowan University. He is the author of *The Making of a Lynching Culture: Violence and Vigilantism in Central Texas, 1836–1916* (2004), which won the Richard Wentworth Prize. He is also the editor of *Lynching Reconsidered: New Perspectives in the Study of Mob Violence* (2008).

Rosa E. Chang works for the National Partnership for Community Training of the Florida Center for Survivors of Torture facilitating training and conducting research. She is a graduate candidate working on her Ph.D. in Sociology at the University of Miami, and her main areas of interest and research include immigrant underinvolvement in crime, images of immigrant groups, and torture recovery.

José A. Cobas is Professor of Sociology at the School of Social and Family Dynamics, Arizona State University, Tempe. One of his most recent articles is

"Language Oppression and Resistance: Latinos in the United States," *Ethnic and Racial Studies* 31 (2008):390–410. He and Joe R. Feagin are the coauthors of *Guardians of Racialization: White Repression and Latino Resistance* (forthcoming in 2010).

Jorge Duany is Professor of Anthropology at the University of Puerto Rico, Río Piedras. In 2007, he was a Bacardí Family Eminent Scholar at the University of Florida. His research specializes in Caribbean migration, ethnicity, race, and nationalism, and his most recent book is *The Puerto Rican Nation on the Move: Identities on the Island and in the United States* (2002).

Joe R. Feagin is Ella McFadden Professor of Liberal Arts at Texas A&M University. He is former President of the American Sociological Association and the author of nearly fifty books. His latest books are *Systemic Racism: A Theory of Racial Oppression* (2006) and, with Leslie Houts Picca, *Two-Faced Racism: Whites in the Backstage and Frontstage* (2007).

Ofelia García is Professor of Urban Education at the Graduate Center of the City University of New York and has been Professor of Bilingual Education at Columbia University's Teachers College and at The City College of New York, as well as Dean of the School of Education at Long Island University. Her latest book is *Bilingual Education in the 21st Century: A Global Perspective* (2008).

Laura E. Gómez teaches at the University of New Mexico in law and American studies. Previously she taught for twelve years at the UCLA School of Law, where she also was appointed in the Sociology Department. Her publications include *Manifest Destinies: The Making of the Mexican American Race* (2007) and *Misconceiving Mothers: Legislators, Prosecutors and the Politics of Prenatal Drug Exposure* (1997).

Jane H. Hill is Regents' Professor of Anthropology and Linguistics at the University of Arizona. Her interests include Native American languages, language and discourse in white racism, and the construction of ideology and identity in narrative and other discourse forms. She has published seven books and more than a hundred articles. Her most recent book is *The Everyday Language of White Racism* (2008).

Cecilia Menjívar is Cowden Distinguished Professor of Sociology in the School of Social and Family Dynamics at Arizona State University. Her research has focused on the interplay of broader structures and the microworlds of everyday life, particularly among Latino immigrants in the United States and women in Latin America. She coedited *Latinos/as in the United States: Changing the Face of América* (2008).

Lisandro Pérez is Professor of Sociology at Florida International University (FIU) in Miami. In 1991 he founded FIU's Cuban Research Institute and served as its director until 2003. He has also served as the editor of the journal *Cuban Studies* and is the coauthor of *The Legacy of Exile: Cubans in the United States* (2003).

Fernando Purcell teaches at the Institute of History at the Pontifical Catholic University of Chile. He has written about transnational migratory processes in the United States during the nineteenth century, with a focus on Chileans and Mexicans in California between 1850 and 1880. He is the author of *Diversiones y juegos populares: Formas de sociabilidad y crítica social. Colchagua, 1850–1880* (2000).

Clara E. Rodríguez is Professor of Sociology at Fordham University. She is the author of ten books and numerous articles on Latinos in the United States. Her most recent books are *The Culture and Commerce of Publishing in the 21st Century* (2007) (a national award winner, soon to be translated into Chinese) and *Heroes, Lovers and Others: The Story of Latinos in Hollywood* (2008).

Nestor P. Rodriguez is Professor of Sociology at the University of Texas at Austin. His research concerns migration, political sociology, global development, and race/ethnic relations. His recent publications include the coauthored article "U.S. Deportation Policy, Family Separation, and Circular Migration," *International Migration Review* (2008), and he is working on a coauthored book with Susanne Jonas on Guatemalan migration to the United States.

Wendy D. Roth is Assistant Professor of Sociology at the University of British Columbia. She received the 2007 American Sociological Association Dissertation Award and is a coauthor of *Rampage: The Social Roots of School Shootings* (2004). Her research focuses on how social processes such as immigration and intermarriage challenge racial boundaries and transform classification systems.

Rubén G. Rumbaut is Professor of Sociology at the University of California, Irvine. He is the founding Chair of the International Migration Section of the American Sociological Association. He recently completed work with a National Academy of Sciences panel on two volumes on the Latin American population of the United States: *Multiple Origins, Uncertain Destinies* (2006) and *Hispanics and the Future of America* (2001).

Elena Sabogal is Assistant Professor of Women's Studies and Latin American and Latino Studies at the William Paterson University of New Jersey. She previously served as Senior Research Associate at the Center for Latin American Studies, University of Miami, and she received her Ph.D. in Sociology from Florida International University.

Zulema Valdez is Assistant Professor of Sociology at Texas A&M University. She examines how group membership (e.g., race, class, gender) affects socioeconomic outcomes in capitalism, especially among entrepreneurs. She has published in the *Sociological Quarterly* and the *Journal of Ethnic and Migration Studies*. Her in-progress book investigates the effects of race, class, and gender on entrepreneurial outcomes.

Clive Webb is Reader in American Studies at the University of Sussex in Brighton, England. He is the author or editor of three books, including *Fight Against Fear: Southern Jews and Black Civil Rights* (2001) and, with David Brown, *Race in the American South: From Slavery to Civil Rights* (2007).

Index